THE CAESARS PALACE COUP

How a Billionaire Brawl Over the Famous Casino Exposed the Power and Greed of Wall Street

MAX FRUMES AND SUJEET INDAP

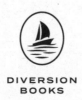

DIVERSION
BOOKS

To Abigail and Jocelyn, and to little Beatrice

———

For more information, email info@diversionbooks.com

Diversion Books
A division of Diversion Publishing Corp.
www.diversionbooks.com

First Diversion Books edition, March 2021
First Diversion Paperback, August 2022
Hardcover ISBN: 9781635766776
Trade Paperback ISBN: 9781635767742
eBook ISBN: 9781635766769

Printed in The United States of America

10 9 8 7 6 5 4 3

Library of Congress cataloging-in-publication data is available on file.
Cover photograph by istock.com
Jacket design by Tom Lau

CONTENTS

LIST OF SELECT KEY CHARACTERS

CAESARS PARENT

CAESARS:

- Gary Loveman (CEO)
- Eric Hession (finance)
- Paul, Weiss, Rifkind, Wharton, & Garrison (legal counsel)
- Blackstone Advisory/PJT Partners (financial advisor)

PRIVATE EQUITY OWNERS

APOLLO GLOBAL MANAGEMENT:

- Marc Rowan
- David Sambur

TPG CAPITAL:

- David Bonderman

FIRST-LIEN BANK LOAN HOLDERS

GSO CAPITAL:

- Ryan Mollett

STROOCK & STROOCK & LAVAN (LEGAL COUNSEL):

- Kris Hansen

FIRST-LIEN BONDHOLDERS

ELLIOTT MANAGEMENT:
- Dave Miller
- Samantha Algaze

KRAMER LEVIN NAFTALIS & FRANKEL (LEGAL COUNSEL):
- Ken Eckstein

SECOND-LIEN BONDHOLDERS

APPALOOSA MANAGEMENT:
- Jim Bolin

OAKTREE CAPITAL MANAGEMENT:
- Ken Liang
- Kaj Vazales

JONES DAY (LEGAL COUNSEL)
- Bruce Bennett

HOULIHAN LOKEY (FINANCIAL ADVISOR)
- Tuck Hardie
- David Hilty

OTHER PARTIES

- Millstein & Co (financial advisor to Caesars OpCo)
- Kirkland & Ellis (legal counsel to Caesars OpCo)
- Richard Davis (Examiner)
- Judge Benjamin Goldgar (US Bankruptcy Court Judge, Northern District of Illinois)

CAESARS STRUCTURE

CAESARS PARENT

Apollo Global Management
TPG Capital

CAESARS OPCO

First-lien bank loans	($5.35 billion)
First-lien bonds	($6.35 billion)
Second-lien bonds	($5.25 billion)
SGN bonds	($0.5 billion)
Unsecured bonds	($0.5 billion)

PROLOGUE

"**G**uys, we've got a $60 million gap to fill."

The room murmured for a moment, then someone shouted, "Jim, it's actually $130 million."

"That's a bad start. We just went backwards," Jim Millstein sighed. This was about to get harder.

Millstein's frustration could be forgiven. This meeting should have been wholly unnecessary. For a generation, Millstein had been one of the top advisors in the world of corporate bankruptcies, first as a lawyer and later as an investment banker. Just a few years earlier, he had served in the Obama administration as the inaugural Chief Restructuring Officer of the United States. But now, on September 23, 2016, Millstein was five years removed from his stint as a Washington insider. He had set up his own firm, Millstein & Co., to capitalize on his sterling reputation and experience. However, he had not fully appreciated just how nasty the restructuring world had become in his absence. After having the power of the US Treasury Department behind him for the better part of two years, he now found himself being mistreated by ex-Ivy League jocks almost half his age.

That morning, he was surrounded by a group of scowling hedge fund managers and their advisors in the offices of the Kirkland & Ellis law firm high atop New York City. Kirkland had a famously impressive set-up for such high-stakes meetings. Entire floors in the Citigroup Center in midtown Manhattan consisted of conference room after conference room, where white marble hallways lined by floor-to-ceiling wood panels gave way to larger open spaces and sprawling views of the city.

Millstein was trying to, once and for all, solve the restructuring of Caesars Entertainment, whose twists and turns had riveted Wall Street. The knock-down, drag-out affair was finally at its endgame. The fighting that had begun more than eight years ago after an ill-timed $28 billion leveraged buyout of the storied gaming company was mercifully being put to rest, along with Millstein's nightmare. The brightest financial minds in the world just had to find an extra $130 million to bridge the gap between what was being offered and what was asked. These investors merely had to pledge back pennies on the dollar to clinch this deal.

"If everyone chips in, the bank debt and senior bonds are good to do the same," Dave Miller said, speaking on behalf of himself and Ryan Mollett. Miller and Mollett—while only in their mid-thirties—had already established themselves as superstar distressed debt investors. Miller was with the feared hedge fund founded by Paul Singer, Elliott Management. Ryan Mollett worked at GSO, an affiliate of the jugger-naut investment firm Blackstone. Collectively, the pair represented dozens of Caesars creditors holding $12 billion of Caesars debt. The two had been bitter adversaries early in the case but had long since made peace.

"Gavin, I need $6 million from your group," Millstein demanded from Gavin Baiera, an executive at hedge fund Angelo Gordon, as politely as one can for such a sum.

Baiera, finding the spectacle comical, could only laugh. The $6 million would be fine but the sheer absurdity deserved at least a chuckle. This triviality could have been handled in a straightforward email.

"I can't talk for the group but I can't imagine we're not going to be OK with this," Baiera said.

Millstein turned to the last group represented in the room. "Ken, that leaves—"

"We are not chipping in!" shouted Ken Liang. This was the moment Millstein had been dreading. There was an old expression in complex restructurings—"just get everybody into a room"—about hashing out a lasting compromise. That approach suddenly did not look so promising.

Millstein had cut his teeth as a lawyer in the mid-1980s just as corporate raiders and private equity firms were emerging on Wall Street. They were called "barbarians," both for their slash-and-burn tactics and their insatiable thirst for profits and glory. Thirty years later, private equity had become a mainstream, if not celebrated, part of the financial establishment. No longer were private equity firms condemned as savages; rather they were earnest entrepreneurs, builders of businesses, and saviors of pensioners.

The distressed debt hedge fund now filled the pirate caricature on Wall Street. The invention of the junk bond had fueled the takeover mania of the 1980s. High yield bonds—or junk—allowed small or risky companies, along with buccaneering raiders, to tap the capital markets from which they had otherwise been closed off. As those deals went bust in the early 1990s, the debt became "distressed," and the "vulture" investor was born. Vulture funds could scoop up the debt of troubled companies for nickels and dimes and take control of over-indebted but otherwise viable companies.

By September 2016, Caesars' debt was almost exclusively owned by these distressed debt investors. These men were not just financial wizards—they had also weaponized the law, using their knowledge of dense legalese in loan agreements and bond indentures to play their hands in both boardroom negotiations and in courtroom showdowns. These funds were now poised to take control of Caesars and make billions of dollars on their distressed debt wagers.

Liang was an executive at Oaktree Capital Management, the $100 billion money manager in Los Angeles co-founded by two of the earliest and most successful distressed debt investors, Howard Marks and Bruce Karsh. Oaktree was one of Caesars' junior "second-lien" bondholders. Liang, like Millstein, was in his late 50s but looked a decade younger. He had been a corporate lawyer for a time before joining Oaktree as its founding general counsel in the 1990s. Over the years, his knowledge of transaction law made him instrumental in navigating distressed-debt transactions. He had also forged a well-earned reputation as an obstinate, if not unpleasant, negotiator.

Millstein had known Liang for two decades and had his share of run-ins with him. Oaktree was about to become a huge winner in the Caesars bankruptcy, so Millstein was hoping for some magnanimity or at least pragmatism. Instead, the two Oaktree representatives at Kirkland that day—Liang had come with his 37-year-old colleague Kaj Vazales—had only brought fury that had been simmering for almost three years.

The central figure in the Caesars brawl was, however, absent from the room. Apollo Global Management had been one of the two principal private equity firms who had acquired the storied casino chain in 2008. Apollo was defined by two traits: genius and impunity. The firm was co-founded by Leon Black, Michael Milken's right-hand man at Drexel Burnham Lambert. Milken had famously invented the junk bond market in the 1980s. After Milken's fall from grace, Black, in 1990, had formed Apollo to exploit the imploding debt markets that Milken and Drexel themselves had wrought.

Over its twenty-five-year existence, Apollo's hallmark had become discerning opportunity where no one else dare tread and then striking deals everyone else was too timid to make. Apollo also liked to play by its own rules, forcing its adversaries to think twice about confrontation. As Apollo's success compounded over the years, only a few ever stood in its way. Apollo had become, unquestionably, the most feared private equity firm in the world.

In the lean years after the financial crisis, Apollo's clever dealmaking had, against all odds, kept Caesars alive in the hope that its fortunes would eventually snap back. Apollo's Caesars investment was led by Marc Rowan, regarded by many as the canniest investor at Apollo and perhaps on all of Wall Street. Rowan's apprentice was a young fireball, David Sambur, whose intellectual horsepower and doggedness left him basically running the casino behemoth while in only his early 30s. Rowan's calm and charm belied his ruthlessness. Sambur, on the other hand, was a pit bull constantly in attack mode.

Together, their gifts kept Caesars afloat longer than any other private equity firm could—or even should—have. Caesars filed for bankruptcy in early 2015 under Chapter 11 of the Bankruptcy Code, leading to a court-supervised free-for-all to determine who would have the right to take control of the revitalized company: Apollo and its partner TPG Capital, or the vulture distressed-debt investors, who happened to be the world's biggest, baddest hedge funds.

The bankruptcy would eventually shine a harsh light on Rowan and Sambur's relentless financial engineering that had sustained Apollo's investment in Caesars. Their machinations had led to credible accusations of a modern day casino heist; fraudulent transfers and boardroom impropriety to the tune of $5 billion in liability. All the while, a complicated game of three-dimensional chess had broken out between multiple creditor groups and the private equity owners. The dispute even migrated to the back rooms of Congress.

For years, it looked like Oaktree would be crushed by Apollo. Junior creditors like Oaktree rarely did well in situations like Caesars. Apollo was masterful at rallying senior creditors to crush those at the bottom of the totem pole. In fact, that is exactly what Apollo had done in joining forces with Elliott and GSO. But through the course of the 2016 bankruptcy case, Oaktree and its running mate, the fabled Appaloosa Management, had methodically outfoxed Apollo in court. Suddenly, they had the mighty Apollo over a barrel. Now Oaktree and Appaloosa were on the verge of making billions for their group. All they had to do in this conference room was to show a little grace and kick back $50 million into the pot. Alas, that was still too much for Liang and Vazales to bear.

"Now guys, there's no need to be unreasonable," Ryan Mollett calmly explained to the Oaktree duo. Oaktree was risking the massive profits all the creditor groups were going to make at the expense of Apollo by not paying their penny. Oaktree needed to be a team player, explained Mollett.

"Go fuck yourself," Liang told Mollett. "We fought our way into this room. All of you were cramming me down for zero fucking dollars during the last two years. Where was 'the team' then? Where is 'the team' on the preferred stock sweetheart deal Elliott is getting now? The rest of you can pay for this. If the deal breaks, fine. If you think it's such a great deal, then give back some of your 120 percent recovery. I'm not reaching into your pocket. Don't reach into mine," screamed Liang.

"Ken, we are at the one-inch line," Mollett pleaded again.

The senior creditors like Mollett's GSO and Miller's Elliott were set to make recoveries greater than 100 percent. Liang's junior creditor group was allocated sixty-six cents on the dollar, which was less than the 100 cent par recovery they were theoretically owed. Still, sixty-six cents was nearly ten times what they were slated to get two years earlier.

The Kirkland conference room had glass windows that made the room visible to the outside lobby but could be fogged for privacy by hitting a switch. For better or worse, the windows remained clear for the duration of the meeting and several lawyers sat outside watching the fireworks involving their clients. One of them remarked that the wild-but-silent gesticulating was reminiscent of a Charlie Chaplin film.

"We are asking you, institutionally, to do the right thing here," Jon Pollock, the co-CEO of Elliott, jumped in.

"Who are you?" shouted the incredulous Liang.

Pollock had not, like Dave Miller, been handling the Caesars investment on a day-to-day basis. There was no particular reason the Los Angeles-based Liang should have known who Pollock was. Still, he was an elder statesman of Elliott and highly respected across Wall Street. Liang was well-known for his outbursts, but this insolence shocked everyone and probably should have embarrassed Liang. Liang, however, was too busy gloating about his triumph in the case and taunting all these putative allies in the room whom he believed had betrayed him.

"Apollo stole from us. They can pay the difference. We are leaving thirty-four cents on the table. We are in the business of loaning money to private equity companies and this would be bad for business," Oaktree's Kaj Vazales interjected, explaining the precedent that caving now could set. Whatever grievance Oaktree had with its fellow creditors, it paled relative to the rage it harbored for Apollo, whose wheeling-and-dealing was the single, defining issue of the bankruptcy. *Oaktree is here to drink the blood of Apollo,* one person in the room would recall thinking at the time.

"Oaktree does private equity stuff too. Maybe next time Oaktree is on the other side of this," Millstein tried to reason.

"Let me know the next time Howard Marks and Bruce Karsh get personally sued and have their personal bank statements subpoenaed," Liang fired back. Lumping the Oaktree founders with Apollo did not sit well with Liang.

Rowan and Sambur, along with David Bonderman, the TPG cofounder, were facing the possibility of personal liability in the case, a highly unusual situation that underscored the severity of the wrongdoing allegations against them. Worse yet, the week prior, the bankruptcy judge had allowed creditors to review their personal financial information to understand their wherewithal to satisfy a potential judgment, a decision that helped prompt this endgame.

But Apollo told Millstein they were not committing any more than the nearly $6 billion they had pledged to settle the Caesars case. The deadline for the deal was roughly 13 hours later at midnight on Friday, September 23.

"I'm disappointed in you, Ken. Oaktree has a reputation for being constructive," Millstein said.

"Well, I'm disappointed in you, Jim!" Liang fired back. Millstein and Liang then retreated to a private side room to continue the negotiation.

"Ken, you've done your grandstanding. Now you are just making a bad deal for yourself."

As a restructuring banker, Millstein was fundamentally a dealmaker: Efficiently get adversaries on board to make a fair compromise and move forward. It was not supposed to be emotional or moral, but rather purely transactional. That's how everybody made the most money. Good and evil and right and wrong did not apply in this world.

But as Liang had already proved, emotion had long overtaken Caesars, and Millstein, as one ostensible referee in the process, had been caught in the crossfire between Apollo and all the creditors. The whole episode was sickening and exhausting to him. The restructuring world had seemed to take a turn for the worse since he had returned from Washington. Too many people—and often twenty- and thirty-something-year-old men trying too hard to prove themselves as tough guys—private equity and hedge fund alike, were fighting merely out of vanity. Most of these funds took money from identical pensions—Texas Teachers, CalPERS, CalSTRS. These fights to the death just moved money from different pockets of the same investors.

Oaktree and Appaloosa, unsurprisingly, had a much different perspective. Vazales stayed in the main room and continued the negotiation with the rest of the creditors.

"We had to claw our way to victory. We've driven this case to its conclusion and you are not spending our recovery," Vazales said. He was a mild-mannered fellow far less prone to theatrical outbursts than his colleague Liang, yet he remained militant. Unlike Millstein, the teams from Oaktree and Appaloosa believed there were higher stakes at play. Private equity firms, they believed—best exemplified by Apollo—had become far too abusive of creditors, wielding legal documents and hardball negotiating tactics as swords to take value from loan and bondholders that simply did not belong to them. To Oaktree and Appaloosa, nothing less than the sanctity of the US capital markets was at stake in this room.

The senior Caesars creditors were not thrilled with Apollo either. But they were less sanctimonious about it and had been begging Oaktree and Appaloosa for months to back off their crusade, which was imperiling a delicate compromise with the private equity firm.

Jim Millstein and Ken Liang returned to the large conference room after their sidebar conversation. Oaktree and the junior bond-holders were not going to budge.

Dave Miller and Jon Pollock quickly left the meeting since there was nothing left to discuss. They knew there was only one way this deal was going to get done in the next 12 hours. Higher powers needed to be summoned—a group of billionaires, who Wall Street types often referred to as the "MoUs": the Masters of the Universe.

After Elliott's exit, Liang and Vazales left to have lunch and debrief at Casa Lever, a Midtown power spot. On the walk over, Liang's phone rang. It was an Oaktree number. The founders of the firm, Howard Marks and Bruce Karsh, were on the line. "Paul Singer just called us and he was just wondering what you guys are doing on Caesars?"

PART I

A NUMBERS GAME

Four assigned seats remained empty each day in class, and Gary Loveman was determined to find out why. He stood at the front of a Memphis conference room a long way from Harvard Business School where he had started as an assistant professor a year earlier in 1989. The prestige aside, the job did not pay particularly well. The real money for HBS faculty came from what he was doing now—teaching executive education seminars at Fortune 500 companies.

The Promus Companies was a hospitality business that had been spun out of Holiday Inn in 1989, the ultimate consequence of an effort to thwart a greenmail campaign waged by a budding Atlantic City tycoon named Donald Trump. The brands within Promus included hotel chains Homewood Suites, Hampton Inn, Embassy Suites, and the gaming company, Harrah's. Loveman and a group of HBS professors were offering a course in consumer marketing. Every Promus executive seemed enthusiastic, except those who were assigned to the four empty chairs. Loveman learned that the four were all part of Harrah's management and were at a bar just adjacent to the classroom Loveman was using at the University of Memphis. He was irritated enough to confront them.

"I'm just curious…You're here in town, and we're having these classes, and people seem to find them interesting, but you guys never show up," Gary Loveman offered incredulously. He expected contrition, but the group instead told Loveman to buzz off. The four were guilty of one of the Harvard hotshot's cardinal sins: the lack of intellectual curiosity.

"What struck me at the time was, here is a business, gaming, that has this elegant, underlying mathematization, which is always where my world has been. It throws off tremendously rich data, real time. And the people who run it are lightweights," recalls Loveman.

At the time, the typical gaming executive had limited formal education and had risen up as a food and beverage manager. As Loveman spent more time understanding Harrah's, he believed casinos were a sophisticated industry held back by unsophisticated operators.

Loveman's elite credentials belied his humble origins. Growing up in Indianapolis, Indiana, the youngest of three in a working-class family, Loveman had experience with financial hardship. His father was a factory worker at Western Electric and his mother was a homemaker.

He attended Wesleyan University in Connecticut, then spent two years as a research assistant at the Federal Reserve Bank of Boston before joining the economics PhD program at MIT. Loveman grew close to Professor Robert Solow, a towering figure in macroeconomics who had won the 1987 Nobel Prize. In 1988, Loveman was considered the top American PhD student in labor economics. His thesis explored the difference in unemployment rates between the United States and Europe. Accepting the HBS professorship made his academic work more practical than theoretical.

PHIL SATRE, LIKE BILL HARRAH, did not care much for Las Vegas. He instead preferred Reno, which, coincidentally, happened to be Harrah's ancestral home. Bill Harrah had fled Los Angeles in the 1930s where his bingo operation on the Venice Beach pier had drawn the ire of local authorities. Nevada had legalized gaming in 1931 and it was Reno, 400 miles northwest of Las Vegas, that became the state's first gambling hotspot.

Harrah's personal life would come to resemble that of many of the colorful entrepreneurs who would dominate the casino industry. A big drinker, he was married seven times to six women, and developed a taste for fancy toys, buying a collection of airplanes and automobiles with the help of the company's coffers.

Satre could not have been more different. Satre was a Stanford graduate and lawyer by trade. He was considered a gentleman in the edgy world of gambling, and after first joining Harrah's in 1980, became chief executive in 1994.

Harrah's had spun out of Promus in 1995, the latest in a string of hotel companies separating from more modestly valued casinos. Satre kept the Harrah's headquarters in Memphis. For years, Harrah's was just four properties: three in Nevada and one in Atlantic City. But in the 1990s, Middle America was becoming more open toward gaming and, more importantly, the tax revenue that came with it. As gaming licenses proliferated in Mississippi, Louisiana, Missouri, Iowa, and elsewhere, it was an advantage to be considered a company from down South. Harrah's would win several riverboat and Native American licenses as they started to come up.

But the company stagnated after that initial wave of regional properties was built. Satre needed a different strategy to keep up with the likes of Steve Wynn's The Mirage, with its pyrotechnics and waterfalls.

His only play was marketing; taking a commodity product—gambling—and getting players to pick Harrah's over and over again. Satre became convinced he needed to look outside the insular casino industry. The marketing wizards of that era were in consumer products and retail, getting Americans to buy paper towels or cheeseburgers by creating brands that were able to build long-term connections with customers.

Loveman continued his executive education courses at Harrah's through the mid-90s while his academic career was taking off. His booming baritone and dry wit made his classes popular and he was racking up teaching excellence awards. In 1994, his Harvard Business Review paper "Putting the Service Profit Chain to Work," written with four other HBS professors, cemented his status as a marketing guru. Drawing upon the examples of Southwest Airlines and Banc One, the paper tied together how motivated employees could create an experience for customers that drives their long-standing loyalty, which in turn can efficiently create massive returns for shareholders.

Satre was intrigued by Loveman's work, and in 1996 invited him to be an ex-officio member of management while keeping his Harvard position. Loveman began shadowing Satre, joining executive meetings when he could. When both were in Atlantic City at a meeting in 1998, Satre asked Loveman if he would be interested in a dedicated role: chief operating officer.

Everything about Loveman—his competitive nature, intellectual curiosity, ambition—pulled him toward accepting this job. Even on the brink of achieving tenure, Loveman had become restless. Satre's offer was for two years—the maximum leave he could take from Harvard—so it was not a long-term commitment. His family was firmly rooted in suburban Boston, and Satre would allow him to commute by private jet to Memphis.

The COO perch gave Loveman the power and credibility to implement his ideas rather than being marginalized in middle management.

"It was critical that I was COO. For what I wanted to do, I needed P&L control," Loveman explained, referring to his autonomy over the spending on the marketing initiatives he would champion.

"I could say to them, 'You will do this,' and they pretty much had to do it," recalls Loveman. "And then once it started working, it made everything dramatically easier. 'Holy shit, look at this, this actually works. We can drive revenue, we can build same store sales, hit our numbers and get our bonus.'"

GARY LOVEMAN'S CAREER AS A casino executive took off in a Memphis pizza parlor. His mission was to understand everything about those people who gambled at Harrah's tables, ate in its restaurants, and slept in its beds, so he could persuade them to never stray.

Loveman wanted to build a data-driven loyalty program where Harrah's would precisely track how customers spent their time and money, and then would direct micro-targeted offers—say, a free room, or steak dinner, or gambling credit—that would get a customer to turn up based on their revealed preferences. This was a Big Data project well before the term had been coined.

With nothing else to do during his weeknights in Memphis, Loveman planted himself at The Memphis Pizza Cafe and sketched out a new loyalty program. He was joined first by Richard Mirman and later, David Norton, who exemplified the type of executive Loveman would flood Harrah's with over the next decade: white men with elite educations who were fluent in concepts like "same store sales," "customer acquisition cost," and "lifetime value of the customer."

Rich Mirman had reached all-but-dissertation status on a math PhD at the University of Chicago and knew Loveman from a case study the professor had written on the management consulting firm, Booz Allen Hamilton. Norton was a Wharton grad working for American Express and had become acquainted with Mirman when they overlapped at Booz Allen.

Harrah's had existing loyalty programs, but they were uneven. Customers simply took their free rooms and dinners and then went across the street to do their gambling.

Using transaction data, the three developed quantitative models to tailor incentives to customers based on what their previous behavior revealed about their habits. In late 1998, just months after Loveman had come on board full-time, the Total Rewards loyalty program pilot was to launch in Tunica, Mississippi. Direct mail was sent to Harrah's customers with differentiated offers based on their hypotheses of customer behavior. "One customer would get $150 a night room rate, another $89 a night, a third might get it comped. We calculated the expected value of a guest before they called," explained one Harrah's executive.

Total Rewards was an immediate success. The local casino managers had little understanding of the underlying calculations but saw revenues jump in response to targeted marketing.

Loveman had found his dream job. Gaming touched customers in so many ways—at card tables, slot machines, hotels, restaurants, spas, golf, nightclubs—and he was running a business in a way that had never been done before. Ever the competitor, Loveman eagerly awaited daily revenue reports that told him if he was winning or losing. The monotony of academia never felt farther away. Loveman was conservative in his personal life, and had a growing family. But Gary grew to enjoy the buzz of the gaming industry and the chance to reinvent it: "Las Vegas was a blast compared to hanging around HBS for nine years."

Harrah's relocated its headquarters to Las Vegas in 1999.

Then, between 1998 and 2002, Harrah's revenues nearly doubled from $2 billion to nearly $4 billion. Its stock price was up 200 percent in that period. In 2002, Satre and the board informed Loveman he was being tapped for the top job. At the age of forty-three, Gary Loveman was the chief executive of what would soon be the largest gaming company in the world. The company had agreed to let him continue commuting to Las Vegas by private jet, keeping his family life separate in Massachusetts.

A unique experiment was about to begin. Loveman, who had never had a corporate job before becoming COO, was to become the public face of a heavily unionized and politically and socially fraught company. He was good in front of a big audience but had to learn to connect with different kinds of people in smaller groups. "Most people thought I'd leave in two years and go back to Harvard. They thought this would be like a kidney stone. It would hurt for a while, and then it would pass," Loveman would quip.

"In those early years, Gary was my hero, he was so smart, he had a booming voice and sharp wit, he was so excited to be CEO, he had grand visions for the company. Everyone was really motivated by him, galvanized by him. It was very heady times," said Jan Jones, who joined Harrah's in 1999 to run government affairs after serving as mayor of Las Vegas.

Loveman would go on to remake the leadership ranks of the company, increasingly finding talent from top business schools and management consulting firms. Loveman made no mystery about whom he favored: "I want to see evidence that someone has achieved a high level of success in some facet of their lives so I can be convinced that they know what a high level is and that they can aspire to it successfully. This could mean having run a business successfully, having run a project successfully, having done well academically, having been a great athlete, etc. If I didn't see any of these things, I probably wasn't very interested."

Harrah's had transformed into a well-oiled machine. The organization from top to bottom was singularly focused on the user experience. Chuck Atwood, the company's chief financial officer in the early 2000s, said, "We were talking about customers, everyone else was talking buildings," referring to the likes of Steve Wynn, Sheldon Adelson, and Kirk Kerkorian.

At the turn of the century, Harrah's spent billions adding regional properties around the country as well as snatching up the iconic Binion's Horseshoe in Las Vegas along with the World Series of Poker intellectual property.

Even after all this wheeling-and-dealing, Harrah's was still an also-ran in Sin City. By the early 2000s, MGM Grand was the dominant player, having acquired Mirage Resorts for $4 billion in 2000 and Mandalay Bay for $8 billion in 2005. Wynn was already plotting a comeback, and Sheldon Adelson's Venetian had opened in 1999.

Loveman's best shot at conquering Las Vegas would be Caesars Palace, which had been built by Jay Sarno, a son of Jewish immigrants who had settled in Missouri. Sarno had started out building motels in the South but after visiting Vegas in the 1950s, believed it needed an upscale property. The Roman antiquity theme was to play to guests' urges for hedonism and decadence. Caesars Palace was built with Teamsters money and, notwithstanding ties to organized crime, Sarno's vision quickly became the most famous casino in the world. Ironically, Caesars, when it was independent, found itself in the middle of the Michael Milken criminal proceedings. The junk bond king had been accused by the federal government of insider trading in Caesars bonds where his firm, Drexel Burnham Lambert, was leading a debt restructuring of the company in the 1980s.

In the summer of 2004, Harrah's announced it would acquire the newly re-christened Caesars Entertainment—which would give it not just Caesars but Bally's, the Flamingo, and the Paris hotel—for $9 billion. Loveman and team would efficiently capture the benefits of putting these new properties in the Total Rewards system. Harrah's stock price continued to soar, which would pique the interest of a different kind of math wizard.

2

KINGS OF LEON

There was little love in the air at Drexel Burnham Lambert this Valentine's Day in 1990. Marc Rowan, then twenty-seven years old, walked out of Drexel's New York office at 60 Broad Street with his office belongings in a cardboard box. The high-flying investment bank had dominated Wall Street in the 1980s with its mastery of the junk bond, a previously misunderstood form of financing for riskier—or more marginalized—companies.

But Drexel's wild ride of the previous decade had ended with an abrupt thud.

On February 13, Drexel filed for Chapter 11 bankruptcy protection after pleading guilty to six counts of securities and mail fraud a year earlier—the fallout of the sprawling and spectacular white-collar crime spree masterminded by its larger-than-life banker, the so-called "junk bond king," Michael Milken. Milken himself was facing ninety-eight counts of insider trading, securities fraud, and racketeering related to accusations of massive self-dealing while running the Drexel junk bond unit.

In his five years at Drexel, Rowan established himself as an uncommonly sharp thinker on finance. After graduating from Wharton with both an undergraduate and MBA degree in 1985, he'd been hired as a junior investment banker, a position which involved plugging numbers into spreadsheet models and drafting investment memos. But his colleagues noticed he was already capable of far more.

His ability to think strategically and devise creative solutions for clients—even in his mid-twenties—was unrivaled. He had secured the flattering moniker, "managing analyst." The term combined the title of "managing director" and "financial analyst," the highest and lowest rungs on the typical project team, given Rowan's ability to run all parts of a deal on his own. "Marc would sit in meetings and then say, 'Let me go home and think about this structure,' and he'd come back with some triple backflip no one else had thought of," according to one senior Drexel banker who was involved in Rowan's hiring.

Drexel's free-wheeling environment allowed Rowan to shine. Yet the firm's scandals and subsequent implosion made his career choice look unwise on that winter day in 1990 (years later Rowan would quip that in his time at Drexel he worked directly for three executives—Dennis Levine, Martin Siegel, and Michael Milken—all of whom went to jail for committing financial crimes).

In the early 1990s, the US was about to enter a recession brought on by higher interest rates from the federal reserve and the crisis among savings and loans—a type of under-regulated thrift where depositors could earn high rates of interest—that proliferated in the 1980s. S&Ls took those deposits, enabled by deregulation, and often invested in risky commercial real estate or Drexel's junk bonds, fueling a bubble that popped in 1990. The unsettled period of 1990 might have sent most bankers to hibernate and wait for a brighter day. For Rowan and a group of Drexel colleagues, it was the perfect time to start a second act.

Michael Milken's crucial insight was that small, speculative companies were shut out of the debt markets for irrational reasons. While a student at the University of California, Berkeley, in the late 1960s, Milken famously came across the studies of W. Braddock Hickman, an American economist who had found that low-grade corporate bonds on a risk-adjusted basis outperformed the high-grade bonds that were typically issued by large-scale, well-known, profitable companies.

Milken's genius as a junk-bond banker and trader was to find both companies who needed capital while also cultivating a coterie of buyers for those bonds who would show up repeatedly to stuff their balance sheets with the risky, high-yield paper. And no buyer of Drexel offerings was as loyal as Fred Carr, who ran a California-based life insurance and annuities firm called Executive Life. Connie Bruck reported in the *Predator's Ball* that by 1983, Executive Life had participated as a buyer in 100 percent of Drexel junk bond offerings. Executive Life eventually held billions worth of junk bonds, using the yields to pay high returns to its policyholders. But by the 1990s, the value of the Executive Life bond portfolio was collapsing just as Drexel failed.

After the Valentine's Day massacre, a group of Drexel bankers took refuge in the Manhattan office of Bennett LeBow, the chief executive of the tobacco company Liggett Group. LeBow was close with Milken, having used Drexel bonds for multiple takeovers. The Drexel group would soon get a fateful proposal from France's Crédit Lyonnais that would alter forever the destinies of both the swash-buckling French bank and Apollo Advisors, the financial firm that the Drexel survivors had formed.

The leader of the Drexel refugees was Leon Black, a husky, brash, Dartmouth and Harvard Business School graduate in his 30s who was running the Drexel merger group out of New York. Black was a native New Yorker born into privilege. But his world shattered in 1975 when his father, Eli Black, then the chief executive of Chiquita banana importer United Brands, leaped to his death from his office in the Pan Am building above Grand Central Terminal. In the days after his death, United Brands was discovered to have made millions in bribes to Honduran officials in order to reduce taxes on banana exports.

At Drexel, Black and Milken formed a formidable duo. Black became the aggressive dealmaker, assembling transactions like KKR's $27 billion leveraged buyout of RJR Nabisco that were then financed by Milken's junk bond group in Los Angeles. The success at Drexel was accompanied by unprecedented compensation for its bankers. Milken himself was taking in hundreds of millions of dollars annually, including $550 million in 1987 alone.

Decades after its birth, Apollo would eventually be identified as having three "co-founders": Leon Black, Marc Rowan, and Josh Harris. The idea that those three alone created Apollo is mythology. Rowan and Harris were too junior to be on par with Black. Over time, however, the two accumulated enough achievements at Apollo to demand and be granted the co-founder title from Black.

Crédit Lyonnais had proposed that Black's group of refugees form a boutique investment bank. But given the economic down-turn, there were few deals to get done. Black and team came up with a better idea: instead of earning commissions and fees as a middle-man investment banker, do deals and earn the profits for yourself. Executive Life, effectively insolvent by 1991, had been seized by the California insurance authorities. California wanted to auction the Executive Life business to shore up policyholders claims with minimal losses. Any buyer would conceivably be helping ordinary Americans while having the chance to profit as the junk bonds rebounded.

Apollo, partnering with an investor affiliate of Crédit Lyonnais called Altus, looked to acquire distressed junk bonds in the Executive Life portfolio at a steep discount, paying roughly $3 billion for a portfolio with $6 billion of face value. The auction of the Executive Life debt portfolio turned competitive, with sharp and deeppocketed investors such as the private equity firm Hellman & Friedman, music executive David Geffen, Texas investor Richard Rainwater, and California entrepreneur Eli Broad all wanting a piece.

Even against such rivals, the Apollo investors had a secret weapon that proved decisive. Black and team intimately knew the details and prospects of the companies whose junk bonds were in the Executive Life portfolio; as Drexel bankers in years past, they had marketed and sold them to the insurer.

Those bonds, which included paper from such companies as Vail Ski Resorts, Samsonite, and Culligan Water, would rocket upwards sharply as the economy improved (though there were occasional duds like Mexican restaurant chain Chi-Chi's). The legend of Apollo was born as a savvy investor in a moment of turmoil.

Apollo had become a trailblazer in the so-called "distress for control" market where it could buy up loans and bonds at steep discounts. When a troubled company restructured its debt, the paper that creditors had accumulated could then be swapped for stock in the reorganized company. If the company then turned around and improved, those credit investors who took on the risk could then make a windfall.

This type of investing took diverse skills—how much could the company be worth, how long will a recovery take, what rights are enumerated in legal documents—and perhaps most importantly, courage and patience to stay the course. Investors had to properly pick which tier of debt was worthless and which tier could be awarded the potentially valuable equity in a reorganized company.

Distressed investing was a natural extension of the junk bond explosion of the 1980s and its subsequent collapse. Loans and bonds were no longer just a passive financing tool that earned steady interest payments; rather, they could be opportunistically bought up and weaponized to take over troubled companies. Financial engineers like Black and Rowan who were experts in valuation, deal structuring, and complex negotiations, were the ideal distressed investors.

Years later, Rowan recalled that when he had joined Drexel, he believed that he was five years too late—all the money had been made and all the fun had. What he said he had learned from the Drexel blow-up and the subsequent birth of Apollo was that, "you want chaos, you want things to be shaken up, you want the system to be brought down and built up again. Just when you think the world is coming to an end and things are never going to get better, that is the time to build a career and build the next great fortune."

"THE PROBLEM WITH THEIR THEORY is that it is obviously wrong," responded David Bonderman. The Securities and Exchange Commission believed Raymond Dirks, a stock analyst, had violated securities law by telling his clients to sell their shares in an insurance company that Dirks believed to be committing fraud. Bonderman, 41, was representing Dirks in the case, and was being quizzed by Associate Justice Byron White of the US Supreme Court during an oral argument in March of 1983.

Bonderman's theory would be validated. Dirks, ten years after being censured by the SEC for his disclosure, was vindicated in 1983 by a six-three vote at the Supreme Court thanks to the zealous advocacy of Bonderman.

Bonderman was still a decade away from making his name as a private equity investor. His life before becoming a billionaire was itself worthy of a movie. He had graduated from the University of Washington in 1963 with a degree in Russian, and was a security guard at the Space Needle for a time. Three years later, he added a law degree from Harvard. He then spent a year traveling the world, having won from Harvard the Sheldon Fellowship, an experience so moving that decades later he would endow a similar post-graduate travel award at the University of Washington called the Bonderman Fellowship.

Bonderman then taught briefly at Tulane Law School before another Harvard fellowship where he traveled to Northern Africa to study Islamic law and learn Arabic. Next was a stint at the Department of Justice in the Civil Rights Division. Finally, in the early 1970s he landed at Arnold & Porter, the powerhouse Washington, DC, law firm. But even as a corporate lawyer, Bonderman still found time to pursue offbeat interests. He became an expert in landmark preservation law doing pro bono legal work and even became vice president of a DC advocacy group called Don't Tear It Down.

Bonderman's civic interest would lead to the biggest break of his career. He became involved in a project in Fort Worth, Texas, to prevent an expansion of a freeway that may have damaged a park and historic area. While in Fort Worth, he became acquainted with oil scion Robert Bass, a member of the famed Bass brothers who had taken their inherited oil fortune and became highly successful corporate investors in the 1980s, most notably in rescuing the Walt Disney Company in 1984 from a raid. In 1985, the brothers—Robert,

Sid, and Lee—established their own separate firms. Bonderman impressed Robert with his intelligence and thoughtfulness, and the lawyer quickly became the third-eldest Bass's deal maven.

Like the Apollo group seizing the Executive Life carcass, Bass and Bonderman would also make hay in the late 1980s failure of California financial institutions. Irvine-based American Savings & Loan, the country's biggest thrift, failed in 1988. The federal government took on much of the toxic assets, selling the remaining "good bank" to Bass for just a few hundred million dollars. Cleansing the toxic bank ultimately cost the federal government more than $5 billion (the cost to taxpayers of the broader S&L crisis was later estimated to be nearly $500 billion). The Bass group later sold the "good bank," rechristened American Savings Bank, for $1.4 billion in stock to Washington Mutual in 1996 (worries about the Bass' sweetheart deal allowed Uncle Sam to get 30 percent of the sale proceeds).

When Continental Airlines was coming out of bankruptcy in 1993, Bonderman could not convince Robert Bass that it was worth resurrecting. Bonderman and a Bass colleague then in his 20s, James Coulter, formed their own vehicle, Air Partners. Through Air Partners, they raised $55 million and partnered with Air Canada to take Continental out of Chapter 11. Bonderman installed Gordon Bethune, a former Navy mechanic, as chief executive who improved the airline's reliability and customer service. By the time Air Partners sold its stake to Northwest Airlines in 1998, it had made more than ten times its money.

In 1993, on the strength of the Continental turnaround, Bonderman, his younger colleague Coulter, and William Price, an executive with experience at GE Capital and Bain & Co., would together form Texas Pacific Group, a private equity firm jointly headquartered in Fort Worth and San Francisco (in the early days, the founders would joke that they had to explain the company was not a railroad).

In its early years, Texas Pacific Group bought such household names as America West Airlines, J.Crew, Ducati, and Burger King. Bonderman also took a personal stake in Ryanair in 1996, where he remained on the board until 2020. On the strength of the Continental investment, TPG developed a reputation less as a slash-and-burn financial engineer and more as an operations expert that could fix and grow underperforming assets. Its 1993 inaugural fund returned an annual rate of 36 percent to investors.

Meanwhile, Apollo's initial 1990 and 1993 funds returned roughly 50 percent. Rowan would boast that Apollo became the largest profit center of Crédit Lyonnais in those years, earning the French institution billions of dollars. Rowan would later wistfully recall those early days of managing a modest amount of capital and the heady returns the Executive Life trade provided: "I remember life was pretty good managing $3.5 billion." But in a pattern that would repeat itself for the next thirty years, the circumstances surrounding clever Apollo trades would prove controversial.

In 1997, a Frenchman named François Marland contacted San Francisco attorney Gary Fontana. Marland had an explosive allegation: The acquisition of Executive Life by the French insurer MAAF was ultimately a sham transaction. Crédit Lyonnais and eventually the French billionaire François Pinault were allegedly the ultimate buyers of the reorganized version of Executive Life and its undervalued junk bond portfolio. The transactions allegedly were "parking agreements" to circumvent American laws designed to prevent foreign-owned entities from buying US insurers.

In 2003, the Department of Justice announced that it had secured guilty pleas from Crédit Lyonnais and other French entities over charges that they had lied to the Federal Reserve about the nature of the Executive Life acquisition. The Department of Justice also announced a $771.5 million deal with the group including Artémis, the entity controlled by François Pinault, to settle the criminal inquiry. Pinault and Artémis were not criminally charged because they were cooperating with the DoJ. Separately, six French individuals were charged with fraud and the Federal Reserve announced its own enforcement action against Crédit Lyonnais, which by then had been acquired by another French bank, Crédit Agricole.

In 2001, California Attorney General Bill Lockyer filed a sprawling lawsuit not just against Crédit Lyonnais and the French parties involved in the Executive Life, but also against Apollo, Leon Black, and other executives for being a party to the Executive Life conspiracy. A year later, however, a federal judge threw out the lawsuit on the grounds that only the California insurance commissioner could bring such a lawsuit. Apollo by then was cooperating with the insurance commissioner and pleaded ignorance of the sham buyers created to purchase Executive Life.

The various litigation surrounding the Executive Life scandal meandered until 2015 and settlements and fines approached $1 billion. The authorities calculated existing policyholders were permanently shortchanged by several billion dollars in their life savings and retirements, while Apollo and its French partners made a windfall buying the temporarily cheap junk bonds.

After the fall of Drexel, for Black and team to so quickly jump into more hot water seemed especially shocking. Apollo's Machiavellian attitude had persisted since the days of Milken, and Executive Life was only the first display of their willingness to push the boundaries of the law when there was a chance to make money.

3

WAKING UP IN VEGAS

Harrah's stock was a puzzle that even Gary Loveman could not solve. Despite its massive revenue and earnings growth through the early 2000s, Harrah's valuation multiple lagged its archrival MGM Grand. And the entire gaming sector traded at a sharp discount to the hotel sector. Harrah's stock had risen steadily to the $40s, from roughly $14 when Loveman had become CEO. Yet Harrah's management did not believe that was anywhere near what the company deserved. Loveman even canvassed his academic friends for their views on the Harrah's discount.

The grind of being a public company CEO was also wearing on Loveman. He thought earnings conference calls with analysts should've been about the company's long-term strategy, but instead involved explaining why the company missed estimates by a penny—a phenomenon that drove the economist in him crazy.

In early 2006, Loveman got a call from Tom Barrack, founder of Colony Capital, a Los Angeles-based real estate investment firm. Colony Capital had sold Harveys Casino Resorts to Harrah's in 2001, and in 2005, Harrah's sold four regional casinos to Colony. Barrack learned about the value of Total Rewards the hard way, as the four casinos' profitability collapsed after they were unplugged from the Harrah's network.

Barrack was previously an investor with the Bass family, famously selling the Plaza Hotel across the street from Central Park to Donald Trump in 1988 for $400 million—a deal that would later nearly sink The Donald. Barrack wondered if Loveman would meet with his friend and former colleague from Bass, David Bonderman. The two met in New Orleans, where the TPG co-founder broached the idea of unlocking the value of Harrah's vast real estate portfolio, including Caesars Palace, clustered at the corner of Las Vegas Boulevard and Flamingo.

The hotel sector was already utilizing the so-called "OpCo/PropCo" model where land and structures were put into a separate "PropCo"—or property company—called a real estate investment trust. The REIT leased the buildings back to the "OpCo," which managed the hotel. REITs avoided corporate income tax and instead paid out big dividends. The package of the PropCo and the OpCo was theoretically supposed to be worth more than the integrated company because of the tax savings.

Loveman was intrigued both by the idea and by Bonderman, who was disheveled, quirky, and cerebral like Loveman himself. Harrah's signed a confidentiality agreement with TPG early in 2006, and both sides looked into their options. Bonderman casually broached the idea of a leveraged buyout and the pair kept in touch, but a $25 billion transaction seemed beyond the realm of possibility.

CHUCK ATWOOD WAS NO NOVICE when it came to financial engineering. Atwood had started at the Holiday Inn in 1980 as a financial analyst before it had even bought Harrah's. He worked his way up to increasingly senior finance roles, including positions in M&A and investor relations. In 1986, to fend off a rumored takeover threat from Donald Trump, Holiday Inn executed a defensive leveraged recapitalization, raising nearly $3 billion of debt using Drexel's famed "highly confident letter." Atwood recalled working on the deal with Michael Milken and his younger colleague, Ken Moelis, who would have his own legendary Wall Street career. The recapitalization was announced on November 13, 1986, the day before Ivan Boesky was arrested on insider trading charges which would later implicate Milken.

In the summer of 2006, Atwood got a call from an investment banker asking if he'd take a meeting with Marc Rowan.

By 2006, Marc Rowan was well past his junior supporting actor role at Apollo. Rowan and Leon Black had quickly established Apollo as a powerhouse in the 1990s. In 1994, Apollo had become a creditor to homebuilder Walter Industries, a company owned by private equity legend KKR. In court hearings in the bankruptcy case, the young Rowan had dazzled with his mastery of the company and its numbers and Wall Street took notice of a rising star.

Apollo's top three men had a complicated relationship. Rowan and Harris were both slender and slight men—under 5'8"—while the hefty Black towered above them at 6'5". Both Rowan and Harris, as their stature grew at the firm, considered leaving to launch their own ventures. They both chose to stay as they extracted from Black better economics, and eventually the co-founder title.

Apollo in many ways adapted the culture of Milken's Drexel. As other private equity firms matured in the 2000s, nearly all but Apollo tried to become more institutionalized and less insular around the founders.

Apollo was, however, run by the triumvirate. The vehicle that controlled Apollo was even called BRH, for Black-Rowan-Harris. Rowan described the firm as "a dysfunctional family with all that implies." The twenty or so Apollo partners all directly competed for capital for deals and compensation. Investment committee meetings to discuss opportunities were rollicking affairs where insults and derision flowed easily from all directions.

The competitiveness led to clever dealmaking, but few at Apollo forged close friendships at work. "Apollo's a place where you go to the office, do your work and go home. You don't really socialize with your colleagues," explained one longtime partner. One Apollo partner once brought a deck on why he deserved more money than certain peers to a year-end bonus meeting with the founders. One Drexel banker and now a Wall Street executive gushed about the talents of Black and Rowan, but then said they would never let their child work in Apollo's cutthroat environment.

Rowan was well-liked. He was charming, glib, and, by billionaire standards, down-to-earth. By 2006, he was married to the former Carolyn Pleva, a fashion designer, and had three sons. By all accounts he was happily married and adored his wife and children. "I married my trophy wife. I come home every day and smile. One of the secrets to my success is being super-pumped up every day," Rowan once said. Rowan even bragged that there had been no divorces among Apollo partners.

Rowan's reputation for feeling secure and comfortable in his own skin proved to be another contrast with Harris. One Apollo partner put it this way: "Josh Harris wakes up in the morning thinking about Marc Rowan. Marc does not wake up thinking about Josh." They had each helped build fortunes at Apollo, but they mostly just stayed out of each other's way. And the way Apollo's culture was set up, that worked just fine.

Atwood took the meeting with Rowan, whom he immediately liked. Rowan was interested in hearing the Caesars story, and Atwood thought the logic of a leveraged buyout was sound—though he did not think a transaction approaching $30 billion would be feasible.

Atwood then arranged for Gary Loveman to meet with Rowan, unaware that Loveman was having ongoing discussions with David Bonderman. Later in August 2006, Loveman and Rowan met in New York Porter House, a restaurant in the Time Warner Center overlooking Central Park. Loveman noticed that Rowan came prepared, seemingly having already thoroughly researched the company. Harrah's was the rare casino group with an investment grade credit rating, and with even ordinary growth projections, the equity returns could be very high in an LBO transaction.

Like Bonderman, Loveman was impressed with Rowan, whom he viewed as eloquent and having a "facile mind," an expression Loveman used a lot. He thought to himself, "I could trade my current smart but less engaged board for this highly engaged, super smart board, it would be good for Harrah's and it would be a good challenge for me to be alongside David Bonderman, Marc Rowan, and Leon Black."

Loveman asked Rowan only a single question that night: "Will you oblige me to run this company for the right reasons or will you force me to run it the way you want to run it?" Rowan assured him that the answer was the former. A leveraged buyout of Harrah's was now in motion.

In a span of two weeks in 2005, the private equity world changed forever. On March 17, Toys R Us agreed to be acquired by KKR, Bain Capital, and Vornado Realty Trust for roughly $7 billion. Eleven days later, SunGard Data Systems announced it would be taken private at a $11.4 billion enterprise value by a six-firm "club"—Bain Capital, Blackstone, Goldman Sachs, KKR, Providence Equity, and Texas Pacific Group. It would, for a short time, rank as the second-largest LBO of all time, only trailing the 1989 RJR Nabisco buyout (by a meaty $15 billion, however).

Leveraged buyout artists had become the richest men on Wall Street by the 2000s, but their province remained public companies that had fallen out of favor or misbegotten divisions of larger conglomerates. Yet the combination of massive amounts of capital that private equity firms were beginning to raise—KKR and Blackstone collectively raised $40 billion for LBO funds in 2006—along with low interest rates meant that plenty of large, stable, corporate stalwarts were suddenly vulnerable to a private equity bid.

Most of these companies were not in need of an overhaul like Continental Airlines in 1993. Rather, their stability allowed them to hold a massive amount of debt that public markets would not tolerate. The debt markets were permissive, giving big buyout firms the greenlight to chase virtually any company. Michael Milken had fantasized about the day he could organize a raid of an IBM or a General Motors and, by 2005, this almost seemed possible.

One private equity executive involved in the Harrah's deal said his analysis at the time showed that historically, 10 percent of companies in the S&P 500 had a blended cost of capital lower than a typical private equity investment. Because of the unique condition of the debt market in the mid-2000s, that proportion had reached 80 percent. "We saw the opportunity to buy Caesars and it was all because the leverage distorted the weighted average cost of capital. It wasn't sustainable. We got deluded," said this person.

SunGard's landmark $11 billion acquisition early in 2005 would have only been a footnote in 2006 or 2007. Such titans as TXU, Clear Channel Communications, HCA, Hilton Hotels, and First Data were all acquired by private equity consortiums in so-called club deals for between $20 billion and $45 billion.

One investment banker to private equity firms recalled the mania of 2005 to 2007. "Debt commitments for LBOs typically took weeks and sometimes months. Now, I'd get a call on a Saturday for a deal announcing next Tuesday. It was hard to keep track if the deal was for $8 billion in total or if the equity check contribution was $8 billion [implying a $30 billion deal]," said this person.

In September 2006, Loveman told Bonderman of the parallel Apollo discussions to buy Harrah's, and both firms decided to team up since the combined equity check needed for the deal was going to exceed $5 billion. In August, Loveman had told some Harrah's board members that the two firms were working on a bid, but didn't inform the full board until early September.

The broader board was not happy to learn of the discussions. For one thing, Loveman was conflicted. Apollo and TPG contemplated the Harrah's management team staying on after the deal. Loveman was both a member of the board accountable to shareholders and also now a bidder for the company. The board also believed Loveman's involvement with one bidding group could chill a full-fledged auction for the company. The company was doing well, and the board also wondered if private equity firms would even have the patience to get onerous gaming licenses.

Still, the board had a duty to consider any bid, and created a special sub-committee of directors who were not part of management to handle the transaction. That committee was made up of several captains of industry including Bob Miller, a long-time grocery executive at Albertsons; Brad Martin, the CEO of Saks; Stephen Bollenbach, the CEO of Hilton Hotels; Frank Biondi, a longtime Hollywood executive at Viacom and Universal Studios; Barbara Alexander, a former Wall Street analyst; and Chris Williams, one of the most senior Black executives on Wall Street at his own investment bank, Williams Capital.

The company signed up advisors to navigate the various conflicts in the deal. The special committee hired Ken Moelis of the Swiss bank UBS to run the auction. After Drexel, Moelis had gone on to a storied career as a Los Angeles-based investment banker at Donaldson, Lufkin & Jenrette; Credit Suisse; and then UBS, where he was running the global banking group.

Apollo and TPG were working with Deutsche Bank, who would be instrumental in organizing the $20 billion of debt financing that was going to be needed. TPG's law firm was New York powerhouse Cleary Gottlieb Steen & Hamilton. Apollo was using Wachtell, Lipton, Rosen & Katz, perhaps the most elite M&A law firm in the world.

Over the course of fall 2006, Apollo and TPG raced to conduct their due diligence. At one point, Loveman invited David Bonderman to a Harrah's charity gala in Las Vegas. A silent auction ended that night with Bonderman spending $300,000 to buy an Aston Martin, raising eyebrows about the men circling Harrah's.

Moelis had been trying to gin up an auction, and by mid-December, the contest for Harrah's was down to the Apollo/TPG group and a rival bid from Penn National Gaming, a small, regional operator that had started out as a single dog track. On December 14, at the UBS office, the special committee invited the Apollo/TPG group to make their final pitch to the board. Apollo brought Leon Black, Marc Rowan, and another colleague, Eric Press. TPG came with David Bonderman and his younger colleague Karl Petersen. Penn National would also get a final meeting.

The committee retreated and decided to see if they could wring out better terms from Apollo and TPG. The sides agreed to a ninety-dollars-per-share price. But the board was worried that state regulators would not approve TPG and Apollo as buyers, so the private equity firms agreed to pay a $250 million fee if they could not get the sign-off. (As the deal became more certain, Leon Black, in an internal meeting, ordered his colleagues to sort out any off-the-books nannies, lest the nosy state investigators start poking around.)

With the go-ahead to negotiate the final contract, the deal machine went into overdrive the evening of December 14. Paperwork

THE CAESARS PALACE COUP • 31

finalizing the merger and complex financing had to be completed. The financing included roughly $6 billion of equity from the sponsors along with $7 billion of bank loans, $6 billion of bridge loans to be refinanced by junk bonds, and $6.5 billion in real estate loans, most of which was provided by JPMorgan through the booming commercial mortgage backed securities—or CMBS—market. $4.5 billion of Harrah's original existing debt would remain. Roughly 100 lawyers, bankers, company executives, and private equity investors— some coming from Las Vegas—descended upon the Wachtell, Lipton office in the CBS building on 52nd Street.

Each of the financings required their own lawyers and bankers who got their own breakout rooms. The size of the transaction required financial commitments from the biggest banks on Wall Street including Deutsche Bank, Bank of America, Citigroup, Credit Suisse, JPMorgan, and Merrill Lynch.

The keys to the ninety dollar bid were the real estate financing and the existing Harrah's bonds.

In order to secure a fully underwritten CMBS real estate loan, Harrah's would effectively mortgage six properties: two in Las Vegas, two in Atlantic City, and two in Lake Tahoe. Because of the hot real estate market in 2006, the debt secured by the six casinos was far greater than what could have been borrowed from a traditional loan or bond. Apollo and TPG had been obsessed with taking advantage of that arbitrage, and so were able to originally secure a $6.5 billion commitment of mortgage debt—about a third of the total Harrah's new financing figure of $20 billion. The commitment for the real estate-backed loan was essentially unprecedented. Real estate financing was not new, but banks had been reluctant to provide a bridge loan strictly based on property valuations, which they were now doing for the first time in the Harrah's buyout—a sign of the excesses that had developed in financial markets.

Crucially, most of the existing Harrah's debt did not have to be refinanced. Because it was not secured by any collateral, suddenly Harrah's could issue senior debt backed by the company's assets. It would do so in the LBO deal, pushing $4.5 billion of existing debt to the bottom of the totem pole in a $25 billion debt stack. This was cruel. Those existing unsecured bonds crashed in price as they were last in line to be repaid. But the maneuver allowed Apollo and TPG to issue new debt more cheaply. And it illustrated one of the key legal principles that would echo through this case: Debtholders' relationship with the company remains strictly contractual. Any rights they have must be bargained for and embedded in documents. The management and board of a company, in contrast, have fiduciary duties which dictate that they maximize shareholder value.

Three days later, on December 17, the exhausted group finally left the Wachtell conference room with the merger and financing documents in place. Penn National's final bid in the form of cash and stock did not quite hit ninety dollars per share, and the board chose the offer from Apollo/TPG.

Ken Moelis gave a formal written opinion to the board that the terms of the deal were financially fair. UBS was in line for a $40 million fee when the transaction closed. Loveman and Atwood told the board that Harrah's management supported the Apollo/TPG bid. The full board then unanimously voted to approve the $90/share offer or $27.8 billion in total.

Apollo and TPG had pulled off, assuming regulators agreed, perhaps the most audacious deal in American gaming history, and one of the ten biggest LBOs to date. Both firms made their reputations as canny assessors of risk and reward, but had seemed to throw caution into the wind, paying a near 40 percent premium to win a tense bidding war. The economy was humming at Christmas 2006, with nothing but clear skies on the horizon.

PUT YOUR MONEY WHERE YOUR MOUTH IS

After a much-needed holiday break at the end of December 2006, Apollo and TPG were back to dialing for dollars in January 2007. On top of $4.6 billion of existing debt that Caesars would keep from before the buyout, banks had committed to $20.5 billion of new debt financing, putting the banks on the hook for the money when the deal reached its final closing. Apollo and TPG had also pledged that they would come up with the remaining $6 billion of equity from their own pockets.

The pair of private equity firms, however, had no intention of footing $3 billion each, a massive slug far too much to put behind any single company. Instead they would rely on co-investors—millionaires, billionaires, other investment funds, large institutions around the world—to join Hamlet Holdings, the name of the legal vehicle Apollo and TPG created to acquire Harrah's. On January 24, the private equity firms arranged a Las Vegas site visit for prospective investors, including tours of Caesars Palace, Harrah's Las Vegas, and the Rio.

In advance of the meeting, Apollo and TPG had circulated a 64-page memo that explained their rationale for the deal, hoping to persuade investors to spend alongside them. Wall Street analysts and observers had been shocked that Apollo, the legendary value investor, had paid a princely price more than 10 times Harrah's 2006 EBITDA, or operating cash flow.

But Apollo and TPG were unworried, as casinos had historically been recession-proof. The investment memo read, "The [Harrah's] performance over the period from 2001–2005 is exemplary as the

Company was operating in an environment of varying economic conditions in the wake of 9/11, the SARS scare, a recession, and the wars in Iraq and Afghanistan." By 2012, the Apollo/TPG model had forecast the company's EBITDA to hit more than $4 billion, 40 percent greater than 2006.

Apollo and TPG forecast that Harrah's aggregate or enterprise value could be as much as $40 billion by 2012, and its equity investment could grow from $6 billion to between $15 billion and $20 billion. The implied annualized rates of return were between 22 and 27 percent, which were typical for LBOs. But those kinds of returns, when applied to a gargantuan $6 billion initial equity investment, created record-breaking absolute dollar profits.

Those numbers got Gary Loveman's attention. Loveman's accrued stock and severance in the buyout totaled nearly $100 million when cashed out. He rolled about a quarter of it back into the deal. Separately, he and the rest of top Harrah's management were incentivized with roughly 5 percent of the company's equity. During the bidding process in 2006, colleagues noticed how attuned Loveman was to his potential profits from the deal. Michael Jensen, an economist who later became Loveman's Harvard colleague, had risen to fame in the 1980s evangelizing leveraged buyouts. His theory was that private equity firms would run companies more efficiently because managers would be given a much larger economic stake in the business. The equity that Loveman and other Harrah's management received exemplified Jensen's theories.

Debt investors were hungry for high-yielding loans and bonds in the mid-2000s. This seller's market meant that the contracts under which Harrah's debt was going to be sold would contain few restrictions, called "covenants," on Apollo and TPG.

The rights of loan and bond holders were spelled out in lengthy loan agreements and bond indentures. The covenants sections explained how companies could issue new debt, sell assets, and pay dividends to shareholders. Creditors wanted to ensure they got paid back first, before any payments to stockholders. But in this era when issuers and private equity firms held all the cards, "covenant lite" debt ruled the day. Harrah's LBO debt would have just a single covenant: the senior secured debt-to-EBITDA ratio test. "This tremendous flexibility should allow the Company to operate through downturns with much less risk of needing bank amendments, further administrative burden, or risk of default," according to the memo.

The co-invest opportunity being marketed in 2007, however, was a strictly passive bet leaving Apollo/TPG firmly in charge of managing

Harrah's day-to-day. More than 30 institutions were impressed by what they saw in Las Vegas in January, and the subsequent pitch from Rowan and Bonderman. These co-investors of the buyout group were, like Apollo and TPG, the smartest, most successful, and most sophisticated investors in the world. They ranged from traditional private equity to hedge funds to Wall Street banks. Funds that put money into the deal alongside Apollo and TPG ultimately included Blackstone, Goldman Sachs, Credit Suisse, Bear Stearns, Deutsche Bank, Oaktree, Silver Point, Oak Hill, and Perry Capital, among several others.

If Apollo and TPG were comfortable investing at a near $30 billion valuation, many less-savvy investors were eager to tag along. The Michael J. Fox Foundation and Bob Kraft, the New England Patriots owner, joined the group. Wealthy venture capital investors from Boston who knew Loveman signed up. From the mid-level on up, Harrah's executives—700 roughly in total—were also given the chance to invest in the LBO. Harrah's hosted a meeting showing the group how their equity multiplied over time; $100,000 could turn into $350,000 over five years, in line with the model Apollo and TPG had shared with the prospective institutional investors. Not every executive chose to buy in, but most did, with one junior executive even committing his entire net worth of $250,000. By the time the equity syndication process was complete, Apollo and TPG were just putting in $1.325 billion each, with the co-investors responsible for $3.4 billion.

IN THE FIRST HALF OF 2007, the economy still was accelerating. TXU, the Texas utility, became the largest LBO ever at $43 billion. In 2007, Harrah's operated in a state of purgatory. The transaction was months from officially closing and transferring ownership. Yet the existing Harrah's team were not free to run the business as before. A shadow board comprised of Apollo and TPG executives was formed. Any big decisions, including spending more than $50 million on an acquisition or casino renovation, required their approval.

Loveman now was getting a taste of what it was like to work with Marc Rowan and David Bonderman, both of whom he had become enamored with in the LBO process.

Loveman noticed that Rowan, at the outset, tended to be deferential to Bonderman, who was twenty years older and, at the time, had more stature. That deference would fade in the coming years. Bonderman was busy with his breakneck globetrotting and extracurricular hobbies, "saving tigers and elephants," as Loveman would say.

Though he'd been the CEO of a multi-billion-dollar casino company, Loveman now felt like he had reached a higher orbit with the private equity glitterati. In 2007, the Harrah's charitable foundation made a $30 million charitable gift to the hospitality school at the University of Nevada, Las Vegas, which Apollo and TPG were happy to approve. The Anti-Defamation League charity honored Loveman, and Rowan and Bonderman wrote big checks and attended the gala.

TPG's annual investor meeting took place each fall in Arizona, at the posh Phoenician resort. There was always an A-list act—Tom Petty or Stevie Nicks—that the white, middle-aged executives could sway to each evening. And Loveman got to sit at the head table with Bonderman and Jim Coulter.

Rowan also introduced Loveman to Hollywood and the Hamptons. Loveman would get a speaking slot at Michael Milken's conference held in Beverly Hills each year as a sort of a modernized version of the Predator's Ball. Loveman met Jimmy Iovine, the legendary music executive who was a friend of Rowan's (Rowan would personally invest in Beats by Dre, Iovine and Dr. Dre's headphone startup that was later acquired by Apple for $3 billion). It was worlds away from leading case study discussions with MBA students.

THE PERSONAL FINANCES AND AFFAIRS of titans like Bonderman and Rowan were not easily disentangled. But if they wanted to own a casino, they were going to have to let regulators into the tent. State gaming commissions were empowered to conduct intrusive background checks with the purpose of rooting out organized crime from the industry. Regulators dug into the private lives of potential licensees, looking for any skeletons lurking in closets.

Loveman found gaming commissioners to be contemptible. In some states, commissioners were political hacks who got their positions through patronage. In others, highway patrolmen or law enforcement officials were empowered and enjoyed wielding power over businessmen. To buy Harrah's, Apollo and TPG were going to have to seek approvals in eighteen different states, a grueling process that alone would have frightened off most Wall Street funds.

But Apollo and TPG had an ace in the hole: Frank Schreck. By trade, Schreck was a Las Vegas gaming lawyer. But he had become one of the most powerful people in Nevada as whisperer or fixer, skilled in the dark arts of shepherding his clients through the regulatory gauntlet. Schreck was the guy in whom casino bosses confided their darkest secrets—mistresses, secret bank accounts—and he made sure those obstacles never got in the way. Schreck himself had been instrumental in convincing gaming regulators that private equity firms could be good owners of casinos.

State regulators were intently focused on ensuring jobs, investments, and charitable contributions were maintained when approving M&A deals. Because casinos were highly regulated and had largely unionized workforces, Harrah's made sure that they donated heavily to the right causes—the NAACP and the like—to maintain warm relationships with people who could potentially cause trouble. It was simply a cost of doing business.

By the time the application for the Harrah's LBO came before the Nevada Gaming Commission for approval in December 2007, the Apollo and TPG executives had received approval in most of the needed states. The process was difficult at times. The Missouri state police sent a contingent to New York to personally inspect Leon Black's world-class art collection worth hundreds of millions of dollars. Missouri was frustrating enough that Bonderman wondered if it was easiest to just sell the two properties Harrah's had in that state. Perhaps the most awkward encounter occurred in that state. TPG senior executive Kelvin Davis apparently shared a name with an ex-convict. To prove that he was not that Kelvin Davis, he was asked to remove his shirt to show he did not have the tattoos that the felon was known to have.

The drill was the same across states for Caesars, Apollo, and TPG. Separate private jets from New York, San Francisco, and Las Vegas would land in Jefferson City or Harrisburg or Jackson or Springfield for a half a day of hearings, and they would get out of Dodge just as quickly. This process of parachuting in and out of small-town America was not dissimilar from when the private equity firms showed up scrounging for state pension cash.

On December 5, the Nevada Gaming Control Board held its first hearing on the Harrah's buyout after a 10-month investigation into the deal, Apollo, and TPG. If a majority of the three-member GCB was supportive, the transaction would move to the Nevada Gaming Commission for final approval.

Frank Schreck opened the proceedings by introducing his clients from Harrah's, Apollo, and TPG. Apollo brought Leon Black and Josh Harris, as well as Eric Press and Anthony Civale, two other executives who had worked on the buyout. Marc Rowan was unable to attend and would appear before the commission two weeks later. It was an unusual if not unprecedented show of force to bring the very highest reaches of the private equity firms. But each wanted to show their commitment by licensing their most important executives.

Loveman spoke first and emphasized how much Harrah's was set to spend in Las Vegas by expanding Caesars Palace, and by starting new developments at the cluster the company had created at the corner of Las Vegas Boulevard and Flamingo. He reminded the commissioners that Harrah's employed 87,000 people and paid $323 million in taxes and more than $1 billion in wages, along with more than $300 million to vendors.

Loveman then sang the praises of Apollo and TPG, with a tinge of his own sardonic wit. "We are pleased to be partnering with two firms that we consider to be the best of the lot…they have a track record of being patient, long-term, value-added investors…I've discovered in my now nearly one year of working with them that they are reasonably well-behaved and show some capacity to learn."

There was a chumminess hanging in the air since the gaming control board already knew Harrah's, Loveman, and Schreck intimately. But the board still had real questions and wanted to ensure that the Wall Street guys were not going to embarrass them—or Nevada. Apollo and TPG were coached to be warm.

In the Q&A session, one board member, Mark Clayton, was curious about how, given the debt, the firms would be able to invest in the business. Press quickly responded that it was easier for a private company to raise capital than a public one. Bonderman, speaking for the first time, broached the re-investment strategy at Continental.

"One of the reasons we have this opportunity," Bonderman explained, "is because of [Harrah's] need for ongoing capital and the public market reluctance to see the long-term value, where we in fact see that as the major value."

Schreck also wanted to vouch for the limited partners who put capital into TPG and Apollo, saying that "from a standpoint of regulatory control, it probably represents the cleanest money that you could get into the gaming industry. It's basically the pensions and funds for firefighters, policemen, and public employees."

Jonathan Halkyard, the company's new CFO who had replaced Chuck Atwood, spoke next about the LBO financing. Halkyard had been an HBS student in the mid-1990s, and had steadily risen through the ranks since joining as an assistant general manager at Harrah's Lake Tahoe. His job was to allay any concerns about the $24 billion of debt the company was going to soon have. "While certainly the level of financial leverage is higher than the company had in the past, I think it's a reasonable amount of leverage. I think the company is going to be able to satisfy its debt obligations fully."

Loveman closed the formal remarks by explaining how wise it was to go private at that moment because "private equity ownership led by these two firms would enhance the capacity of our business to continue to develop what has become at least a different approach to a large gaming company operation…I am today before you even more enthusiastic about those prospects than I was at the time in December [2006]."

The discussion materials that Harrah's shared with the board described the fees Apollo and TPG would extract from the company as they owned it. First there was a $300 million deal fee the two firms would split for simply closing the deal. There were also annual monitoring fees leveled at one percent of EBITDA that would accrue to firms.

The commission asked what exactly Harrah's was getting in return for roughly $30 million a year. "We…between our two firms in a given year we pay very, very large fees to Wall Street," explained Eric Press of Apollo, "and therefore have tremendous access and negotiating leverage with various providers of financing and tend to spend a lot of time working with our portfolio companies optimizing their capital structures, sourcing additional capital…[A]nother area simply by virtue of the nature of the business that we are in as private equity firms where we will spend a lot of time with the Harrah's team is on future acquisitions and capital allocation opportunities."

Dennis Neilander, a lawyer and chairman of the gaming control board, then announced he would support the buyout, explaining that the commission had done a study of several deals the two firms had completed. He was also comfortable with the Harrah's debt load. "And while this company at the end of the day [is coming] out with a higher blended interest rate is certainly a much more leveraged company than it is today, it doesn't rise to the level where it's going to cause me regulatory concern."

Next to support the bid was board member Mark Clayton, who said that "both of the funds have had one or two investments that struggled, but rather than cut and run from those investments, our record indicates both funds stayed with those investments and nurtured them along for a lot longer than otherwise could have been required."

Randall Sayre, another member, added, "Mr. Loveman might take some exception to this, but Harrah's is our baby, too."

The three commissioners then approved the buyout application.

On December 20, the buyout went before the Nevada Gaming Commission, whose five governor-appointed members took up licensing matters sent to it by the Control Board. Rowan, famous for avoiding neckties, made an exception for these important discussions.

Rowan humbly discussed how Apollo's ownership of Vail Resorts had demonstrated the firm's long-term orientation and that according to the firm's calculations, 92 percent of their investments had demonstrated a positive rate of return. "But rarely is it straight up," he said. "We often take a detour along the way...there is a business cycle, there is an economic cycle, there is competition. There is a thrust and parry to dealing with all that. And I think having done this over seventeen years, having lived through a number of business cycles, having lived through some pretty catastrophic events including owning a large hotel chain in the aftermath of 9/11 has taught us a great deal of patience..."

Halkyard again stated the leverage was manageable, though he shared a new statistic that showed what little slack Harrah's would have: "The ratio of our total operating cash flow to our annual interest expense which is about 1.5 times also compares quite favorably with a number of transactions that have been done recently..." A ratio of cash flow to expenses below two times historically had been considered on the edge.

With those assurances out of the way, there was still time for banter. Commissioner Arthur Marshall teased Rowan and Loveman, "I want to warn both of you since our chairman here is a Harvard man and Mr. Loveman is a Harvard man, you can always tell a Harvard man, you just can't tell him very much."

The gaming commission went on to unanimously approve of the buyout, along with the licenses for the Apollo and TPG executives. Commissioner Marshall, who was nearly eighty years old, ended the session with his personal memories of Bill Harrah. "Harrah's has really been a legendary company in this state. I'm proud you are continuing that legend."

5

A BRIDGE JUST FAR ENOUGH

Gary Loveman could still play economist when necessary. At the December 2007 hearing, Nevada regulators were curious about his thoughts on the state of the suddenly wobbly American economy.

Loveman, who was also a board member at FedEx and Coach, said: "The trends out of all these businesses, not ours but these others, are disturbing for me…and I would just add finally that as I think about events that influence consumers, there are some of these that are linear like gas prices go up five cents and then ten cents, and I think that has not had a particularly damaging effect especially on our business, and then there are others that are really discontinuous where someone says I can't sell my house and if I had to I would take a big loss or my children can't get a mortgage for their first home or my job is at great risk. I think these kinds of very discontinuous events tend to make consumers quite wary and in turn the businesses that service those consumers quite wary…I think the next few months will be demanding."

Whatever Loveman's view on the economy, Harrah's needed to sell its $20 billion of debt in early 2008 to close the buyout. In the intervening 12 months, the capital markets had already been upended. The LBO boom had suddenly withered.

In the typical LBO, the most senior debt would be in the form of a term loan that matured in five to seven years. Banks in the 1980s created a process called "syndication" where loans were sold by arranging banks among a wide pool of buyers, other banks, insurers, mutual funds, and even securitized into so-called collateralized loan obligations.

LBO financing could be lucrative. Harrah's estimated that the total transaction expenses for the $28 billion deal would exceed $1 billion, with much of that going to the half-dozen banks responsible for assembling the debt financing. The loan syndication process, along with refinancing the bridge financing into junk bonds, unloaded the risk off the bank's books. But the gig only worked if the financial markets did not seize up between signing a deal and closing it months later. If the banks could not unload the debt, it would be stuck on their own balance sheets. On a $20 billion loan, even a 5 percent haircut was worth $1 billion.

When banks made their Caesars commitments in December 2006, they agreed with Harrah's on the interest rates and other terms of the debt. In the race to get deals done between 2005 and early 2007, little attention was paid to the fine print in M&A contracts and financing papers. With financial markets and the economy roaring, there was little chance that a buyer would attempt to walk away.

When Eric Press explained to the regulators in December that the management fee to Apollo and TPG went toward strong-arming the Wall Street banks, he was not kidding. The Harrah's deal was one of the massive LBOs that comprised more than $300 billion of deal financings that sat in limbo. Six banks involved in the Harrah's financing—Bank of America, Citigroup, Credit Suisse, Deutsche Bank, JPMorgan, and Merrill Lynch—were about to be on the hook for the Harrah's debt as the biggest financial crisis in eighty years was unfolding.

In January 2008, Apollo and TPG needed their six banks to display some courage. Sometimes private equity firms and banks were in sync on trying to back out of deals, as both stood to lose money on acquiring a damaged business. But in the case of Harrah's, Apollo and TPG wanted to get it done and were willing to play hardball.

Ultimately, Harrah's avoided having to get tough with the banks, and Apollo and TPG compromised. Harrah's gave the banks a little more flexibility on the interest rates at which they could sell the debt to ease the syndication process. The covenants on the debt still remained minimal. On January 28, 2008, more than a year after signing the merger agreement, Apollo and TPG were now officially the proud owners of Harrah's. Shareholders received ninety dollars per share in cash, a valuation that the company would not even come close to seeing for nearly a decade.

Apollo's willingness to get Harrah's across the finish line did not mean, however, that it always was willing to live up to signed contracts. In July 2007, an Apollo chemicals company, Hexion, announced a deal to acquire rival Huntsman Corporation for a total value of nearly $11 billion. Leon Black and Josh Harris had coveted Huntsman for years and had personally negotiated the transaction with Jon Huntsman, a devout Mormon from Utah who had founded the company in 1982. The final deal negotiations occurred at the Huntsman vacation house in Deer Valley in the presence of two US Senators from Utah, Orrin Hatch and Bob Bennett.

By early 2008, Huntsman's prospects deteriorated from the previous summer. A highly leveraged acquisition was now unappetizing to Hexion, and Apollo got cold feet.

On June 18, Hexion disclosed that it had obtained an opinion from valuation firm Duff & Phelps, stating that the combined Hexion/Huntsman would be insolvent. The consequence of that opinion would prevent Deutsche Bank and Credit Suisse from fulfilling their financing commitment. Hexion also filed a lawsuit in Delaware asking a judge to allow it to walk from the deal paying no more than the $325 million reverse termination fee.

Jon Huntsman told the *Wall Street Journal* the two Apollo cofounders "should be disgraced." His son Peter, who was CEO of Huntsman, said of Apollo, "if this is their way of conducting business, it's absolutely pathetic."

Delaware Chancellor Stephen Lamb was not impressed with Apollo's act either. The evidence at trial showed how Apollo and Hexion appeared to have manipulated the solvency opinion, not telling Huntsman in advance it had retained Duff & Phelps and never seeking Huntsman's inputs on its financial projections. Duff & Phelps' notes from the pitch meeting—found during discovery—had the phrase "get out" scribbled on them, along with, "1) Notice the insufficient capital to close. 2) [Apollo] hiring D&P to support that notion."

Lamb ruled that Apollo/Hexion had "knowingly and intentionally breached" numerous covenants under the contract, writing in his opinion, "If one man intentionally kills another, it is no defense to the charge of murder to claim the killer was unaware that killing is unlawful." Lamb ordered Apollo and Hexion to live up to the pledges made in the merger contract, or otherwise face damages.

Apollo and its litigators at Wachtell Lipton had a separate legal inferno on its hands. Huntsman had sued Apollo—along with Leon Black and Josh Harris—in Texas, Huntsman's home state, for backing out of the deal, claiming that Huntsman was entitled to $3 billion in damages.

However, cooler heads prevailed. Apollo and Hexion settled by

December 2007, with Black and Huntsman personally negotiating the detente. Huntsman would get $1 billion split between Apollo and the two funding banks, Deutsche Bank and Credit Suisse. Apollo also agreed to help Huntsman in its separate pending Texas litigation against the two banks, for conspiring with Apollo to breach the merger agreement (the banks would separately settle with Huntsman for $1.7 billion).

Jon Huntsman's 2015 autobiography devoted a full chapter to the Apollo saga, entitling it simply "The Double Cross." It offered such lines as, "Our earlier experiences with Bain and Blackstone proved there is no honor among thieves or among Wall Street shops. Apollo was no exception...Matlin [a Huntsman board member] had warned us Apollo would attempt to shaft us and Apollo did not disappoint... the route Apollo chose for saving itself was duplicity."

PART II

6

PROJECT RUNWAY

The lawyer deposing Chuck Atwood in a New York law office asked the now-former Harrah's CFO to flip through some printed emails. Atwood was in the middle of a lawsuit concerning a Bahamas casino project Harrah's was trying to exit. The lawyer was attempting to goad Atwood into saying something unflattering about private equity. And those messages between Apollo and TPG executives may have been good enough to get Atwood to take the bait. Executives at the two firms were using unflattering language and disparaging the near thirty-year Harrah's veteran. Atwood had no clue Apollo and TPG felt that way about him.

He then knew it was time to move on from Harrah's, even after Marc Rowan apologized for the language of his underlings. Atwood had enough stature that Rowan and David Bonderman attended his retirement dinner later in Las Vegas. Mr. Atwood, and several other executives who left in 2008, may have had the right idea. The optimism about an economic recovery Gary Loveman spoke of to the Nevada Gaming Commission in 2007 was misplaced.

Apollo and TPG spent a fortune buying Harrah's because the business was thought to be impervious to swings in the economy. But with America reeling from record unemployment, foreclosures, and massive losses in home equity and the stock market, there was little appetite for consumers to visit casinos.

From the moment the buyout closed, Harrah's was on its heels. The company had only experienced rapid growth for the decade Gary Loveman had been there. Loveman thought to himself, "We have been trained to drive a Ferrari and now we are stuck in a Kia."

Management skills, he had come to believe, were not symmetric; just because you knew how to grow a business did not mean you could be the one to shrink it.

While Harrah's was coming to grips with the new reality, Loveman was trying to figure out his new bosses. As he had noticed in 2007, Apollo and TPG had differing management approaches. He got along well with Rowan, who was quick and decisive. TPG was trickier. Once, there had been questions about why Harrah's management was pricing rooms at the Rio more modestly than perhaps they should have. Loveman showed the two firms how Rio could then drive customers to other higher-end Harrah's property like Caesars Palace. With Apollo, the math immediately clicked. With TPG, it took rounds and rounds of the same presentation with little breakthrough.

Harrah's employees below the top levels of management were often intimidated by the private equity guys. The Apollo and TPG teams consisted mostly of white men with degrees from fancy schools. Even as Loveman had raised the bar for the talent at Harrah's, there were many managers whose backgrounds were modest and whose careers had advanced steadily over the years within the company.

But ultimately, most Harrah's employees had decent experiences with both firms. The TPG team tended to be warmer and friendlier, but many employees almost preferred the no-nonsense, direct style of the Apollo executives.

THE MONUMENTAL TASK OF TURNING Harrah's around was going to require all of the tools available across TPG and Apollo, each a master of different domains. TPG, which resurrected Continental Airlines, focused on the so-called "left side of the balance sheet" where the company's physical assets were enumerated. Its operational expertise could be used to make Harrah's leaner and meaner.

Apollo, its core strength in financial engineering, would take on the right side of the balance sheet, where the liabilities and equity details of the company were listed. Marc Rowan once said, "It's all about if $A = L + E$," referring to the famous accounting identity that states that a company's book value of assets is equal to the sum of its liabilities and its equity. "If your assets are worth more than your liabilities you will find someone to bridge the liquidity gap."

In 2008, operating profit was down already a third from 2007. Financial leverage worked both ways. If the company performed well, Apollo, TPG, and the co-investors could have easily doubled their $6 billion equity investment. But the $24 billion of debt also gave the company little wiggle room if it got into trouble.

Between 2007 and 2009, overall visitors to Las Vegas fell by nearly seven percent, but gambling revenue fell by nearly 20 percent. Americans were still coming to Sin City, but it was a different crowd spending far less money. That was obvious when the Harrah's management team walked around the properties. Some guests at the check-in line at Caesars Palace now brought their own beer-filled coolers. The corporate convention business had become a lifeblood of Las Vegas, particularly from Wall Street. With the US banking sector on the ropes, junkets essentially collapsed overnight. In 2006, 6.3 million convention goers visited Las Vegas. In 2009, that figure was down to just 4.5 million.

Washington seized on the politics and optics of the banking bailout that saved Wall Street while millions of Americans were forced from their homes due to foreclosures. In early 2009, the newly inaugurated President Barack Obama said in a speech, "You can't go take a trip to Las Vegas or go down to the Super Bowl on the taxpayer's dime." (A year later, he turned to American consumers remarking, "You don't blow a bunch of cash in Vegas when you're trying to save for college.")

TPG's job was to get the assets in the $A = L + E$ identity to be worth more. From its famed operations group alone, the firm had sometimes devoted as many as ten professionals to work on Harrah's, to say nothing of the investment team and capital markets group who were also grinding away. There was a sense that Harrah's was flabby. Its largely uninterrupted success and growth never created much urgency on costs. There was natural fat to cut, and the operations group had sophisticated "lean" management approaches to wringing out savings, applying lessons learned from throughout the TPG portfolio.

The work was as simple as following housekeepers around for a day and tracking how they cleaned a floor full of rooms. The insights could be quite basic; most of the housekeeping staff were Latino women. One of the most demanding physical tasks was simply removing bedsheets to change out and wash. TPG came up with the idea of using "strippers"—men whose sole job was to go room to room stripping the bedsheets off before housekeepers arrived. Staff break rooms tended to be centralized in massive casinos. Instead, TPG found that installing satellite rooms reduced downtime and increased productivity.

JUST A COUPLE MILES NORTH of the Stratosphere casino at the very northern edge of the Las Vegas strip resides a non-descript trailer complex that may be as high-powered an office space as there is in the city. It is home to the offices for Culinary Union Local 226, an affiliate of Unite Here. The Culinary Union represents 60,000 housekeepers, valets, janitors, cooks, and bartenders—nearly all the daily workers that keep a casino running (with the exception of dealers)—in Nevada and Atlantic City. The Culinary Union's trailers double as a museum, the walls littered with photos of members proudly posing in their casino uniforms. The union's advocacy and scale had won healthy wages and benefits, and unionized casino jobs, despite the physical demands, were coveted, even if gaming CEOs quietly cursed organized labor.

The union had negotiated a strong contract in 2007 that was set to expire in 2012. The contract called for annual wage escalations but the union—viewing the carnage from the financial crisis—agreed to defer the increase for one year in exchange for extending the contract through 2013. The hope was that the recovery would be in full bloom by then and workers would have a strengthened bargaining hand.

In many ways, casino workers were insulated from the Great Recession. Their wages were fixed by contracts and their benefits stayed in place. There were layoffs, but rules around severance, seniority, and hiring back workers mitigated the pain. Many workers felt the downturn at home; many workers, particularly women, had suddenly out-of-work spouses who were in the once-booming Las Vegas construction sector. Still, Harrah's would shed several thousand jobs.

The recession, along with the crushing interest expense, forced the company to make tough choices on where to spend precious cash. They first examined the properties where ordinary improvements could be pushed to a later date. Loveman had been less focused on the casino "box," and some believed the Harrah's properties already looked tired. One member of the executive team said, "The properties were becoming embarrassing. Rooms at the Paris hadn't been touched in twenty years. The original tower at Caesars Palace was a scary place."

Harrah's had committed to finishing the new Octavius hotel tower at Caesars Palace and spent $1.1 billion in capital investments in 2008. By 2010, capital investments had dropped to just $160 million. One bellman at The Paris described the years after the Apollo/TPG takeover: "It felt ugly after the buyout. Before you could service the guest, it was a great place to work before those private equity guys took over."

Attrition and hiring freezes meant that employees were often forced to do the work of two people. Customers were suddenly facing longer lines to check in and have their luggage delivered, which proved stressful both for guests and the remaining staff. Holes in the wall weren't fixed because maintenance crews were let go, and there was no money for repairs anyway. Duct-taped carpet was evident everywhere. The system for delivering and bussing room service orders broke down, leaving carts of food scraps next to elevators and guest rooms, leading customers to complain and forcing the union to intervene.

"[M]oves to aggressively implement cost savings across the property platform in areas such as staffing levels, direct mail, comps and cash back awards is concerning as well," wrote Deutsche Bank analysts in 2008. "While management may consider these actions necessary, we believe these actions will aggravate an already discouraged work force and degrade properties, in some cases in great need of repair."

The Harrah's workforce generally had enjoyed good relations with Gary Loveman. He may have been an elitist when it came to academic credentials, but he was otherwise unpretentious. The union and employees owned shares in the company and would attend the annual stockholder's meeting. Caesars line workers were even given photocopies of The Service Profit Chain, the paper that had put Loveman on the map and which touted the importance of basic interactions with the customer. The kinship between CEO and worker that had been one of the pillars of Caesars' success was now wobbling.

The job was weighing on Loveman as well. He continued to commute from Boston, doing his best to keep his professional problems out of his personal life. But he was putting on weight and aging quickly. He also knew he had to be positive and put on a brave face with employees when everything was looking grim. "They should see a CEO who was confident, not tired and dejected. If the buffet chef in Joliet only sees you once a year, you need to be 'on' all the time," Gary thought to himself.

Harrah's was slashing hundreds of millions in annual costs, but it needed revenue to stabilize. The biggest challenge to that was the meltdown in Atlantic City. AC had been roughly one-third of Harrah's EBITDA at the time of the buyout. Gaming was slowly being legalized along the mid-Atlantic, which was known at the time of the leveraged buyout. Harrah's four AC properties made it the number one player in the market, and even the 2003 opening of the Borgata, the first new development in years, had not slowed Harrah's position. But the financial crisis led to neighboring states aggressively handing out licenses, desperate for the tax revenue. In 2006, total Atlantic City gaming revenue exceeded $5 billion. By 2013, that figure had dropped below $3 billion, and Pennsylvania was on its way to becoming the second-largest gaming market behind Nevada.

New capacity was its own problem in Las Vegas. The cycle for building resorts lasted several years and in the early 2000s, with no sign of financial crisis and with Sin City booming, all the big players launched major projects. MGM had its City Center extravaganza, its 16 million square-foot enclave of hotels, casinos, condominiums, shopping, and commercial office space. Steve Wynn built Encore as a follow-up to Wynn. Las Vegas Sands opened Palazzo. New York developer Ian Bruce Eichner opened the hip Cosmopolitan down the street from Caesars.

Between 2001 and 2011, Las Vegas expanded from 127,000 rooms to 150,000 rooms even as demand had softened considerably. Hotels were not only sensitive to occupancy rates but also to the so-called ADR, average daily rate. The ADR, which had climbed to $140 per room before the crisis, was down to below $100. There was no way to grow cash flow enough to get from underneath the debt load. Fortunately, Apollo had expertise in what needed to be done next.

THE HARRAH'S BOARD HAD GATHERED in Atlantic City in the spring of 2008. For Leon Black, this was not the time to be worrying about what other people would think. Of the $21 billion of new debt the company had issued to complete the LBO a few months ago, $1.5 billion was in the form of so-called "PIK toggle" bonds. PIK stood for payment-in-kind. Holders of this debt were owed a coupon payment of around 11 percent each year. However, Caesars had an option. Instead of paying in cash, it could issue new debt instead. If the PIK option was invoked in a given year, the debt balance to be repaid would grow from $1.5 billion to $1.65 billion to reflect the interest payment added to the principal amount.

Exercising the PIK was a no brainer. The mortgage market meltdown was in full swing, and every dollar saved at Harrah's counted toward preserving liquidity. Bonderman and Jim Coulter were, however, less convinced than Apollo. Exercising the PIK would irritate bondholders and would signal that Harrah's management was already worried about the business just months after closing the deal. They also worried about the precedent, and what it would signal about TPG as a firm. Ultimately, Harrah's agreed to invoke the PIK election in July 2008—though emails between Apollo's and Harrah's executives showed that the private equity firms were indeed interested in applying "spin" to the announcement to avoid "[news] stories combining 'Harrah's' and 'bankruptcy' in the same sentence."

Fortunes in private equity were just as much about making home run investments as avoiding big losses. At some point, Apollo and TPG knew, the financial crisis would end. The economy would recover, and Americans would start traveling and spending again. They just had to buy enough time and enough breathing room at Harrah's for that turnaround to happen. And Apollo, with its heritage at Drexel, knew all the tricks of the trade to "extend the runway"—the metaphor that private equity used to describe tinkering with the debt stack to create more space for the company to get airborne.

Loveman used to pore over casino data every morning to see how Total Rewards was bringing in repeat customers. Now, in constant tricky refinancing negotiations, the Caesars executive team would gather around fax machines, celebrating when documents from banks would roll in. Board meetings would erupt in applause when Apollo could report that he had convinced lenders to ease financial covenants.

As expected, the six banks who participated in the Harrah's 2008 LBO financing took huge baths on the deal, with paper losses extending into the billions. These so-called "hung bridges," bridge loans that could not be quickly syndicated to mutual funds and other institutional buyers or refinanced as junk bonds now created an opportunity for a particularly aggressive type of scavenger: the distressed debt investor.

DISTRESSED DEBT HEDGE FUNDS AND private equity firms—which included Apollo and TPG—were happy to scoop up Harrah's paper, and paper from other LBOs gone bad, for fifty and sixty and seventy cents on the dollar from besieged banks. The distressed debt industry had slowly emerged in the 1980s. The federal bankruptcy reform enacted in 1978 made Chapter 11 bankruptcy a far more efficient forum for re-organizing companies. In the 1980s, commercial banks and insurance companies were typical corporate creditors who were mostly looking for ways to get paid back. But in the aftermath of the junk bond collapse, more specialized funds were created to buy troubled bonds and loans.

Distressed investors in those early years were considered misfits, those who could not get jobs in investment banking or as corporate raiders. Yet the newness of the distressed market allowed these early investors to make fortunes. Distressed debt was the natural extension of Milken's insight about mispriced risk and reward in the junk bond market.

By 2008, the distressed debt market was a mainstream asset class with hundreds of billions of dollars dedicated to the strategy. Those buying the hung LBO bridge loans were not necessarily seeking to take over companies. These funds could lock in solid returns for limited risk. And certain early investors in Harrah's paper from 2008, like Oaktree and GSO Capital Partners, would go on to be long-term investors in the company.

The mix of distressed investors and traditional bond and loan investors now holding Harrah's paper, from the likes of Fidelity and Vanguard, created opportunities for wheeling-and-dealing. Apollo had two goals: slash debt where possible, or at least push out maturities to further in the future.

To reduce debt, Harrah's could go into the market and buy back bonds and loans at discounted prices. Buying back a bond at fifty cents reduced debt by one dollar of principal, immediately creating fifty cents of equity value. This was economically efficient but required cash to be diverted from capital expenditures and other priorities.

Harrah's other option was so-called exchange offers. It could, for example, offer new paper worth $80 million to holders of $100 million of debt, which would mature three or four years later, in exchange for a higher ranking in the debt stack. To induce holders to make the trade, Harrah's could push up the interest rate and offer extra fees.

In December 2008, Harrah's exchanged $2.2 billion of existing debt for new debt with a face value roughly half of that. In March of 2009, it exchanged $3.7 billion of new debt for then-outstanding debt of $5.5 billion. At the same time, the Harrah's operating company and the separate entity that housed the CMBS debt were buying back debt in the open market.

Harrah's also needed help from the federal government. The company's discounted debt purchases were reducing the company's leverage but had created tax liability when the company was already running low on cash.

After a call from Marc Rowan, Jan Jones, the former mayor of Las Vegas who ran public affairs for Harrah's, went to work. Jones, along with Apollo's longtime Washington lobbyist Norm Brownstein, pressed Nevada Senator Harry Reid and Max Baucus, the chair of the Senate Finance Committee, for relief. The campaign worked. The American Recovery and Reinvestment of 2009, also known as the "stimulus package," included a provision for the "cancellation of debt income" that deferred taxes on debt repurchases. At the next

Harrah's board meeting after the bill's passage, Loveman mentioned the CODI provision in the stimulus bill. Rowan and Bonderman rose to their feet and applauded Jones for getting the results they wanted.

"YOU ARE GOING TO BUY Planet Hollywood?"

Harrah's workforce's collective reaction to Gary Loveman's M&A idea was not exactly exuberance. Harrah's had already imposed layoffs, suspended 401(k) contributions, and scaled back property maintenance, including in employee dining and break rooms. Loveman was sympathetic to the backlash. But he also knew the company could not sit still if it wanted to grow out from underneath $24 billion of debt.

While Harrah's had been strategically buying back its own debt at a discount, it had been carefully examining the debt of other troubled rivals. In 2009, Harrah's began acquiring the junior mortgage debt of the Planet Hollywood hotel and casino from the likes of Goldman Sachs for fifty cents on the dollar or less. Ultimately, Harrah's spent $70 million to acquire $300 million of debt, which it then converted into a controlling equity position by early 2010. There was a remaining $550 million senior mortgage that would be left in place at a low interest rate, making it a low-risk bet.

A young executive at Apollo, David Sambur, had been looking at various distressed casinos like Las Vegas's Fontainebleau and Atlantic City's Revel to plug into Harrah's. Those were poor fits, and nixed by Harrah's management. Planet Hollywood, however, would be the property that both Apollo and Caesars could agree on. Planet Hollywood could be its own distinct "box" away from OpCo where its cash flows and debts did not become enmeshed in the overleveraged Harrah's.

Planet Hollywood's location at the intersection of Flamingo and Las Vegas Boulevard put it directly in the cluster of existing Harrah's properties. It drew a younger crowd and there were possibilities for expanding into entertainment. Planet Hollywood would eventually pay off big time for Harrah's, generating nearly $200 million a year in net cash flow after being acquired for less than $100 million. The Harrah's leadership was impressed that Sambur, the thirty-year-old Apollo junior executive, had pulled it all off.

Harrah's canniest acquisition, however, would not be a casino or a plot of land. Rather, it was a Quebec lawyer with an entrepreneurial streak.

Mitch Garber had been a lawyer in Montreal through the 1990s before helping create a successful payment processing business. In 2006, Garber became CEO of Party Gaming, whose Party Poker unit was the largest online poker business in the world. Party Gaming was a smashing success and naturally tied with Garber's background in payments. It also had run afoul of US laws on online gambling and settled with the US Department of Justice for $105 million in 2009. Garber left Party Gaming in 2008 and announced he was joining Harrah's just days after the 2009 settlement with the DoJ.

When Harrah's acquired Binion's in 2004, it also got the World Series of Poker brand, moving the showcase tournament to its Rio property off the strip. Loveman thought they could do much more with the World Series of Poker, most notably offering real-money, online tournaments that could be worth billions—and Garber was the man to expand the Caesars empire online.

In 2006, the US enacted the Unlawful Internet Gambling Enforcement Act, which Harrah's was determined to overturn with its army of lobbyists in Washington. Harrah's would clash for years with Sheldon Adelson, the man behind Las Vegas Sands, who was also making a name for himself in Macau. Adelson was hell-bent on preventing online gaming and committed his own fortune to stop it. In that stalemate, Garber had an idea. With the advent of smartphones, games on mobile devices were taking off. What if Harrah's pivoted into social, just-for-fun casino games for mobile phones?

In 2011, the company spent $115 million to acquire an Israeli mobile games start-up called Playtika. Loveman believed the online business could be the next big thing in gaming whatever broader changes the traditional casino business was enduring, and that Garber was the guy to figure it all out.

FOR JOHN PAULSON, THE FINANCIAL crisis had been anything but miserable. Paulson had believed the housing market was overvalued and bet against mortgage-backed securities. The wager netted his funds $15 billion in 2008 and cemented Paulson, a once obscure figure, as an immediate billionaire and legend. In the years after the crisis, he believed that Las Vegas was poised for a big comeback and had made savvy bets on MGM Grand stock, becoming the company's second-largest shareholder.

Harrah's stock was not listed since the LBO closed in 2008, so Paulson's next best option was to buy the company's unsecured bonds which—because of their position at the bottom of the capital stack—made them most resemble equity. But Paulson wondered if there was a better trade to make. An executive at Paulson & Co,

Ty Wallach, knew Marc Rowan and had run into him at the Milken Global Conference in Beverly Hills in spring 2010. Over the following months, the firms structured a way for the hedge fund to get the equity exposure Paulson wanted.

Apollo had found its own success as a distressed debt investor. It had bought up the discounted loans of troubled chemicals maker LyondellBasell from Wall Street banks, eventually accumulating a large position of control in the company's 2009 bankruptcy. Apollo spent $2 billion buying up debt, which turned an eventual profit of $10 billion after LyondellBasell restructured its balance sheet and took advantage of the fracking revolution in the early 2010s. It would prove one of the great trades in the history of private equity, and model what Paulson hoped to accomplish at Caesars.

Paulson had bought unsecured debt held by a Harrah's affiliate for roughly sixty-six cents on the dollar. In total, Paulson, along with Apollo and TPG funds, then exchanged $1.1 billion worth of unsecured bonds for 16 percent of equity in the Harrah's parent company. Paulson was getting that tenth of the Harrah's equity at a valuation of roughly $4.5 billion. Importantly, the exchanged bonds were now owned by the Harrah's parent and were not officially retired obligations; the OpCo would still be effectively sending cash up the chain to the ParentCo in the form of interest payments.

In conjunction with the deal, Harrah's filed an IPO prospectus in August. Public equity could become a currency to further reduce debt. As part of the IPO and to play up its luxury image, Apollo and TPG changed the company's official name from Harrah's to Caesars Entertainment Corporation, and thereon the company was always referred to as "Caesars."

Paulson's enthusiasm for Caesars was, however, not broadly shared, even as the company had knocked off its overall debt balance to $21 billion and had pushed back major debt maturities until 2015. On a roadshow across America, the company tried and failed to sell its shares to the public at a valuation greater than $5 billion, less than the buyout price, but more than the valuation for which it had exchanged its unsecured bonds. Apollo would execute dozens of capital markets transactions between 2008 and 2013. Yet, with the business still deteriorating—particularly Atlantic City—it was hardly making a dent. It was time for Apollo to try something more daring.

LEON BLACK NEEDED A FAVOR from Gary Loveman. He wanted a blowout sixtieth birthday bash, and wouldn't it be great if Elton John performed? Most Americans were still suffering the effects of the financial crisis; but it was good to be at Apollo, after the LyondellBasell win and the firm's own IPO in early 2011.

Elton John had a residency at the Colosseum theatre at Caesars Palace since 2004. Gary Loveman connected the two and for a million dollars, Elton happily performed at the party in Southampton in August 2011. According to the *New York Times* account, Lloyd Blankfein, the Goldman Sachs CEO, bumped into Steve Schwarzman of Blackstone at the party and teased him about his infamous 2007 birthday extravaganza while tying it to Black's. "Your sixtieth got us into the financial crisis. Let's hope this party gets us out of it." Black wisely chose not to have his party in Las Vegas.

Bonderman, on the other hand, believed Sin City was the perfect place to celebrate his big day. His legendary sixtieth party in 2002 began at the Bellagio and later migrated to the Hard Rock for the musical portion of the evening. For his seventieth in November 2012, he wanted to go all out again.

This time he happened to be the co-owner of a casino chain that had a property worthy of a private equity billionaire. After scouting Caesars Palace, Bonderman instead chose Wynn, believing it had the needed space.

"David, you don't have to do this at a portfolio company and this is totally your call. But I have to say this is going to be demoralizing to the workforce that the principal owner of the property is having his party at a competitor down the street after going through layoffs, 401(k) cuts and no raises. It isn't going to go down well," Gary Loveman pleaded.

Embarrassed TPG executives reached out to Loveman to offer sympathies. The party ended up being even more spectacular than previous soirees. The entertainment included Robin Williams, John Fogerty, and Paul McCartney. Guests were put up at the Wynn and were each given $1,000 that they could donate to a charity of their choice. The party made news highlights and Loveman, wounded by Bonderman's decision, would be asked for years about why exactly the TPG founder did not choose the casino he owned.

A PARTY AT THE MUSEUM of Modern Art proved more problematic for Leon Black and Apollo. On the evening of May 15, 2007, the crowd included New York heavyweights such as Mayor Mike Bloomberg, Henry and Marie-Josée Kravis, Caroline Kennedy, Carl Icahn, Barry Diller and his wife Diane von Furstenberg, and Vera Wang. The MoMA was hosting its annual black-tie "Party in the Garden" fundraiser, and the evening's honorees were Leon and Debra Black and Martin Scorsese. The entertainment would be provided by Jay-Z, who, like Black, was a native New Yorker.

Among the A-list New York glitterati, the two most important guests that evening in Black's mind may have been a pair of non-descript, middle-aged men from California. Leon Shahinian was a senior executive at CalPERS, the massive California state pension that had invested in Apollo funds since the mid-1990s. Shahinian had come to the MoMA fundraiser with Alfred Villalobos, a former board member of CalPERS who had since become a private equity "placement agent." Placement agents were hired by private equity firms like Apollo to help them connect with the pools of capital who would be the backbones of their funds. Leon Black ran into Shahinian that evening and told the CalPERS executive he was glad he could make it.

Shahinian rented a tuxedo for the MoMA festivities, but his remaining out-of-pocket expenses were limited. Rather than taking a commercial flight, he joined Villalobos on a private jet for the 5-hour trip. At the time, CalPERS was examining buying a stake of Apollo and Shahinian was part of the team on the project. Apollo had hired Villalobos to represent its interests with CalPERS. It looked to be an odd arrangement, given that Apollo and CalPERS had done business together since 1995—and Apollo's sparkling investment returns should not have required much help finding investors.

According to evidence gathered later, Black had met the two Californians in the hours before the MoMA event at Apollo's office at 9 W 57th, just up the street from the museum. In June, a few weeks after the party, the CalPERS investment committee met. Shahinian recommended that the pension invest $700 million into the Apollo management company given their long, mutually successful relationship. He failed to mention, however, that he had just returned from an all-expenses-paid New York trip a few weeks earlier, or the three wine and champagne bottles, including one from the MoMA event, that Villalobos had given him.

In July 2007, two months after the MoMA event, Apollo announced it had sold 9 percent stakes to CalPERS and to the Abu Dhabi Investment Authority, another long-time backer, for $600 million each, roughly valuing Apollo at $6 billion and confirming the billionaire status of Black, Rowan, and Harris. The stake sales were precursors to an IPO of the entire firm. In 2006, Apollo had listed an affiliate on an Amsterdam exchange, an entity called AP Alternative Assets, which it referred to as AAA. AAA was a way for ordinary investors to get access to private equity funds. A portion of AAA had even invested in the Harrah's deal.

The sheer amount of cash floating around private equity meant that there was plenty of money for hangers-on well down the food chain—like Villalobos—who made themselves gatekeepers between investment professionals and the bureaucrats who controlled the purses at pensions.

For the MoMA junket, Villalobos was reimbursed by Apollo for $8,000 in hotel costs, $1,500 in car service fees, and $50,000 for the private jet charge. Additionally, Apollo paid Villalobos's firm $13 million as a placement fee for the ultimate CalPERS investment in Apollo.

A month after the museum party in New York, Leon Shahinian gave a presentation to the CalPERS investment committee recommending the deal. Shahinian was later put on leave in 2010 after his interactions with Apollo came to light and he eventually quit CalPERS.

In April 2010, Apollo and CalPERS announced that the private equity firm would lower its management fees by $125 million over the next five years and agree to no longer use placement agents to secure capital commitments.

But the storm was only just gathering. A few weeks later, Villalobos and Federico Buenrostro, the former CalPERS CEO, were charged by the California Attorney General over a massive bribery and fraud scheme. The state alleged Villalobos illicitly offered kickbacks to Buenrostro to pour billions of state money into the funds of his clients. Between the state's indictment and an outside report completed by a law firm in 2010 for CalPERS, the lucrative relationship between the pension, Villalobos, and the investment community became clearer.

Overall, the state paid nearly $1 billion a year to external managers just in fees, which explained why investment firms found placement agents worth the trouble. Villalobos had been paid $60 million by external investment managers seeking CalPERS dollars. In 2006, Apollo's new general counsel, John Suydam, had instituted a new policy regarding the firm's placement agents. He wanted agents to have a form signed by the institution who was getting a capital commitment so that relationship could be disclosed to both Apollo and any of its limited partners in a fund. After Apollo instituted this policy, Villalobos tried and failed to get CalPERS investment staff to sign the form.

Villalobos then went to Buenrostro illicitly and did forge several Apollo forms. The documents signed were plainly inauthentic, but

Apollo accepted them and paid more than $20 million to Villalobos. Apollo paid roughly $40 million in placement fees in total to Villalobos, according to the California indictment, with $20 million or so coming from payments associated with the sham CalPERS disclosures.

A 2012 Securities and Exchange Commission action against Buenrostro and Villalobos depicted Apollo as a victim. "Buenrostro and Villalobos not only tricked Apollo into paying more than $20 million in placement agent fees it would not otherwise have paid, but also undermined procedures designed to ensure that investors like CalPERS have full disclosure of such fees," said John M. McCoy III, Associate Regional Director of the SEC's Los Angeles Regional Office.

In 2015, Buenrostro was charged with corruption and fraud and ultimately pled guilty, admitting to taking $250,000 worth of gifts and travel. In 2016, he was sentenced to 54 months in prison. Buenrostro was also set to testify against Villalobos in his trial on the charges. But in early 2015, Villalobos took his own life at a shooting range, at age 71 and in poor health.

His suicide spared Apollo potentially embarrassing revelations at trial about the firm's relationship with Villalobos. Still in 2013, CalPERS committed $500 million to Apollo's eighth flagship fund.

In less than two decades, Apollo had been in the middle of two enormous California scandals—Executive Life and CalPERS—and had avoided sanction both times. But that track record was not going unnoticed. Dan Walters, a longtime columnist for the *Sacramento Bee*, wrote in July 2014, "Two big deals and two big scandals. Leon Black claimed ignorance of shady dealing in both, but maybe it's time for officials to stop doing business with him."

NOT THAT INNOCENT

Caesars Entertainment Corporation (Parent)	
Caesars Entertainment Operating Company (OpCo)	**Property Company (PropCo)**
Forty-six casinos, including Caesars Palace 	The Flamingo The Paris The Rio Harrah's Las Vegas Harrah's Atlantic City Harrah's Laughlin

Caesars corporate structure immediately post-LBO.

"**P**lease do not refer to the Greece joke. I would prefer to keep it vague," TPG's Tim Dunn wrote to Gary Loveman in an email in August 2012.

Dunn was acting as temporary CFO of Caesars, and in a meeting had compared how the company resembled the European nation that could not repay its debt. The company simply needed more time to reach escape velocity. The reality of a possible bankruptcy was starting to sink in, and Apollo, TPG, and Caesars management were extremely sensitive about chatter of the company going under.

In August 2012, an Apollo analysis noted multiple problems: the Caesars OpCo debt had only a single covenant, the senior secured leverage ratio. But the numbers indicated that profitability was so low at Caesars that covenant could be breached as early as October 2014. EBITDA was at $1.5 billion, $300 million less than the interest expense at OpCo, and the excess cash that Caesars possessed could finally run out in 2014. And even if OpCo debt maturities could be pushed out to 2015, the commercial mortgage, or CMBS, debt at the PropCo was coming due sooner. The presentation ended not with an answer but a question: "What should Apollo and TPG's strategy be and is there an appetite/thesis around future investment?"

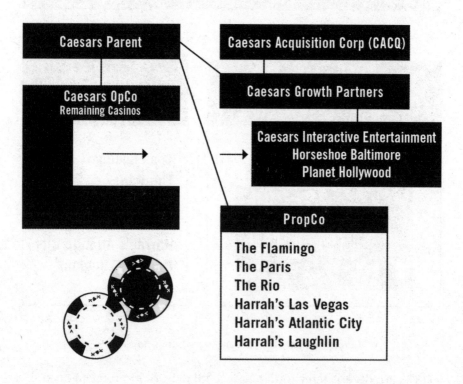

Caesars corporate structure post-Growth transaction.

In December 2013, a group of executives wandered the floor of the New York Stock Exchange in logoed bathrobes. The men ran

Hilton Hotels and were wearing Hilton outfits. Like Caesars, the hospitality chain had been bought out by private equity in 2007 for more than $25 billion. The company was now going public, and had the honor of celebrating their good fortune at the high cathedral of American capitalism. The buyout had been so successful, Hilton's owner, Blackstone, would eventually make more than $10 billion in profit.

But it had hardly been an easy path. Hilton had floundered in the years after the financial crisis, as Caesars had, putting Blackstone's $5.5 billion equity investment in jeopardy of being wiped out. But a rising star at Blackstone, Jonathan Gray, made a bet that Hilton could recover. In 2009 and 2010, Blackstone threatened and cajoled creditors into taking haircuts on their position while the firm put in another near $1 billion of equity. Gray wagered correctly and Hilton snapped back quickly, a feat that had not gone unnoticed at Caesars.

Marc Rowan had formed his own creative idea to throw more money into Caesars. Caesars had finally been able to list its shares in early 2012, in an almost embarrassing offering that raised less than $20 million. All those co-investors, including Loveman's friends from Boston, finally had a chance at cutting their losses. Caesars was in such poor shape that Jimmy Lee, the legendary banker at JPMorgan, could not underwrite the deal at the valuation Gary Loveman demanded. Even with the prospects of the interactive gaming business, mutual funds were going to run away from the $24 billion debt pile and there was no end in sight for the hemorrhaging of cash. Caesars then turned to its B-list advisors, Credit Suisse and Citigroup (Loveman would later tell Lee that he had been correct all along on the market view on Caesars stock).

But what if Apollo and TPG created a new Caesars vehicle, free and clear of its legacy problems? Investors, including the two private equity firms, could put in cash. New debt could be raised. The combined capital could be funneled into buying assets from OpCo. Most crucially, the new vehicle would be untainted by the mess at the existing Caesars, giving investors the confidence to invest. An August 2012 Apollo presentation hinted at this structure, calling it "limited partnership financing."

Two months later in October 2012, Rowan and David Sambur had mostly fleshed it out. In a new presentation, Apollo described a plan to "invest equity to buy a controlling stake in strategically valuable unencumbered assets." Put more plainly, Caesars had parts of the business that were doing well, particularly in Las Vegas. Maybe

Apollo and TPG could rescue those assets, and there would be a way to create more overall value to pay off existing Caesars debt?

Rowan had, however, planned for the contingency where Caesars never got out of the abyss. This new vehicle he was proposing had the benefit of also putting Apollo and TPG in a stronger position with creditors. On one slide, Apollo wrote, "A transaction like this is the only way we see to 'have our cake and eat it too'…if things do not work out, our position is substantially improved vs the status quo… cash invested in [the] partnership grows over time, thereby increasing value and 'war chest' upon a potential restructuring event."

If Caesars simply declared bankruptcy then, at the end of 2012, creditors would take control of the company, and Apollo and TPG would have been totally wiped out. Rowan was trying to avoid that disastrous scenario by playing offense. By creating this new partnership and taking some Caesars casinos for the partnership—a war chest as he put it—Apollo and TPG immediately would have more negotiating leverage against OpCo creditors down the road. Possession was nine-tenths of the law. Rowan sensed a big fight was upcoming with hedge funds. It was best to start planning for the battle.

Apollo was playing this close to its vest. TPG later would deny they ever were told that one purpose of the new Caesars partnership idea was to create potential negotiating leverage later (though Bonderman would say, from his point of view, there was nothing inappropriate about that approach). Apollo eventually shared the analysis with Loveman later that month. Curiously, the version the Caesars CEO received contained none of the bullet points or slides about creating negotiating leverage against creditors in a bankruptcy scenario.

On November 12, 2012, Loveman went to the broader Caesars parent board to explain the creation of Caesars Growth Partners. He had a script and a twenty-nine-page presentation which highlighted how the deal could efficiently raise cash to invest in properties while also creating liquidity to keep creditors satisfied. At no point, however, was the board apprised that Apollo viewed the Growth Transaction as a way to posture with creditors later as necessary.

Paul, Weiss, the law firm brought in by Apollo to advise the Caesars parent company, then explained the mechanics of the transaction. A new company called Caesars Growth Partners would be formed and be owned by two entities. One owner would be the Caesars parent corporation that was publicly listed after the February 2012 IPO and controlled by Apollo and TPG. The second owner would be a new company called Caesars Acquisition Corporation. The Caesars parent would have a 58 percent stake in CGP, which it would get in exchange for contributing the interactive digital business, CIE, that was run by Mitch Garber. The Caesars parent would also transfer to Caesars Growth Partners the $1.1 billion of bonds that Paulson & Co., Apollo, and TPG had exchanged in 2010 for shares in the Caesars parent.

Caesars Acquisition Corp, the new public company, would target raising $1.1 billion in a so-called "rights offering." Current shareholders of the Caesars parent would have the right to buy shares in CACQ. If existing shareholders participated, they could maintain the same stake in both public Caesars companies. CACQ would purchase a 42 percent stake in Caesars Growth. With the cash that was raised in the rights offering, Caesars Growth would buy Planet Hollywood and the Horseshoe Baltimore, the latter a new casino under development, from OpCo.

Even for a guy with a PhD from MIT, it was a lot for Loveman to swallow. There were all sorts of questions about how arrangements across all the Caesars companies would work. But the cleverness was apparent and there was a sense of desperation even among the Caesars team, who did not quite grasp all the features of the deal. After the presentation, which effectively explained how assets were going to be shuffled out of the OpCo, two Caesars executives leaned in close to each other and half-jokingly wondered about "fraudulent conveyance," the elephant in the boardroom.

Fraudulent conveyance was the idea that either assets or liabilities would be sold or transferred to benefit the shareholders of a company at the expense of creditors. Owners and boards of directors had broad discretion to exercise their so-called "business judgment" to maximize shareholder value. But the law was trickier for debt-laden companies, and solid legal advice was going to be as important in this transaction as Apollo's financial wizardry.

By 2013, Tim Donovan, the Caesars General Counsel, was concerned about how much he could trust Caesars' lawyers at Paul, Weiss. The firm had advised him that there was no need for independent directors to form a special committee that could recommend and negotiate the Growth Transaction. Caesars, Apollo, and TPG were effectively on both sides of the deal, selling assets between each other. The conflict would typically require the independent directors of Caesars to represent the Caesars public shareholders not affiliated with Apollo and TPG. Establishing an independent committee was a routine practice, yet Paul, Weiss suggested that it was unnecessary. Avoiding a special committee also happened to be a move that could make it easier for the deal terms to be favorable to Apollo and TPG.

For Paul, Weiss, Apollo was slowly becoming a dream client. Paul, Weiss, Rifkind, Wharton & Garrison had been in business since 1875, and was one of the pillars of the New York legal establishment. Its lawyers represented Wall Street banks and Fortune 500 companies in their thorniest matters. The firm had carefully cultivated an image for high-mindedness. Its staff served, before or after their Paul, Weiss tenures, at the highest levels of government, and contributed their talents to pro bono civil rights work and other various civic and social causes that required elite legal skills. Its alumni included the likes presidential candidate Adlai Stevenson, US Supreme Court Associate Justice Arthur Goldberg, and Ted Sorensen, White House adviser to President John F. Kennedy.

In the 1980s, Paul, Weiss's legendary partner Arthur Liman had represented Revlon in its fight with corporate raider Ron Perelman, who was using Drexel-issued junk bonds in a take-over. And later when Michael Milken needed a criminal lawyer, he went to Liman and another Paul, Weiss litigator, Martin Flumenbaum, to defend him in the case brought by the Department of Justice.

Brad Karp was a junior associate at Paul, Weiss in the 1980s, a protégé of Liman and Flumenbaum. By 2010, he was an accomplished litigator who had ascended to position of firm's chairman. He was best-known for defending Citigroup in cases arising from the Enron and WorldCom scandals, as well Smith Barney, the brokerage it acquired in the 1990s, in the infamous "boom boom room" sexual harassment scandal.

Karp also had the charm and media presence of a politician (he himself was a power broker in the Democratic Party), and liked to remind others of Paul, Weiss's exalted history—even as it represented deep-pocketed institutions accused of wrongdoing that harmed ordinary people. In a 2017 interview with *Bloomberg Law*, he said, "I came to appreciate that industries and companies that are demonized at various points in time have a special need for zealous representation in order to level the playing field."

Karp and another top Paul, Weiss litigator, Lewis Clayton, had been brought on board by Apollo in 2008 after an adverse decision in the legal fight to escape the Huntsman Corp buyout. The firm was tasked with settling the remaining parts of the case.

For all of Paul, Weiss's success and prestige, it had a hole. While the firm had a vaunted litigation practice that represented the likes of the NFL and Exxon in high-profile courtroom battles, it lacked a commensurately prestigious deal-making group. Paul, Weiss's leading M&A lawyer was Robert Schumer, the brother of the New York senator Charles Schumer. Even as he was well-regarded, there were few stars alongside him.

An opportunity eventually presented itself: What if Paul, Weiss could be a one-stop shop for Apollo, providing every conceivable service a big private equity firm needed? Apollo treasured finance lawyers who were experts at drafting bond indentures and loan agreements that were wired with all the flexibility Apollo liked. In the Harrah's buyout, the underlying documents that run for hundreds of pages each had been drafted by attorneys at O'Melveny & Myers. And that group of O'Melveny lawyers kept working on Caesars assignments after the Apollo/TPG buyout closed.

In May 2011, Karp made his move. Paul, Weiss snatched six elite O'Melveny partners—a group whose ties to Apollo were already established. Years earlier, Apollo had been close with another law firm, private equity boutique O'Sullivan Graev & Karabell. Los Angeles-based O'Melveny acquired New York-based O'Sullivan in 2002, making O'Sullivan's top lawyer, John Suydam, head of its M&A practice. In 2006, Suydam left O'Melveny to become the general counsel at, of all places, Apollo.

Bringing over a large group of lawyers from other outfits risked upsetting the culture that firms carefully tried to maintain. Karp was making the bet that the lucrative relationship with Apollo was going to be worth the risk.

The key pieces of the O'Melveny raid were a pair of financing experts, Greg Ezring and Mark Wlazlo. Both were celebrated as "mad scientists" skilled at drafting the kind of loose documents that Apollo liked. Debt buyers preferred to put companies on tight leashes, restricting things they could do when it came to issuing new debt or paying dividends to shareholders that would harm their chances of repayment. The fight over the language included in the papers was intense. In the boom markets of 2006 and 2007, however, companies like Caesars were able to mostly win out with "covenant-lite" terms thanks to the skills of Ezring and Wlazlo.

Tim Donovan ultimately called another law firm, Wilson Sonsini, for a second opinion that would eventually convince Paul, Weiss to agree to the independent committee.

The three independent Caesars Parent directors formed a "Valuation Committee" that would approve the creation of Caesars Growth Partners and the terms of the sale. One director was Jeffrey Housenbold, chief executive of Shutterfly, the online photo album company. Another member was Chris Williams, founder of one of the few Black-owned investment banks, who had been a director of Harrah's in the years before the LBO. The third board member was Lynn Swann, the former Hall-of-Fame wide receiver for the Pittsburgh Steelers who had become a businessman and a football analyst.

The Valuation Committee was going to go up against Apollo and TPG, who were representing Caesars Growth Partners (CGP did not exist so it did not have its own board of directors). As its investment banker, the committee hired Evercore, a boutique firm started in 1996 by Roger Altman, who had served in Bill Clinton's Treasury Department.

Evercore's work was not just about advising on and negotiating the best deal it could for the independent directors and independent shareholders. It was going to provide a letter to keep Chris Williams, Jeff Housenbold, and Lynn Swann out of legal trouble. Evercore's contract with the Caesars Valuation Committee called for it to make as much as $8.5 million—some of that fee fixed for providing a "fairness opinion," and some of that fee discretionary should their clients, the independent directors, be pleased with its work. The fairness opinion was a letter that stated that the financial terms fell within a range of reasonableness. One of the two fiduciary duties directors had was a "duty of care" requiring that they essentially try hard on behalf of shareholders. Hiring an investment bank to give a fairness opinion in an M&A deal had effectively become mandatory for a board to demonstrate due "care."

The private equity firms naturally wanted to pay as little as possible for the properties, and sharing a forecast with lower profits could justify the lower price. The independent directors and Apollo/TPG clashed over the financial projections for the casinos and CIE through early 2013. By March, Rowan and Bonderman had grown irritated with the Valuation Committee. The process was dragging out and the committee's expectation on value for the casinos and CIE was far too high. On March 14, Apollo and TPG sent a letter to the committee threatening that if a deal wasn't clinched by April 4, the sponsors may walk away from the Growth Transaction "in order to permit Caesars the ability to access the capital markets."

David Bonderman was upset enough to call Roger Altman, the Evercore founder, to register his displeasure. Altman then checked in with Eduardo Mestre, the leader of the Evercore team on the Caesars assignment. Later Bonderman would explain, "There was a general notion that Evercore was a day late and a dollar short in everything they did and it took them forever to get anything done."

These assignments were fraught for investment banks. Evercore's clients were the independent directors—and by extension the ordinary shareholders—of Caesars. But Apollo was a big, powerful institution that hired Wall Street advisors all the time. And while investment banks had a job to do, they were aware that crossing powerful private equity firms could be expensive in the long run.

By mid-April, the sides appeared to have agreed to terms: Planet Hollywood and Horseshoe Baltimore would be sold to Caesars Growth for $360 million together. The bond portfolio contributed would be valued at $749 million. CIE, the mobile gaming business, would be valued at at least $525 million with a chance for another $230 million if it performed well through 2015. If the rights offering raised the maximum target of $1.182 billion, Caesars Acquisition Corporation would own 43 percent of Caesars Growth, with the Caesars parent company owning 57 percent.

On April 21, Evercore shared its valuation analysis of the latest terms of the Growth Transaction with the Valuation Committee. Williams, Housenbold, and Swann unanimously agreed the deal represented fair value. The next day, Williams, the committee's chair, shared the conclusion with the broader Caesars parent board, which was largely made up of Apollo and TPG directors. Apollo and TPG were relieved that the Growth Transaction was finally on track. But there would soon be an unexpected wrench thrown into the deal.

THE FRIENDS OF THE APOLLO and TPG billionaire founders could be an annoyance for the Caesars management team. Rowan would, from time to time, try to get the company to hire the latest buzzy chef that he had met in the Hamptons. And since Caesars was having trouble bringing in a more youthful crowd, Apollo arranged a meeting with Gary Vaynerchuk, a celebrity influencer and digital advertising entrepreneur. Rowan was also close with the nightclub tycoon Victor Drai and pushed the Caesars team to do deals with him.

Rowan had developed an important insight about the future of Las Vegas. Gambling was going to become a far less important draw. Even as visitors returned to pre-crisis level, gambling revenue was not recovering. Younger demographics cared less about sitting in front of a slot machine than they did about dining, shopping, dance clubs, and pool parties. Those experiences were going to be the future of Las Vegas.

Rowan believed the company could create a hub for millennials on the opposite side of Las Vegas Boulevard from Caesars Palace. Harrah's had bought Imperial Palace in 2005 for $370 million and was spending hundreds of millions to turn that area into a hotel and casino called the Quad. According to an investor presentation, the Quad was to be "reposition[ed]…from a lower-tier product to one targeting younger guests and trend seekers…and to appeal to the Las Vegas region's growing Generation X and Generation Y clientele." Adjacent to the Quad was a project called the Linq, an open-air shopping and dining area to feature the world's tallest Ferris wheel called the "High Roller." Bill's Gambling Hall & Saloon, next door to the Quad and the Linq, was renovated and rebranded The Cromwell. At the top of The Cromwell was a pool and nightclub called Drai's, developed by Rowan's pal.

Tariq Shaukat, a McKinsey partner whom Loveman had recruited in 2012, was running marketing for Caesars. He and his team were looking for ways to drive traffic to Caesars properties. Sin City tended to attract stars past their peak, performers who wanted a gig easier to manage than a tour. And while the music residencies at Caesars Palace Colosseum—notably Celine Dion and Elton John—had been successes, Shaukat believed they needed a younger act to fit in with the company's new image on the other side of Las Vegas Boulevard. Wynn and MGM had raised the stakes with DJ residencies starring David Guetta and Calvin Harris. A washed-up performer would not create the buzz Shaukat needed.

The Caesars solution: Britney Spears. Britney was about a decade off her peak and her life had been messy in recent years. A thirty-six-hour marriage and divorce in Las Vegas, another marriage, two children, another divorce, and bouts with mental health episodes culminated with her fortune being put into a conservatorship managed by her father, James Spears.

Amidst the drama and heartbreak, Britney was still releasing albums, going on tour, and even getting $15 million a year to be a judge on the *X Factor* singing competition. But the high school and middle school kids who grew up during her turn-of-the-century peak were now in their twenties and thirties, and just the kind of customers Caesars needed. And they had the right venue at Planet Hollywood. All Shaukat and Loveman had to do was convince the private equity firms that a shaky casino business should take a flier on an, at-times, troubled and fading pop star.

TPG was initially unenthusiastic. The private equity firm's Hollywood connections said Britney believed she would struggle to appear on stage several times a week and the financial projections were uncertain. Apollo was, however, more positive.

Las Vegas residencies were great opportunities for talent. Performers did not have to travel. Usually they got a healthy up-front guarantee plus a big share of incremental ticket revenues, and sometimes a cut of merchandise and food and beverage. The real benefit for the property was to drive traffic to the hotel, casino, restaurants, and bars. Loveman believed in his team's analysis and went to bat for getting Britney, spending some of his political capital. And that proved enough for Apollo and TPG to sign off in 2013.

Caesars made a deal with Britney for ninety-six shows to be performed over two years, with the performer getting $4.8 million upfront. Caesars then had to get the venue just right. Planet Hollywood owned a large theater called "PH Live at Planet Hollywood," which was operated under a third-party lease. Caesars was able to buy out the lease and transform it for the stage Britney wanted at a total cost approaching nearly $35 million. But re-doing the theater allowed it to host artists on the nights Britney was not performing. Planet Hollywood would hold the touring rights to Britney for two years and ensure she was doing nightly meet-and-greets, which drove high rollers.

One Caesars executive, Tom Evans, wrote to Eric Hession, then Caesars treasurer, "This deal is one of the most favorable residency deals in our history by any measure, whether considering the number of years, number of shows, or upfront payment amount." The enthusiasm for what the show could bring was, however, tempered by the complication it was creating for the Growth Transaction. Planet Hollywood was being sold by the Caesars OpCo to Caesars Growth, and anything that made it more valuable should have made the purchase price go up.

Rowan and Sambur had found the previous negotiations with the Valuation Committee and Evercore to be exhausting, and Sambur even referred to the Britney deal as a "Pandora's Box." In early June, Eric Hession wrote an email to David Sambur, Michael Cohen, a Caesars lawyer, and Greg Ezring and Mark Wlazlo, the Paul, Weiss lawyers, wondering if there needed to be another fairness opinion since the Britney deal, codenamed Project Songbird, was creating incremental value at Planet Hollywood. Two days later, Greg Kranias, a TPG executive, emailed his colleagues Kelvin Davis and Kendall Garrison, along with Gary Loveman and Tariq Shaukat asking, "We are supportive of the Britney deal, but as you know, do not want to increase the purchase price of the PH asset. Is there a way to set this up so we can be 100 percent guaranteed that happens?"

On June 7, Shaukat messaged Hession, writing, "Kelvin agreed to base + britney + ph live if there is no valuation impact on cgp/ph."

Hession wrote back, "I don't think we can say that without talking to Evercore unfortunately."

A month later, Caesars was at an impasse. TPG did not want to pay any more for Planet Hollywood and re-open what had already been a bruising negotiation. The new Caesars CFO was Don Colvin, a Scot who spoke with a strong brogue and had worked in finance roles at various semiconductor companies. Colvin wrote an email on July 7 to Shaukat and Hession saying, "We can call Evercore tomorrow. I had good contact with them and we just cut them a huge check so I am optimistic they will be responsive."

One interpretation was that Colvin believed Evercore could be manipulated because of its fees though Colvin later said he only meant that Evercore would respond quickly. It was a tricky situation. Evercore's client was not Caesars, it was the independent directors; but it was Caesars whose funds were being used to pay Evercore. Nancy Bryson, an Evercore banker, was later asked if Evercore would simply yield to the wishes of Caesars. She responded, "[T]hat's not how we operate. I mean, if we thought the valuation needed to be updated, we would have updated it."

Bryson, and the rest of the Evercore team as it turned out, did not think the Planet Hollywood valuation needed to be updated. Marty Cicco, another Evercore banker, spoke with Hession and Colvin in July 2013 and was told the revenues and profits associated with Songbird may not have covered the investment costs of signing Britney and remodeling the Planet Hollywood theater. This was odd since Caesars management had lobbied the private equity firms to approve Songbird. If it was a money loser, why did they bother? Apollo and TPG ultimately approved Project Songbird on July 10, 2013, and the renovation at Planet Hollywood began later that summer with the hopes of Britney beginning her run late that year.

Later, several flaws were discovered in Evercore's financial analysis of Project Songbird. The primary Evercore valuation model never included the revenue and profits associated with the Britney Spears residency. Caesars management tried to convince Evercore it was a "break-even" project, even as a separate analysis by the bank valued it between $10 million and $20 million. Cicco later even admitted that Evercore was "trying to solve backwards" the value of Songbird as neutral. Caesars, in fact, was constantly revising upwards its projections for Planet Hollywood throughout 2013, but those updates never made their way to Evercore.

Finally, in October 2013, the full Caesars parent approved the deal after the Valuation Committee stated that it had not changed its support for the terms agreed to six months prior. Then, Evercore rendered its fairness opinion. The Valuation Committee and

Evercore had relied upon projections that had been prepared in late 2012, a full nine months ago. In that time, Planet Hollywood had far exceeded expectations. Evercore had asked for the latest projections, and the company, inexplicably, did not provide the latest forecast—and Evercore did not push back to receive updated numbers. The consequence is that in the last period of the forecast period Evercore was given, EBITDA for Planet Hollywood was $131 million. In October 2013, the figure had been revised upward 26 percent to $165 million, which meant CGP could have been asked to pay far more for the property. Additionally, Evercore's analysis never had the revenue benefits from Britney Spears.

Tim Donovan, the Caesars General Counsel, had wisely introduced a special Valuation Committee to negotiate the Growth Transaction. The committee had, at least prior to the Project Songbird fiasco, bargained hard as evidenced by the frustration of Apollo and TPG. Still, no one considered whether the Caesars OpCo, where the creditors resided, deserved to have an independent voice in approving the deal.

The Growth Transaction closed on October 21, 2013, and CGP immediately launched the rights offering allowing Caesars parent shareholders to commit new dollars to Caesars Acquisition Corporation, the new public company that would own 43 percent of CGP. On November 18, 2013, the offering closed with $1.2 billion raised, of which $458 million came from Apollo and TPG. Most investors in Hamlet Holdings—Apollo, TPG, and the co-investors—were happy to put new cash into this new vehicle despite the nightmare of the previous five years.

The outlines of the transaction were first announced in April 2013. Over the course of the year, shares of the Caesars parent had gone from under eight dollars to more than twenty dollars. The Caesars parent held a board meeting in November 2013 after the Growth Transaction closed. Apollo shared an analysis of how much they thought the assets sold to Caesars Growth would be worth in three years: CIE would be worth $820 million up from the just-paid $525 million; Planet Hollywood would be worth $579 million up from the current $280 million; and the Horseshoe Baltimore $260 million up from $80 million. Even accounting for discounting back to present value, Apollo believed that Caesars Growth had gotten a steal.

At five thirty a.m. on September 17, 2013, Britney Spears was hovering over the southern Nevada desert in a helicopter. She was to announce live on *Good Morning America* her residency at Planet Hollywood. "Britney: Piece of Me" was to begin three months later.

Greeting her were 1,330 young women dressed as schoolgirls in an homage to her Lolita persona in the video for ...*Baby One More Time*, her 1998 breakout hit. The women were holding flip cards that, when turned over, displayed two massive images of the star. GMA host Sam Champion tried to speak with Britney while she was in the helicopter as the cards were flipped but got no response. Britney had gotten airsick from the turbulence.

Smoother air was imminent. In the following days, ticket sales for the show surged well ahead of expectations. Tariq Shaukat wrote to the board that tickets were selling at "2x the pace of Celine and Elton's shows in the last two years, and over 4x Shania's residency launch, making it the fastest residency sale in recent memory." It was a huge win for the Caesars management team who had taken the chance on her. VIP packages were selling out, website traffic and hotel bookings were way up, and the eventual 2014 results were ahead of the forecast. Britney's shaky career got a huge boost as well. She found a platform that would make her an A-list star again.

Gary Loveman thought Rowan had pulled a rabbit out of a hat. Caesars should have been in bankruptcy two or three years ago. Instead, the Caesars stock price was, somehow, more than double its IPO price from eighteen months earlier. "I do not know where Caesars Acquisition Corp stands in your personal hierarchy of great ideas, but it was one fucking good idea. Thanks," beamed Loveman in an email to Rowan.

The Apollo co-founder was just getting warmed up.

8

CERP'S UP

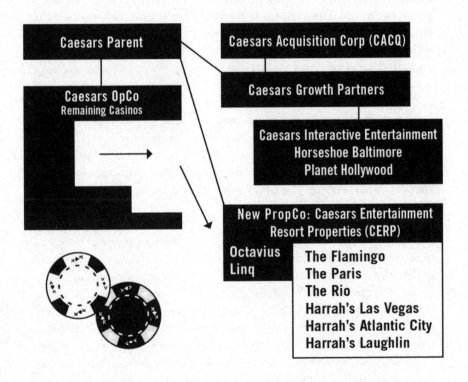

Caesars Parent	Caesars Acquisition Corp (CACQ)
Caesars OpCo Remaining Casinos	**Caesars Growth Partners**
	Caesars Interactive Entertainment Horseshoe Baltimore Planet Hollywood
	New PropCo: Caesars Entertainment Resort Properties (CERP)

Octavius
Linq

The Flamingo
The Paris
The Rio
Harrah's Las Vegas
Harrah's Atlantic City
Harrah's Laughlin

Caesars corporate structure post-CERP transaction.

"It's just a bunch of buildings."

Gary Loveman would dismissively mutter the sentiment, even to investors. By 2013, Marc Rowan was referring to those same buildings as a "guillotine" hanging over Caesars' head. As a part of the original 2008 leveraged buyout, Harrah's had split up its casinos between two vehicles. On one side was OpCo, which had tens of properties financed with $18 billion of traditional debt. On the other was a PropCo, which borrowed $6.5 billion in commercial mortgage-backed securities debt and held six casinos: Flamingo, Paris, Rio, Harrah's Las Vegas, Harrah's Atlantic City, and Harrah's Laughlin. The PropCo financing provided needed flexibility to Caesars. Once PropCo made interest and principal payments on the mortgages, excess cash could be distributed to the separate OpCo to meet its needs. The Caesars parent—whose shareholders were Apollo, TPG, its co-investors, and by 2012, the public shareholders—owned the equity in both subsidiaries.

Loveman's contention was that the heart of the Caesars empire was in the algorithm of Total Rewards, not in the physical structures of the company. The PropCo had still been a useful tool, though the clock was about to strike midnight—its debt was soon to come due with no easy way to refinance it. The financial markets just did not want that kind of real estate debt anymore. Caesars' private equity owners now would need to pay off PropCo with more traditional bank loans and bonds.

If the PropCo did not get refinanced quickly, its lenders could foreclose on the six properties, effectively forcing the bankruptcy of the Caesars parent—the guillotine Rowan referenced. Apollo had been doing yeoman's work in pushing out OpCo debt maturities and keeping hope alive on the other side of the house. The PropCo debt dilemma threatened all of that.

By mid-2013, the key holders of the PropCo debt were hedge funds and distressed debt experts. The largest holder of PropCo debt was Oaktree, which was invested heavily across Caesars—including OpCo bonds and a co-investment in the parent equity. Other key holders in PropCo debt were the Blackstone credit affiliate, GSO Capital, Black-Rock, and Omega Advisors. Through discounted buybacks over the years, Caesars had been able to knock down the PropCo CMBS debt balance to $4.5 billion. But a compromise needed to be struck with those sophisticated creditors over the remaining balance. Because of the decline in the value of the underlying PropCo casinos, an "equity gap" had opened up, and it needed to be plugged.

Solving the PropCo problem was straightforward enough. The $4.5 billion of debt had to be supported by a reasonable amount of cash flow, and the current six casinos were not capable of producing it anymore. Apollo's initial calculations of this "equity gap" were massive: more than $1 billion of value needed to be found. Marc Rowan and David Sambur ultimately concluded that sending properties that

OpCo owned to the PropCo was the best solution. They focused on the Linq and the Octavius Tower, the latter one of the new wings of Caesars Palace.

The Linq was the millennial hub that Rowan had envisioned across Las Vegas Boulevard from Caesars Palace, and included a casino/hotel, the High Roller Ferris wheel, and a shopping and dining promenade. Linq was set to debut in 2015. Octavius had opened in early 2012 and had cost nearly $900 million to develop.

TPG, however, didn't love the idea of taking the two prized assets out of OpCo, instead thinking cash might be a better plug. Octavius was a tricky asset to jettison. It was connected to the broader Caesars Palace and selling it off could damage the value of the OpCo crown jewel. David Bonderman pushed back on the idea in an email to Marc Rowan: "Alienating the [Octavius] Tower by selling it or leasing it to someone else for a long term is likely to turn out to be a bad idea. The Octavius Tower was planned and built as an integral part of our core property, and I suspect that losing control of that will be value destructive over time."

Even Caesars management was getting nervous about breaking up Caesars Palace. Eric Hession wrote to David Sambur and his deputy Alex Van Hoek, wondering if only the Linq could go. Van Hoek wrote a short email acknowledging Hession's concerns and that Apollo was dead set on transferring both the Linq and Octavius Tower.

Even TPG seemed to have been reduced to the occasional cameo appearance. Greg Kranias later explained how the arrangement worked with his firm: "As a general matter, Apollo took the lead on capital structure matters and then once an idea actually progressed to the point where it looked like they wanted to do real work on it and flesh it out, they would actually raise it with us. They would continue to lead it and then they would bring it to us very close to the point of approval so that we could understand it and be in a position to recommend it or not."

At one point, a Citigroup banker working on the deal emailed Sambur asking if TPG was up to speed. Sambur responded curtly, "No—I didn't waste my time with TPG."

THIS WAS GOING TO BE an assignment like no other for Mike Kramer and his longtime deputy, Josh Scherer. Kramer ran the restructuring investment banking practice at Perella Weinberg Partners, where he and his team had been early recruits when the firm formed in 2006.

The restructuring investment banking business had taken off in the 1990s as companies and creditors were more actively seeking to bring bankrupt companies back to life. Boutique banks were ideal places for restructuring experts as the big Wall Street houses were often conflicted by their large trading operations.

Kramer had been the original head of restructuring at Perella Weinberg. A large man with an ego to match, he had been one of the best bankers in America for troubled companies since the 1990s. Joe Perella and Peter Weinberg, both graduates of Harvard Business School, were Wall Street blue bloods and Kramer—having been an intern at boutique bank Houlihan Lokey after graduating from lowly Cal State Northridge—was in some ways an odd fit at their firm. But his ability to bring in deals was undeniable.

Restructuring banking was often about developing creative financings and structures to keep companies alive to fight another day. But what Apollo was proposing appeared unprecedented to Kramer and Scherer. Apollo wanted to sell the Linq and the Octavius from OpCo to the new PropCo vehicle called Caesars Entertainment Resort Properties, or CERP. The rub: no cash or stock was to change hands.

Rather, the only payment would be for purely theoretical costs that the OpCo would "avoid" if PropCo were forced to default on its debt. PropCo shared in certain Caesars overhead costs and Apollo argued that if PropCo defaulted and left the system, those onerous costs would fall back to OpCo. Avoiding a default would be avoiding those costs…and *that* would be the form of "payment." Perella's job would be to render an opinion to the Caesars OpCo board, who was "selling" the two casinos, that it was reasonable not to receive any cash for them.

The terms of the assignment were so unusual that Perella hired its own law firm, Weil, Gotshal & Manges—its neighbor in the General Motors Building across from Central Park—to negotiate its contract with Caesars. These discussions started in August but were not finalized by early September when Perella shared its first draft opinion with Caesars. It was not a traditional fairness opinion, but a letter stating that Caesars OpCo was receiving "reasonably equivalent value," a phrase that was crucial in heading off future allegations of fraudulent transfers.

On August 12, 2013, Apollo formed its first views on the valuation of the deal. In a presentation created by Alex Van Hoek and shared with David Sambur, Van Hoek valued the equity of Linq and Octavius—sent to CERP from OpCo—as worth $729 million. OpCo was to get two pieces of value in exchange from CERP. OpCo would be on the hook for $140 million of annual expenses if PropCo went under. If that figure could be avoided through this deal, Apollo said that was worth in total a present value of $1.3 billion. Separately, in the creation of CERP, the Caesars parent would no longer guarantee the lease payment PropCo was making. The Caesars parent guaranteed the debt for the OpCo, so if suddenly the PropCo guarantee went away, Apollo reasoned that the remaining OpCo guarantee was worth an additional $4.4 billion.

All told, these two avoided costs added up to $5.7 billion. They were so speculative that Van Hoek applied a 90 percent discount to them, valuing these non-cash benefits at $570 million. The two casinos were worth $729 million, so the trade with CERP was still at a net loss to the OpCo.

Given the inadequacy, the next day Sambur and Van Hoek tried again. Moving some dials in the spreadsheet, the value of the saved operating costs went up to $1.8 billion from the previous $1.3 billion. At the same time, lowering the value of other inputs to the transferred Linq and Octavius brought down their total value to just $585 million. The adjustments made little sense from a conceptual point of view, and it seemed as if Sambur and Van Hoek had simply manipulated the spreadsheet to solve for the desired answer.

Even the discount that had been applied before on the guarantee release value was cut out. Sambur and Van Hoek were now arguing the deal was providing a whopping net benefit to OpCo in excess of $6 billion—up from $570 million the day before—even as OpCo received no cash in the deal.

On August 14, Sambur shared the terms of the CERP transaction—as it was now known with the Perella bankers. Apollo explained to Scherer and his colleague, Cody Leung, the mechanics of the exchange.

Perella immediately saw the problem. The firm needed to get their opinion through an internal committee that signed off on such matters. Gary Barancik, who chaired Perella's opinions committee, wrote an email to Josh Scherer that day after reviewing the Caesars presentation. He immediately grasped the punchline. He wrote that Apollo believed "that they can transfer up to $6.2 billion of assets for no consideration."

By the end of August, Perella's discomfort with these initial terms was clear. Scherer was not going to give Apollo any credit for the release of the lease payment guarantee—which Apollo had valued at more than $5 billion—given how nebulous it was. The avoided operating costs from preventing PropCo's default were also being knocked down some. The Perella fairness committee was additionally insisting that some sort of hard currency be included alongside these abstract cost savings.

At the same time, OpCo creditors got wind of the CERP transaction and were making inquiries of Caesars investor relations. An investor relations employee emailed Caesars executives Eric Hession, Michael Cohen, and Jacqueline Beato, writing, "the question around what compensation we are giving to OpCo for Octavius/Linq is gaining momentum." The company decided it would disclose that it had received a fairness opinion for the deal without releasing its details.

The math that anxious investors were doing was simple. Hession himself valued the two casinos leaving OpCo along with bonds that OpCo had now agreed to take as hard currency. The deficit from the deal on that calculation was between $300 million and $500 million. The only way to make the equation work was to ascribe value to the avoided costs. Citigroup was working with Apollo to drum up new lenders who would provide CERP the nearly $5 billion in new debt. The new debt would mature in seven years instead, replacing the soon-coming-due $4.5 billion in CMBS debt and $450 million in debt that Octavius and Linq carted over to CERP as part of the deal. Citi, too, became concerned about how all the puts and takes worked. In a September email, David Sambur wrote to Greg Ezring of Paul, Weiss, that Citi was now even "chirping about fraudulent conveyance risk factor."

Meanwhile, the fight dragged on between Perella's lawyers at Weil, Gotshal and Caesars' lawyers at Paul, Weiss over the precise terms of the opinion. Perella was trying to legally protect itself while finding a way to issue the unorthodox opinion. Even a standard fairness opinion is filled with caveats and disclaimers that water down the integrity of the final product. This opinion was proving particularly thorny.

Perella wanted to include an assumption that avoided costs were a legitimate form of consideration. But Paul, Weiss argued that if such a view was offered as an assumption, the opinion was meaningless because that was precisely what Caesars wanted Perella to conclude—and therefore could not also be an assumption. To solve that impasse, Apollo held a conference call with Perella without Paul, Weiss on the line to deliver their message. Within days, Perella and Paul, Weiss somehow ironed out their differences.

Just before eight p.m. on October 9, 2013, Gary Loveman was sent a PowerPoint deck explaining the CERP transaction, codenamed Project Citizen. It was the first time he had seen these materials and he had until six thirty a.m. to review them before the OpCo board—just himself and Michael Cohen, the Caesars lawyer—were to approve the deal. OpCo was to get a $150 million bond portfolio along with $450 million worth of debt forgiveness for borrowings of Linq and Octavius. The value of the avoided operating costs by keeping the PropCo properties in the Caesars system was valued at $378 million. The release of the lease guarantee by the Caesars parent was listed as a piece of consideration, but Perella held firm and refused to put any value on it.

In a 45-minute board meeting early October 10, Loveman and Cohen agreed to the deal. Later in October, CERP closed on roughly $5 billion of new financing to pay off the outstanding PropCo debt that had originated with the original buyout.

Even after the deal, the Caesars investor relations staff was feeling the heat over both the CERP and Growth Transactions, which were both consummated within days of each other in October 2013. Analysts at Royal Bank of Canada wrote late that month of the two deals, "We believe these transactions will create some confusion in the near-term as investors attempt to understand the impact on cash flow among the various subsidiaries."

Some OpCo investors were not confused at all. Shawn Tumulty, a respected credit investor at Franklin Mutual Series, wrote an email to the Caesars investor relations account, writing, "Several of the recent asset sales have taken place at EXTREMELY questionable valuations (in fact, the value that OpCo received in the transaction with CERP appears ridiculously low…)."

What was clear to Caesars bean counters was the accounting damage that the transfer of Linq and Octavius had created. Diane Wilfong, the Caesars controller, wrote an email to senior management in December of 2013 saying that the deal would "stand out like a sore thumb on the OpCo financials." The book value of the two properties was $550 million, and selling them seemingly for $150 million was going to blow a hole in the equity section of the Caesars balance sheet.

Rowan and Sambur were steadfast in their support for the CERP deal, which they believed solved the puzzle of refinancing the $4.7 billion of PropCo debt. In their view, PropCo was the most existential threat to all of Caesars: Its default would have brought down the curtain on the entire company. Yet, between the Growth Transaction and CERP, three prime Las Vegas assets—Planet Hollywood, Linq, and Octavius—had left OpCo.

And while Apollo insisted that all Caesars creditors had benefited from the deal, the OpCo creditors owning nearly $20 billion in debt had no voice in those two transactions. Paul, Weiss was even having inklings that it might be problematic. The Caesars OpCo still had no independent directors, and there had been no formal analysis of the solvency of OpCo—or formal discussion of any of the legal risks that either the Caesars parent directors or OpCo directors faced if OpCo was approaching bankruptcy. Lewis Clayton, the Paul, Weiss litigator, wrote in a July 2013 email just as the CERP deal was taking shape, "if [OpCo] isn't [solvent], then we may have a fiduciary duty to OpCo creditors that could be violated by using Octavius and Linq assets to support a sister corporation."

9

FOUR PROPERTIES OF
THE APOCALYPSE

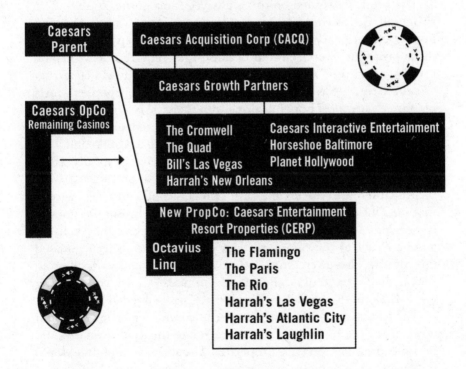

Caesars corporate structure post-Four Properties transaction.

After the stress of the Growth and CERP transactions, by the fall of 2013 Apollo came to one undeniable, wrenching conclusion: the Caesars OpCo was still going to run out of money the next year. Both previous deals were legally fraught, and Caesars had only bought a reprieve of a few months. Caesars' fundamental problems of too much debt and nowhere near enough cash flow persisted and were exacerbated with four casinos out the door. The senior secured leverage covenant ratio was set to be breached in 2014, and according to an internal presentation that David Sambur shared with Caesars management, the Caesars OpCo was projected to burn an astounding $2.5 billion of cash between 2014 and 2016. Sambur forecast that the company needed $4 billion to pay off debt and pay interest over that time. The Caesars OpCo had to keep selling casinos and the buyer was destined to be Caesars Growth.

There was, however, another option: declare bankruptcy. Apollo and TPG were running on a treadmill that kept speeding up. Any other private equity firm would have cried mercy. But Rowan and Sambur were in far too deep to just give up now.

The two firms settled on three Las Vegas properties to sell—The Cromwell, Bally's, and the Quad—along with Harrah's New Orleans, hoping to get nearly $2 billion of cash. The company insisted that those properties were selected because they required heavy capital spending that the OpCo could no longer support. It was clear that Caesars Growth was getting the prime Las Vegas properties whose prospects were most hopeful, along with Caesars' best regional asset, the New Orleans Harrah's. Growth was supposed to be liberated from the OpCo's problems and it was evident that Apollo and TPG were giving the new company the best possible chance to succeed.

On the Tuesday before Thanksgiving 2013, the Caesars parent board gathered to discuss the cash crunch. Apollo and TPG agreed that the OpCo needed a cash infusion immediately. But the Caesars owners had a much grander plan than just casino divestitures. It was getting closer to the time for a large-scale restructuring negotiated directly with Caesars creditors. Before those talks could start, however, Caesars had a handful of chess moves to make. This board meeting was to float those trial balloons. But first, Caesars needed $2 billion.

The Caesars parent formed a special committee of independent directors at the board meeting to negotiate the sale of what would become known as the Four Properties. The special committee would only have two independent directors: Lynn Swann, who had already served on the committee that approved the Growth transaction, and Fred Kleisner, a longtime hotel executive who had joined the Caesars parent board in the summer of 2013 and had served on another Apollo-affiliated board.

As in the original Growth Transaction, Apollo and TPG were on both sides of the deal—OpCo was to sell the casinos to Caesars

Growth, which the two private equity firms also controlled. The conflict was obvious. OpCo's equity was worthless, and any profits the sponsors had at Caesars were tied up in Caesars Growth and CERP. As such, Apollo and TPG's objective was to have Caesars Growth pay as little as possible for the Four Properties while OpCo creditors would want as much cash as possible.

As in the CERP and Growth deals, OpCo would not get any say in the transaction, as the special committee only spoke for the Caesars parent.

Early in the week following Thanksgiving, Gary Loveman contacted Mitch Garber, now the CEO of Caesars Growth, where Garber's digital gaming unit resided. Loveman told Garber that OpCo would be offering Cromwell, the Quad, Bally's Las Vegas, and Harrah's New Orleans to Caesars Growth. The committee hired lawyers from Reed Smith, a Philadelphia firm. And in this latest transaction, the Caesars special committee hired another boutique firm, Centerview Partners, at a fee of $5 million, as its investment banker. Lynn Swann had worked with Centerview during his stint as director of Heinz Corporation. Swann had contacted Blair Effron, the co-founder of Centerview, who passed on the assignment to colleague Marc Puntus, a longtime restructuring advisor. Puntus knew Marc Rowan well from fundraisers both had attended for AIPAC and the Friends of the Israeli Defense Forces. Puntus's client was not Apollo in this instance, or even Caesars. Rather, his job was to protect the independent public shareholders of the parent company, though not the OpCo creditors.

Caesars Growth would have Caesars Acquisition Corporation, its publicly listed parent, negotiate the Four Properties deal on its behalf. CAC's special committee had three independent directors. One was Don Kornstein, a former investment banker at Bear Stearns who had been a director at Gala Coral, a UK-based gaming company that Apollo controlled. Phil Erlanger, a PhD from Wharton, was a longtime investment banker at Barclays and Lehman Brothers covering private equity firms—including Apollo. The lead director for CAC would be Marc Beilinson, a Los Angeles bankruptcy lawyer who had reinvented himself as restructuring consultant and professional board member. Beilinson was smart, experienced, aggressive, and close with Marc Rowan.

There could be no leisurely pace on the Four Properties deal. Deloitte, the firm's auditor, was considering giving a "going concern" warning in Caesars' annual report filing with the SEC to be submitted in March 2014. The going concern language would prompt an immediate default of Caesars' OpCo debt and could trigger an immediate bankruptcy. Caesars needed the Four Properties deal to be announced in two months' time in order to keep those dominos from falling.

By late January, Centerview had completed its due diligence and in its first valuation presentation told Kleisner and Swann that the Four Properties were worth between $1.9 billion and $3.5 billion. Two days later, Beilinson countered, saying Caesars Growth would only pay $1.6 billion. The banker for Caesars Growth, Lazard, however, put little faith in the financial projections that Caesars management had prepared.

Most interestingly, Beilinson, in his counteroffer, asked that the Total Rewards loyalty program, as a part of the deal, be put into a new "bankruptcy remote" vehicle. The fear was that if the Caesars OpCo, where Total Rewards was housed, filed for bankruptcy, its relationships with the Caesars properties at Growth and CERP could be threatened or terminated. Kleisner would later claim he was shocked by the request for Total Rewards. The Caesars parent special committee countered back with a $2.75 billion figure and stated that Total Rewards would not be transferred out.

But Kleisner's hardline did not last long. The original forecasts that Lazard doubted, known as the "January Business Plan," came from the company's standard budgeting process that had been completed late in 2013. Lazard made significant "haircuts" to the plan, believing that the capital requirements and growth rates embedded in the Four Properties forecasts were too rosy. Kleisner, after a board meeting on January 31, 2014, inexplicably felt uncomfortable with the January figures, telling Swann they needed to critically assess the numbers since Caesars had missed its targets before.

The Caesars finance staff believed that there was pressure from Kleisner coming to knock back the numbers. It was unusual for such a request to come from the board in the context of selling assets; Kleisner and Swann's job was to get the highest possible price for the Four Properties.

Later the Caesars finance staff would say that a revised set of projections was driven by Fred Kleisner. Rob Brimmer, a Caesars executive, said, "We only changed the numbers because—we only presented an alternative case because Fred [Kleisner] asked us to."

By February 5, 2014, they had circulated a revised forecast known as the February Business Plan which had reduced the aggregate EBITDA figure by 12 percent. The February Plan was built strictly for the Four Properties transaction, with other previously created forecasts used for planning executive bonus targets.

The OpCo needed cash quickly and Kleisner believed that more credible projections were necessary to close a deal. The natural question was, however, if Kleisner was willing to agree to a deal with Caesars Growth on any terms. The committee had no discretion in picking the casinos included in the Four Properties or considering alternative transactions, similar constraints that were present in the Growth Transaction and CERP.

By February 10, the Caesars parent had a deal with Caesars Growth to sell the Four Properties from the OpCo to Growth for $2 billion, less the assumption of nearly $200 million in debt, a purchase price at the bottom of the range Centerview had given in its first valuation analysis just weeks earlier. Later in February, Centerview gave its fairness opinions to the board. Neither Apollo, Paul, Weiss, nor Caesars decided, however, that it was necessary that OpCo have its own directors or hire its own advisors to vet the terms.

Most controversial would be the treatment of the Total Rewards intellectual property that was within the OpCo. Loveman's Total Rewards was the glue between the various Caesars properties. Apollo and TPG had specifically not sold any OpCo casinos in the Growth, CERP, and Four Properties transactions outside the family. They believed the casinos were far more valuable within the system.

An OpCo bankruptcy threatened all that. In a bankruptcy, OpCo might be free to change the terms of how non-OpCo casinos used or paid for Total Rewards. Apollo, TPG, and Paul, Weiss were worried enough that by late 2013 they were already at the drawing board, coming up with contraptions to keep access uninterrupted to Total Rewards for the new Caesars entities—CERP, Caesars Growth—that had been created.

Per the agreed-upon terms agreed, OpCo contributed a license that would not charge a royalty to another new vehicle, Caesars Entertainment Services (fully transferring the underlying IP was a bridge too far, legally). But the license arrangement seemed to be effectively the same thing. OpCo would own 69 percent of CES while the other affiliates, Caesars Growth and CERP, would own the rest. The latter two contributed $65 million for their stakes. The ostensible benefit to OpCo was that capital expenditures for Total Rewards would be split among the three companies but there was no valuation put on Total Rewards. Just how easily Total Rewards was lifted out of OpCo would soon become one of the creditors' harshest grievances.

Apollo insisted that the Four Properties deal was keeping the Caesars OpCo alive. The problem, however, was that basic analysis showed that the company was made worse off. A February 2014 analysis from Centerview showed that the transaction was only temporarily forestalling a bankruptcy filing. The bankers concluded that, because of the Four Properties transaction, the Caesars OpCo would lose nearly $3 billion in revenue and more than $700 million of EBITDA, respectively, between 2014 and 2016. Most damningly, debt would only drop by $185 million because of the incremental borrowing the company would need to make to stay afloat. Overall, debt to EBITDA would spike from a hefty 14x to a shocking 18x (anything over 6x was precarious).

The math was straightforward, and outsiders were noticing. Goldman Sachs wrote in a March research note, "We continue to believe that the sponsors do not want to file any subsidiary in the Caesars org structure [for bankruptcy], especially not OpCo since we believe this could create significant litigation risk related to arguments about fraudulent transfer of assets (a stated risk in CAC's S-1), among other things, as well as regulatory risk with state gaming authorities which control their gaming licenses."

There was one final chess move left for Apollo to execute in what had been a dizzying set of events over the course of a year. Rowan and Sambur were insisting that the flurry of asset sales of prime Caesars properties was faithfully executed to ensure that Caesars creditors were duly paid back. The sincerity of that proposition was becoming more questionable by the minute.

10

SHOT OF B-7

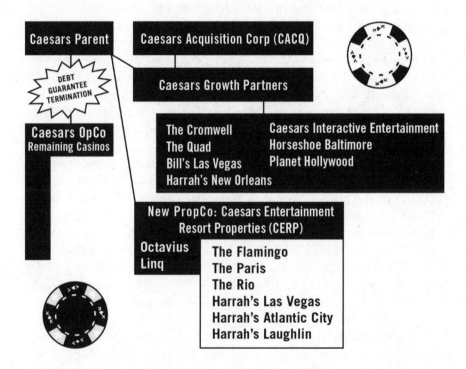

Caesars corporate structure post-B-7 transaction.

As his Princeton lacrosse teammate snatched the loose ball and desperately heaved the ball across the field, Ryan Mollett could see the trouble unfolding. The Princeton Tigers were taking on Towson State in the NCAA semifinals on a rainy May afternoon in 2001. More than 20,000 fans had gathered at Rutgers Stadium in northern New Jersey to watch the action.

Princeton was a perennial lacrosse powerhouse, but on this day the team was having trouble shaking off the scrappy squad from Maryland. With the lacrosse ball now drifting across the field, Princeton was about to be caught awkwardly with too many players on the defensive side of the field. An offsides penalty could have swung the momentum to Towson and proved decisive in a tight game. But Mollett, just named the Ivy League Player of the Year, quickly sensed the unfolding disaster and sprinted onside to keep the balance of players between zones correct. Moments later, Mollett stole the ball from an attacker and quickly tossed it to a teammate who slammed home the game-winning shot in a 12–11 victory. Two days later, Princeton took home the championship in a tight battle with Syracuse.

Mollett would go down as one of the all-time great Princeton lacrosse players. After graduation in 2001, he played professional lacrosse for a few years. And like many "lax bros," he ultimately took an office job where it would keep the competitive juices flowing: Wall Street. After earning an MBA at Yale in 2007, he first went to BlackRock and then joined GSO Capital in 2011 as a distressed debt specialist. Mollett's ability to clearly see and appreciate the field of play amidst chaos would come in handy.

GSO, like Apollo and so many credit investing firms, had its roots in Drexel. Bennett Goodman—the G in GSO—had joined Drexel in the mid-1980s out of Harvard Business School. In 1988, Goodman moved to Donaldson, Lufkin & Jenrette, where he would help build out its junk bond business. Later in the 1990s at DLJ, Goodman would hire Tripp Smith (the "S") and Douglas Ostrover (the "O"). In 2005, five years after Credit Suisse swallowed up DLJ, the trio formed GSO Capital Partners to be a corporate lender and credit investor. Three years later, in 2008, Blackstone bought GSO for nearly $1 billion.

By early 2014, Ryan Mollett and GSO had been involved in Caesars' debt for years, buying the hung bridge loans in 2008, then participating in the 2013 transformation of the Caesars PropCo into CERP. Mollett had gotten to know David Sambur well. The two were, on the surface, quite different. Mollett was blond, 6' 2", two hundred pounds, and while an accomplished athlete, a friendly, affable fellow off the field. Sambur, a diminutive 5' 7", was a whirling dervish of nervous energy.

In early 2014, the duo was trying to help each other out. Caesars needed more cash. The $2 billion proceeds from the Four Properties sale would not be enough to pay off 2015 debt maturities and avoid breaching the ratio of senior debt to cash flow, the single covenant that OpCo had to meet.

Caesars had the ability to borrow more through senior loans. But with no bank willing to lead that effort, Sambur needed a bold buyer to jump in first, and GSO would fit the bill. If Mollett could extract the economics he wanted from Sambur, this could be a sweet deal. But Sambur needed more than money from Mollett.

When Harrah's initially sold the OpCo LBO debt in 2008, and in the dozens of financing transactions, there was one key structuring feature consistent across all the legal documentation: The $18 billion in loans and the bonds were borrowed at the OpCo level where the casino assets were held. This gave comfort to debt buyers that they had a direct claim on those assets if Caesars ever faltered. Apollo and TPG also offered another form of so-called "credit support": The parent Caesars, which owned 100% of OpCo, would "guarantee" the repayment of those loans and bonds of OpCo. The guarantee allowed Caesars to borrow more cheaply because creditors knew another entity, the Caesars parent owned by Apollo and TPG, was like an umbrella protecting OpCo debt underneath it.

The value of the guarantee was ceremonial at first. The value of the parent company was largely tied up in the equity of OpCo, which sat below the OpCo debt. If OpCo debt was in trouble, OpCo equity was in worse shape—so the guarantee did not mean much as there was little independent value for OpCo creditors to chase. However, the creation of Caesars Growth and CERP changed the equation. The parent had stakes in those two, giving it a few billion dollars of value independent of OpCo which had still retained Caesars Palace and various regional properties

The guarantee was a constant, nagging dilemma for Apollo and TPG. In a hypothetical bankruptcy, the guarantee was likely to be invoked and the parent assets were going to be seized by creditors including the casinos and IP that had been shifted out of OpCo. But maybe Ryan Mollett could help Rowan and Sambur solve this dilemma.

Since the 2008 LBO, Caesars had borrowed six different tranches of bank loans. By 2014, its pending seventh would become known as the "B-7." Sambur, however, needed more than money this time. He was desperate to amend the underlying legal document known as the credit agreement so that the parent guarantee on the bank loans was severed. Sambur also wanted to weaken the senior secured loan covenant that required the ratio of OpCo senior debt to cash flow be raised from 4.75x to 7.25x to avoid covenant breach. GSO and another money manager, BlackRock, would then commit to buying a big chunk of the loan. The OpCo would throw in $315 million in cash it had in its coffers, and $1.8 billion in loans and bonds of OpCo would be paid back.

Mollett was listening. The bank loan was senior debt, and he was not obsessed by the fine print. And most importantly, Sambur was making it worth his while. For their support of what might have been an unpopular deal, GSO and BlackRock would be paid nearly $130 million in extra fees. Mollett agreed to get behind Sambur's plan; of the $1.75 billion B-7 term loan, GSO and BlackRock collectively bought $820 million. These anchor orders successfully induced other hedge funds and institutions to feel safe enough to put in orders as well, and despite objections by creditors who saw it as a "terrible deal," Apollo rallied more than enough buyers.

Caesars again relied on the wizards at Paul, Weiss to draft the revised loan agreement with all these features. For technical reasons, the guarantee on the bank loans could not be fully severed. Rather it could only be watered down to something called a "guarantee of collection," which forced creditors to spend years in court trying to enforce it, unlike the traditional "guarantee of payment" which was enforceable immediately after a default.

The B-7 deal came at a cost. In total, Caesars paid an enormous $219 million in fees to raise the $1.75 billion. Then the interest rate on the B-7 loan was a generous 9.75 percent while paying off debt that was mostly cheaper. As a result, annual interest expense for the OpCo went up by $43 million. The debt repurchase could have been more efficient as well, as Caesars used the new cash to buy back debt at greater than 100 cents on the dollar when it was trading in the market at far less. Worse yet, $450 million worth of bonds bought by OpCo at 100 cents were held by Caesars Growth, making it appear that Apollo and TPG were scratching the back of another company they controlled.

Mollett knew the details were not pretty, but it was not his problem. GSO and BlackRock got their windfall. Corporate restructuring could be about ruthlessly cutting side deals and picking off individual players all to divide and conquer.

WE USED TO BE AN *investment bank*, grumbled Steve Zelin and Mike Genereux. Zelin and Genereux were restructuring bankers at Blackstone, a firm best known for managing more than $200 billion across private equity, real estate, credit, and hedge fund assets by 2014. But Blackstone's small, plucky deal advisory business was the firm's heritage.

Blackstone's founders Pete Peterson and Steve Schwarzman were top dealmakers at Lehman Brothers before departing together after a power struggle in 1985. They then formed Blackstone in the hopes of becoming an investing powerhouse. Blackstone's private equity unit would eventually take off in the 1990s, making Schwarzman and Peterson billionaires. But in the early years, Blackstone survived as an investment banking firm putting together deals for corporate clients.

Integrating a massive investing firm with one that dispensed deal advice had its shortcomings. Blackstone had initially angled for a position working with senior bondholders like Elliott. But there were multiple conflicts of interest to resolve. Blackstone had been a co-investor in the original 2008 buyout alongside Apollo and TPG, owning a few percent of the Caesars parent. And GSO was a major holder of Caesars debt in multiple entities. The decision to stay out of advising a creditor group had been escalated to the highest levels of the firm: Steve Schwarzman, Tony James, and Blackstone's general counsel. Blackstone decided that the firm did not want to take a role adverse to its equity position. It was an odd decision, the restructuring team believed, since GSO's existing debt position was already adverse to the firm's equity position.

Around the same time, David Blitzer, a senior Blackstone executive, called Apollo co-founder Josh Harris to ask if there was a role for Blackstone advising Caesars itself. It was an easy phone call for Blitzer to make, as he and Harris were co-owners of the Philadelphia 76ers and New Jersey Devils franchises. By March of 2014, Blackstone had been hired to represent Caesars in restructuring negotiations.

Zelin and Genereux quickly gleaned that Rowan and Sambur wanted to avoid bankruptcy. Instead, Apollo was looking to create optionality and maximize negotiating leverage against the various creditor groups. The B-7 financing was already underway when Blackstone was hired. Blackstone, which had been speaking with Caesars creditors in the previous year, gave Sambur a few pointers on how to manage the negotiations. Otherwise, Sambur handled it himself (GSO's Ryan Mollett would call Blackstone just a few floors away at 345 Park Avenue, from time to time, to vent about the young Apollo executive he was clashing with).

WHILE THE B-7 FINANCING WAS designed to help terminate the parent guarantee on Caesars OpCo debt, it was only the first step in a complicated recipe. Caesars had modified the parent guarantee on $5 billion of bank debt. But next Apollo had to sever the parent guarantee on the remaining $12 billion of bond debt (and ultimately it became a condition of GSO and BlackRock funding the B-7 so no other creditor had a guarantee). And for that, Sambur needed Blackstone's help.

According to bond legal documents called indentures, the parent guarantee fell away if the Caesars OpCo was no longer a 100%-owned subsidiary of the Caesars parent. The underlying principle was that a parent need not be accountable for debt in a related entity in which it did not fully own. The answer then was for the Caesars parent to find minority investors for OpCo.

Selling equity of the OpCo, however, was practically problematic. If the Caesars OpCo debt was trading well below 100 cents on the dollar, the lower-ranked equity, by definition, should be worthless. In April 2014, Blackstone made a presentation to the Caesars parent board about the benefits of selling stock in the OpCo, noting that it could facilitate a restructuring but also that "it contractually releases [Caesars parent] from liability for approximately $14.9 billion of OpCo debt and thus protects $2.5 billion of [parent] equity value for shareholders." Blackstone also noted that "there might be hostile responses from [OpCo] creditors," something that would prove later to be a spectacular understatement.

Rowan later insisted the sale of stock "was one of the easiest ways for us to delever...to come up with an interesting exchange transaction that can further reduce debt." Even David Bonderman did not buy that line, later saying the release of the bond guarantee was "a catalyst for constructive debt reduction negotiations in the future" because it "changes the leverage dramatically if you are not liable for $15 billion worth of debt."

As investment bankers, Blackstone offered their professional views of what OpCo equity could be worth. Under any traditional valuation method, OpCo stock was—unsurprisingly—worthless. The only way OpCo stock had any marketability was as an "option" that, regardless, could not "be reliably quantified today," Blackstone wrote. Zelin and Genereux explained that the only buyers for this paper would be funds who already were involved elsewhere in the Caesars capital structure who were to otherwise benefit from the termination of the bond guarantee. The trick then would be to explain to these investors that buying this intrinsically worthless OpCo stock would save their other investments.

Apollo identified three such funds in late April 2014. The first prospective buyer of OpCo equity was Paulson & Co, who had participated in the bond exchange in 2012 and had vastly overrated the value of Caesars parent stock then. Paulson now agreed to buy about 1 percent of OpCo for roughly $1 million. Paulson was so worried about the optics of buying worthless OpCo stock that it negotiated for a provision that would prevent it from being liable should Caesars creditors try to sue later.

The second buyer was Scoggin Capital Management, another Caesars parent shareholder who also bought 1 percent.

The third buyer of OpCo equity also had bigger bets elsewhere at Caesars. But the scale of Chatham Asset Management's other positions, in light of the stock sale and the simultaneous B-7 transaction, was on an entirely different level of daring. Chatham years later would become a household name for another investment it made in 2014—buying control of American Media, the publisher of the supermarket tabloid *The National Enquirer*. But in early 2014, it was an obscure hedge fund with close ties to New Jersey governor Chris Christie. Chatham was named for the town in north Jersey where its office was located. It, along with Appaloosa Management and Omega Advisors (whom Chatham partnered with on American Media), formed a set of elite hedge funds that had clustered near each other in the Garden State.

Unlike Scoggin and Paulson, who had made their calculations based on how their parent equity would benefit, Chatham's angle centered on its OpCo debt investments. At the beginning of 2014, Chatham held just under $300 million of OpCo junior debt. But through the course of the first four months of that year, that figure would rise as it steadily was buying junior bonds.

Chatham was following closely the flurry of maneuvers by Apollo to keep Caesars alive. After the Growth Transaction, Chatham executive Greg Roselli wrote to a contact at the Nevada Gaming Control Board, "the new spinoff company (which is Caesars Growth Partners) is going to start picking the best properties out of OpCo to help force the lenders to take a haircut."

On March 3, when the Four Properties transaction was announced, Roselli wrote to another colleague at Chatham that the deal "extends the liquidity profile but doesn't change the story for the [junior bondholders] in the long run; and now [Caesars Growth has] stripped the best assets. (New Orleans does very well)."

Through April, Chatham kept adding to its OpCo bond position and only on April 30 did Chatham get restricted from trading as Sambur informed the fund of the pending B-7 loan and OpCo stock sale. By the end of April, Chatham owned more than $400 million of junior bonds.

Chatham's debt purchases proved timely. In late April 2014, David Sambur told Chatham founder Anthony Melchiorre and Roselli that he was pursuing both the sale of OpCo stock and the B-7 term loan. Roselli would later say that Sambur had told him during the call that the $1.75 billion B-7 loan would be used in part to buy back junior debt, just the kind that Chatham was holding. Chatham also later claimed that the OpCo stock was "an attractive investment," though it had done no analysis on it.

Melchiorre ultimately agreed to take the biggest chunk of OpCo stock, $4 million worth. Chatham also bought $50 million of the B-7 term loan with the juicy 9.75 percent interest rate. As part of those movements, Chatham had $412 million worth of junior bonds bought out by Caesars for $435 million. When the B-7 and 5 percent stock sales of OpCo were simultaneously announced on May 6, Caesars bonds took a dive because the parent guarantee no longer was in place. It was an extremely convenient break for Chatham that the bonds it owned were the ones that were paid off for greater than 100 cents on the dollar. Chatham's canniness would eventually raise questions about what exactly Sambur and Melchiorre arranged.

As for the Caesars parent stock held by Apollo, TPG, and the likes of Paulson and Scoggin, the shares jumped by 14 percent after the announcement on May 6 while the OpCo debt plunged. These market reactions were significant. Apollo repeatedly claimed that its aggressive ploys were to the benefit of creditors. But when the stock that it held spiked upward and debt prices plunged, those statements were shown to be contrary to the market reality. As in all the previous transactions, the Caesars OpCo creditors got no independent voice when the Caesars board approved the B-7 and the sale of the 5 percent of the OpCo stock in April 2014.

Motivation aside, the termination of the bond guarantee was a breathtaking moment. The mechanics required meticulous work from Apollo and Paul, Weiss. And the sheer audacity was most shocking of all. Debt guarantees were sacred and not supposed to be casually jettisoned. The B-7 and the OpCo stock sale felt like an even harsher "fuck you" toward Caesars creditors from Rowan and Sambur than even the Growth, CERP, or Four Properties ever did.

There had to be at least some modicum of trust between private equity firms and the debt investors on the other side of them. By May of 2014, it felt like the distressed debt world, never a place for the faint of heart, had become an even more savage jungle. Caesars creditors had been constantly bracing for the next diabolical move from Apollo. These latest transactions, however, represented an escalation. Rowan and Sambur had found ways to flip individual creditors and then pit them against others:

- Give GSO and BlackRock tens of millions in fees.
- Allow Chatham, Paulson, and Scoggin to profit from their other Caesars positions.

And from now on, every other creditor had to worry if their foxhole mate would, at the right price, defect to Apollo's side of the battlefield.

11

PIXIE DUST

"We are your problem. But we are your solution, too," Andrew Dietderich calmly explained to Lewis Clayton, Alan Kornberg, and Jeff Saferstein, all senior Paul, Weiss lawyers representing Caesars.

Dietderich was an attorney at Sullivan & Cromwell, perhaps one of the three best Wall Street law firms. S&C was not a bankruptcy specialist like Kirkland & Ellis or Paul, Weiss, but it had a handful of partners like Dietderich who typically represented companies that had esoteric disputes among creditors. In Caesars, however, a group of investment funds needed his help. Dietderich loved complex corporate restructurings. To him it was like playing speed chess— rapid-fire decision-making where there was constant feedback to each player's moves.

And on this summer afternoon in 2014, Dietderich thought he had Apollo and Paul, Weiss in checkmate. S&C represented a group of four funds who owned a couple hundred million dollars of Caesars unsecured bonds. There were roughly $1 billion of these bonds outstanding that had been issued before the 2008 Caesars LBO.

Compared to the senior bank loan, senior bonds, and junior bonds—which collectively totaled more than $15 billion—these "legacy" bonds were trivial. But Dietderich's message that day to Paul, Weiss was that his foursome was about to derail Apollo's painstaking plan to keep control of Caesars.

"We think you should buy all our bonds at par," Dietderich explained to the Paul, Weiss team, along with Apollo's David Sambur, who had joined the meeting in the Paul, Weiss conference room. The meeting was in a space called the "Jury Room" across from the firm cafeteria and for some reason Sambur was sloppily eating a bowl of cereal. On May 6, 2014, Caesars announced the B-7 loan along with the 5 percent stock sale. The sum of those transactions was to have released the parent guarantee on all the Caesars bonds outstanding, or so Paul, Weiss had believed.

In the days after May 6, two Sullivan clients—Bluecrest Capital Management and Goldman Sachs—asked Dietderich to assess the validity of the guarantee release. Reviewing the indenture for the unsecured notes, Dietderich concluded that the 5 percent stock sale, in fact, had not properly terminated the guarantee. He wrote to Paul, Weiss telling them as much.

In this meeting, Dietderich had an offer to make to Sambur: Caesars could simply buy out all the unsecured bonds at par, and there would be no need to litigate the legal vagaries of the 5 percent stock sale. Dietderich knew Kornberg well, and liked and respected him. But he also believed that Paul, Weiss was in deep with Apollo and had gotten too cute with the parent guarantee termination.

The indenture governing the legacy bonds held by the Sullivan clients was different than the documents for the LBO bonds. According to the language in the legacy indenture, the bond guarantee could be terminated if OpCo "ceases to be a 'wholly-owned subsidiary' of the [parent] under SEC Reg S-X."

SEC Regulation S-X allowed the OpCo and the Caesars parent to file single, consolidated financial statements. Dietderich's legal argument was that since Caesars had been and wanted to continue using single, consolidated financial statements for the parent and the OpCo, the guarantee could not be so easily released with the sale of the 5 percent of OpCo stock. Indentures were not supposed to be like other legal contracts, he believed. Norms and expectations of the market mattered here, and there was no prevailing view that guarantee terminations could or should be so simple to pull off like Caesars just had.

"This either is a real guarantee or its securities fraud," Dietderich told Paul, Weiss and Sambur.

Paul, Weiss disagreed. It called the parent guarantee a "guarantee of convenience." The guarantee was a mere formality to streamline financial reporting. OpCo creditors had no expectation it was enforceable. Still, the guarantee release was a critical issue that Rowan and Sambur had to get correct or their investment would be wiped out.

Worried that the 5 percent stock sale had not severed the bond guarantee, Apollo had gone to Plan B. In late spring 2014, Apollo created a so-called "Performance Investment Plan" for OpCo employees where the company would distribute 6 percent of OpCo shares to ostensibly motivate the top several hundred Caesars executives. After the PIP, the Caesars parent would only own 89 percent of OpCo, underscoring that OpCo was no longer a wholly-owned subsidiary and that the guarantee had been terminated.

But the circumstances around the PIP were bizarre. The timing was rushed, OpCo was not even public, parent company stock would have been easier to pass out, and there were tax problems created for ordinary employees—some of whom paid out-of-pocket taxes owed to the IRS. The biggest problem remained the same as the 5 percent stock sale weeks earlier: OpCo stock was worthless. The PIP seemed like a sham transaction. In a June 2014 text message to Rowan, Sambur even admitted as much in writing: "No one wants [OpCo] stock. It's like saying we will pay them with pixie dust."

In this brewing legal fight with Sullivan, Apollo knew that it did not really matter whose legal interpretation of the legacy notes indenture was correct. If Sullivan were to make a public spectacle, it could be fatal to Apollo's position at Caesars. Sambur knew he would have to buy off Dietderich's clients, the "solution" that Dietderich had cryptically referred to earlier. There would be an easy way or a hard way to pay this ransom, and there was no doubt which one David Sambur was going to pick.

CAESARS WAS THE KIND OF case that had brought Jamie Sprayregen back to Kirkland & Ellis. In the summer of 2014, Caesars had called Kirkland after finally reaching the conclusion that OpCo needed its own separate legal advisors outside of Paul, Weiss. For years, Sprayregen had been considered the most commercially successful corporate bankruptcy lawyer in America. But in 2006, he left Kirkland, his home for the previous sixteen years, to try his hand as a restructuring banker at Goldman Sachs. Sprayregen was humble enough to ask Goldman if he could participate in junior analyst training in order to properly understand and appreciate all the work that bankers did (Goldman declined to let him do so). It was not usual for top lawyers to give it a shot as bankers. Sprayregen was also such a legend that while at Goldman, the most senior members of the storied firm would often stop by to pay their respects.

But by 2009, Sprayregen was back at Kirkland. The financial crisis had hit, and it was clear Wall Street was going to be a far less fun and lucrative place in the coming years. A huge bankruptcy wave was coming out of the Great Recession, and it would be fun to be the top bankruptcy lawyer around.

And besides, Kirkland was run like a rollicking investment bank. The Chicago-based firm had first made its name as a corporate litigation specialist. For years, its most famous face was Kenneth Starr, the right-wing lawyer, former US Solicitor General, and special prosecutor who investigated President Clinton in the Whitewater and Monica Lewinsky scandals.

Kirkland had yearned, however, to be a deal-making powerhouse. It built a practice working with medium- and large-sized private equity firms. The deals from these firms were not often blockbusters but provided steady revenue in multiple areas of law. Kirkland, unlike its New York rivals, was not hidebound when it came to running the business. It eschewed the "lockstep" compensation model where all law partners made the same money each year. Kirkland instead paid rainmakers based on the business they brought in—and they were expected to bring in a lot. Partners who underwhelmed were ushered out. New talent was aggressively brought in for top dollar.

Sprayregen had joined Kirkland in 1990 after stints at smaller firms. (He had been rejected from Kirkland the first time he applied, and he eventually had the rejection letter framed and mounted in his office at the Kirkland headquarters.) Restructuring was not a formal group when he joined the firm, but it was an auspicious moment. American companies were struggling after the 1990 recession, and there was the nascent marketplace of investment firms using Chapter 11 to bring companies back to life.

Sprayregen, while soft-spoken, was intense and driven. He was an avid runner even in the Chicago winters. He regularly completed marathons in under four hours. He was constantly shuttling between Chicago and New York. Rivals noted that he was dialed into multiple conference calls even while in board meetings.

The New York firms who were strong in traditional corporate M&A mostly did not focus on bankruptcy, creating a market opportunity for Kirkland. By the 2000s, Kirkland, Skadden, and Weil, Gotshal began to dominate highly lucrative "debtor" work, representing bankrupt companies in Chapter 11. The most complex cases—like Caesars—required the deployment of dozens of lawyers having expertise in not just bankruptcy law but tax, real estate, and virtually every other corporate law specialty. And Sprayregen sat at the top of the Kirkland machine.

Kirkland was hired in early July by OpCo's two new independent directors, Steve Winograd and Ronen Stauber. The arrival of independent directors was a watershed moment. Apollo and Paul, Weiss had insisted for years that the Caesars parent and OpCo shared identical interests. Now there was an acknowledgement that OpCo was at least approaching insolvency and its creditors needed to be protected. There were immediate questions about how tough Winograd and Stauber were going to be in checking Apollo and TPG. The tardiness of their arrival made it feel like the security guards had showed up after the bank vaults were largely emptied.

There was also the question of how dedicated these security guards were going to be. Winograd had been an investment banker at Drexel in the 1980s working for Leon Black and supervising Marc Rowan. Winograd then went to join Blackstone in the late 1980s, but had fallen out of favor with Steve Schwarzman after leading a disastrous investment in a steel company. Winograd would then bounce around several investment banks over the next twenty-five years putting together deals for PE firms, including Apollo. Winograd would deny that he and Marc Rowan were close friends, but admitted they were involved in the same charities and that he had invited Rowan to parties he had hosted.

The other independent director, Ronen Stauber, had his own ties to Apollo. Stauber had been an executive at Cendant, the hospitality conglomerate built by Henry Silverman, a longtime friend of Leon Black, who would later become an Apollo executive (Realogy, the 2007 Apollo buyout, was a castoff part of Cendant). After Cendant, Stauber had worked at Pegasus Capital, the investment firm of Craig Cogut—a Drexel executive and Apollo co-founder who had worked closely with Leon Black on the controversial Executive Life rescue. Like Winograd, Stauber had charitable connections to Rowan. The standards for independence in corporate law were lax and Apollo were happy to take advantage.

The independence of Sprayregen, Winograd, and Stauber was going to be tested right away in the summer of 2014. Sambur had developed a plan to fix the guarantee issue in the legacy bond indenture. Sullivan had arranged for a group of four funds—Goldman Sachs, BlueCrest, Aurelius Capital Management, and Angelo Gordon—to sell a portion of their legacy unsecured notes, which had been trading at roughly fifty cents, for 100 cents on the dollar back to Caesars. The Caesars parent and Caesars OpCo would spend roughly $150 million in cash to buy back those bonds. The Caesars parent would also surrender $400 million worth of the same series of unsecured bonds it owned. These bonds together formed a bare majority of the legacy notes—51 percent. This bare majority then agreed to amend the indenture to sever the bond guarantee.

Such horse-trading between companies and creditors was not unusual; Caesars had been doing it for years to stay alive. But this transaction reached a whole new level of aggression. Typically, all holders of a debt issue got the chance to decide whether or not they would participate in such a cash-out offer, a structure that even Dietderich of S&C had even initially proposed. Instead, Rowan and Sambur wanted to complete this deal in the cheapest and the most incendiary way—cutting out the 49 percent minority from the buyback.

Within the OpCo board, Winograd and Stauber formed a two-person Special Governance Committee whose job it was to approve any conflicted transactions between OpCo and the Caesars parent. On August 8, 2014, the committee had its first meeting on this so-called Unsecured Notes transaction. By August 12, the two had approved the deal. The OpCo was spending just $80 million to reduce debt by $500 million. The trickier question was around the release of the guarantee. The release disabled the rights of $12 billion of Caesars bonds. Winograd and Stauber came to believe that severing the guarantee would prompt a comprehensive restructuring. The thinking was that a Caesars parent no longer burdened with the crushing guarantee obligation would then make big monetary contributions to a settlement with creditors. That scenario was plausible, but it was a generous reading of the mindset of Rowan and Sambur, who had been merciless for years toward creditors. With two friendly directors now calling the shots, Apollo got the benefit of the doubt.

SHELL GAME

Matt Ragsdale was getting in a run at the gym on the afternoon of August 12, 2014. It was after four p.m. and since the markets had closed for the day, the thity-four-year-old distressed debt investor at Greenwich-based MeehanCombs LP figured it was a good time for a workout. But in the middle of Ragsdale's run, his phone pinged with a new email—Caesars had just released an 8-K with the SEC, a filing type that shared important company news.

Ragsdale read the filing, which contained a bombshell for his firm's position in Caesars. The filing described the transaction where Apollo got 51 percent of the unsecured noteholders to release the guarantee in exchange for that favored group of four hedge funds having their legacy unsecured bonds taken out at par. MeehanCombs was a known holder, and there had been whispers of such a deal in the works. But it was customary for such buybacks or exchanges to be offered to all holders, so firms like MeehanCombs would get a shot to join such a deal. David Sambur had other ideas. It would become clear that MeehanCombs was indeed left out of the group being offered the deal. It was time for MeehanCombs, and the group of hedge funds caught on the outside looking in, to get their own lawyer.

JIM MILLAR WAS TIRED OF not getting respect. Millar was a top partner in the bankruptcy practice at Drinker Biddle & Reath, a scrappy, mid-tier law firm based in Philadelphia. Based in New York himself, Millar often ended up the representative of minor creditors trying scratch

out recoveries among giants in big bankruptcy cases. The glory typically went to A-list firms like Kirkland & Ellis, Weil, Gotshal, or Jones
Day. Yet Millar believed that he was every bit as talented as the big
boys. Caesars was going to be his opportunity for the headliner role
he had long craved.

In mid-August 2014, Millar got a call from Nomura Securities, a
client he was representing in another LBO gone bad, Energy Future
Holdings. Nomura was a holder of the Caesars OpCo legacy unsecured notes and wondered if the Unsecured Notes Transaction was,
indeed, legally permissible. Millar did some digging and noticed
the Caesars fact pattern resembled another case from fifteen years
prior called *Federated Strategic Income Fund v. Mechala Group*. Mechala,
a Jamaican company, was attempting a complex debt restructuring
that included the release of a bond guarantee and asset transfers to a
new company. Bondholders who agreed to the deal would get nearly
fifty cents on the dollar. Those who did not would be left holding a
claim on the existing company that had been left an "empty shell"
after the asset sales.

A dissenting investor, Federated, sued to block the deal. The relevant law in question was an obscure Depression-era statute called
the Trust Indenture Act of 1939, an addendum to the Securities Act
of 1933. The TIA had been enacted to protect creditors in restructurings completed outside of bankruptcy court where a judge supervised
the proceedings. According to the TIA, any bond restructuring that
changed the core terms of the debt—principal, interest, maturity—
required unanimous consent of holders. A New York federal judge
granted a preliminary injunction ruling that the Mechala restructuring would likely be impermissible.

Based on the *Federated* ruling, Millar was convinced that the Caesars Unsecured Notes deal was a violation of the TIA. On September
3, 2014, Drinker, Biddle filed in New York federal court, *Meehan-
Combs Global Credit Opportunities v. Caesars Entertainment Corporation
and Caesars Entertainment Operating Company*. Millar's case appeared
weak. Rarely did creditors prevail in such situations. But serendipity
was about to strike.

ANDREW MILGRAM WAS NO BOY Scout, so to speak, despite having
achieved the rank of Eagle Scout as a teenager in the 1980s. He
remained an active Scoutmaster in his adopted hometown of
Greenwich, Connecticut. But in the distressed debt world, he
had acquired a reputation as a troublemaker. Milgram was a managing partner of Marblegate Asset Management, which he had

co-founded in 2009 with two partners. Marblegate was considered a gadfly firm, while Milgram himself was an outspoken, personable, if arrogant, man.

Milgram had become an expert in troubled, for-profit education companies. These schools were once Wall Street darlings, but now their predatory practices had drawn the scrutiny of regulators. As they ran into financial trouble, they sought to restructure debt. But for-profit schools could not file for Chapter 11 bankruptcy because their lifeblood, federal student loan programs, would be cut off. Milgram's insight was that because bond restructurings needed to be completed outside of court, a holdout hedge fund could have outsized power.

Education Management Corporation was just the type of for-profit school that Milgram was monitoring. EDMC had been acquired in a $3.4 billion leveraged buyout in 2006 by Providence Equity Partners and Goldman Sachs. It had $1.3 billion in secured debt, and $200 million of unsecured bonds at an operating subsidiary guaranteed by the parent company. The business was faltering, and the company needed to quickly reduce its debt balance.

The company and its advisors came up with a solution: The junior bondholders could unanimously agree to take a 67 percent haircut on their bonds. To force any stragglers to agree or be wiped out, the company would move all its assets to another company, which would belong to the creditors who signed up for the deal. Holdout creditors would be left with a claim on the old company which had become an "empty shell." The deal had been cleverly structured to ensure that holdout creditors still technically maintained their existing paper without modification.

Every Education Management bondholder agreed to the deal—except Marblegate, which held just $14 million in bonds. If the restructuring was completed, Marblegate bonds would be worthless because there was no remaining business to either support Milgram's debt or for him to foreclose upon. To Milgram, this was a clear violation of the Trust Indenture Act. In late October 2014, Marblegate sued in New York federal court to get an injunction blocking the debt exchange.

Holding up the EDMC restructuring was not making Milgram any friends.

"You're going to be considered a black hat in the industry…You'll be in the same camp as Paul Singer and Steve Feinberg," one banker told him.

"You just named a couple of billionaires. If you're threatening that I'm going to become a billionaire doing this, that's not much of a threat," Milgram fired back.

Milgram found the distressed debt ecosystem to be too chummy. Too many funds wanted to get along and then go play golf together afterwards. Milgram believed his job was to make money for his investors. If it rubbed others the wrong way, that was their problem, not his.

Milgram's instincts proved to be correct. On December 30, 2014, US District Court Judge Katherine Polk Failla ruled that the EDMC restructuring was likely at odds with the Trust Indenture Act, allowing for a future trial. According to her opinion, "…the Trust Indenture Act simply does not allow the company to precipitate a debt reorganization outside the bankruptcy process to effectively eliminate the rights of nonconsenting bondholders."

The decision, even if preliminary, was a game-changer at Caesars. Jim Millar was convinced his TIA claims were better than Milgram's. If the Caesars parent's guarantee terminations were to be nullified, the Caesars parent stood to go bankrupt. Apollo and TPG's investment would be wiped out. Jim Millar, lawyer to a ragtag group of creditors, was suddenly the man of the hour in the Caesars case.

13

CHASING WATERFALLS

"*Rid yourself of fear. Rid yourself of fear.*" Dave Miller kept whispering the mock chant, really a mock narration, while filming his best friend, Kaj Vazales, who stood atop a jagged cliff. Vazales was set to attempt a risky ski jump in front of a gathering crowd well off of the marked trail at the Alta resort in Park City, Utah. It was 2003 and Vazales, having trouble making it as a professional golfer, was considering other paths in life including getting a regular job and putting his Harvard degree to use. An expert skier, the annual boys ski trip with Miller and some other friends was a chance to ponder the future.

Vazales made the leap as the crowd gasped. Miller briefly cheered, until he saw his friend land hard and his body crumple. Vazales was knocked unconscious and fractured several bones. Ski patrol would have to come with a sled to ferry him down the mountain. Though he would recover, the fall wiped away any thoughts of more stunt skiing, and the effects of Vazales's injuries were debilitating enough that crouching down to survey putts was no longer possible. This was the right moment to transition to high finance like his friend Miller, who had been making a name for himself since the pair graduated from Harvard together in 2001.

The friendship of Miller and Vazales seemed to be defined in the snow. Both were sophomores at the exclusive Deerfield Academy in rural Massachusetts when a dispute over a video game turned into a snowball fight and wrestling match. From that tussle a lifelong friendship blossomed. Both would go to Harvard and join Delphic, one of the Harvard finals clubs (Miller's sport ended up being heavyweight crew after an ill-fated attempt to join Vazales on the golf team). After graduation, Miller landed at Peter J Solomon & Co., a boutique investment bank focused on the consumer sector. After two years as a junior banker, Miller made a move to join the powerful hedge fund Elliott Management in 2004, where he was steadily moving up the ranks in the distressed credit investing group (ironically, in the weeks before joining Elliott, Miller had his own serious skiing injury trying to race the much-faster Vazales).

Soon after he recovered from his daredevil injuries, Vazales got himself a job at Houlihan Lokey, an investment bank that would advise on restructurings like the ones Dave was investing in. And three years later, Kaj became an investor himself at one of the biggest firms in the distressed investing industry, Oaktree Capital Management.

IN 2014, MORE THAN A decade after the fateful ski trip, Dave Miller was noticing Oaktree's heavy position in the Caesars junior debt. It seemed like his friend Kaj Vazales was standing, once again, on that cliff with either glory or disaster waiting below. Miller was going to keep his distance from Kaj's Caesars position. Instead, he eyed the senior part of the Caesars OpCo capital structure: the $12 billion of combined first-lien bank loans and first-lien bonds. The values for this higher priority debt had traded down into the 90s and 70s, respectively, in early 2014, as holders were fleeing, afraid of what crazy scheme Apollo had up its sleeve.

But David Sambur's furious wheeling-and-dealing had captured Miller's attention. Miller could not ever recall seeing such aggression from a private equity firm. It was becoming clear to him that Apollo was executing a meticulous plan to grab value from OpCo and daring the creditors to stop them.

Miller belonged, however, to a firm that relished such a fight. Elliott Management had been formed in 1977 by Paul Singer, then a Harvard-educated corporate lawyer. For years Singer's focus had been trading convertible bonds, instruments that combined fixed income securities and equity options. Elliott took on distressed investing in the 1980s and the analytical, legally intensive nature of the work made it a natural fit for Elliott.

Singer was not afraid of messy situations that even other smart investors did not have the patience for. His firm was willing to make a big bet to make money but also confirm its philosophy on how capital market should function.

In a legendary battle with the government of Argentina that started in 2001 over a debt restructuring, Elliott famously seized an Argentinian naval vessel that had docked in Ghana. Argentina called Elliott's actions "extortive" and referred to the firm as a "vulture fund."

The Argentina litigation did not conclude until 2016 (Elliott was largely vindicated and took home an estimated $2 billion of profit). But by 2014, Elliott's reputation as a savvy, aggressive, and persistent debt investor was secure; if Elliott was willing to go to war with Argentina, Apollo was not going to spook them.

Given the sheer size of the Caesars OpCo capital structure—$18 billion of debt across different tiers—Dave Miller knew creditors were going to have to organize to challenge Apollo. But in the meantime, Elliott was going to start its own due diligence. Elliott prided itself on how many hours and dollars it invested to answer every conceivable contingency before placing its bets.

Engaging four law firms to review bond indentures and loan agreements, Elliott set out to understand their provisions about collateral, liens, and guarantees. Miller wanted to know all the details of Caesars' paper, down to whether the company's very gaming licenses counted as assets that could be seized. Elliott's analysis made it comfortable enough to eventually buy more than $1.25 billion of senior bonds and nearly $650 million of senior bank loans together, making it the largest single creditor of Caesars.

The junior creditor group led by Oaktree and another Los Angeles-based hedge fund, Canyon Capital, had been working with its lawyers and bankers for months plotting strategy. And by March 2014, the dozens of hedge funds and mutual funds that owned the more than $10 billion of senior Caesars bank loans and bonds needed its own advisors. Private equity owners of troubled companies know they maintain two immediate advantages even as their investment is deteriorating. First, even if their equity was becoming near worthless, they still kept control of the company and could swing for the fences to save their investment. And second, their creditor adversaries are often dispersed and disorganized. Suddenly, with the announced sale of the Four Properties in early 2014, Caesars senior creditors were scrambling to protect their interests, wondering if they were too late.

The senior bondholders (many held first lien bonds and loans) chose the law firm Kramer Levin Naftalis & Frankel to represent them. Leading the Kramer Levin team was Ken Eckstein, one of the most experienced corporate bankruptcy attorneys in America who specialized in representing creditors. Eckstein had come of age in the 1980s working on such cases as Texaco and Eastern Airlines, and more recently he had represented Elliott in the Argentina litigation. Kramer's immediate task was to rally as many senior creditors as possible of the $12 billion group. The stronger block they could show Apollo, the far more seriously their demands would have to be taken.

On April 3, just days after getting hired, Kramer Levin wrote a letter to Caesars sharply criticizing the Four Properties deal. The purpose of the letter was to put a stake in the ground. The senior creditors needed to put Apollo on notice. Jones Day, a law firm representing junior creditors, had sent their own letter two weeks earlier.

Paul, Weiss and Caesars now were concerned. These protests could derail the closing of the sale of the Four Properties deal, which OpCo needed both for the cash and to avoid the accounting opinion that would have triggered a default. The lenders who were providing financing to Growth were growing nervous too. If these transactions were fraudulent, there was a chance the casinos would have to be shipped back to the OpCo.

THE LOUISIANA GAMING CONTROL BOARD had a meeting scheduled for April 24, 2014, in Baton Rouge, Louisiana, to consider the Four Properties sale that included the Harrah's New Orleans property. Dissenting creditors would get the chance to address the board. The hearing would prove a dramatic moment: the first public clash between Caesars and the company's creditors, who now fully believed they were being mugged by Apollo.

The creditors flew their representatives out to Baton Rouge where they made their way to the LaSalle Building, a twelve-story limestone structure that welcomed visitors with a row of stained glass featuring the magnolia state flower above the entranceway. The hearing took place in the LaBelle Room, a cavernous space that rises four stories. Footfalls on the marble floors echoed through the open spaces.

Speaking for the junior creditor group would be Sidney Levinson, a Jones Day bankruptcy attorney, along with a Houlihan Lokey banker named William Hardie III, better known by his nickname, Tuck. The group had raced from another gaming board hearing the day before in Mississippi. Hardie happened to be a New Orleans native who still kept a home in the Big Easy.

City slicker bankers and attorneys tended to stick out like a sore thumb in these proceedings in small-town America. But good ol' boy Tuck Hardie would be right at home.

Hardie and Levinson were able to raise enough doubts to get the board to hold off approving the sale of Harrah's New Orleans. Caesars, having received approval from Nevada, went ahead with the sale of the three Las Vegas properties for $1.3 billion on May 5.

On May 19, the Louisiana regulators met again with both Caesars and the creditors. If the company could push through the sale of Harrah's New Orleans to Caesars Growth, they could once again regain the upper hand. If the regulators, however, bought the fraudulent transfer argument, Apollo's entire strategy could unravel.

Neither side was leaving anything to chance at the hearing. Caesars brought John Payne, the highly respected head of Caesars' operations in the South, to make their case. Tuck Hardie and Sid Levinson again showed up to the hearing, as did Ken Eckstein from Kramer Levin for the first-lien creditors. Payne opened with his long-standing ties to Louisiana. He had been at Caesars for fifteen years, starting as the general manager at the Lake Charles property before taking the helm as GM of Harrah's New Orleans in 2002.

Sid Levinson explained a set of events that would become the metaphor for all the Caesars creditor groups who felt like they were being victimized. In closing the Four Properties transfer at the last minute, Caesars left behind within OpCo a parcel of Bally's Las Vegas that housed a laundry facility that was found to have environmental liabilities. Levinson tried to extend the metaphor to the three Louisiana properties: "…like the potentially toxic laundry facility in Nevada, they're leaving behind the North Louisiana properties that they apparently regard as subject to liabilities."

Regardless, Hardie and Levinson knew they had already lost.

The board seemed skeptical that the woes of hedge funds were Louisiana's problem, asking Eckstein why the bondholders failed to negotiate tighter documents. It was an awkward question, as the creditors were seen as hedge fund speculators who were not going to elicit much sympathy whatever the merits of their arguments.

Tim Donovan, the Caesars general counsel, noted that even with the earlier grievance letters sent by Jones Day and then Kramer Levin to the company, "while they're here today arguing against the transaction, they have yet to file a lawsuit…this is a contractual dispute, and the proper forum for a contractual dispute is a court of law."

A few minutes later, the chairman of the Louisiana Gaming Control board said, "You know I haven't heard a lot of good alternatives here. I mean we are damned if we do, and damned if we don't. But the fact is from my view, we have to protect the interests of the state citizens…" He introduced a motion to pass the resolution and the board unanimously approved the sale of Harrah's New Orleans.

At this point, the litigation that Tim Donovan was tempting looked like the creditors' only hope to get their money back.

THERE WAS AN EXPRESSION AMONGST creditors about dealing with Apollo: Everyone comes to the table with a gun, but Apollo is the only party who puts it on the table before the meeting starts.

Little did Kris Hansen know that this was literally true. As he walked into an early meeting with Apollo in August, he noticed a collection of muskets on a side table in a hallway outside of a conference room high atop 9 West 57th Street. "Don't pick them up," Apollo's David Sambur told him. "They're antiques. Fifteenth century."

Hansen led the restructuring group at Stroock & Stroock & Lavan and had won the role representing the senior loan holder group who by now had formed a group separate from the senior bondholders. By bankruptcy lawyer standards, Hansen was mild-mannered. The son of a fireman, he was trim and fit, he resembled a young Danny Ainge, the former basketball star.

He had been in sticky situations before—once receiving a death threat while representing creditors of a Donald Trump casino. Hansen was close with Ryan Mollett's GSO Capital, as well as other key loan holders including Franklin Mutual Advisers and Och-Ziff Capital Management.

Hansen was thrilled to have found a role on Caesars. In the years after the 2008 buyout he had been counseling Fortress Investment Group and Franklin Mutual on the dizzying number of refinancing and balance sheet transactions Caesars had been conducting. There were worries in the spring of 2014 that Apollo would transfer out the crown jewel, Caesars Palace, which Hansen advised would be too brazen a move (and one that would not entirely come to pass). Hansen also believed that the B-7 term loan was a "booby trap" and that hedge funds should stay away. Whatever his analysis of the legal documents, his warnings were not heeded, and the demand for the B-7 was through the roof. A few months later, restructuring negotiations were now beginning, and it was time to start brainstorming solutions.

On this day in August 2014, Kris Hansen had made his way from the Stroock office next to the South Street Seaport in lower Manhattan over to meet Sambur at Apollo's Midtown headquarters. This meeting with Sambur and Paul, Weiss was mostly supposed to be a simple meet-and-greet. Both sides were going to feel each other out to see if there was a deal to be done. Elliott and the first-lien bonds had already started talks with Apollo. The negotiation with the more senior loan holders should, theoretically, have been simplest. They were at the top of the totem pole and would expect to be paid 100 cents plus interest, all in cash.

Who is this guy? Hansen wondered of Sambur a few minutes in. Hansen calmly explained his client's position. Instead of just nodding and playing it cool, Sambur, a mid-level private equity guy more than ten years younger, decided to give Hansen a lecture in bankruptcy law.

Sambur explained to Hansen how the guarantee of collection differed from the guarantee of payment, and why accruing post-bankruptcy interest was going to be a problem for loan holders. His supreme confidence was surprising given that Apollo's equity was deeply impaired and the savviest investors in the world—carrying $18 billion worth of debt—were ready to go to war.

"LISTEN, IT'S A GREAT DEAL for you. But I hope Caesars doesn't go south," Ken Liang warned Ken Schneider and Alan Kornberg, the senior partner who managed the Oaktree relationship and senior bankruptcy partner, respectively, at Paul, Weiss. "If it does, it could be our Waterloo. And I don't know who Napolean is. "

In 2011, Liang was a top executive at Oaktree Capital Management, the Los Angeles-based fund manager that was one of the elite credit investors in the world, managing almost $100 billion. Paul, Weiss had just lured the ace group of financing lawyers from O'Melveny & Myers, a Los Angeles-based firm trying to be a big player on Wall Street. That raid was about to cement Paul, Weiss's relationship with Apollo, which Liang knew would be a massive financial windfall for the law firm.

This Paul, Weiss gambit was going to be tricky. Apollo, Oaktree, and Paul, Weiss were already deeply intertwined. Trouble at Caesars could jeopardize those relationships, as Liang had just speculated with Schneider and Kornberg. Liang had been close with Kornberg since the 1990s. What's more, Oaktree had been a major Caesars creditor since the 2008 buyout, purchasing various Caesars securities over time. Oaktree had also been using Paul, Weiss as legal counsel for years, and Liang had discussed the Caesars debt papers with Ezring at O'Melveny since the 2008 buyout.

Now that Paul, Weiss had lured the O'Melveny team, Caesars was about to be a Paul, Weiss client, and Liang understood that Oaktree needed another lawyer. Oaktree would pay Paul, Weiss perhaps a few million dollars a year. Apollo could be worth many, many multiples of that. But Liang had an uneasy feeling that things were never going to be the same for the trio.

Howard Marks, the co-founder of Oaktree, was never a Drexel employee. But as a consistent buyer of Drexel junk bonds in the 1980s while an investment manager at Citigroup, he eventually became like family to Leon Black. And their wives, Nancy Marks and Debra Black, would become especially close.

In 1978, after years as an equity analyst at Citigroup, the bank asked Marks to look into the nascent junk bond market that Michael Milken was creating in Los Angeles. Marks eventually moved to LA in the late 1970s to start up within Citigroup what was thought to be the first institutional junk bond fund. In 1985, Marks jumped to Trust Company of the West, also in Los Angeles, one of the largest fixed income investors in the world. Marks would sour on TCW. In 1993, Marks and a handful of top TCW executives and dozens of employees left to form Oaktree Capital Management (Marks chose the name because his vacation home near Santa Barbara was in an area histori- cally named "Las Encinitas," Spanish for "little oak trees").

The split was ugly, with TCW unhappy about the mass defection. There was no litigation, but the "Marks salad" in the executive dining room was quickly renamed the "TCW salad."

Marks had developed a reputation as a sage of the financial mar- kets. His periodic letters to investors became must-reads, not only for his often contrarian ideas, but also for his wit and storytelling. Marks would become the face of Oaktree—with investors and the public. Bruce Karsh, one of his trusted TCW colleagues who had started his career at an attorney at O'Melveny & Meyers, would be Oaktree's chief investment officer.

Ken Liang, who had also started his career as an O'Melveny attor- ney, joined Oaktree with Marks and Karsh, serving as the firm's first general counsel. Liang emigrated from Hong Kong as a child, first landing in New York for a few years in 1969, before settling in South- ern California. His immigrant parents pressured Ken and his twin brother to choose safe professions, and Ken chose the law while his brother became a physician.

Liang's legal training ultimately saw him switch to a role assisting Oaktree investors in corporate restructurings. Liang developed an understanding for the game theory behind multi-dimensional fights. "Ken could see what was coming around the corner," explained one colleague. Liang also developed a reputation as an obstinate nego- tiator not afraid to throw bombs as necessary to advance Oaktree's position. "Ken is a screamer, he could take wholly irrational positions and then storm out of a room," described one adversary who would face off with him regularly.

"You hear Ken's voice on the phone and all you can do is sigh," lamented another rival.

That style clashed at times with the more diplomatic Karsh, but Liang's unique skills made him a valuable commodity at Oaktree. (He also kept a large stash of M&M's in his office that made him popular with his colleagues and softened his reputation.)

Oaktree quickly became a successful distressed investor with notable wins in the early 2000s, including the luggage brand Tumi and US movie theater chains including Regal, Loews, Edwards, and Landmark. By 2010, Oaktree was managing more than $80 billion of capital, mostly in locked-up funds that allowed it to be a patient investor.

HE WAS A LONG WAY from Harvard Yard. Sleeping in his car in the hinterlands of Florida, Kaj Vazales was determined to chase his dream, which happened to involve chasing a golf ball across the American South. Vazales's golf game had blossomed while he was a boarding school student at Deerfield Academy in the late 1990s. At Harvard he eventually became the captain of the school's team. While his fellow Class of 2001 classmates went off to grad school or to corporate trainee programs, Vazales was going to give professional golf a shot.

Golf's minor leagues are a long way from the glamour of the PGA Tour. The prize money was marginal while the competition was fierce. Vazales was taking his shot at the Hooters Tour, a mini tour in Florida where the top performers could perhaps graduate to the Web.com tour, the circuit just below the PGA Tour. To save money, Vazales would sometimes sleep in his car.

Vazales's parents were successful physicians who had staked him, but he was determined to make it on his own. He had occasional success, once co-leading an Arkansas tournament after the first round. Still, Vazales understood that he was not going to make it in the professional golf world; while a good ball-striker, he did not make enough lengthy putts. "It was eye-opening to see how good I had to be," he said. "I realized I wasn't even close. It was humbling. It was a lot of failure for someone who hadn't experienced much failure. But I met a lot of good guys and saw parts of America I wouldn't have seen otherwise."

Vazales also attributed his substandard play to his attitude on the course; when things were going well, rather than gaining confidence, he would expect the worst.

That mindset may not have been conducive to success as a professional athlete, but it prepared him for life as a distressed debt investor. Vazales eventually went to work for boutique bank Houlihan Lokey in 2005 and then joined Oaktree in 2007.

By early 2014, Vazales, who led Oaktree's investment team on Caesars, had that familiar feeling of dread. Had Oaktree bought Caesars' debt far too soon? After the original Caesars LBO in 2008, Oaktree had bought both senior bank loans and junior bonds at discounts, believing that the company would snap back, and the debt would eventually trade up sharply. "This is a good business, with a bad balance sheet," he liked to say.

The junior bonds that Oaktree owned were trading at just forty cents on the dollar at the end of 2013. But Vazales and Ken Liang were becoming increasingly worried that Apollo had a systematic plan to siphon value away from creditors.

Caesars kept reassuring them that the parent guarantee remained in place, and as long as it existed, Oaktree had nothing to worry about—the transferred casinos were still under the umbrella of the broader Caesars empire. With the operating company hopelessly underwater, the only support holding up debt prices was the guarantee of the parent. And all sides knew it.

But the chatter around the guarantee was only continuing to grow. Wall Street analysts were mixed on the prospects of what would be almost incomprehensible provocation. "In our view, Caesars will not release the parent guarantee with a goal to file [the Caesars OpCo for bankruptcy] and reduce debt," wrote Goldman Sachs in October in 2013. Later that month, Barclays disagreed, writing, "We believe CZR could potentially execute a transaction in the future that removes this guarantee…"

The termination of the guarantee had been the subject of discussion from even the previous year. *Covenant Review,* an influential debt trade publication staffed with former leveraged finance lawyers, speculated as early as 2012 that the parent guarantee could be terminated.

Against this ominous backdrop, Sambur and Apollo thought they had the upper hand with the junior creditor group that included Oaktree. In 2014, Sambur and the second-lien group began swapping proposals about some kind of exchange offer where the junior bonds would swap into a new convertible bond, perhaps get some modest amount of cash, and get some Caesars equity as upside. The value of the package was perhaps twenty to thirty cents on the dollar. That was not great, but there was the distinct possibility that in a bankruptcy the junior paper would be rendered worthless.

Ken Liang was skeptical of these early 2014 discussions with Apollo. What was the point of a one-off negotiation with a canny operator like David Sambur? Apollo, Oaktree, and all the investors and advisor banks created intricate spreadsheets described as "waterfalls" that calculated how much offers were theoretically worth. Variables included how much the company was worth, and then how that value spilled downward from senior creditors to junior creditors to shareholders. Sambur's arithmetic underlying his offer was dubious with all its moving parts and inflated value of the company. The number it added up to, according to Oaktree's own analysis, was less than the current trading price of the debt.

But to Liang, the math was beside the point. Caesars was in deep trouble with so many disparate stakeholders. What it needed was an all-hands-on-deck restructuring that solved all these simultaneous equations. Instead, Sambur was playing whack-a-mole.

Against that skepticism, Liang and Vazales flew to New York in early 2014 to meet with Sambur at Apollo. Liang and Vazales had both encountered Sambur during the CERP transaction and Liang also knew him from other deals. Also joining the meeting were investors from Canyon Capital. Canyon was a highly successful Los Angeles-based hedge fund that managed $24 billion invested in a wide variety of securities. Canyon's founders, Mitch Julis and Josh Friedman, had been executives at Drexel in the 1980s and remained close with the Apollo founders.

Canyon's Julis, Todd Lemkin, and a more junior analyst, Chaney Sheffield, all flew in from Los Angeles. Sheffield, tall, blond and in his mid-30s, was out of Central Casting. A high school baseball phenom in Southern California, Chaney had starred on the pitcher's mound at Harvard. He was a year behind Vazales and the two, along with Dave Miller, became friendly as members of the Delphic finals club. After college, Sheffield landed at Morgan Stanley before joining Canyon. He had become a sector expert in gaming, and made a series of large wagers in casinos, believing a cyclical recovery was due after the financial crisis.

In the New York meeting, Sambur reiterated that his current offer was better than what the Oaktree junior creditor group would get in a bankruptcy. Liang remained dubious and delivered his message. "David, there is nothing wrong with a settlement. But it's hard to just settle with one or two guys with all these other pieces out there. We are going to need a higher yield security with a different collateral package. I'm not sure what currency you have. Why would we reduce our claim when no other group is? I don't see how you can get this done and still keep the company."

The meeting was cordial but terse, lasting less than thirty minutes, and Oaktree suspected Apollo mostly intended to feel out the junior creditor group. Oaktree was happy to telegraph that they were willing to fight this out in bankruptcy if necessary.

"We've gotta be all over this," Mitch Julis said, pressing Liang to start litigating with Caesars. Mitch Julis's sudden militance proved surprising to Oaktree. Liang was not necessarily opposed; after all, he was usually cast as the brawler. But he knew there was a process to follow that would take time.

The next day back in Los Angeles, Liang got a call from Oaktree co-head Bruce Karsh. Mitch Julis had called Karsh to say Canyon did not believe Liang was showing the resolve to take on Apollo, and Julis gave Karsh the "dare to be great speech." Karsh was unsure what posture Oaktree should adopt. In Liang's experience, the Masters of the Universe tended to care about what the other MoUs thought of them. Liang explained the situation and asked Karsh if he really wanted to get in the middle of this food fight, both within the second-lien bond group and, ultimately, with Apollo. Because if they did, Liang warned, Oaktree might wind up going it alone.

"Bruce, if you want, call Mitch and tell him I fucked up. But let's not count on Canyon being there at the end. They will fade like the worst golf shot," Liang said. He'd had previous sour experiences with that firm.

Next to pick up the phone was Apollo. Marc Rowan and Leon Black made calls to the Oaktree brass. Liang believed that these moments when Apollo went over his head only confirmed the strength of Oaktree's arguments. Apollo had its cudgels, as well as a gift for preying on the pain points of its adversaries. Apollo ominously reminded them that Oaktree and Canyon depended on deal flow from Apollo that they could be excluded from in the future.

On March 3, 2014, Caesars announced the sale of the Four Properties. Additionally, Caesars disclosed that the Total Rewards IP was also leaving OpCo. The junior bonds traded down to twelve cents on the dollar on the news.

Vazales and Sheffield crunched the numbers and calculated that the terms of the four casino sales were laughable. The implied valuation multiples were just a skinny seven or eight times off of depressed EBITDA. David Farber, a debt analyst at Credit Suisse, arranged a briefing at Caesars Palace in Las Vegas with Caesars finance chief

Eric Hession and his colleague Jacqueline Beato, a former Deutsche Bank investment banker and Harvard Business School grad who managed investor relations. Both passionately defended the fairness of the transactions and how creditors would benefit. Vazales was struck by Beato's confrontational tone. She sounded like she was simply reciting talking points written for her by Apollo.

The second-lien bondholders had written the letter to Caesars objecting to the Four Properties deal and had also tried to intervene at gaming commission hearings. Yet even as war raged, peace talks continued in the background. Sambur had not given up on an exchange offer with the biggest junior bondholders, Oaktree, Appaloosa, and Canyon.

Kaj Vazales was hopeful there was a deal to be cut. But on May 6, an 8-K filing from Caesars landed in his email inbox. The OpCo had raised $1.75 billion through a new term loan and it had sold 5 percent of the stock—the B-7 transaction. The sacrosanct parent guarantee had been purportedly terminated. Vazales happened to be in New York at the time, and after he received the news, he numbly wandered the streets of Manhattan.

Sambur had been stringing them along only to drop this bomb. The second-lien bonds dropped to single digits on the dollar. The guarantee that had been hoisted for years as an assurance to creditors was gone with the stroke of a pen. It was obvious now that Sambur had been working all along with the other senior bank loan creditors like GSO. Now, with the new cash from the B-7, it appeared Caesars would skirt a bankruptcy where a judge might have held Apollo to account.

A few days later, Sambur made a conciliatory call to Vazales, insisting that Apollo was still willing to cut a deal with the Oaktree group. "You just screwed us, why should we do a deal with you?" Vazales screamed, wondering if he would ever have his shot at vengeance.

"IT'S A GOOD THING IT'S a public place, so if one of us kills the other, at least there will be witnesses," David Sambur half-joked on the phone. Sambur needed a friend, and was breaking the ice with Dave Miller of Elliott. Elliott's and Apollo's offices were diagonal to each other across 57th Street, and they agreed to meet for breakfast at the restaurant at the nearby Four Seasons Hotel on July 30, 2014.

Negotiations with the Oaktree group were effectively dead by the summer. Dealing with the senior bank lender group, led by GSO, was a slog. They were asking for at least 100 cents on the dollar, a figure that Sambur was not prepared to pay.

Sambur's next option to keep Apollo's investment alive was to look in the middle at the senior bondholders. Elliott had quickly become the biggest player in the senior bonds, with a position approaching $1 billion. Perhaps Sambur and Miller could come to an understanding over orange juice and eggs.

The Leon Blacks and Paul Singers were the public faces of firms like Apollo and Elliott. The day-to-day work, meanwhile, was handled by men (alas, it was almost always men) like Sambur and Miller in their 30s. The intelligence of this cohort was undeniable—but their maturity, judgment, and experience varied.

On paper, Sambur and Miller were somewhat similar, down to their first names. Both went to elite private universities (Emory for Sambur, Harvard for Miller), graduating one year apart in the early 2000s. After spending two years in investment banking, both quickly had gone on to become successful investors at top firms earning millions of dollars each year.

But that was where the similarities ended. Sambur superficially reminded many of Marc Rowan—short, dark hair, Jewish, and razor sharp when it came to complex finance. Still, he had little of Rowan's charm. One could not help but like Marc Rowan; one often could not help but cringe at David Sambur. He always operated at Defcon One. Ordinary interactions turned into sieges with Sambur. He was not for chit-chat or back-slapping; it was what you could do for him or what he was going to threaten to do to you.

That posture, combined with his brilliance, had worked for him as a buyout investor at Apollo. But now he was running point on Caesars, one of the most complicated, multi-party restructuring negotiations in Wall Street history, where Apollo needed him to be smooth and strategic.

Dave Miller, as was his practice, displayed little emotion at breakfast. His consistent poker face and periods of unbroken silence led some to believe he was mildly autistic (he was not). Miller liked that the Elliott culture felt more academic than anything else. He did not mind dressing like a college student, even for key negotiating sessions. Sometimes Miller's shirt was untucked, a result he blamed on his six foot four frame. At this time in Miller's life, he favored hoodies and an informal pair of Clarks. Unlike Sambur, who had been married since he was 25, Miller had remained a bachelor. And notwithstanding his boarding school heritage, whether it was Domino's Pizza, Taco Bell, or McDonald's, Miller loved fast food.

Sambur was relieved that Miller would meet him. And Miller was open to the idea of Elliott joining forces with Apollo. The juxtaposition of the two firms was notable. Elliott was a hedge fund that took tradable stakes in securities and was less interested in acquiring and running companies in the way Apollo did as a private equity firm. In their respective worlds, each institution's brilliance, conviction, hardball tactics, and ultimately profits, terrified their opponents into submission.

Miller's potential alliance with Sambur was, unsurprisingly, not going to come cheap. The first-lien bond group that Elliott led represented what was the "fulcrum" security. The senior bonds likely could not be paid back in full in cash given the depressed value of the Caesars OpCo. This impairment meant they would not get 100 cents on the dollar for their claims or would have to take equity or stock in the reorganized Caesars. Being an impaired creditor was not ideal. But it opened up the possibility to a creative solution.

Miller was also something of a savant when it came to financial engineering for troubled companies. He already had some ideas how he could help solve Sambur's problems to Elliott's benefit. For now, though, Miller only had one request: he wanted Caesars to file for bankruptcy as soon as practicable, perhaps by the end of 2014. The OpCo was making hundreds of millions of dollars of bi-annual interest payments to the junior creditor group, cash Miller believed belonged to Elliott and the senior creditors. And the quicker bankruptcy arrived, Miller believed the Apollo shenanigans would stop.

Sambur was surprised by this idea. The Caesars OpCo had just executed the messy $1.75 billion B-7 loan to forestall a bankruptcy. It had a decent amount of cash left over after paying off some other debt with the loan proceeds. A bankruptcy was perhaps in the cards for late 2015, at the earliest. But he hoped with the new runway, Caesars profits would snap back and there could be a successful out-of-court deal between all the creditors that kept Apollo's investment alive.

A bankruptcy would be a wild card for Apollo. Creditors would have new power and a judge could order all sorts of things, including an investigation into all the Caesars dealmaking. But it was an opportunity, too. If Sambur could convince enough creditors to go along with his restructuring plan, Apollo could stay in control of Caesars and, once and for all, eliminate the threat of the junior creditors. Miller's ideas were interesting enough, so Sambur agreed they should keep talking. Miller's stone face belied an intricate plan that was now in motion.

THE MAJOR NEW YORK LAW firms liked to keep at least a floor dedicated just to conference rooms. The best firms had space overlooking sweeping vistas of Central Park or the Statue of Liberty to impress visitors, almost signaling that "important work is being done here in these rooms." On September 14, 2014, a little more than a month after the Sambur/Miller breakfast, the first meaningful meeting between Caesars and the senior bondholders took place in one such cavernous conference room at Paul, Weiss's office on 6th Avenue and 53rd Street.

It was time to get serious on a restructuring accord that Sambur and Miller had previously discussed. Caesars' advisors—Paul, Weiss and the Blackstone investment bank—and the bondholders' representatives at Kramer Levin and investment bank Miller Buckfire had been having low-level discussions for weeks. In these preliminary stages, these agents were crucial, acting as buffers for their clients. These bankers and lawyers had worked closely for years in the tight-knit restructuring community, and could lay the groundwork for later crucial negotiations.

Importantly, once these substantive principle-to-principle talks commenced, investors like Elliott would have to become "restricted," disallowing them from trading in and out of their positions due to their possession of material, non-public information.

"You can keep Caesars Palace, and we're giving you $100 million, not a penny more," sternly warned Mike Genereux of Blackstone, who wanted to emphasize that his client remained firmly in control. "And we're not going to pay twice."

The bondholders in the room included Elliott, as well as other large holders like JPMorgan, Pimco, and BlackRock. These terms were not what they had in mind when they got restricted.

Blackstone had shared a 45-page PowerPoint deck that it had been working on with Apollo for weeks. The first slides simply described the dire situation at Caesars. Interest expense of nearly $2 billion was double the size of cash flow. Annual free cash flow was running at negative $1 billion. Profits had fallen so sharply since 2007 that debt-to-EBITDA had spiked to a sky-high 18x.

Page twenty-five of the deck finally summarized the nitty-gritty of three proposals. The details were complicated, but ultimately it was all dead-on-arrival to the bondholders. Among the ideas proposed was another OpCo/PropCo structure, but with a twist. The real estate of the Caesars properties would be put into its own company and trade separately as a so-called real estate investment trust—a new angle for Caesars, inspired by another casino operator. In 2012, Penn National Gaming had formed a REIT subsidiary, which turned into a big hit. REITs traded at higher valuations and creating one as a new PropCo could be a way to magically create value for Caesars creditors.

The REIT had been broached by Miller before, and he now had other more pressing objections. The Caesars restructuring always contemplated that Caesars parent would pay some sort of "settlement" to creditors over allegations of fraudulent transfers in the Growth, CERP, and Four Properties deals. The Apollo proposal contemplated a modest $400 million payment to make the allegations go away. It was really only a $100 million payment, where the creditors believed the fraud totaled into the billions. Adding to the egregiousness of the proposal, Apollo and TPG were suggesting they would remain owners of the casinos that had been transferred and would then get full immunity from any liability for wrongdoing.

Marc Rowan's appearance at the meeting was significant, and he was there to deliver a message. "The best-case scenario if you don't take this deal, you sue us for years and the first-liens get $2 billion," he said, referring to a potential win in fraud litigation. "Essentially one third of the $6 billion in claims is what that would be, so for this group, you get $600 million and what are the assets going to look like then?" He believed litigation would be fruitless for creditors.

Over the next several weeks, both Caesars and the bondholder group continuously kept trading proposals and counterproposals. The existing mistrust with Sambur and Apollo was only getting worse in these settlement talks. Because the Caesars business was in such poor shape, the recoveries for creditors would come in the form of some cash, new debt, and stock across multiple Caesars companies. This required various assumptions and calculations on all the moving parts. When Apollo would, for example, assert in a meeting that the first-lien bond recovery was ninety cents on the dollar, a closer examination by Dave Miller or his bankers would conclude it was really worth eighty-five cents or eighty cents. The fuzzy arithmetic would even get its own nickname: "Sambur math."

By now, all the creditor groups had been at the table at some moment with Sambur and were slowly getting accustomed to his unique negotiating style. His command of every detail around the Caesars business and capital structure was masterful. But just how he played Apollo's hand perplexed his adversaries. Both Rowan and Sambur had a habit of declaring preliminary offers as "best and final," only to quickly come back with an improved offer.

Sambur had to be the alpha personality in the room, the center of attention, where nothing could happen without his approval. He sometimes would fly off the handle for no particular reason and theatrically storm out of conference rooms. His performances quickly became lore. This became complicated for his affable junior Apollo colleague, Alex van Hoek, who never knew when he should rise and walk out with Sambur. In one meeting with the loan group, Sambur tried to storm off only to trip and fall, dropping the stack of papers he was holding.

Pratfalls aside, Sambur could even frustrate his allies. In most restructurings, bankers and lawyers tried to make as much progress with the other side's advisors as they could. But Sambur had a habit of freelancing. He would call up Ryan Mollett and Dave Miller and try to come to terms. But his advisors at Blackstone (one of whom affectionately referred to him as a "pet rattlesnake") or Paul, Weiss would be in the dark. Without knowing what goodie Sambur had passed out, they ended up looking foolish.

The bigger problem, however, was that the restructuring was so complex that there was no way to keep track of the latest offer on the table: Give a penny to, say, the loan holders, and there was no easy way to follow the ripple to the various bondholders.

By late October 2014, Apollo's September bluster was a distant memory. A settlement with the senior bondholder group was slowly taking shape. The sides had largely agreed to bifurcate Caesars into the OpCo/PropCo. The devil was very much in the details, and Miller still had a few tricks up his sleeve.

WHILE DAVE MILLER AND DAVID Sambur were breaking bread, Canyon and Oaktree knew they could not simply sit still. The risk was that Apollo and senior creditors were going to cut a deal that left the junior bondholders holding the bag. Strongly worded letters were not going to cut it anymore; it was time to go big and hit hard. Tim Donovan, the Caesars general counsel, had taunted creditors before the Louisiana regulators in the spring, rhetorically wondering why the bondholders upset about the Four Properties deal had not filed a lawsuit?

Donovan got his wish on August 4, 2014. Jones Day launched its shot across the bow, filing an eighty-one-page complaint in Delaware, where Caesars was incorporated, targeting all the major Caesars entities, and naming the key board members—Gary Loveman, Marc Rowan, David Bonderman, and David Sambur—as defendants.

"The net effect of the transactions…has been to divide Caesars into two segments—one, a 'Good Caesars,' consisting of Growth Partners and Resort Properties that owns the prime assets formerly belonging to OpCo, and the other, a 'Bad Caesars,' consisting of OpCo which remains burdened by substantial debt and whose remaining properties consist primarily of regional casinos that are unprofitable or far less profitable than those taken from OpCo by the Sponsors," read the lawsuit.

David Sambur was caught off guard. He emailed Caesars' lawyers telling them to get their own lawsuit against creditors out right away. "Pls file asap. Don't wait," Sambur urged. For months Apollo knew that creditors might go to court asking a judge to intervene at Caesars. This lawsuit from Caesars asked for a so-called "declaratory judgement" in New York State Court, where they requested a judge to rule that the company's asset deals had been appropriate and that the creditors pay damages for harassment (the delay of the sale of Harrah's New Orleans was costing Caesars $200,000 in bridge loan expenses).

This countersuit offered its own incendiary prose. The list of targeted hedge funds included the likes of Canyon and Oaktree, but also more fringe creditors. They were accused of "maliciously and repeatedly" making "unfounded threats," "bogus allegations," and "false statements" meant to "bloody up" Caesars.

Yet the most interesting aspect of the lawsuit was not the allegations, but rather the plaintiffs. The Caesars parent company, controlled by Apollo and TPG, naturally initiated the suit. But, surprisingly, the OpCo joined the lawsuit as well. Apollo and Paul, Weiss, now attuned to the corporate governance controversy surrounding Caesars, had just appointed Ronen Stauber and Steve Winograd as the first-ever independent directors to the OpCo board.

Among their first acts, Stauber and Winograd began an investigation into the Caesars asset transfers to determine if there had been any fraud or misconduct. Because that investigation was just getting under way, the two abstained from joining a vote of the OpCo board on whether to join the countersuit. Still, the rest of the OpCo board—Gary Loveman, Eric Hession, and the Apollo and TPG representatives—voted to join the lawsuit, which proved to be enough. OpCo was now investigating Apollo's assets transfer while simultaneously asking a judge to say there was nothing untoward about them. For creditors, it was just another data point illustrating the conflict between the Caesars OpCo and the Caesars parent.

14

GUITAR HERO

Emotions were running red hot on all sides in late 2014. Both the senior bond and senior bank loan groups were fighting tooth and nail to get the best settlement deal with Apollo, and ultimately with each other, to get the biggest piece of a shrinking pie.

Ken Eckstein, the lawyer for the Elliott senior bondholder group, would call up Kris Hansen, his counterpart with the bank loan group, wondering why the two creditor groups were not marching in lock-step against Apollo. "Our interests are different. You guys want to own the company. We just want to par plus accrued interest in cash," said Hansen, explaining their diverging interests.

Michael Barnett, an executive at Och-Ziff Capital Management, was a key member of the loan holder group. The Och-Ziff office was at 9 West 57th (a few floors below the Apollo space) and diagonal from the Elliott building. And from time to time Barnett would be dispatched to see Miller and take his temperature. Sometimes, Ryan Mollett from GSO would join the discussions. They were all men in their mid-30s who naturally got along well.

But politeness aside, there was clear envy in the bank loan group developing toward Elliott and the windfall that they were negotiating toward with David Sambur. The loan holders, fairly or not, believed that they deserved a better deal than the one Elliott and Dave Miller were getting. But even within the bank loan group, there was some division. Silver Point Capital, a sharp-elbowed hedge fund out of Greenwich, had been accumulating bank debt based on an aggressive interpretation of the loans' seniority. Silver Point began to worry that the group's ringleader, Ryan Mollett of GSO, would go soft. The bank loan group should be asking for the moon, Silver Point believed and did not want Mollett to prematurely cave to Apollo.

Sambur thought he sensed some cracks within the loan holder group. If he could peel off a few big holders, then just maybe he could muscle them into a settlement. Even a few pennies shaved off meant hundreds of millions of dollars that Apollo and TPG would keep, or that they could use as currency with the junior creditors. Sambur started working the phones trying to make customized pitches.

Shawn Tumulty, a world-class triathlete, worked at Franklin Mutual Series, a part of the big asset manager Franklin Resources. Sambur would call Tumulty and ask him why he was putting his lot with these buccaneering hedge fund characters when he was operating a vanilla mutual fund.

Sambur happened to know Michael Barnett of Och-Ziff socially as well. Barnett had to endure the Sambur hard-sell at any social gathering while the case was proceeding.

Sambur's more natural approach was to simply use brute force. He was prone to sending a nasty email at all hours of the night, explaining how his opponents, sometimes addressed as "motherfuckers," would be vanquished. It made him effective in some ways. But his intensity did not make him friends or build trust, and it was increasingly clear he was going to need both in Caesars. The bank loan group members, meanwhile, were becoming increasingly tight-knit. They would share Sambur's missives and chuckle.

At one point, Sambur had even tried to engineer a side deal with Mollett. Apollo thought there was a way to create an extra payment to GSO, if it could win its support for a settlement with the bank group. As the key holder, if GSO signed up, the others would likely follow. Mollett had been concerned about the deal that Elliott was looking to strike with Sambur, and he was fearful those senior bondholders were going to get a better deal than his loan holder group. Sambur was trying to exploit that sensitivity. Maybe there was some special security or payment he could pass out to GSO? In the B-7 term loan, GSO and BlackRock got big fees to sign up first for the deal. But the circumstances were now different. Mollett was part of a group, and striking a quiet deal on his own would not be taken kindly.

Mollett struggled with the decision. Ultimately, he could not pull the trigger and said thanks but no thanks to Sambur. "I have a long time in the industry," Mollett told his adversary. "I can't do this."

Mollett quickly convened a phone call with his fellow loan holders, explaining what had happened. Mollett joked to the group, "I'm literally living a Taylor Swift song, 'We're never ever, ever getting back together.' I feel like I have to break up with him every time."

The bond that the loan holders had developed tightened even further—as did their resolve to squeeze Sambur for everything they could.

AT THE ELLIOTT HOLIDAY PARTY on December 11, 2014, Samantha Algaze could not totally free her mind from work. Algaze, twenty-six, was one of the few women investors at Elliott and in the distressed debt industry in general. Her place on the Caesars deal team was almost an accident, as she had been attracted to Elliott by its stock activist investing group. She would joke that when she joined Elliott in 2013, after starting her career at Deutsche Bank, she barely knew how to calculate a bond yield (it was strictly a joke: she was razor sharp and a Wharton graduate). Caesars would be one of her first distressed debt assignments. But she was a quick study and had a penchant for details and she quickly made herself indispensable to Dave Miller. Her job was taking the deep legal analysis that outside lawyers had provided and translating it into a spreadsheet model that was the underpinning of the hundreds of millions of dollars Elliott had plowed into Caesars debt. Spending virtually all her time on Caesars, Algaze came to know the details of the case as well as anyone, and soon found herself holding her own in heated negotiations with men sometimes twice her age.

That evening, Algaze periodically checked her phone for emails. At 10:14 p.m., a press release crossed the news wire, stating that the informal committee of bank loan holders—GSO, Franklin Mutual, Och-Ziff, and Silver Point, among others—had let non-disclosure agreements with Caesars expire, meaning settlement negotiations had ceased due to a lack of progress. As part of this "cleansing," the loan holders chose to disclose the terms of the latest settlement along with seventy-five pages of PowerPoint documents that had been shared during the previous weeks of negotiations.

The bank loan group's bowing out of negotiations was no shock. Their headline settlement value was 100 cents, but only about a third was in cash. Worse, the fine print in the contracts underlying the paper was so problematic that even Caesars advisors would later admit that it was "a shitty document." Kris Hansen had reviewed the legal documents that Paul, Weiss had shared prior to this cleansing, and his revisions were so vast that his markup was filled with red ink.

An hour later, around 11:31 p.m., another press release dropped. A single member of the Elliott bondholder group was also terminating its own NDA. Included in this press release was another 500 pages of PowerPoint decks and terms sheets that charted the evolution of the talks that had started in September. The talks were well-known, but the details were not publicized until now.

The name of the single bondholder who wanted out of the group was not shared in the release—but it was BlackRock, the trillion-dollar asset manager. *The Wall Street Journal* even ran "BlackRock Gives Up Leadership Role in Restructuring Talks for Caesars Unit" as its headline the next morning.

The next day, Caesars, in an SEC filing, wrote, "Notwithstanding the actions by Non-Extending Creditors, the NDAs with certain First-Lien Bondholders have been extended and [Caesars is] continuing discussions with them with respect to finalizing the material economic terms of a Restructuring." There still was momentum to finalize a deal with the Elliott group, and the pressure was squarely on David Sambur and Marc Rowan to sign at least one major Caesars creditor group.

"THE LOWER THE DEBT TRADES, the less downside risk there is." This was the gallows humor the junior bondholder group featuring Canyon and Oaktree was deploying to comfort themselves. The junior bonds were only continuing to collapse through 2014. While they had started the year in the fifties, by late autumn they had plummeted to below twenty cents. The Caesars business, five years on from the financial crisis, was still moribund. And it was becoming clearer that Apollo was going to take Caesars into a bankruptcy, possibly with support of two of the three major creditor groups, leaving the junior group with a ten or fifteen cent recovery.

And while Canyon had been talking tough in the spring and early summer about taking the fight to Apollo, they'd lost their stomach for a fight. Canyon founders Mitch Julis and Josh Friedman conceded that Apollo had the deeper pockets. Their relationship with the Apollo co-founders went back to Drexel, and it would be an ugly fight with people they considered friends.

Todd Lemkin and Chaney Sheffield of Canyon liked a certain expression: "structure determines behavior." Canyon was a hedge fund that marked its returns monthly. Unlike Apollo and Oaktree, which were structured as "locked-up" funds that had seven- and ten-year lives, Canyon fund investors could redeem their money every quarter—meaning that the firm had the pressure to generate returns more quickly. In late 2014, Canyon decided that they now had a better angle to generate returns at Caesars than the second-lien bonds.

BlackRock began to dump first-lien bonds and Canyon was able to grab $300 million worth at seventy cents on the dollar. Lemkin and Sheffield figured that the senior bonds were a safer bet, and told Ken Liang of Oaktree they wouldn't be joining the fight even as they also bought more second-lien bonds given the low prices.

Liang was disappointed. He felt abandoned at this gut-check moment, though he had predicted months earlier that their fellow LA-based firm would ultimately back off. Things were getting tense at Oaktree as well, as the junior bonds continued to dive. Bruce Karsh had a habit of walking directly past Liang's office to discuss the investment—and whether it was worth exiting—with Kaj Vazales, the other leader on the Caesars team. Liang would then wander over and try to get Karsh to buck up. "If you want, Bruce, just mark the position to zero if that's easiest. But let's stay in and hold on. We've got a shot here so I say we just ride this out."

Oaktree ultimately decided to stand firm. But with Canyon putting down its sword, Oaktree needed to assess the gumption of their remaining allies. And that took them to a nondescript New Jersey office park where a kindred spirit awaited.

DAVID TEPPER DID NOT CARE to be in the club. Fierce independence was not always easy on Wall Street, but over the course of a career it would prove liberating and lucrative for him. Tepper grew up in a humble family in Pittsburgh. He was a star junk bond trader at Goldman Sachs in the late 1980s and early 1990s. Tepper, however, did not quite fit in at Wall Street's most elite shop. He clashed with his boss Jon Corzine, a future Goldman CEO, US senator, and New Jersey governor, who would not promote him to partner, the exalted inner circle at Goldman Sachs.

Tepper left Goldman with a couple of colleagues in 1993, to start a new firm. He initially wanted to call the firm Pegasus, but that was already taken. He then flipped through a horse book looking for another moniker and decided on "Appaloosa," in part for strategic reasons: brokers in the early '90s sent out "runs" or security price quotes via fax machine in the morning. With the name Appaloosa, Tepper was to be at the top of the distribution list.

Apart from its consistently high returns often exceeding 20 percent annually, Appaloosa developed a certain reputation. It made a handful of concentrated bets in corporate debt or equity and sovereign securities, commodities, or other macroeconomic-based instruments, all based on Tepper's strong convictions and instincts. Tepper became a cult favorite because he spoke his mind plainly and came across like a fun, ordinary guy who happened to have hit it big as an investing genius. On his desk he displayed a pair of brass replica testicles that a former employee had given to memorialize big gains from the bankruptcies of Enron, WorldCom, and Conseco in 2003.

The US banking sector would be the source of Tepper's greatest triumph. In early 2009 after the bailouts of the previous fall, the worst had passed for the banks; rather than being nationalized, they would slowly recover alongside the US economy. Tepper started buying the stock and bonds of Citigroup and Bank of America, along with mortgage-backed securities. David Bonderman had tried the same bet nine months earlier when TPG led the $7 billion rescue of Washington Mutual, only for that investment to get fully wiped out in September 2008.

The rally Tepper anticipated was not immediate, and Appaloosa took some heavy paper losses. But eventually he was vindicated to the tune of a staggering $7.5 billion in profits. Tepper's share of the profits totaled $4 billion, one of the greatest hedge fund hauls in history.

Tepper had started enjoying some of the trappings of wealth. In 2004, the business school at his MBA alma mater, Carnegie Mellon University, was named after him in conjunction with his $55 million donation. He had bought a minority stake of the Pittsburgh Steelers, the hometown football team of his youth. In 2007, Tepper's fiftieth birthday was held at the Mandarin Oriental hotel across the street from Central Park and featured Sheryl Crow, with whom he sang on stage.

In a 2010 profile in *New York Magazine,* Tepper famously asked the writer, Jessica Pressler, what to do with his billions. "'What do you think I should do with it?' he asked me. 'I could buy an island. I could buy a private jet—but I have NetJets. I could get myself a twenty-two-year-old!'"

Tepper, the richest man in New Jersey and wealthier than the three Apollo founders combined, had been married for years and had three children. His primary home was a relatively modest place in Livingston. But in 2010, he bought the Hamptons beachfront estate of one-time nemesis Jon Corzine for $44.5 million, then tore it down to build a new vacation house that would be completed in 2015 (the property belonged to Corzine's ex-wife at the time). Tepper perhaps could forgive but he did not forget, and he was not afraid to play a long game.

One place Tepper was, however, not breaking the bank was on Appaloosa office space. The firm, which had fewer than fifty people despite managing more than $10 billion, occupied the second floor of a nondescript low-rise building across the street from the famed

Short Hills, New Jersey, shopping mall. The bland location suited Tepper and one of his key lieutenants, Jim Bolin, who would spearhead the firm's Caesars team.

Bolin had worked with Tepper on the Goldman Sachs trading desk in the early 1990s and joined Appaloosa shortly thereafter. In the aggressive, macho world of distressed debt investors, Bolin was different. He wore glasses, talked softly, and resembled a librarian or a park ranger. He lived in Morristown, played golf at a public course in Hackensack, and would not be caught dead in the Hamptons if for no other reason than he could not tolerate the traffic. His passion outside of work was the guitar, which he had studied classically at Washington University in St. Louis in the 1980s. Bolin had built a notable collection of the instrument, particularly the vaunted custom Gibson L-5s, an instrument of musical legends like Paul Simon, Mark Farner, and Django Reinhardt.

Bolin was also a painstaking, meticulous investor, and Tepper and Bolin formed a powerful duo. In a 2010 interview with *Institutional Investor*, Tepper described Bolin as "the best pure analyst on Wall Street." Both had been through the wars and simply were not going to be swayed by Apollo's extracurricular lobbying. "Most firms on Wall Street are happy to take crumbs from Apollo. Appaloosa may be the one firm that is not," explained one large Caesars creditor.

In 2013 and 2014, as Apollo was moving assets out of the OpCo, Bolin had taken notice. Those deals, according to his analysis, were done on nowhere near fair terms. Throughout 2014, Appaloosa was accumulating the junior bonds as prices kept falling, eventually scooping up nearly $1 billion worth in face value. Between a rebound at Caesars and the litigation value in pursuing fraudulent transfers, the upside on the junior Caesars debt could have been enormous.

Ken Liang of Oaktree had found a soulmate in Bolin. When David Sambur tried to strongarm Liang into taking twenty cents on the dollar, he responded by telling the young Apollo investor he was, instead, happy to litigate this case. "David, I love these facts. There are like eight deals here that are going to get challenged. I only have to win one of them, you gotta win 'em all."

Most Caesars creditors agreed with Liang's assessment. But virtually none had the guts to take on goliath. Apollo had been able to pick off enough other hedge funds, and believed it was only a matter of time until everyone else gave in. Appaloosa and Oaktree, however, had other ideas. Like every other creditor in Caesars, they wanted to make money. But by the end of 2014, they both were also out to exact justice.

FIRST DERIVATIVE

*"Every day you woke up and the Caesars contract went wider,
you were like what the fuck does someone else know that you don't?"*
—Wall Street swaps trader, 2014.

Dave Miller had smartly calculated that Apollo, as it tried to work out a restructuring in 2014, would be desperate for allies. The senior loan holders, led by Ryan Mollett of GSO, were driving a hard bargain for 100 cents plus interest. The second-lien bonds, led by Oaktree and Appaloosa, were so furious that their only play was litigation. Elliott, in the middle as a senior bondholder, had decided cooperation—at least its version—would be a shrewder way to play. Elliott had a strategy to make a windfall return but not take money out of Apollo's pocket. But Miller required something from David Sambur: put Caesars into bankruptcy.

Derivatives are securities whose value is tied to or derived from other underlying securities. Put options and call options on stocks, for example, allowed investors to wager on whether stock prices would rise or fall without actually owning the stock. Miller was going to use derivatives to juice his Caesars returns. His derivative choice was the credit default swap, or CDS. Buyers and sellers of CDS were betting whether companies could repay their debts in full. In this case, purchasing CDS would pay off if Caesars defaulted or went bankrupt.

Banks created CDS to keep debt on their books while offloading risk. A young JPMorgan executive, Blythe Masters, had created CDS to help the firm hedge default risk related to a $5 billion loan to Exxon. A buyer of CDS is effectively purchasing insurance that pays off if a company defaults. For example, if a bond of a bankrupt company settled at twenty-five cents, the CDS seller would owe the buyer seventy-five cents to make them whole.

Products that allowed market participants to hold risk in the form and quantity that they preferred were supposed to increase efficiency across the board. But on Wall Street, a good idea tended to be abused. Banks, insurers, and hedge funds were writing and buying CDS to the tune of trillions of dollars by the mid-2000s—activities that were largely done outside of the watch of regulators. AIG, the massive global insurer, had sold CDS on more than $500 billion of assets, including $78 billion of securitized mortgage debt called CDOs. Those underlying mortgages soured in 2008, and AIG had no way to come up with the payout it owed. It ultimately led to a $182 billion bailout and seizure by the US Treasury. Warren Buffett labeled CDS as "weapons of financial mass destruction" and their opaque, complex use and scale worried market observers.

Dave Miller's CDS gambit at Caesars was less menacing but would soon become a key subplot. The early 2015 Caesars bankruptcy filing Miller craved looked like a longshot. Caesars had just raised $1.75 billion in the B-7 loan transaction led by GSO and BlackRock. There was enough liquidity to get the company to at least the middle of 2015.

All this created an opportunity for Miller. CDS protection that paid off in the case of a default before the second quarter of 2015 was dirt cheap in the market. Ryan Mollett was confident a Chapter 11 filing was still far off, so GSO risked a portion of their fee by selling the CDS protection, taking the opposite side of Miller's bet. BlackRock, the other key party in the B-7 loan, did the same thing.

Miller started to slowly buy, and as 2014 progressed, market chatter grew that Elliott—and only Elliott—was buying what was called "front-end" or "short-dated" credit default swaps, accumulating as much as a half billion worth of CDS protection. Only Elliott seemed to be confident Caesars would default in less than a year.

Apollo was aware of the adjacent skirmish between Miller and Mollett. It was not thrilled about the sideshow wreaking havoc with its company, but Sambur needed Miller—and Miller believed that his CDS bet was perfectly aligned with his underlying debt positions.

Amid the delicate negotiations, Elliott dropped another bomb. On November 25, it filed a lawsuit against Caesars in Delaware, asking the court to appoint a "receiver" to take away control of the casino company from Apollo and TPG. It was a sneak attack—Elliott referred to it as a "commando operation"—that not only caught

Apollo off-guard, but also surprised other fellow senior bondholders, none of whom were alerted by Elliott which was worried about disloyal members of its group. Jeff Saferstein, a bankruptcy partner at Paul, Weiss representing Caesars after the lawsuit dropped, emailed Ken Eckstein of Kramer, Levin—who represented the senior bondholder group. "Bizarre they [Elliott] would commence this. Not helping the dynamic." Eckstein tersely responded, "We just learned about this after it filed. Will report later."

Elliott had hired the aggressive litigation firm Quinn Emanuel, who did not disappoint. Choice phrases in the 200-page complaint included "unimaginably brazen looting and corporate abuse," "devised a scheme to cheat creditors of their rightful recoveries," and that, "The fox has not only been put in charge of the hen house; it has barricaded the door and has even paid itself a salary." Rowan and Sambur were stunned. Apollo also knew it needed an ally and had nowhere to go. Elliott had Apollo over a barrel, and everybody knew it.

"We just laughed. Elliott is amazing," explained one advisor to the company. Elliott was beating Apollo at its own game: finding a weakness and repeatedly exploiting it.

After Thanksgiving, Apollo and Elliott resumed their negotiations. The bank loan group led by GSO was back at the table, too. The bad blood, the rivalries, the recriminations, the litigation all hung over Caesars going into the holiday season, with little sign of peace on earth and goodwill toward men.

RUBICON CROSSED

On December 19, 2014, Dave Miller finally broke David Sambur. Caesars put out a press release announcing a Restructuring Support Agreement (RSA) in place with the steering committee of senior bondholders that was led by Elliott. The plan was largely in line with the terms that had been disclosed in recent weeks.

The Caesars OpCo would slash its debt balance from $18 billion to $8 billion. The OpCo and PropCo would be formed out of the remaining casinos with OpCo. But all the properties that were now at Caesars Growth and Caesars Entertainment Resort Partners would stay put. They would remain out of the reach of the OpCo creditors, and stay owned by Apollo, TPG, and public investors. (A few days later, Caesars Growth and the Caesars parent even said that those two companies that had been kept out of the reach of OpCo creditors would merge, and would be valued at more than $3 billion.) The senior loan holders were to get 100 cents on the dollar, a figure they disagreed with given all the non-cash pieces allocated to them. The senior bondholders' package was worth ninety-four cents, again with only a fraction in cash. The junior creditors were to get only nickels, with nothing in cash.

The press release boasted that the Caesars parent was contributing $1.45 billion toward the settlement, though creditors found the math on that issue dubious. $1 billion of that figure was to buy in all the equity of OpCo and a portion of PropCo at cheap valuations. Only $400 million was allocated in cash with no strings attached. The "absolute priority rule" in bankruptcy law stated that equity holders had to be wiped out if the higher-ranking creditors were forced to take haircuts on their debt. Apollo and TPG were, however, avoiding that rule by having the Caesars parent put in new money to buy equity.

Apollo and TPG, the firms themselves, were not contributing to the settlement. Still, all legal claims for fraud and other wrongdoing against the private equity firms, and even the individuals like Rowan, Bonderman, Sambur, and Loveman—who were board members—were prohibited.

The RSA documentation seemed to be the usual dense legal jargon. However, some noticed three seemingly innocuous provisions that—when taken collectively—punctuated Miller's victory over Sambur. First, Caesars had agreed to file for bankruptcy in mid-January. On December 15, the company announced it was skipping a $225 million interest payment to junior bondholders, which foreshadowed the bankruptcy filing, but the press release now confirmed it. The bankruptcy filing would ensure that Elliott's credit default swap bet would pay off.

The second notable feature described a $300 million convertible preferred stock instrument in PropCo that was going to be made available to certain senior bondholders like Elliott for purchase, ostensibly to use the cash from selling the preferred to reduce the leverage on the reorganized OpCo. But Miller had secured another windfall: The convertible preferred was to be "backstopped" by those bondholders who signed this RSA, meaning they would fund the $300 million if no other buyers could be found. The pricing of the security was cheap relative to its value, meaning every backstop party would be happy to subscribe to it and pocket the free money. Additionally, the backstop parties got separate fees on top. Most importantly, the security itself had various absurd features like dividends that were paid in more PropCo equity.

The final key point in the RSA indicated that the torture was not even close to being over for Apollo. The agreement called for Caesars to reach certain "milestones" in the bankruptcy process to keep the deal terms in place. Caesars would need to have a full restructuring approved within months of filing for bankruptcy. Otherwise, the RSA would automatically terminate and Sambur would have to agree to a new deal with Miller, where he could extract even more pounds of flesh. Even Caesars advisors at Paul, Weiss and Blackstone referred to the document as "Swiss cheese."

According to the press release, Caesars was "continuing to work to obtain additional support from its other creditors." But getting that support quickly would be rough. Sambur had taken a very specific approach to negotiations in 2014. Apollo took the position that it could hold one-off negotiations with the various creditors and through sheer force get each group to submit.

After Sambur had seemingly given away the store to Elliott, Mollett was furious that there would be no deal with the bank loan holders anytime soon. As for the junior bondholders, Liang of Oaktree and Bolin of Appaloosa were ready to go to war in court. Additionally, Apollo would eventually confront numerous minor creditors as well.

Apollo's other problem was that the business continued to deteriorate. EBITDA across the Caesars empire had dropped nearly a tenth to $1.7 billion in 2014, the latest in a string of years worse than the last. Interest expense had ballooned to $2.5 billion for the year.

Sambur had so few chits to give up to creditors, and now all the shell games from previous years were going to be scrutinized in bankruptcy. The last few months of 2014 had been a nightmare. The holidays were a time for Sambur and Rowan to rest up and get ready for 2015, which was set up to be an even rougher year. The one advantage Apollo had wielded since 2008 was control over Caesars. But within days, that too would evaporate.

PART III

BIG GAME HUNTER

Lewis Ranieri and Michael Bloomberg had a disagreement in early 1979. Should their twenty-year-old ace intern Bruce Bennett accept his admittance to Harvard Law School? Or should he stay on full-time at Salomon Brothers, where the two were senior executives? During his summers, and then in his spare time at Brown University, Bennett had been writing computer programs in the language FORTRAN to model paydown of mortgages backed by the government agency Ginnie Mae. Ranieri believed that consumer mortgages could be traded like bonds. (Ranieri would later be immortalized in Michael Lewis's memoir, *Liar's Poker.*) But first, Ranieri needed to understand everything he could about how borrowers repaid home loans. He had Bennett analyzing mortgage data from stacks of tapes.

Bennett had taught himself programming at his high school in Rockland County north of New York City. His father was an engineer at Lipton Tea, and Bruce had inherited an analytical mind. The job at Salomon was dumb luck. With no family connections, Bennett had been rejected by virtually every other Wall Street firm. Bloomberg believed if one got in to Harvard Law School they should go to Harvard Law School, while Ranieri wanted him to stay at Salomon. Bennett ultimately enrolled at Harvard as a twenty-one-year-old. But for months after matriculating, he was still programming on the side for Ranieri—just as the mortgage-backed securities revolution was taking off. After his first year, Bennett spent his summer at Wachtell, Lipton, the New York M&A powerhouse firm.

For someone of Bennett's talent, the typical route would be to a Wall Street law firm. But his professor from a bankruptcy course,

Vern Countryman, would mention Bennett's name to George Treis-ter. Treister's firm, Stutman Treister and Glatt, took Bennett and a few other promising students to dinner, trying to persuade them to spend their summer at their small Los Angeles firm.

Bennett, who had only been to California once before, gave it a shot, eventually returning to Stutman full-time after graduation. Even in Bennett's early years there, the firm gave him his own cases to run, both small and large. Los Angeles, with the emergence of Drexel, suddenly had become an epicenter of finance. Bennett worked a series of high-profile cases in the 1980s—Dome Petroleum, Campeau and Federated Stores—in the wake of the bankruptcy reform legisation passed in 1978. But the case that made him a star was not even a corporate situation.

In the early 1990s, Orange County, California treasurer Rob-ert Citron had made a series of complex investments on behalf of both the county and local municipalities. He took billion-dollar bets through Merrill Lynch that wagered on interest rates staying low. Those investments soured unexpectedly, forcing the county into an emergency bankruptcy. Bennett, by then married to another high-powered lawyer with a newborn at home, got a call at four a.m. on December 6, 1994, asking if he could take on the case. He rushed to the Santa Ana courthouse, fifty miles away. A colleague later had to find an ATM to withdraw cash needed to pay the filing fee.

Bennett's task over the next eighteen months was to fashion a complex deal to pay off creditors as best as possible, allowing the county to stay solvent but also allowing it to access the municipal bond markets again. His aggressive legal theories and hardball tac-tics shocked creditors and debt ratings agencies. Yet by June 1996, Bennett—who, at just thirty-eight, had received glowing profiles in the *Los Angeles Times* and the *New York Times*—shepherded the bruised Orange County out of bankruptcy.

Bennett's brilliance was undeniable. He could quickly discern the core issues in a complicated case. His background in math and finance allowed him to understand the numbers better than most lawyers. And while most lawyers were either classified as dealmakers or litigators, Bennett was the rare attorney who could negotiate a contract in the boardroom but also go to court and cross-examine a witness.

In the middle of the Orange County saga, Bennett abruptly left Stutman to form his own boutique, enabling him and his partners to capture the bulk of the millions in fees for themselves. Bennett had by now decided to make Los Angeles his home. He developed a

reputation as a combative creditors lawyer who would battle companies to get the best possible recovery for his hedge fund or mutual
fund clients. Bennett, however, bristled at the notion that he was just
a courtroom brawler, quick to point out that he had won the *American Lawyer* magazine's Dealmaker of the Year honor but had never
been recognized as Litigator of the Year. Bennett was proud of cases
like the bankruptcies of City of Detroit and the Los Angeles Dodgers
baseball team. They were unorthodox situations where he did not
represent particular creditor groups, but was charged with solving
the entire case.

He had carved out a nice life in California and while his practice
was global, he wondered if his estimable stature would have been
greater if he had been based in New York. Bennett's accomplish-
ments elicited respect, despite his perceived arrogance. Bennett
always had to have the last word, always had to be the smartest guy in
the room. Many wondered if living so far away from the center of the
action had created this chip on his shoulder.

The assignment for the Caesars second-lien bondholders would,
however, suit Bennett perfectly. The case was legally and financially
complex. Junior creditors' only chance at a meaningful recovery
required the pursuit of intense litigation. Appaloosa and Oaktree by
now were spoiling for a fight, and were ready to turn Bennett loose
on Apollo. It would be the perfect pairing of lawyer and client.

INVOLUNTARY REACTION

"**B**ut we are not drawing first blood," Ken Liang explained to Bruce Karsh, his boss at Oaktree. "They've already named us in the lawsuit that they'd filed last August. It's not like we're going to throw the first punch. It's already been thrown."

The group holding second-lien Caesars bonds was in a tough spot at the end of 2014. It began to appear that Apollo and TPG would stay in control of Caesars, leaving the junior creditors with scraps. Elliott had signed its peace treaty with Caesars. GSO was now not far behind in laying down its arms. Caesars' legal strategy to keep control of the company was now turning to steamrolling Oaktree and Appaloosa by buying off every senior creditor. In the Chapter 11 process, companies tended to have an advantage over holdout creditors. The bankruptcy code aimed to help companies reorganize and preserve jobs and while creditors got a voice, judges often preferred to help companies exit quickly, an orientation that was beneficial to Caesars and Apollo.

Liang was terrified that the tide had turned on his group before their counteroffensive was even underway.

Yet there was a way for the junior bondholders to begin to seize back the momentum: a so-called "involuntary bankruptcy petition." Companies themselves normally filed the papers for bankruptcy, picking the court venue and the date they preferred. In an involuntary proceeding, however, creditors could force the filing if they believed a company was not paying their debts "as they came due." As it happened, Caesars had intentionally skipped a $225 million interest payment on December 15. Liang believed the second-lien group had to consider making a preemptive strike.

Involuntary filings were risky, however. They could create havoc at companies caught off guard, and Liang worried about the effect on the 70,000 workers across the Caesars empire. There was also potential legal liability for creditors bringing a frivolous involuntary claim. And an involuntary could create blowback during delicate, ongoing negotiations. The Oaktree founders, meanwhile, were concerned about the broader reputational damage from spearheading such an aggressive gambit. Howard Marks and Bruce Karsh also worried about their personal relationships with the Apollo founders, who would undoubtedly be furious.

Liang pointed out to Karsh that the Caesars situation was already ugly. Caesars had already sued Oaktree; this was gut-check time for the junior creditors. They had been screaming bloody murder about Apollo's asset transfers for months, and it was time to put up or shut up. "If you don't believe all the stuff we said about the asset moves and everything else, we need to step aside," Liang implored Karsh.

Apart from the tactical advantage of putting Caesars into bankruptcy, there were substantive reasons to do it as soon as possible. The company itself was likely to voluntarily file on January 15, 2015, per its agreement with Elliott. In October, the Elliott group had also secured a portion of the company's cash for itself. If Caesars filed for bankruptcy on January 15, 2015, that lien on cash would be legally permissible. Any bankruptcy filing before that date, however, allowed all other creditors to claim that cash.

There was an even more important reason to prevent Caesars and Apollo from dictating the bankruptcy filing: federal bankruptcy courts were not all the same. Judges had enormous discretion in how they ran cases. In a messy case like Caesars, the judge's idiosyncrasies could swing the outcome. Apollo needed a friendly judge who would quickly bless the RSA it had signed with the Elliott group, and then would pressure holdout creditors like Oaktree to jump on board. Just as important was the "circuit" a bankruptcy court belonged to. A Caesars restructuring deal would include "third-party releases," keeping Apollo and TPG from facing liability for alleged wrongdoing. Certain circuits were more forgiving of such releases.

Just where Apollo would file Caesars had become its own parlor game. The junior creditors were hearing rumors about courts all over America. Caesars rival Station Casinos had gone through an easy case in Reno, Nevada, where a judge approved a plan that kept the Fertitta brothers, the original owners, in charge. Liang wanted to avoid a venue like that.

The other Caesars scuttlebutt was around midwestern locations, perhaps Indiana or Illinois, where Caesars had local casinos. Indiana had little experience in big cases, but Chicago could be intriguing. It was the hometown of Kirkland, and over the years had its share of blockbusters such as United Airlines and Kmart. Crucially, it was in the Seventh Circuit, where the case law was generous on third-party releases.

Bruce Bennett of Jones Day was even playfully teasing Marc Kieselstein, his friend and a Kirkland & Ellis bankruptcy attorney, about the Windy City. Bennett sent a Vimeo video made by his son Noah in an email on January 7. At the end of the message Bennett wrote, "PS it looks like Kirkland thinks I need to experience more bad weather: Caesars in Chicago?"

Kieselstein wrote back, "I'm sure you will find Chicago very hospitable. What's -35 wind chill between friends?"

By early January, Liang had gotten Karsh and Marks on board for an involuntary filing. But the salesmanship was not done. The filing required three courageous firms to put signatures on the page. Appaloosa was a certain signatory, but Liang needed a third.

Centerbridge Partners, a prominent New York investor, had been buying up hundreds of millions of dollars of the second-lien debt in late 2014. While Centerbridge was confident in the legal case that the junior creditor group was building, it was unwilling to go as far as to sponsor an involuntary bankruptcy filing.

The third signatory was found in Liang's own backyard: Tennenbaum Capital Partners was a Santa Monica-based hedge fund that had been a Caesars junior debtholder since 2009 and Jones Day's Bruce Bennett had asked if they would support the involuntary filing. David Hollander, the Tennenbaum executive responsible for the Caesars investment, had been a lawyer at O'Melveny with Liang years ago, and he had clashed with Apollo in another deal where there were allegations of fraudulent transfers. The firm playfully nicknamed that situation "Little Caesars." Hollander understood the urgency of the involuntary filing and signed on the dotted line.

Five days later, on Monday, January 12, an involuntary bankruptcy petition for the Caesars OpCo was filed in the United States Bankruptcy Court for the District of Delaware with signatures from Jim Bolin, Ken Liang, and David Hollander. The junior bondholders were off the sidelines and back in the game in a big way.

PRIDE GOETH BEFORE THE FALL

Hero Named Gary was the title of the children's book. Gary Loveman was being honored in early October 2013 by the Public Education Foundation, a Nevada think tank focused on school policy in the state. Each year, an illustrated story book was created to describe the life of the guest of honor. Loveman's 2013 edition took the reader sweetly through his childhood in Indianapolis, college and grad school in the Northeast, all the way to his CEO tenure at Harrah's and Caesars—making sure to note his wholesome family life and charitable interests.

There was, however, no mention of the LBO, the $24 billion of debt crushing the company, and the never-ending fight to turn around the business. Before the first section, a caption noted that the book had been funded through donations from TPG, Marc Rowan's family foundation, and Teneo, the politically connected PR firm that represented Caesars.

A year later in the fall of 2014, the goodwill between Loveman and the two private firms was gone. In 2013, Caesars thought it was on its way to securing a license for a new casino in Massachusetts. But a 558-page report from the state's gaming commission questioned the company's "suitability," effectively killing its bid. It was an embarrassment for Loveman in his home state, and his credibility in the boardroom never really recovered.

As the company careened toward bankruptcy, Apollo and TPG were finished with Loveman. The wheeling-and-dealing Apollo had engineered was predicated on a business turnaround. But the company kept underperforming. Law enforcement had raided Caesars

Palace in the summer breaking up a World Cup betting ring that had been set up by an Asian guest unbeknownst to management. The negative publicity ended up crushing high roller visits from Chinese guests for much of the year. Then an expensive promotional campaign that Loveman and his team implemented in 2014 had backfired. Loveman's intermittent presence in Las Vegas had become untenable as the business was in its worst shape ever.

Loveman had grown weary after years of the constant struggle to keep Caesars afloat. At a Caesars gathering in New York in August of 2014, Loveman informed the directors he was ready to begin his transition out of the company. "I don't want to do this forever," he told the board, hoping they'd find a successor together.

Neither Loveman nor Apollo/TPG, however, had been grooming an heir apparent. But by late 2014, the wheels were moving quickly to find a new boss who could guide the company through bankruptcy and impose operating discipline that had been missing for years.

On February 4, 2015, Caesars made the news public in a lengthy press release noting Loveman's academic career (he was described as "Dr. Loveman"), the creation of Total Rewards, and reminding the market that over his tenure the company's enterprise value rose from $8 billion to nearly $30 billion at the time of the 2008 LBO (no mention that enterprise value had since cratered). Loveman had been battered by the LBO years after at first believing he was going to make a fortune. Still, he had been treated well on the way out the door and was mostly at peace with leaving the company he had built. Acceptance of his successor would be another matter.

"GARY, YOU NEED TO TELL the board that this guy is terrible and he's going to destroy the company," begged one C-level Caesars executive. Some hoped the new Caesars CEO could be sacked before he really started. And no one was more outraged about the new guy than Loveman himself. Apollo had tapped Mark Frissora, a longtime industrials executive, to take over through an unusual transition. Frissora was to become "CEO-designee" at first, and then ascend to the official CEO job five months later in July. Loveman was to stay in a largely ceremonial role as Chairman of Caesars.

Apollo was having a difficult time finding candidates for the top spot, and Frissora would have had a hard time finding any job at any other public company. In September 2014, he had left as CEO at Hertz Global citing "personal reasons." In fact, Hertz was in the middle of a massive accounting scandal where the rental car and equipment company was facing accusations of inflating profits. Carl Icahn had taken a near 10 percent stake and was making noise. Another hedge fund said Frissora had "lost all credibility."

To his surprise, Frissora got a call from an executive search firm just two weeks after leaving Hertz. They asked if he had interest in the Caesars job. He met with Rowan, Sambur, and Bonderman. Apollo claimed it would be a brief six-month bankruptcy, and the job would be fun. Frissora had been the CEO of two public companies, Hertz and auto parts maker Tenneco, and was new to gaming. But Hertz had gone private in a $15 billion LBO in 2006, so he had experience working with private equity. Until the accounting scandal, Hertz had prospered under Frissora. Rowan and Sambur were hoping an experienced operator could impose business discipline they believed Loveman had not.

Frissora's appointment felt like a direct rebuke to Loveman and his loyalists, since the two could not have been more different. Loveman had his rumpled professor aesthetic, whereas Frissora wore flashy suits. Frissora would hit the gym during the workday and his tight dress shirts elicited jokes that the buttons were at risk to pop off at any moment.

Frissora was no intellectual or visionary. But he was happy, unlike Loveman, to relocate to Las Vegas. He had been coming to Sin City for years for pleasure, and loved the scene, the action, and the accoutrements of being the boss of the most famous casino in the world. For the first months of his tenure, he took temporary quarters at the Octavius Tower at Caesars Palace, which Apollo had infamously transferred out of OpCo in the CERP refinancing deal. Despite the Hertz accounting scandal, and that it looked perhaps worse with the fraud allegations hovering over Caesars, Rowan and Sambur felt lucky to have someone they viewed as a disciplinarian take over for Loveman.

Loveman had met Frissora during the interview process at the request of Apollo and TPG after which Loveman reported back his discomfort. He transparently resented Frissora in those early months of 2015 while he remained lame duck CEO. Loveman and Frissora's offices were just down the hall from each other on the mezzanine level at Caesars Palace, overlooking the resort's swimming pools. If Frissora saw an employee go into Loveman's office, he would later quiz that person on the discussion.

What most offended Loveman and frightened the remaining executive team was Frissora's lack of intellectual curiosity about the gaming business. "Mark never got into the details of the industry, the terminology, how the marketing worked," Loveman said. Frissora, unlike the former professor, Loveman, required hours of preparation before he could make remarks to the group.

The remaining executive team quickly decided that their best bet was to keep Frissora as far away from the business as possible, leaving the day-to-day operations to the long-tenured staff. It would be tricky, however, since Frissora was now the new face of the company.

Yet, in the middle of the CEO transition in early 2015, something amazing happened: the Caesars business snapped back. In November 2014, a group of top Caesars executives—Tariq Shaukat, Tom Jenkin, Blake Segal, and Rob Brimmer—had gathered in a conference room. They were given a simple task: the Caesars OpCo needed to hit $1.096 billion of EBITDA in 2015. The company's Total Rewards experiments had not gone well in 2014, so the group made the tough choice to dial promotions back down.

In the first quarter, EBITDA hit $275 million—a jump of almost 15 percent—as the company slashed marketing spend by a quarter. In 2015, Caesars also started to make improvements that had been postponed for years, and the customer response was quite favorable. There was a direct link between updated rooms and rates that Caesars could charge. In 2015, the Caesars average daily room rate jumped from $114 to $127, which alone was worth $90 million of annual EBITDA growth. The company finally seemed like it was turning the corner.

But the good feeling was tempered. Loveman was still on the way out. Apollo and TPG were upset that the turnaround had taken so long. If the inflection point had been in the middle of 2014, the company would have had far more bargaining leverage with creditors.

Frissora was suddenly feeling uneasy. The company was roaring back, but it was based on a strategic plan from Loveman's team. The executive team noticed that Frissora, once he assumed power, started to lash out to assert his dominion. At one meeting of the senior leadership team, he demanded that executives be at their desks by eight a.m. Frissora's edict made little sense for a casino company. Marketing executives, for example, had to be at the casinos late at night or on weekends. But Frissora felt he had to show people he was boss and that he was running a tighter ship.

Frissora's suspicion of his new colleagues put his own behavior in the spotlight. The Caesars valets started to note his movements, which included late arrivals, early departures, and his gym and massage sessions during the middle of the workday. On his first day as chief executive in July, Frissora, an automobile enthusiast, had a

Bentley delivered to Caesars Palace—an episode that rubbed many at the beleaguered company the wrong way.

Apollo and TPG were aware of Frissora's antics. But the numbers were finally improving at Caesars, and Frissora was easy to keep on a tight leash. The business plan was simple: cut marketing costs and, since the bankruptcy suspended all debt obligations, take the $2 billion allocated each year to interest expense and instead use it to remodel dilapidated hotel rooms.

Later in July, Hertz released its delayed 2014 annual report, where it restated multiple years of financial results. Hertz damningly wrote, "Our investigation found that an inconsistent and sometimes inappropriate tone at the top was present under the then existing senior management that did not in certain instances result in adherence to accounting principles...In particular our former Chief Executive Officer's [Frissora's] management style and temperament created a pressurized operating environment at the Company, where challenging targets were set and achieving those targets was a key performance expectation."

Nevertheless, Loveman's near decade-long relationship with private equity was now largely over, apart from his ceremonial title. His name was associated less with the revolutionary marketing science he had brought to Las Vegas and more with the largest casino bankruptcy of all time. And the final indignity, the men whose respect he so deeply craved, Marc Rowan and David Bonderman, had replaced him with a man for whom he had nothing but contempt.

"OUR DEBT IS ACTUALLY AMONG the best performing out there among private equity firms," explained Michael Konigsberg. The head of Apollo's capital market group, Konigsberg served as a liaison to investment banks and credit investors who bought the debt financing of Apollo LBOs. It was spring 2015, and Apollo was showing some humility. The firm had scheduled a series of meetings—a roadshow, effectively—with institutional investors who had watched the Caesars escapades in horror. Because Caesars debt was so big, it became a part of high yield indices forcing many asset managers to buy it. Once Caesars filed for bankruptcy the debt was no longer part of benchmarks. Portfolio managers were then able to sell off Caesars holdings and were relieved to get off the roller coaster.

Apollo rarely betrayed any contrition, but internally, there was a growing sense it may finally have gone too far. Apollo partners were reading the headlines about "looting" at Caesars and wondering if Rowan and Sambur's scorched tactics were damaging the broader firm. Debt investors noted that Apollo deals required higher interests to get done as there was an expectation that Apollo companies that ran into trouble would fall into legal fights.

Apollo had, however, sent the likes of David Sambur as well as the head of private equity, Scott Kleinman, to deliver a defiant message on this apology tour: the debt of Apollo portfolio companies performed quite well in reality, and there was no reason for alarm: Creditors had benefited from Apollo's ability to turn around troubled companies.

"BANKRUPTCY EQUALS EMBARRASSMENT. IT IS embarrassing to you as a company, it is embarrassing to us as a state, it is embarrassing to gaming," Dr. Tony Alamo lamented. As chairman of the Nevada Gaming Commission, Dr. Alamo presided as Caesars went before the regulatory body in late March 2015 to discuss fallout from the bankruptcy filing. Eric Hession, the Caesars CFO, explained that the original LBO was "spectacularly poorly timed," and annual EBITDA since 2007 had gone from nearly $3 billion to under $2 billion.

Any explicit criticism toward the company or Apollo/TPG, however, was largely muted. The commission's harshest sentiment seemed to regard Gary Loveman's commuting arrangements. "And I hope your new management, your new CEO who will be more engaged, hopefully live here. The absentee thing has always bothered me when a CEO of a company that is home-based in Las Vegas, Nevada, doesn't work here, doesn't live here," said Chairman Alamo.

As Apollo faced its own reputational hazards, there was a public relations disaster brewing both for Caesars and the Nevada Gaming Commission. Sixty-three former Caesars employees, whose tenures dated back decades, were part of a special pension called a "supplemental executive retirement plan." Its total liability was just $33 million. However, once the company filed for bankruptcy, Caesars stopped paying the benefit. One of the employees whose SERP payment was halted, Ken Houng, appeared before the gaming commission that day alongside his daughter.

Houng, nearing the age of eighty, relied on the SERP payment to survive. He had started at Caesars in the 1980s as a host to bring in high rollers from Asia (according to his daughter, "He brought in customers that would come in and lose millions every trip."). SERP beneficiaries had become "unsecured creditors" of the Caesars estate. And unsecured creditors were at the back of the line behind the first-lien loan holders, the first-lien bondholders, and the second-lien bondholders. The RSA that was in place with the senior bondholders contemplated a recovery for unsecured creditors at just ten cents on the dollar.

In addition to appearing before the commission, Houng and his daughter wrote a letter to the judge explaining their plight, a document that was then publicly filed on the court docket. As Houng's daughter wrote, Gary Loveman had taken home more than a hundred million dollars in total compensation from Caesars over the years: "Why should [my father] be penalized because current Caesars executives have mismanaged funds and have not paid their creditors?"

Houng was getting a cold introduction to the realities of the Chapter 11 process. Lawyers, bankers, and other advisors got their millions in fees paid by the bankrupt company while executives often received retention bonuses; but creditors at the bottom of the totem pole often got wiped out. Mark Frissora had signed a four-year contract after the bankruptcy filing that paid him an annual base salary of $1.8 million, the chance for an annual bonus of $2.7 million, plus one million shares worth of stock options. The gaming commission asked Tim Donovan, the Caesars general counsel, what could be done for Houng. But Houng had no recourse, and any attempts to jump the line would be swatted down immediately. "Caesars is not the villain here," shrugged Donovan.

SPLIT SCREEN

No Wi-Fi, no problem. Kris Hansen had plenty of material to read and ponder on his flight from Newark to O'Hare. Earlier that morning, on January 15, 2015, Caesars lawyers had filed a voluntary bankruptcy petition in a Chicago federal court, just three days after the junior creditors filed their own involuntary bankruptcy in Delaware. The result of the competing actions was chaos. Each court would hold opening hearings on the same day. The law firms involved sent representatives to both proceedings. Flights from New York to Chicago were packed with lawyers who knew each other, as was the Acela from Manhattan to Wilmington.

That day, Hansen welcomed the lack of in-flight internet; he had time to catch his breath and figure out the best tactics for his loan holder group. He believed his clients were in a strong position wherever this bankruptcy was going to be decided. They were at the top of the Caesars capital structure and had not signed up for the settlement deal in December that senior bondholders like Elliott had. As such, Hansen's loan holder group were now "free agents" and could either play hardball with Apollo or, at the same time, try to partner with the junior creditors on some other creative deal. But for now, Hansen just had to make sure that this case ended up with an experienced judge.

Delaware was Hansen's preference. The judge who had been assigned in the involuntary case, Kevin Gross, was well-respected and had handled such cases as the Los Angeles Dodgers and Trump Entertainment—and Hansen knew him well. Chicago, on the other hand, was a wild card, and not just because of the winter weather.

While Hansen and his legal team from Stroock & Stroock had been involved in the settlement discussion with Apollo and Caesars weeks earlier, drafts of the legal documents had stated the chosen bankruptcy venue would be Delaware. As the negotiations progressed, Hansen noticed that the venue line had been left blank.

More than a decade ago in 2003, Hansen had represented creditors in the case of a company called Advanced Lighting Technologies in the Chicago bankruptcy court. The experience was a nightmare. The case passed to a newly appointed bankruptcy judge, Benjamin Goldgar, who had just been plucked from the Illinois state attorney's office. Judge Goldgar was inexperienced. And with so many aggressive and experienced lawyers in the Caesars case, there was the risk that Goldgar, if picked, could get pushed around and lose his handle on the proceedings. Goldgar, Hansen thought, focused on all the wrong issues. Hansen got the impression Goldgar could be overmatched in a big case with big personalities. In the Advanced Lighting case, Hansen had advised his clients to quickly settle as Goldgar had been so unpredictable.

As soon as his plane touched down at O'Hare, Hansen turned on his phone to a deluge of messages. Bankruptcy judges in the Northern District of Illinois are randomly assigned after the company's counsel files the Chapter 11 using the electronic filing system. At the time, there were nine available bankruptcy judges. Hansen only really wanted to avoid one.

"OYEZ! OYEZ! ALL RISE FOR the honorable Judge A. Benjamin Goldgar!" the clerk announced before a stunned group of dozens of lawyers and bankers in downtown Chicago. What the hell was this, the 1800s? Kris Hansen already knew what everyone else was about to see—Goldgar was going to be a mess.

Hansen discovered who was going to be the judge about an hour before when his plane landed. As he rushed to grab a taxi, he called his partner Ken Pasquale, who was attending the Delaware proceeding that morning.

"Goldgar we can't have," Hansen quickly explained to Pasquale. The hearing was just about to begin in Delaware at ten-thirty a.m. East Coast time, while Judge Goldgar, seemingly oblivious, had gone ahead and scheduled a Chicago hearing an hour and a half after that: eleven a.m. central time.

At Hansen's direction, Pasquale quickly prepared remarks he would make to Judge Gross in Delaware, while Hansen made his way to downtown Chicago. Pasquale stepped into the Delaware courtroom and delivered his remarks to Judge Gross, announcing to anyone listening that the loan holders were totally against Chicago as a venue.

"We find it, frankly, shocking that the debtors would have filed a case in Chicago, based on what we believe is a—while it may be proper technically—but it is one joint venture entity that—one affiliate in Chicago, when Delaware is plainly the most appropriate forum," Pasquale began. It was a surprising statement. Virtually everyone in the case believed that the involuntary filing was a silly stunt pulled by Bruce Bennett and his junior creditor clients.

But Pasquale was only getting started. He accused the Caesars OpCo of forum shopping. "We believe they did that because they perceive a benefit with respect to third-party release law. And that, of course, is going to be a big issue in this case, in light of the transfers that you've heard referred to today."

The backlash was swift. While still in traffic nearing the Chicago courthouse, Hansen received an incensed email from Paul, Weiss's Alan Kornberg about what had just happened in Delaware. Hansen started drafting an email to Paul, Weiss, warning of Goldgar.

Before Hansen could finish, Ken Eckstein of Kramer Levin, who was representing Elliott and the first-lien bondholders, was calling. Eckstein, counseling the only group to have struck a deal with Apollo, was clearly agitated but he tried to stay measured over the phone. "What are you doing, don't you know we have $470 million in liens riding on this?" Eckstein scolded Hansen.

Eckstein was referring to $470 million of cash that had been allocated to the senior bondholder group that he represented. The cash transfer had occurred in mid-October 2014 and had to be completed ninety days before a bankruptcy filing, according to the bankruptcy laws. The January 15 Chicago filing was outside that ninety-day window, but the Delaware filing was not—Eckstein's group needed the case in Chicago to keep the cash.

Hansen did his best to calmly reply.

"Ken, this is much bigger than just four hundred million. This is about us getting par plus accrued. Besides, your guys are going to run the company," Hansen replied. Hansen then arrived at the stately 219 Dearborn building and headed straight to the courtroom with just minutes to spare. He was met by an irate Paul Basta.

Basta, Jamie Sprayregen's deputy, was running the Caesars case on a day-to-day basis for Kirkland & Ellis, the OpCo's law firm. Understandably, Basta was not happy about Stroock seemingly endorsing the Delaware venue.

"How dare you, you son of a bitch, we worked together, we have a relationship!" he started to shout. In the courtroom hallway, onlookers watched in disbelief. "I can't believe you would take this approach." Basta was shaking, looking like he might start throwing punches.

Hansen delicately fired back, "We have a right to do what we want, so put it away, Paul!"

A minute before the hearing would start, they all awkwardly made their way into the courtroom. It would take maybe thirty seconds before Basta realized Hansen might have been onto something with Judge Goldgar.

After his own pretentious entrance, Judge Goldgar took his seat, elevated several feet above the rest of the court, and the clerk introduced the case.

"Taking up all matters on Caesars Entertainment Operating Company, Incorporated, and all related cases," said the clerk.

Composing himself, Paul Basta stood up. As he'd done dozens of times, Basta began explaining the background of the Caesars case, hoping to set the tone.

"Good morning, Your Honor. I am Paul Basta from the law firm of Kirkland & Ellis. We are proposed counsel to Caesars Entertainment Operating Corporation and its affiliated debtors. I'd like to thank the Court for hearing us on such short notice—"

"You're welcome," Judge Goldgar cut in, appearing to throw off Basta's rhythm.

"Your Honor, let me just—before we even get into the introductions, we're in an interesting procedural posture, because there's a hearing going on as we speak now before Judge Gross where certain of our second-lien noteholders had filed an involuntary case a few days ago. And under Rule 1014, Judge Gross is presently conducting a hearing on whether to stay these proceedings," Basta continued.

"Yes, I know."

"No stay has been issued yet, and we're prepared to proceed."

"Right."

"We had—Your Honor, with a case of this size and magnitude, it would be typical, and, we thought, helpful to give an overview of the situation. I think we heard before court today that it might be the Court's preference to proceed right to the first day relief. Happy to proceed at your direction. It's a complicated situation. We've given the Court a tremendous amount of paper. If you'd like me to give an overview, happy to do that. We think it would be helpful." Basta framed it as an offer, though such an overview was rarely refused in New York and Delaware.

"Well, my view is that there are two things: evidence and not evidence," Goldgar stopped Basta in his tracks.

"This is not evidence," Basta replied weakly.

"Yes. And so if it's not evidence, I don't know what purpose it would really serve."

Basta blinked. Behind him, Hansen strained not to smirk.

"Look, the purpose—it's definitely not evidence," Basta reasoned. "It's akin to an opening statement in a trial. Really, the purpose of it, it's a distillation of the first-day information memorandum. But there's a lot of complicated transactions that occurred and complicated entities. It's really just to give the Court a summary. It's not evidence by any means. It is typical. But if the Court views it as not helpful, I think there's no reason—"

"Well, how long did you have in mind?"

"I don't know, Your Honor. Half an hour?"

"I don't see why I need a half-an-hour speech about this case."

"Okay."

"You know, I am acquainted, to the extent the time available allowed me to be acquainted, which was not very much, with the motions and their general nature. And I don't see any reason why we shouldn't get to them. If it turns out I need information along the way, you can provide it to me," Goldgar said with finality.

Basta, now shell-shocked, sat down. Goldgar seemed to have his own thoughts on how a mega-bankruptcy case should be run, and they did not resemble those of everyone else in the room.

Moments later, a Jones Day attorney, who was representing the second-lien group, stood up and blurted out something about the rival hearing in Delaware.

"Good morning, Your Honor…We're the proponent of the involuntary bankruptcy in Delaware. I think it's appropriate at this time, before any relief is granted, that we provide a report of our understanding of what happened in Delaware this morning. And my colleagues—"

Goldgar cut him off, "Has something happened?"

"I believe it has, Your Honor."

"Oh, all right," Goldgar sounded amused.

Judge Gross was about to rule on whether or not they should at least pause the Chicago proceedings, the lawyer told him, but Goldgar seemed dubious. "So you're suggesting we recess until we have a print order from him?"

"Or at least the benefit of his ruling, which, as I understand it, is coming imminently."

"Well, how imminently is imminently?" Goldgar asked. He turned to the US Trustee, an objective overseer from the Department of Justice who is part of every major bankruptcy, asking her whether she thought this was real.

"Judge, they did start the hearing at nine-thirty."

"They did?"

"Yes. So it's been ongoing. We've been getting real time reports from our office, who is neutral but appearing, obviously, and monitoring it. So I have been getting reports. It has been proceeding. I don't know how close they are to conclusion. I've got to believe that in an hour, we probably will have a decision from Judge Gross," the trustee told him.

Goldgar agreed to take a break for lunch while the tense parties awaited the Delaware decision. The court was abuzz. The lawyers either dialed into the Delaware court or kept checking their phones for updates. No one had ever experienced anything like this.

The first-day hearings in a Chapter 11 case were crucial but typically perfunctory. Motions were brought to allow employees and "critical vendors" to keep being paid in order to keep the business functioning and prevent any further loss of value. Instead, precious time was being spent on deciding a court for Caesars.

In Delaware, Gross provided an elegant solution: He ruled that Goldgar should decide all of those first-day issues, at least temporarily, and then Judge Gross would conduct a trial at a later date to determine where Caesars could proceed with its bankruptcy.

The venerable Delaware judge even provided some much-needed diplomacy: "I might also add that I did have an opportunity to speak with Judge Goldgar this morning, and I can assure everyone that this is anything but a battle of judicial egos," Gross said.

Back in Chicago, the whiplashed lawyers reassembled in Goldgar's courtroom, where Goldgar seemed pleased with Gross's decision. He proceeded to sign off on all the important measures needed over the course of the next few hours.

As the hearing wrapped up, Kramer Levin's Ken Eckstein made another attempt to provide some sort of overview of the case, suggesting parties come back at a later date to cover the points of contention. "So coming back to allow people to give me the overview of the case I wouldn't let anybody give?" Goldgar shot back.

"Essentially you're right, Your Honor," Eckstein demurred.

In what would become a recurring theme, Goldgar's next response caused some further head scratching. Lawyers weren't sure if they were supposed to respond or if the judge was just thinking out loud.

"So 'cover' means sort of have a nice chat, in other words. Well, I suppose we could do that. It strikes me as unorthodox, but maybe I'm the unorthodox one. I wouldn't rule that out. We're certainly going to have to have a status hearing, and maybe that's the next thing to discuss...I don't know, of course—there are hearings and there are decisions, and the decisions don't always necessarily follow the hearings that swiftly...But I really need time to digest these things. I didn't get very much time at all today to digest things. I was able to figure out this case had something to do with casinos," he quipped.

"But I do like to read people's materials and consider them. And I imagine people like their materials to be read and considered." Goldgar ultimately decided to hold such a hearing at a later date. "Of course, we may not be in a position for me even to do anything except say hi. I don't know. It depends on what happens in Delaware. But I just want to do this in a sensible way."

He adjourned the court, mercifully, and an exhausted group made their way onto the frigid streets of Chicago. After the hearing, Eckstein, Basta, and Hansen stood together. A local lawyer who had witnessed the spectacle—including the near fisticuffs in the morning—asked, possibly without irony, "So is this how you New York guys do it?"

"We have a relationship," Basta replied with a smile. Eckstein could only laugh.

21

STORM JUNO IS GONE

"**S**torm Juno is gone. Storm Caesars Entertainment rages on," proclaimed Judge Kevin Gross of the Delaware bankruptcy court, kicking off the final day of the two-day trial to determine Caesars' venue on January 27, 2015.

The brutal Nor'easter that had pummeled the East Coast was nothing compared to the storm inside Judge Gross's Wilmington courtroom. Kirkland was desperate enough to want the case in its hometown that it had politicians from Illinois send letters to Gross trumpeting Chicago. Observers in court laughed when Bruce Bennett, who filed the involuntary petition, dryly noted to Gross that Bennett himself "could subpoena the mayor of Wilmington, the governor of the state of Delaware and the general manager of the DuPont Hotel," the latter referring to the luxury lodging where lawyers and bankers stayed when in town.

The right judge and the right federal circuit could be the difference between winning and losing, and Bruce Bennett was going to play what few cards his junior creditor group had. In his remarks to Gross, Bennett impassionedly explained to the judge that Caesars was "cramming people down" and depriving his hedge fund clients from suing Apollo and TPG. "And, recall, we have a plan that's been accepted by exactly one group of creditors and opposed by every other," Bennett said, pointing out that Caesars had only agreed to terms with the Elliott senior bondholder group.

It was quickly evident just how different Wilmington would be from Chicago. Most big cases ended up in either the New York or Delaware bankruptcy courts, and in the small world of restructuring, professionals were at ease—if not downright chummy—with the judges. Kris Hansen, the lawyer at Stroock, considered Judge Gross a friend, and had been in front of him in several big cases. When Hansen first spoke at the hearing, no introduction was necessary. "Mr. Hansen, good morning. It's nice to see you, as always," greeted Judge Gross.

Even the lawyers on the phone joined the lovefest. When one of Kirkland's lawyers, Ryan Preston Dahl, spoke up over the phone, his colleague in court, David Zott, identified him. "That's Mr. Dahl, Your Honor."

"Yes, I know Mr. Dahl," said Gross elatedly. "I was here for the birth of his son." Zott laughed, "Now we're definitely beyond the evidence."

Kirkland's lead lawyer, Paul Basta, fresh from his humiliation in Chicago two weeks earlier, noted how familiar Kirkland was with Delaware: "So let me just start, Your Honor, to just describe how difficult it is to show up as a lawyer from Kirkland & Ellis before this Court to advocate for a venue other than Delaware."

"Each case is on its own merits," Gross played along.

"Each case is on its own merit," Basta repeated, and launched into his argument. "And you have heard a—that we're not a very popular debtor. Right? We're not very popular."

"I would say that's true," responded Gross.

"And you heard a long laundry list of complaints about how our debtor has not lived up to its fiduciary duties, has engaged in improper activities, has not engaged with junior parties in the capital structure, and is generally bad…Nothing they said had anything to do with venue. Everything they said we do was that we're bad."

Basta was feeling like himself again, given room to run. "But if we fly to Chicago, we're still going to be bad. The flight isn't going to make a difference. So unless Your Honor has a better moral compass than the Court in Chicago, it's unclear what all these allegations of bad acts has to do with the venue choice. And what I'd like to do is I'm going to hand to Mr. Bennett, I have a short chart that outlines all the bad things that we've done. I've actually never done this in my career, but…"

Basta retrieved a set of papers that outlined the infractions Caesars and Apollo had been accused of. "So this is—this is what I call the bad debtor," Basta said, waving the paper. "It's not evidence. It's just something to help walk through the argument."

Basta had a point. Whatever bad things Caesars was accused of, it was not required that the case be heard in the court of Bruce Bennett's choice.

Judge Gross took the papers from Basta and mused, "This is rather unique, I would say."

Now with a full head of steam, Basta continued. "It is unique," he said, walking through all of Bennett's arguments against him, concluding, "And none of this has anything to do with venue. Nothing. That's going to happen here or that's going to happen in Chicago. It's the same issues that are going to have to be worked through."

Judge Gross was thoroughly enjoying himself. "I just can't get the Leroy Brown song out of my mind since you've been talking about being so bad."

Next to speak was Jim Millar, the attorney representing the group of holders of the Caesars unsecured notes who had been left out of the transaction in August, when a select group of hedge funds had negotiated a sweetheart deal with Apollo. Millar had, in some ways, become the most important lawyer in the case, even if his clients were only minor creditors. Millar had filed the lawsuit in September on behalf of the fund MeehanCombs, alleging that the deal David Sambur cut had violated the Trust Indenture Act. Early in January 2015, New York federal judge Shira Scheindlin, drawing upon the fresh *Marblegate* decision, ruled that Millar's lawsuit could move forward.

If Millar could eventually win his lawsuit, it would completely upend the bankruptcy case—it would leave the Caesars parent on the hook for more than $10 billion of the OpCo's debt. Millar figured Kirkland, like Apollo and TPG, wanted his lawsuit shut down and that a hometown Chicago court would help them do so.

"James Millar of Drinker Biddle & Reath on behalf of the Ad Hoc Group of 5.75 percent and 6.5 percent notes," he began, having dialed in from his Connecticut home. "Fairness implicates all of the so-called bad debtor conduct that they want you to view as irrelevant to venue. Even though they ignore it, I'd like to offer, Your Honor, a very elementary notion of fairness that applies to the facts here. Your Honor, let's say I take two of my children to the toy store. And I buy one of them a toy and I don't buy the other one anything. We walk out of that store. The one that didn't get a toy is going to look up at me and say three words, and everyone listening to this call and everyone in the courtroom knows exactly what those words are."

Judge Gross was willing to play along. "It's not fair," he said.

Millar confirmed, "That's not fair. You got it." Referencing an exhibit handed to the judge, he noted how "three big holders of the legacy Harrah's notes received par plus accrued interest on many of their bonds. While my clients, who had the very same notes, were not even offered that deal. In simple terms, Your Honor, that's not fair. Now, Your Honor, the debtor wants the court's help in getting to Chicago so that it has a better chance of implementing its scheme to avoid any collateral damage."

A new voice spoke next. Tom Lauria led the bankruptcy practice at White & Case and tended to represent creditors in bankruptcy cases. Lauria was a loud, aggressive, profane litigator not afraid to throw bombs on behalf of his clients, who were often hedge funds holding near-worthless paper. Lauria lived in Miami where he frequently hung out with David Tepper. Lauria happily leaned into this reputation with business cards that read, "WALK IN. FUCK SHIT UP. WALK OUT."

Lauria's clients held $500 million of so-called Subsidiary Guarantee Notes. The bonds were guaranteed by certain Caesars subsidiaries, but otherwise were considered "unsecured" and were trading at ten cents on the dollar.

"It's a pleasure to have you back here," Gross welcomed him.

"It's good to be here, despite the fact that I flew here from Miami," said Lauria.

"You're headed the wrong way, I think," Gross said.

"Yes, indeed."

Lauria and Judge Gross were, of course, acquainted.

Lauria offered his full support for Delaware.

"OpCo's creditors and those of its subsidiaries should not be made to pay OpCo's lost bet. To put a twist on a well-known phrase, what happens in Wilmington, stays in Wilmington."

"I like that, Mr. Lauria," Gross said approvingly.

"THE INTEREST OF JUSTICE NARROWLY supports a determination that the involuntary petition and Illinois cases should proceed before the Illinois Court." Judge Gross gave his oral decision on January 28. This decision was a gut punch to Bruce Bennett of Jones Day, who had sought the involuntary on behalf of the Appaloosa/Oaktree group—particularly since multiple creditors groups had publicly agreed that Delaware should be the venue for the Caesars case.

Adding to the sting, Judge Gross's remarks seemed to indicate that the judge had sympathy for Bennett's substantive arguments about wrongdoing at Caesars.

"The Court also readily recognized that the debtors' conduct leading to its voluntary filings, on its face, is suspect. There are serious allegations raised, both in the involuntary petition and pending lawsuits, that the debtors' controlling equity holders, Apollo Global

Management, LLC, and TPG Capital, LP, engaged in a series of self-dealing transactions, transferring very substantial assets out of the reach of creditors," he said. "The Illinois Court is fully capable of recognizing, if they exist, breaches of fiduciary duty and fraudulent activity."

Bennett was heartened that someone important understood his case against Apollo and TPG. Now he just had to convince a wild-card judge in Chicago of the same thing. The second-lien creditors decided not to appeal, believing it was time to make their case.

22

A THOROUGH EXAMINATION

Bruce Bennett would have some early good fortune in Chicago. The Office of the United States Trustee acted, on behalf of the Department of Justice, as a watchdog over the bankruptcy system. At the outset of a case, the US Trustee would typically appoint an "Official Committee of Unsecured Creditors." Unsecured creditors had no collateral, and included the most junior bondholders as well as vendors. Unsecured creditors for Caesars included the likes of the Earl of Sandwich restaurant, who had locations in Caesars casinos; IGT, the slot machine maker; and the National Retirement fund, which ran pension programs for certain Caesars retirees.

The Unsecured Creditor Committee (UCC) could investigate the company in Chapter 11 and its fees for bankers and lawyers were paid for by the bankruptcy "estate," making it a powerful body. Bennett was hoping to muscle a few of his clients onto the UCC so they would have a louder voice in the process. But Kirkland did not want Oaktree or Appaloosa anywhere near that kind of power. It argued that the second-lien bondholders, because of their lien, were not really unsecured. And that since there were $5.5 billion worth of second-lien bonds, they would exercise disproportionate power.

The US Trustee in the case, Patrick Layng, agreed. But then he did something almost unheard-of: he gave the second-lien bondholders their own, distinct committee officially known as the Official Committee of Second Priority Noteholders. Jones Day and Houlihan Lokey would now have their fees paid by the estate. The committee would include Appaloosa, Oaktree, Centerbridge, and Tennenbaum, and it would have a massive platform to prosecute its case. Kirkland attempted to disband the committee, citing the resulting cost and complications. But Goldgar chose not to overrule the US Trustee. Suddenly, Chicago was not looking so bad for Bennett.

Now that he had the momentum, Bennett played perhaps his strongest card. There was really only one way for his group of junior bondholders to get more than peanuts in a recovery. They needed independent fact-finding that confirmed their belief that Apollo/TPG had "systematically dismantled OpCo by stripping them of many billions of dollars of cash and assets," as they had alleged in a February 2015 court filing.

Bennett's best shot was to get the court to appoint a so-called examiner—a third-party authority figure—who had been given the power and resources to dig deep into everything that happened at Caesars in 2013 and 2014. For example, an examiner appointed in the 2012 bankruptcy of energy company Dynegy had found wrongdoing against Carl Icahn, who was a major shareholder. After a report was published, Icahn quickly ceded the case to creditors. Bennett wanted the same thing, moving the court for an appointment of an examiner with a broad scope and authority to investigate all the pre-bankruptcy transactions.

Imperiling Bennett's play, the OpCo independent directors—Steve Winograd and Ronen Stauber—suddenly wanted an examiner, too. On February 13, 2015, the pair, along with their legal representitives, Kirkland & Ellis, filed their own motion seeking an examiner. But they wanted one with a much more limited scope than Bennett. He worried that Kirkland was trying to co-opt him with a soft-pedal inquiry.

Winograd and Stauber's Special Governance Committee had launched its own separate investigation into the Caesars asset transfers after they had been appointed to the OpCo board in the summer of 2014. That investigation, with limited time and discovery rights, determined that the OpCo had fraud claims against the Caesars parent worth between $1 billion and $2.3 billion, a pittance compared to what Bennett's group thought they were worth.

In the RSA that OpCo had signed with the Elliott senior bondholder group in late 2014, OpCo had secured what it believed were financial contributions from the Caesars parent it valued at $1.5 billion. Now, in February of 2015, Kirkland did not want an examiner going on a fishing expedition for months on end, an outcome they described as a "value-destructive litigation free-for-all." The senior creditors had already secured a decent deal for themselves, and whatever bad things Apollo and TPG may have done, they did not want the junior creditors to upset that deal.

Kirkland was in a tricky spot. Jamie Sprayregen was supposed to be representing all creditors, but by trying to narrow the scope of an examiner, he seemed a lot closer to Apollo and TPG's position than junior creditors Appaloosa and Oaktree.

OpCo was asking for an investigation that lasted just 120 days and cost only $10 million, with no access to the most sensitive "privileged" Caesars documents, which Winograd and Stauber's committee never got access to either. OpCo said in its court papers "that empirical evidence supports the position that defining the scope of the examiner's role up front saves the estate time and money."

Bennett was apoplectic. The fix was in, he thought: OpCo was looking for a whitewash. He had come to accept that he was in for a nasty fight with Apollo and TPG. But he was slowly realizing that Kirkland and the independent directors would gang up on him to force the junior creditors to take a bad deal.

In a February 13 filing, Kirkland wrote that "... although controversial, the Challenged Transactions generated more than $2 billion in liquidity for the Debtors, extended maturities for more than $10 billion in debt that previously matured before 2016, and allowed the Debtors to pay approximately $2.2 billion of interest and $2.6 billion of principal on their debt—including approximately $1 billion of interest and $1.5 billion of principal to second-lien and unsecured noteholders." These were the very transactions Bennett believed were fraudulent, and Kirkland's job was to fight for the junior creditors, not be stooges for the private equity firms.

Judge Goldgar ultimately sided with Bennett. On March 12, 2015, Goldgar granted a motion to appoint an examiner with broad power to review more than a dozen of the controversial transactions the Caesars parent engaged in since the LBO. The order allowed the examiner to hire its own staff and advisors. There was no hard cap on expenses or time. The examiner was supposed to submit progress reports every 45 days, and a final report within 60 days of finishing the investigation. Goldgar ordered all sides to "use their best efforts to coordinate their investigations and avoid interference or needless duplication."

The Caesars parent had, like OpCo, fought for a limited examiner. In a February court filing, it wrote, "the evidence that will be presented to the examiner (and ultimately to the Court) will demonstrate that the transactions the second-lien Committee attacks were entirely proper." It was a bet Bruce Bennett was ecstatic to take.

WITH HIS BACKGROUND, THERE WOULD be no need for a glossy deck of slides. Richard Davis merely submitted his resume with a cover note attached. It would prove to be more than enough. It was February 2015, and the US Trustee was looking for an examiner for the Caesars bankruptcy. Davis was one such wise man, an *eminence grise*, the kind of guy made for blue ribbon commissions. In a forty-year legal career, he shuttled between elite posts in the public and private sectors. Davis had been a junior Watergate prosecutor, an Assistant US Attorney, an official in the US Treasury Department, and had been called to offer expert testimony in the impeachment proceedings of President Clinton.

Davis then spent decades at law powerhouse Weil, Gotshal & Manges as a star litigator working on such matters as the Argentina debt restructurings in the 1980s. After leaving Weil, Davis had met with the United States Trustee, telling the agency he would be interested in Chapter 11 assignments.

Davis did not mind messy cases. And the trustee was looking for an examiner to dig into the flurry of Caesars transactions Apollo and TPG had cooked up in the years leading up to the January bankruptcy filing. Given his place in the New York firmament, Davis had existing connections to parties in the sprawling Caesars situation. Weil had represented Drexel Burnham and Fred Joseph, its chief executive, in its early 1990 bankruptcy and related litigation. In 1992, Davis had helped federal Judge Milton Pollack craft the $1.3 billion settlement that junk bond king Michael Milken had agreed to in order to end litigation brought by Drexel.

Davis could recall how unhappy Leon Black had been with his massive multimillion-dollar bonus in the last days of Drexel. Later, Black was one of the Drexel executives asked to put partnership interests back into the settlement pot. He recalled that Brad Karp, now the chair of Paul, Weiss, had been a junior lawyer representing Milken. Davis had since gotten to know Karp well, as both were involved in the New York Legal Aid Society. At the organization's 2014 gala the Society had, in fact, honored Karp and Josh Harris, the Apollo co-founder.

While other applicants for the Caesars examiner post submitted lengthy PowerPoint decks with graphics and pictures, Davis's sparse submission would be plenty. Instead of flying to Chicago, he completed his interview over the phone while nursing a back injury. But that proved enough to get the job. At his March 25 retention hearing in Chicago, the US Trustee introduced Richard Davis to Judge Goldgar.

"Are you game for this?" Goldgar asked Davis as the courtroom erupted in laughter.

Davis nodded his head.

"Very good. I'm happy to grant the motion. You're in."

"IS THIS A PAGE FROM the Kirkland & Ellis website?"

"I've never been on our website," answered Jamie Sprayregen.

"Okay. Do you know who maintains the website?"

"No," said Sprayregen.

"Do you know how materials are posted to the website?"

"No," Sprayregen repeated the second time.

"Okay. Good. We'll move on."

Sprayregen, as one of America's leading bankruptcy lawyers, was too busy to sweat the details of Kirkland & Ellis's internet presence. His questioner in the Chicago bankruptcy court on April 23, 2015, was Geoff Stewart, a litigator at Jones Day, the firm representing the junior second-lien bondholder group. Stewart's colleague Bruce Bennett was attempting get Jamie Sprayregen fired.

After the OpCo had filed for bankruptcy in January 2015, Kirkland was set to represent it and play the crucial role of managing the restructuring and settlement negotiations with Apollo and TPG for all creditors.

Bennett was worried about that. Kirkland had the dominant private equity practice, a group that helped buyout firms raise money and then execute LBOs. That work dovetailed nicely with a bankruptcy practice. But the coziness with private equity had been a longstanding question for Kirkland.

Sprayregen was an expert at putting together cooperative restructurings where deals came together quickly. Caesars, alas, was not going to be that kind of a case. This was a brawl where the private equity firms were facing real charges of misconduct. The debtor lawyer needed to be willing to throw a few punches at Apollo and TPG if necessary. Bennett believed that Kirkland was not up to that task. He remembered that Kirkland had fought his efforts for an expansive examiner.

After the January bankruptcy filing, there had been a meeting in the late winter at Kirkland's office in New York where Bennett became convinced that Sprayregen was in the tank for Apollo/TPG. The Kirkland team had shared the results of its Caesars prebankruptcy asset transfers investigation, and why they thought the $1.5 billion contribution that the Caesars parent was making to the settlement merited giving Apollo and TPG full legal releases from liability. Bennett thought the six-page analysis was so shoddy that he had no choice but to challenge Kirkland's role.

Kirkland's retention as debtor's counsel was going to be lucrative, likely earning the firm tens of millions of dollars. Its fees would be paid by the Caesars' "estate," the surviving company. But per the bankruptcy rules, its retention had to be approved by Judge Goldgar. Accordingly, Kirkland had to attest that it was unconflicted in representing OpCo. Even for an aggressive litigator like Bennett, challenging Kirkland like this was a big decision. The banker and lawyer community in the bankruptcy world was small and tight-knit. Today's adversary was tomorrow's ally. A mutual non-aggression pact had informally developed, where advisors would fight hard for their clients but would avoid making accusations of corruption against one another.

Bennett, however, cared little about such decorum. He swung a big enough bat that it did not really matter what other lawyers thought of him. Still, he had other concerns about challenging Kirkland. A fight over advisors could distract from his primary case against Apollo and TPG.

He ultimately made a simple calculation: If he did not challenge Kirkland's neutrality, he would tacitly be approving their work for the rest of the case. Given what he had seen so far in the case, that was not an option. On February 25, 2015, the second-lien bondholders committee filed an objection to the retention of Kirkland, asserting that "K&E does not meet the rigorous standard for disinterestedness applicable to Debtors' counsel under 327(a) of the Bankruptcy Code."

Judge Goldgar scheduled a two-day hearing in late April to consider Kirkland's retention. The first day was the main event with Jamie Sprayregen as the sole witness. One of the top bankruptcy lawyers in America was challenging, in open court, the integrity of another. Sprayregen was first questioned by his longtime colleague David Zott, a top litigator for Kirkland who was leading the in-court effort on the Caesars assignment. Goldgar held the hearing in his courtroom. It was packed by those wanting to witness an unprecedented heavyweight fight.

Sprayregen explained that Kirkland had never represented Caesars or Hamlet Holdings, the vehicle through which Apollo/TPG owned Caesars. The firm had little business with Apollo and TPG or their portfolio companies, somewhere less than one percent of its annual revenue. Kirkland was representing the board of General Motors, which included David Bonderman, and when that came to light, Bonderman got his own lawyer as a part of his GM responsibilities.

Sprayregen also emphasized that Kirkland was absolutely willing to sue Apollo and TPG if it came to that. Responding to the junior creditor group's concern that it would "take a dive" or "pull punches," Sprayregen answered, "That assertion is completely incorrect from both a legal and an ethical standpoint. Kirkland & Ellis has complete freedom, either through waivers or lack of client relationships, to initiate a litigation against any party affiliated in any way with Apollo or TPG."

In May 2015, Judge Goldgar unsurprisingly ruled that Kirkland could serve as the Caesars OpCo counsel. The law was clinical on the issue of disinterestedness, and Jones Day offered no smoking guns. Goldgar wrote that the evidence presented to prove that Kirkland and the OpCo "are really in the pocket of Apollo and TPG" was "thin at best."

But all was not lost for Bennett. The trial had demonstrated to Judge Goldgar the tightrope that Kirkland was walking.

23

NEXT MAN UP

Marc Rowan had plenty of Caesars headaches in February 2015, and the last source of pain he needed was someone on his own side. Perella Weinberg Partners had been representing the Caesars OpCo alongside Kirkland & Ellis since the previous summer. As OpCo's investment banker, Perella was going to be crucial in negotiating with hostile creditors in the Chapter 11 case, and there was a mountain of work to get done. But a brewing internal soap opera at Perella was about to become Apollo's problem.

On February 15, 2015, Perella fired Michael Kramer, Josh Scherer, and two other senior restructuring bankers after the firm's leadership uncovered what it believed to be the group's plot to quit Perella and form their own rival boutique, allegedly a violation of their employment agreements. Through 2014, while the restructuring group was doing well, Kramer's relationship with Peter Weinberg was dramatically deteriorating and Kramer had been stripped of some management responsibilities. Kramer was known to be a difficult personality and he never really meshed with the blue-blooded Weinberg.

On Sunday, January 11, 2015—the same week of the dueling Caesars bankruptcy filings—senior members of the Perella Weinberg restructuring group had gathered at Kramer's sprawling estate in New Canaan, Connecticut. Weinberg and Joe Perella would later get wind of the meeting. They concluded that the group was finalizing plans to jump ship.

A month later, Perella and Weinberg made a decision to fire the foursome. Litigation between Kramer's team and Perella would extend for years as Kramer and friends argued that they had been fired simply because Perella wanted to improperly seize $60 million in equity they held in the firm.

But at that moment in February 2015, Weinberg wanted nothing to do with Kramer and his team and was willing to withdraw Perella completely from Kramer's live deals. Marc Rowan was not pleased. Bankers left their jobs all the time, but firms kept clients happy by allowing departed bankers to stay on existing deals in exchange for splitting the fees.

Rowan sent a scathing email to Kirkland on February 25, stating, "Perella needs to be an adult and put the client first." Rowan began negotiating directly with Peter Weinberg to keep the Kramer team as the financial advisor to Caesars OpCo. It was, however, awkward and perhaps inappropriate for Apollo to choose the OpCo investment banker since they controlled the parent Caesars.

On Tuesday of that week, after Weinberg and Rowan spoke by phone, Weinberg sent over a draft term sheet delineating how the Kramer team could keep working on Caesars. Weinberg's terms included a provision where Perella would keep 85 percent of the fee, even as the exiled Kramer bankers would do most of the work. Kramer asked that his group get between 40 and 60 percent of the fee.

On Wednesday morning, an exasperated Rowan wrote back before departing for Israel. Weinberg, as a condition of allowing the Kramer bankers to stay on at Caesars, would force them to relinquish any legal claims they had against Perella in connection with their terminations. Why was Peter Weinberg trying to drag Caesars and Apollo into his personal war with Mike Kramer, wondered Rowan: "[T]he client is being harmed while Kramer and Perella fight it out," he wrote. "I urge you and your partners to reconsider your position before OpCo retains another advisor. Please feel free to forward to those involved internally as this needs to be resolved quickly one way or the other. Tks. MR."

Investment bankers were usually at the feet of private equity firms, and for Weinberg to even consider crossing a heavy hitter like Marc Rowan seemed unthinkable. On Friday evening just before six p.m., Perella's lawyers at Weil, Gotshal sent a formal letter terminating Perella's engagement with the Caesars OpCo after no compromise could be struck.

"ARE YOU IRA MILLSTEIN'S KID?"

Jim Millstein was about to graduate from Columbia Law School in 1982, but his employment prospects were complicated by his father. Ira Millstein was a senior partner at Weil, Gotshal & Manges and one of the most important corporate lawyers in America. Ira had served a stint in the Antitrust Division in the Department of Justice in the early 1950s before landing at Weil, helping turn the once-Jewish firm into a powerhouse that competed toe-to-toe with the old-line WASP firms that represented Wall Street and Fortune 500 clients. Millstein counseled the likes of General Electric and Westinghouse. Like his contemporaries Marty Lipton and Joe Flom, Ira Millstein became a leading thinker and voice on corporate governance. And by the early 1980s, he was imposing enough to make life difficult for his son.

Jim Millstein at first did not contemplate a career in law. After graduating from Princeton, he went to graduate school at Berkeley to get a PhD in political theory. But he soon discovered that even with his top-notch CV, the odds of getting a full-time faculty position were slim. Jim Millstein left Berkeley with a master's degree and admission in the first-year class at his father's alma mater, Columbia.

After law school, his father's long shadow kept Jim from jobs at Midtown firms like Wachtell and Skadden. He was told to try his luck downtown, and he eventually landed at Cleary Gottlieb Steen & Hamilton. One of his first assignments was a loan syndication deal for an offshore oil drilling contractor, Global Marine. The debt-laden company, which had also issued junk bonds underwritten by Drexel, would quickly be overwhelmed by both its balance sheet and falling oil prices. Millstein, while not yet a Chapter 11 expert, was tapped by creditors of Global Marine because of his knowledge of the company. The case took more than two years to finish, and involved many of the biggest bankruptcy lawyers in the country. Millstein would become hooked, spending more than fifteen years at Cleary and becoming one of the stars of the field just as it was blossoming in the late 1980s and 1990s.

In 1999, Millstein decided to try his hand at the finance side. He joined Lazard Frères as an investment banker, where he would eventually lead its restructuring group. Millstein was erudite and ambitious and had always maintained a deep interest in politics and public policy. He had represented the United Auto Workers in labor negotiations and had done several sovereign debt or state-owned enterprise restructurings. In 2008, members of the Obama presidential campaign called Millstein to get his thoughts on the financial markets as the financial crisis was unfolding.

After the election, Millstein assisted in the transition between the Paulson and Geithner Treasury departments, as the US government had taken large stakes in banks and auto companies to bail them out. The Treasury was going to need private sector experts to manage the portfolio it had amassed, and President Obama appointed Millstein the first Chief Restructuring Officer of the United States. Millstein spent two years at the Treasury, where the bulk of his time was spent fixing AIG, the insurance company whose credit default swaps mischief required a near $200 billion bailout. By the time the US government sold all its stake in AIG, the government had recorded a profit of over $20 billion.

In 2011, Millstein returned to investment banking, forming his own boutique firm, Millstein & Co. In 2014, Millstein had pitched for the Caesars OpCo mandate that went to Perella Weinberg.

Nine months later, Millstein was the rare restructuring advisor who did not have an existing role in the Caesars case. But with the soap opera at Perella, Millstein's free agency was suddenly an asset. In late February, Millstein got a call asking if he would take over the assignment for OpCo. He was excited to step in, blissfully unaware of the bad blood in the case.

For nearly thirty years, Jim Millstein had been one of the most important men in the bankruptcy world. He loved the intellectual challenge of assembling a complex deal and was supremely confident in his ability to clean up messy situations. Millstein had been through countless wars on Wall Street and in Washington. But there was no good preparation for the Caesars circus, of which he had just become ringmaster.

24

GIVE PEACE A CHANCE

"It would be one of the greatest messes of our time," Jim Millstein explained in a sworn statement to the bankruptcy court in May 2015. Millstein had been the OpCo financial advisor for less than three months. His goal in this deposition was to convince Judge Goldgar to keep the Caesars parent out of a separate bankruptcy, one that certain OpCo creditors were trying to force to gain the upper hand. Millstein, along with Kirkland & Ellis, wanted Judge Goldgar to halt multiple lawsuits that sought to enforce the parent bond guarantee on $11 billion of debt. The Caesars parent was only worth a couple of billion dollars and those lawsuits, if successful, would have bankrupted it and, in the process, upended the OpCo bankruptcy, thereby creating the "great mess" that Millstein predicted.

The Caesars case was already a mess. Millstein and his colleague Brendan Hayes would walk into meetings and negotiations and wonder *why is everyone so angry with each other?* And the contempt was not just between the private equity firms and the hedge funds. Millstein noticed the ill will between GSO and Elliott, who had been on opposite sides of the credit default swap trade in 2014. Elliott had also grabbed a windfall in its RSA, which made it that much harder to shore up a deal with the senior loan holders who felt cheated by Elliott's terms. And then there was the ongoing war waged by the Bruce Bennett-led second-lien bondholders against essentially everyone. And somehow, against that backdrop, Millstein was supposed to craft a deal.

Step one was to create some breathing room. Chapter 11 was supposed to produce that safe haven. One of the key features of the bankruptcy code was the so-called "automatic stay" of litigation.

Lawsuits against the debtor were halted or "stayed" while the parties tried to hash out a restructuring. The problem for Caesars was that the most important lawsuits in the case were not against the bankrupt OpCo, but rather against the Caesars parent—the publicly listed company majority-owned by Apollo and TPG who had guaranteed the OpCo debt.

It was possible that Caesars would lose the parent guarantee litigation and have to make good on more than $10 billion of OpCo debt. On January 15, 2015, Judge Shira Scheindlin of the Southern District of New York refused to dismiss Millar's lawsuit on behalf of MeehanCombs and other holders of the Caesars unsecured notes. Scheindlin, citing the *Marblegate* decision, wrote, "I find that the complaint's plausible allegations that the August 2014 Transaction stripped plaintiffs of the valuable Caesars parent Guarantees leaving them with an empty right to assert a payment default from an insolvent issuer are sufficient to state a claim…"

In March 2015, Bruce Bennett decided that his clients had their own bond guarantee claims and quickly filed a lawsuit in New York federal court. Bennett's case was different than Millar's, and would prove one of the quirkier moments of the Caesars case. Millar's clients had their bond guarantees released when three favored hedge funds owning 51 percent of the unsecured legacy bonds agreed to amend their indenture to kill the bond guarantee. Those hedge funds got much of their debt bought out at 100 cents, leaving pennies for those left out—Millar's clients.

The second-lien bondholders, however, had their bond guarantee released in a different way. In May 2014, Caesars OpCo sold 5 percent of its stock to the three hedge funds Paulson, Scoggin, and Chatham; thus, the OpCo was no longer "wholly-owned" by the Caesars parent. Bennett had noticed that the indenture language on releasing the guarantee was worded in a peculiar way. There were three distinct methods for release of the parent guarantee listed in the indenture: first, sell OpCo stock, which had happened. Second, sell OpCo. Third, pay off all the OpCo debt.

Between the second and third options in the indenture's verbatim legal language, the word "and" appeared. Did that mean that all three conditions had to be met for the guarantee to be released? It was ambiguous, so the junior bondholders argued in their guarantee lawsuit, among multiple points, that since Caesars had not satisfied all three, the guarantee must remain in effect. If any of the guarantee terminations were valid, all of the bonds would no longer be under the umbrella of the Caesars parent.

Paul, Weiss would, however, argue that the indenture language was meant to be "disjunctive" not "conjunctive," and as such only one condition was required. Caesars went as far as getting the lawyer who drafted the indenture, at the firm Cahill Gordon & Reindel, to provide an affidavit affirming that the release only required a single condition to be satisfied. Distressed debt investing often hinged on readings of these complex, esoteric documents. But even if Paul, Weiss and Caesars were correct in their interpretation, the mere overhang of this lawsuit was a mortal threat.

"YOU'RE ALL GOING TO BE questioning witnesses, is that it?"

Judge Benjamin Goldgar was, yet again, annoyed with the lawyers in the guarantee lawsuits. Goldgar was holding a two-day trial starting on June 3, 2015, over a so-called 105(a) injunction. 105(a) of the Bankruptcy Code gave a judge the broad power to halt litigation against parties not formally in Chapter 11 if such a time-out would promote a successful settlement.

Judge Goldgar asked who was going to be arguing this issue. Three Kirkland lawyers presented themselves, followed by no fewer than ten other attorneys from other firms. "It's going to be very difficult for the court reporters here, as well as the cast of thousands," Goldgar commented.

Eventually, Kirkland's lead litigator David Zott called Jim Millstein to the stand to testify on the behalf of their mutual client, the Caesars OpCo. Millstein and Kirkland were not representing Apollo, TPG, or the Caesars parent, but were trying to strike a deal that was best for all Caesars stakeholders. Still, that meant sometimes taking sides. By arguing for the injunction against the multiple parent guarantee lawsuits, Millstein was aligning himself with Apollo, TPG, and the senior creditors who had struck settlement deals.

Millstein should have been an effective advocate and an honest broker. He had become one of the pioneers of the restructuring business as a lawyer, a banker, and finally in government as the first Chief Restructuring Officer of the United States. With his short, white hair, clear-rimmed glasses, and calm, erudite demeanor, Millstein oozed gravitas.

Zott referred to Millstein's deposition testimony taken before the June hearing.

"Now, you've seen some messy situations. For example, AIG as one example, and the financial crisis. In your deposition, you mentioned that a CEC bankruptcy would be one of the great messes of our time. Do you stand by that?" Zott asked.

"Yeah," Millstein replied. "I think the—I think what we did with AIG, thankfully we had no—did not require the intervention of a court. But I think the commencement of a bankruptcy by the Caesars parent would create a forum, a litigation forum, which may not certainly be rivaled in my experience." Millstein then predicted, accurately, "The opportunity for litigation would be—it would proliferate."

Goldgar interjected and asked about the difference between the lawsuits on the bond guarantee and the fraud lawsuits on the casino transfers.

"I mean, I think that's why it's one of the great messes of our time because we would have the defendant be the subject of a bankruptcy, and so we would be litigating for the return of property from one estate in favor of another estate," Millstein clarified. Millstein explained that the $12 billion in guarantee litigation outside of bankruptcy would be competing with the claims over fraud in the bankruptcy.

But Goldgar was dubious. "Fraudulent transfer actions would be stayed," he countered.

"They would be," Millstein admitted.

"We'd just have claim litigation," said Goldgar.

"Well, but we would argue for equitable relief to our bankruptcy judge," Millstein responded, almost exasperated that Goldgar didn't see that these lawsuits would all be pursuing the same pool of money.

Zott jumped in, "Well, we'll try that one another time," and added quickly, "Hopefully we're not going to try that one." Goldgar caught his slip, "One thing at a time." "Yes, let's take them one at a time, yeah," Zott said nervously.

The rest of the hearing, Goldgar continued to interject with his own questions.

The Kirkland attorney had to change tactics. If hyperbole wouldn't work, then maybe details would. Zott tried a more direct question to Millstein. "Why do you believe continuation of the guarantee litigation would disrupt that process?"

Millstein regrouped and tried again. "Well, because the allegedly guaranteed parties are trying to jump the line. They're trying to— they're trying to alter the priorities that would otherwise prevail in the bankruptcy, and to compete with the debtors' claims against the Caesars parent arising out of many of the same transactions of which they're a litigant."

But Judge Goldgar wasn't having it. "Isn't that what guarantees are for? This is why people get them."

"Yeah, that's right," Millstein responded, trailing off.

There was a circularity to the Caesars case that was difficult to comprehend—as Goldgar's questions demonstrated. A parent company existed, an OpCo company existed, and just where the value and the legal claims resided could seem a mystery.

"But the—there is a more—there is a more complicated conversation about that," Millstein went on. "At the time these guarantees were given, there was nothing in the Caesars parent. The value that sits in the Caesars parent really resided in the OpCo. The value that could be obtained today came from the debtors…And so if we recovered our fraudulent transfers, if there are fraudulent—if they really were fraudulent transfers, the guarantees would be of absolutely no value to these parties because at the time the guarantees were given it was a holding company. It had nothing in it other than the equity in OpCo.

"And it's only through a series of transactions, which the estate is asserting or could assert that Caesars parent has independent value to those guarantee claims. So what these creditors are trying to do is compete with fraudulent conveyance claims that the estate has, and be a beneficiary of those fraudulent conveyance claims by seeking a separate recovery on their guarantees."

Millstein then added, "And in that sense, they're jumping the line. If they're successful, they're jumping the line and getting ahead of the estate, and, therefore, really interfering with the priorities it would otherwise obtain in the bankruptcy."

Zott then chimed in: "You mentioned—when we first met and started preparing, you mentioned a John Lennon song. Do you remember the song?"

"Which one? 'Give Peace a Chance'?" Millstein responded.

Goldgar interjected with lyrics from a different John Lennon tune: "Imagine all the people, living life…" drawing laughs from the courtroom.

Without irony, Zott said, "I think he got it right. What was the song?"

"'Give Peace a Chance,'" Millstein confirmed.

"Is that what you're saying here?" asked Zott.

Millstein, not catching on, said, "Oh, no. I'm saying that the highlight of a bankruptcy proceeding is where the fruit of a plan of reorganization will be produced. And to allow—you know, to start spreading seeds outside the bankruptcy proceeding is—to let, you know, a thousand flowers bloom outside the bankruptcy case is basically going to make this case very difficult to resolve."

Zott's friendly questioning ended lamely, setting the stage for Geoffrey Stewart, the Jones Day litigator for the second-lien bonds, to tear into Millstein. Stewart made it clear his clients were not looking for peace but rather their version of justice. Stewart suggested the junior bondholders intended to pursue not just the parent company, but Apollo and TPG—and even the individuals who were responsible for the controversial transactions.

"Now, is it fair to say that you're aware of the claims that have been propounded against the officers and directors…for breaches of their fiduciary duty?" Stewart began.

"Yes," Millstein tersely answered.

"And under the RSA [the existing Elliott deal]—the RSA is going to give releases [of liability] to a number of people, correct?"

"Yes."

"These will be general releases, right?"

"Correct."

"Not limited in any way. It's general across-the-board releases, correct?"

Millstein started to nod. Affording him no respect, Stewart said, "You have to say yes or no. The reporter can't pick up a nod of the head."

"Yes, I understand that," Millstein responded, not quite masking his agitation.

Stewart pressed the issue that the private equity firms largely seemed to be getting off the hook and not paying anything for being absolved from wrongdoing. "And Apollo, how much is it paying for its release? TPG, how much is it paying for its release?" Stewart asked rhetorically. "Do you deny for a minute that the…estate could pursue these other entities to get the significant contribution from them if the Caesars parent weren't able to pay it?"

This would become the central theme of the second-lien bondholders for the rest of the case. Potential liability for fraudulent transfers could total into the billions and flow all the way up to Apollo, TPG, and even personally to Marc Rowan, David Sambur, and David Bonderman. In exchange for broad releases of liability, Jones Day wondered what exactly were the private equity firms putting into the settlement pot?

"Do you question for a minute whether this group of men is or isn't able to pay a judgment against them if it's rendered in the amount of several billion dollars? Do you know?"

Then Stewart got to his point. "You do understand, and I'm not sure you agree with what I'm about to say, but you do understand, don't you, that there's quite a large number of creditors in this case who believe the RSA was…a sweetheart deal to exonerate the Caesars parent from serious tort liability for a low price and let it grab these assets out of bankruptcy? You know that's how a lot of the creditors feel, don't you?"

"They want more. That's not surprising," Millstein said dismissively.

"No, not that they want more," Stewart corrected. "That's not my question. That they feel something different. That this was a deal that was engineered between a parent and a sub[sidiary] before we ever came to this courtroom, that gives a remarkably good deal to that parent, and exonerates it from liability for billions of dollars of transfers, it doesn't make it pay very much money, and gives sweeping releases to everybody who got near those transfers—you know that's how a lot of the creditors feel, don't you?"

Picking up on Millstein's phrasing from earlier, Stewart went for the kill. "You said, by the way, that would be, what, a world class mess or something like that? You used a word like that."

"Yes."

"Isn't it true that this mess was made by the Caesars parent?"

"The corporate structure," Millstein tried to deflect.

"Sir, yes or no."

"Well, I'm—"

"No, seriously. This is a very simple question. Yes or no, was it made by the Caesars parent or wasn't it?"

Kirkland's Zott jumped in, pleading with Judge Goldgar, "He started answering the question, then he got cut off."

"Well, he was because he's not answering the question," Stewart insisted.

"Well, how do we know. He didn't…" Zott fought back.

"Because he didn't say yes or no. He started giving a speech," Stewart interrupted.

Zott objected, but Goldgar had no sympathy for Kirkland or Millstein at this time. "It's overruled. You can answer the question, sir."

"This mess had many fathers," was the best Millstein could come up with.

GIVEN THE COMPLEXITY OF THE guarantee litigation and how it fit into the broader bankruptcy case, it would take weeks for Judge Goldgar to rule. In the interim, the significance of his pending decision only grew. On June 23, 2015, Judge Katherine Polk Failla ruled in the *Marblegate* case that the complex restructuring contemplated by Education Management Corporation violated the Trust Indenture

Act. She wrote that the EDMC restructuring "gave dissenting bond-holders a Hobson's choice: take common stock or nothing. In effect, Marblegate bought a $14 million bond that the majority now attempts to turn into $5 million of stock, with consent procured only by the threat of deprivation without resort to the reorganization machinery provided by law."

The ruling was not a shock, as Judge Failla had telegraphed it when she denied a motion to dismiss in December 2014. In her latest ruling she even cited Judge Scheindlin's preliminary ruling in Jim Millar's *MeehanCombs* lawsuit surviving a motion to dismiss in January 2015.

EDMC immediately appealed Failla's ruling to the Second Circuit, but that decision could be months away. In the meantime, the *Marblegate* ruling would throw the entire out-of-court bond restructuring marketplace into chaos, since many such deals involved coercive tactics that the court criticized.

Suddenly, Jim Millstein's warning that Caesars could be in a "mess" looked like a real possibility. If Goldgar allowed the parent guarantee lawsuits to go forward, creditors were poised to quickly win based on the new *Marblegate* precedent.

At the hearing on July 22, 2015, Goldgar announced his decision on the injunction. "I don't consider the testimony that denying the stay would lead to 'one of the great messes of our time' as evidence," Goldgar explained. The guarantee lawsuits could proceed. The stock price of the Caesars parent collapsed immediately, falling 40 percent at the prospect of its now pending bankruptcy. Goldgar had repudiated Millstein's theory on how best to resolve the Caesars case.

25

THE METER IS RUNNING

Why were there so many Kirkland & Ellis lawyers milling about his courtroom, Judge Benjamin Goldgar wondered. Kirkland lawyers from Chicago and New York swarmed every Caesars hearing. Most of them did not even have to speak in court; they merely took up valuable bench space. Kirkland had become perhaps the best bankruptcy firm in the world because it had dozens of lawyers in every conceivable specialty it could throw at cases like Caesars. CEOs and directors tended to be risk-averse, and nobody ever got fired for picking Kirkland. By 2015, most bankruptcy judges had made their peace with the bonanza of legal and advisory fees that defined Chapter 11 cases. Benjamin Goldgar, however, would not be so permissive.

Goldgar required adjustment from all the lawyers in the case. They had grown accustomed to experienced judges who knew how to take control of the Chapter 11 process to reach some kind of settlement. Goldgar, the lawyers in the Caesars case believed, was less than commanding. He focused too much on form over substance. He liked to pontificate on seemingly random matters and sweat the trivial points. The case never had a rhythm, starting from the January first-day hearing when Goldgar shut down Kirkland's ace lawyer, Paul Basta. Since that moment, Kirkland had been knocked off balance.

Kirkland, like all the professional services firms representing either the Caesars OpCo or one of the officially sanctioned creditors' committees, had its fees paid by the bankruptcy "estate"—that is, the surviving Caesars OpCo. But in exchange, the advisors were required to submit their fees for approval by the court. Given the scale of the case, the US Trustee and other parties agreed to a five-person "fee committee" consisting of representatives from the Caesars OpCo, the US Trustee, and the two official creditors' committees.

The committee's job was to vet the fee applications and submit their feedback to Judge Goldgar. The committee was led by Nancy Rapoport, a University of Nevada law professor who had served as a fee expert in several Chapter 11 cases. She charged $21,000 a month plus expenses for hiring law students and recent law graduates to help her sift through the fee applications.

Those applications were not slim documents. Kirkland's first fee application filed in July 2015 ran more than 1,900 pages—it tallied every hour that its lawyers billed, along with costs for expensed meals, taxis and cars, hotel rooms, and photocopies. For the period between the bankruptcy filing on January 15, 2015, and the end of May, the firm was asking for $21.4 million in fees to be approved along with nearly $800,000 in expenses. The firm had a total of 64 professionals working on Caesars, between lawyers and support staff with top partners Jamie Sprayregen and Paul Basta billing at $1,325 per hour. More than $200,000 in expenses alone was for printing charges.

The fee committee had filed its first report at the end of August 2015. The report highlighted general issues with fees and expenses submitted in the case, such as pricey partners charging for low-level research. Rapoport had discussions with the various advisors to better understand their charges and often accepted their explanations. Still, several firms trimmed their fee requests and changed their billing based on her feedback (Kirkland had, for example, accepted lowering its fees by $170,000).

In its second report filed in late December 2015, the fee committee "found fewer areas of concern." However, it still questioned billing practices, including why "numerous people attend[ed] meetings and hearings." In the section devoted to Kirkland's latest fee request, the reports cited a few areas of concern but after hearing the firm's explanations, the committee "concluded that the fees and expenses…should be allowed as reasonable or necessary."

Judge Goldgar was less convinced. In an order signed two days before Christmas, Goldgar noted that the fee committee report expressed concern about all the Kirkland lawyers attending Caesars hearings and that he wanted an explanation. On January 6, 2016, Kirkland filed its response, writing, "Given the multi-faceted issues and many stakeholders in these contentious cases, however, that often requires having multiple attorneys present at hearings or meetings of particular importance or relevance to the attorneys' role on these cases."

The filing went on to detail what several attorneys, including many from New York, were doing at an important June hearing in Chicago, even as many of them "did not have a speaking role." For example, Nicole Greenblatt, one of Kirkland's lead partners handling Caesars, stayed for three nights in Chicago at the Langham Hotel down the street from Kirkland's Chicago headquarters. Greenblatt would spend thousands of hours on Caesars and it made perfect sense for her to be present for key hearings. But Goldgar focused on how she had expensed $1,200 for her three night stay at Langham though she never spoke in court during the hearing.

In most big bankruptcies, no judge would subject a top law firm and its top lawyers to the humiliation of justifying their court attendance. In its filing, Kirkland agreed to voluntarily reduce its fee request by $3,492 to reflect three employees' non-essential billed work. Kirkland was still asking for more than $13 million in fees and $350,000 for the four months between June and September.

Goldgar took up the matter of Kirkland's fees at a January 20, 2016, hearing: "I'm willing to sign the order [Kirkland fee request] but I am still a little bit concerned because there are an awful lot of Kirkland lawyers at these hearings. And there are lawyers there who are not calling any witnesses at all. And I see lawyers, frankly, on their smartphones during the trial. So they are not watching the trial. Now, I don't know if they are taking notes about the trial or whether they're sending settlement offers to the committees or whether they're playing 'Boom Beach.' I can't tell. If it's the latter, I would be disturbed."

David Seligman, the only Kirkland restructuring partner who topped Greenblatt in time spent on Caesars, told Goldgar that the firm took the billing feedback seriously and added earnestly, "And your point about the smartphones, I'm an old-fashioned guy that writes on a yellow notepad but some people do take notes on their phone." Goldgar and Seligman continued to discuss the perils of mobile devices in court, and Goldgar ultimately granted the application.

DON'T STOP "TILL" YOU GET ENOUGH

Amy Till, an Indianan in her early 20s with a young family, needed a cheap car. Scraping together $300 for a down payment, she and her husband went to their used car dealer and drove off with a used 1991 Chevrolet S-10 pickup truck for only $122 twice a month. They financed the remaining $6,426, which included the price of the truck, fees, and taxes, at a hefty 21 percent interest rate.

Just a year later, in October 1999, the Tills were in default on their car payment and jointly filed for bankruptcy in the hopes of keeping their vehicle and working out a payment plan with their lender. The truck by then was worth less than the loan. The Tills' plan proposed to repay the claim in full over seventeen months at a 9.5 percent interest rate. But their lender rejected that plan, insisting on the 21 percent that was the standard subprime rate.

Remarkably, one of the Tills was part of a labor union that paid for its legal fees, and they fought their lender all the way to the US Supreme Court. On May 17, 2004, in a 5–4 decision, the Supreme Court ruled that the Tills should only have to pay the 9.5 percent rate, not the "eye-popping" 21 percent, adopting a so-called "formula approach" to working out replacement debt under the Bankruptcy Code. The highest court had just ruled that secured creditors, in this case the subprime auto lender, could be forced to take back replacement debt with a below-market coupon.

"YOU MOTHERFUCKERS, DID YOU NOT see what I did in Momentive? I will *Till* the shit out of all of you."

David Sambur was threatening holders of the Caesars OpCo

loans. And while Sambur was definitely not Amy Till and Caesars was not a used pickup, the precedent from the *Till* case would be useful to him. It was late on a Friday in December 2014, and talks between Apollo and the loan holders had stalled. Elliott and the other senior bondholders were about to strike a sweet deal, and the loan holders led by Ryan Mollett of GSO were furious that they were going to get the short end of the stick.

In addition to the Till case, Sambur's message referred to the bankruptcy of another Apollo portfolio company, a chemicals maker called Momentive Performance Materials, that the private equity firm acquired for $4 billion in 2006 from General Electric. Momentive had filed for bankruptcy earlier in 2014 and the company's job cuts had been a public relations nightmare for Apollo.

In the Momentive bankruptcy fight, Sambur had effectively used the *Till v. SCS Credit Corp.* precedent to force senior creditors to take replacement debt with a lower interest rate than the rate that was negotiated when the loan was first made. This made the lenders worse off. While forcing unattractive terms on holdout junior creditors was called a "cramdown," imposing poor terms on senior creditors was known as a "cram up." Sambur was now threatening to call the same play at Caesars.

Mollett was first amused and then angered by Sambur's tack.

The loan holder group had serious demands. They wanted as much cash as possible for their $5 billion in claims. They also wanted accrued interest for the pendency of the bankruptcy at a rate far higher than what Sambur was now offering. The impasse remained through January 2015, and the group had even drafted a civil RICO conspiracy lawsuit against Caesars in the spirit of Elliott's inflammatory lawsuit in Delaware two months earlier.

On January 29, just two weeks after the involuntary and voluntary bankruptcies, the loan holders convened with Apollo and Caesars at Kirkland & Ellis's office in the Citicorp Center on Lexington Avenue. Having throngs of people in these meeting rooms could be awkward, because people talking at opposite ends of the table could be 100 feet away. Key members of the ad hoc bank group, Ryan Mollett of GSO, Michael Barnett of Och-Ziff, and Shawn Tumulty of Franklin Mutual, represented the creditors. The group's advisors from Stroock and Rothschild were also in attendance. Karim Moolani, a young executive at Silver Point Capital, the firm that had been pressuring Mollett and the core bank group to get more aggressive, showed up.

Apollo sent both Marc Rowan and David Sambur, signaling the importance of the discussion. They hoped that a deal could be struck soon, as Apollo had bigger fish to fry in the bankruptcy.

The master of ceremonies would be Paul Basta, the Kirkland partner representing the Caesars OpCo. Basta explained that Caesars could meet some of the loan holders' demands, but more aggressive treatment on accrued interest was not feasible. Kirkland's M.O. was all about finding a deal quickly, so Basta pivoted to his main point: Debtors such as Caesars were given "exclusivity" in bankruptcy, the right to first propose a restructuring plan. It would last 120 days, and it gave Caesars a leg up in negotiations. Basta warned the loan holders that it was in everyone's interest to come together quickly.

"People have to make decisions on whether or not they work this out quickly or fight for years. It's key for us not to lose exclusivity and we need these things to get a deal done," Basta said. Aiming for an emphatic finish in these closed talks, Basta didn't mind getting a little coarse: "There comes a time in every case where you have to shit or get off the pot."

Sambur then stood up and aimed to take back control of the meeting. "Thanks Paul, that was great. Good job laying that out," Sambur began. "And for the avoidance of doubt, *I'm here to shit.*"

The lenders and their advisors looked at each other, shaking their heads. Sambur had a gift for making an awkward situation even more so.

"Who is this twelve-year-old talking to me," muttered Chaim Fortgang, referring to the baby-faced (at thirty-four) if pugnacious Sambur. Fortgang was a legend in the bankruptcy world. Now in his late sixties, he had worked as an advisor to Silver Point since 2004. But in the 1980s and 1990s, he was a pioneering creditor lawyer at Wachtell, Lipton—often clashing with Harvey Miller, the famed debtor lawyer at Weil, Gotshal. Fortgang's intellect was enormous. But so was his penchant for outrageous behavior. Fortgang had once thrown a bagel at an opposing investment banker, telling him, "This is what you['re] entitled to!" Another time, Fortgang threatened to rip out the tongue of an opposing lawyer and stomp on it. He ultimately left Wachtell in the early 2000s.

By 2015, his appearance had grown unkempt. His hair was long, he had grown heavy, and as an Orthodox Jew, wore a kippah at all times. In meetings, the junior analysts and young lawyers would wonder who the oddball old guy at the table was. But he remained a sharp thinker and strategist and was valuable to the loan holder's group.

On phone calls leading up to this meeting with Apollo, Fortgang had already lived up to his reputation, shouting into the phone, "Fuck this, fuck this deal, you understand you're entitled to post-petition interest!" Sambur eventually grew tired of Fortgang's antics and would later tell Moolani in advance of future meetings to "leave Chaim at home."

The core negotiations between Caesars and the loan holders were conducted by Sambur and Ryan Mollett. Mollett spoke up: "We have your latest proposal, why don't you step out and let us talk among ourselves." Apollo and everyone else but the loan holder team walked out.

"Ok, we can give 'em a little bit here but the fact remains that they keep drawing lines and stepping over them," Mollett said, referring to Sambur's infamous habit of breaking his word.

"We're not going to take a haircut on everything," Mollett continued. "It's just an argument over cash versus other currency, so it should be an easy negotiation." The more militant faction pressed Mollett to not give an inch. But the majority preferred to at least offer a minor concession, in the form of giving up so-called "default interest," the higher rate of interest a company sometimes owes if the company goes into default.

If this accommodation helped shorten the Caesars case to say, six months, default interest in such a short period would not matter much. Within the room, there was worry, however, that a drawn-out bankruptcy would hurt the group. Their capital would be tied up while they were earning a more modest rate of return. But the dovish faction won the day and conceded on the default interest as long as they got everything else, including assurances that the financings necessary to pay them off would go through—"schmuck insurance," as it was called.

Apollo and the rest filed back into the conference room, and Mollett tried to break the tension with some levity.

"From your perspective, you say you want us to 'shit or get off the pot,' so I have a proposal that should bring a little 'movement' to the situation," Mollett said, tickled with his own wordplay. He turned to his GSO colleague Jason New and the group's lawyer, Kris Hansen, for some reassurance, but his double entendre had fallen flat.

Mollett shifted to a more serious tone. "In many ways we are easy. We don't care about the REIT, we don't care about backstop financings or capital raisings. We want cash and couldn't care less about the other stuff. So we'll consider not charging you default interest. But you guys are in a tough spot."

Mollett's point was that their demands were simple: all cash with interest, but they would budge a little on the interest rate.

Sambur was furious. The 100-cent offer on the table, even if mostly in new debt, was more than generous.

"We brought everyone here, made concessions, and now you say you are not giving anything? Thanks for that, I'm out of here." Sambur picked up his papers and marched out of the conference room. Marc Rowan looked on silently and let the meeting dissolve, but shortly after, he dragged Hansen, Barnett, and Mollett into a separate room.

"Look, this is just business at this point, but we can't let this go on," Rowan told them. "We have to find a way to get to a deal but there are certain lines we just won't cross in terms of value. At some point there's nothing in it for us."

Mollett was irritated by Rowan's hardball. Apollo wanted not only a get-out-of-jail free card, but also to keep as much of the company as possible. The free pass should have been more than enough for them.

"I get it. But you need us. We have a guarantee and we will chase you. And by the way, you are getting a legal release out of this, so you should be happy to get $0," Hansen responded. "You need to deal with your true opponent, who are the second-liens. They're your antagonists."

Rowan nodded, "OK, I appreciate it. We'll try and get to a deal."

IT WAS GOOD TO BE Dave Miller in the summer of 2015. While all the other creditors were playing demolition derby by either scrambling to cut deals or litigate with Caesars, he was playing with house money. By deftly forcing the Caesars bankruptcy filing, his credit default swap bet had paid off handsomely. Elliott had never publicly acknowledged its position in Caesars derivatives, but market participants had estimated the firm's profits in the hundreds of millions of dollars. If that was not enough, the RSA he had negotiated with Sambur came attached with all sorts of goodies like the convertible preferred backstop for the new PropCo's equity that was pure windfall.

Remarkably, everything he had won could only get better. In order to remain effective, the RSA he and his fellow senior bondholders had signed required Caesars to reach milestones by specified dates. Those milestones included filing a detailed restructuring plan with the bankruptcy court and getting a so-called disclosure statement approved, which would trigger a plan confirmation process by Judge Goldgar on or before August 2015. Given that Caesars had little traction with the other creditors, there was no chance these milestones were going to be reached. That meant the RSA would lapse, giving Miller the chance to take another pound of flesh from Sambur. By August 1, 2015, Caesars announced it had renewed the first-lien bond RSA with improvements for Elliott and its friends.

MARC ROWAN SLOWLY STOPPED BEING Apollo's public face of the Caesars effort. The private equity firm made the fateful decision to let thirty-five-year-old David Sambur be the man on the ground. On some level it made sense. He had been working on the Caesars investment for a decade. His boundless energy and his mastery of the business and the financials was encyclopedic. His career and life had blossomed in those years. By 2015, Sambur and his wife had two daughters and a son (he was known to dote on them in the early evenings and then, after they went to bed, work into the wee hours). He had now ascended to partner at Apollo. In 2015, he sold his apartment on the north side of Madison Square Park for nearly $6 million and purchased a $15 million home on 68th Street, just off 5th Avenue. Creditors, however, got wind of Sambur's prosperity, and feeling that he had stolen from them, began to joke about who was going to seize his residence by the end of the case.

A lighter touch from Sambur was, however, not forthcoming. At another negotiation with the loan holders committee, GSO's Jason New would face Sambur's wrath. The deal with the loan holders called for them to get new debt in the reorganized Caesars. The reorganized Caesars had to make lease payments to the new PropCo REIT that actually owned the properties.

The loan holders were worried that the lease payments were senior to their interest payments, and wanted to understand the priority. "Can you explain to me how the waterfall works?" New simply asked. Sambur lost his cool and snapped, "We are here to a cut a deal and you are asking basic questions!"

"The lease is senior, I don't think you are right," New clapped back when Sambur said interest on debt was senior. The discussion moved on, but New learned his interpretation was correct.

Sambur's wrath continued at another large gathering at Paul, Weiss that included first-lien bondholders like Elliott, Pimco, and the usual bankers and lawyers. Sambur's nemesis from Elliott, Dave Miller, was arguing for tight covenants on the lease payments PropCo was getting. The first-lien bondholders like Elliott were getting the bulk of their recovery in PropCo, so naturally Miller was interested in protecting the lease payments. Miller had been a stubborn negotiator and finally Sambur exploded, "Are we going to just stand here masturbating all over each other or are we going to get a deal done?" The room of perhaps 50 people fell silent. Paul, Weiss and the Blackstone bankers suggested it might be time to end the meeting.

Sambur's fire was not limited to the hedge funds. On a large conference call, Kramer Levin lawyer Danny Eggermann—the senior associate working around the clock on Caesars—pointed out that Sambur wanted more lenient treatment for Apollo than for creditors for a similar clause in a financing document. Sambur—not knowing who Eggermann was—screamed into his phone, "Who the fuck just said that? Who's the fucking wise guy?" Ken Eckstein, Eggermann's boss, softly spoke up to defend his colleague.

In mid-2015, Millstein & Co. was brokering a new RSA between Caesars and the Elliott senior bondholder group. They were close to a deal, with just a single issue outstanding: a guarantee of lease payments from the Caesars OpCo to the PropCo that the bondholders would own. Ken Eckstein, the attorney representing the bondholders, insisted that the guarantee be one of payment, not collection. Miller, as often was the case, said little; but his position was clear. After an hour, the bondholder team left, leaving Jim Millstein and his colleagues, along with Apollo and Paul, Weiss, to debrief.

"That was a good meeting. It sounds like they're going to come around to our point of view that they'll accept the guarantee of collection," Sambur pronounced to the people who remained.

Millstein shook his head. That was decidedly *not* what Elliott had communicated. "David, you and I must have been in different meetings because that's not what they said," Millstein corrected. "They said they'll only accept guarantee of payment."

Sambur glared at Millstein and then started screaming. "Fuck you! Fuck you! FUCK YOU!"

Everyone in the room was mortified. Jim Millstein was old enough to be Sambur's father. He was one of the deans of the restructuring industry, a top staffer in the Obama administration, and, above all, a gentleman.

"David. If that makes you feel good to get all those 'fuck yous' out of your system, keep saying them," Millstein calmly responded.

Sambur then stormed out and everyone else in the room sat there embarrassed.

"You guys are going to deal with him because I'm done," Millstein told his colleagues Brendan Hayes and Daun Chung.

Millstein was not personally offended, but the Caesars situation had turned into a grind. Neither Apollo nor Oaktree/Appaloosa wanted to give an inch, and he was caught in the crossfire.

Millstein occasionally would speak with Rowan or visit him at his office to discuss the case. He even asked the Apollo co-founder to rein in Sambur, who had been a nightmare—not just for Millstein, but for Sprayregen and Kirkland, along with all the creditors who had been dealing with his histrionics for years. The unpleasantness was hurting the prospects of solving the case, since Millstein believed that a solution would require at least some cooperation and good faith.

The Sambur/Rowan dynamic was intriguing. In 2006, Sambur was just in his mid-20s and the junior guy on the team. By 2015, Sambur still reported to Rowan but was now a senior executive. One Caesars banker had happened upon a shouting match between Rowan and Sambur in 2014. The banker later asked Rowan why he tolerated Sambur's seeming insolence. Rowan explained that Apollo encouraged lively debate and that the best ideas should win. It was never personal. Rowan was the ultimate decision-maker on Caesars. And those who were closest to Apollo really believed, despite Rowan's charm and Sambur's rough edges, that *Sambur* was the more pragmatic party, while his boss, *Rowan*, was the militant.

Rowan demurred to Millstein's request. The good cop/bad cop system had its merits, and Rowan was already backchanneling with the likes of Bruce Karsh and David Tepper. There was also deep respect for Sambur within Apollo for keeping Caesars alive for so long. He was flawed, but at the end of the day he embodied what Apollo thought it was: brilliant, unrelenting, and fearless. And if that rubbed other people the wrong way, that was their problem.

IN THE SUMMER OF 2015, an old face emerged in the proceedings. TPG thought it could help break the impasse with the loan holder group since there was far less hostility toward it than Apollo. Rick Schifter was now leading the restructuring effort for the other primary owner of Caesars. Schifter, in his late 60s, had been a lawyer at Arnold & Porter in Washington, DC, where he had met David Bonderman. They had worked together on the Braniff bankruptcy, and Schifter would join TPG in its early years. Schifter was a cerebral man, and his age and demeanor made him Sambur's opposite.

At a meeting over the summer, Schifter, with Rowan and Sambur present, tried to lower the temperature. "Tell us what you need and we'll try to make it happen."

With Schifter's guidance, the loan holders and Apollo finally came to terms. The two parties dispatched their respective lawyers to paper the deal into a formal restructuring support agreement.

The bank loan had largely been cohesive, staying tight to take on Sambur. But a crack would eventually open up. After GSO, the second largest lender was an aggressive hedge fund, Solus Alternative Asset Management, who had a $500 million loan position.

A section of the RSA declared no party of the agreement could support an alternative proposal or "*take any action materially inconsistent with the transactions expressly contemplated by this Agreement... including, without limitation, commencing, or joining with any Person in commencing, any litigation.*"

On the side, as hedge funds do, Solus had quietly purchased a smaller position—less $50 million worth—of Caesars unsecured notes and was secretly helping pay for the pivotal MeehanCombs lawsuit over the bond guarantees. Solus could not, theoretically, on the one hand sign the bank loan RSA and on the other, keep paying for the parent guarantee litigation.

Until this point, Ryan Mollett and the rest of the loan group were not aware that Solus had this side position. Mollett was infuriated that Solus had taken this position without informing him, jeopardizing what he felt was a cohesive group. Patrick Hambrook, the young investor at Solus who was leading the Caesars effort, would connect with Mollett to try and smooth things over. Hambrook was in his early 30s, had ascended from a modest background—the son of a New Hampshire state trooper—and had joined Solus as a gaming industry expert from a small investment bank.

Hambrook explained that the unsecured notes investment was from another "side pocket" fund and not adverse to their loan position, so really it was not relevant. Mollett strongly disagreed and felt deceived. Mollett felt that if the MeehanCombs lawsuit was successful it could hurt the bank group's recovery. Mollett looked into whether he could sue Solus. Ultimately he swallowed his rage and decided it was better to just move on, though the chilliness between him and Hambrook would continue.

On August 21, 2015, Caesars announced the bank loan RSA. It was nominally worth 108 cents on the dollar, an improvement over the 100 cents that was embedded in the bank loan holder-rejected December 2014 RSA with Elliott. Improvements included getting far more in cash recoveries than in new takeback debt and better guarantees on the debt they were taking on the OpCo.

As a joke, the loan holder group presented Ryan Mollett with a set of mock lyrics to Taylor Swift's "We Are Never Ever Getting Back Together" as a memento, since Mollett had once mentioned that he felt like he and Sambur were living a Taylor Swift song.

Whatever the brain damage, the bank loan RSA was a win for Apollo. It took too long to accomplish, but they had deals in place with the two most senior pieces of the Caesars capital structure, which together represented $11 billion of a total $18 billion of debt. Rowan and Sambur finally had some momentum in the case. Caesars had even signed up an RSA with a splinter group of second-lien bondholders that contemplated a twenty-seven-cent recovery. Those signatories were less than half of the group, and this RSA would expire quickly. But it showed that not every junior bondholder was following the scorched-earth path blazed by Appaloosa and Oaktree.

MR. ROWAN GOES
TO WASHINGTON

"I have Amanda Fischer from Maxine Waters's staff on the line," Sarah McIntosh said from her boss's office doorway. Marblegate Asset Management was located in a sleek but nondescript office building in the hedge fund capital of the world—Greenwich, Connecticut—just across the street from the town hall. A classic distressed investing hedge fund, Marblegate scoured America for struggling companies whose troubles presented an opportunity. McIntosh worked for Andrew Milgram, the firm's chief investment officer, and on November 30, 2015, as usual, he was going through a list of distressed retailers that could be headed for a cliff.

Milgram turned to McIntosh, raising his eyebrows and giving her his full attention. It was the second unexpected phone call that day. Earlier, a *New York Times* reporter had called asking if Marblegate had any thoughts on some of the language that was being inserted into an upcoming piece of must-pass legislation. Milgram had no idea what she was talking about at the time. But now the head of the House Financial Services Committee was reaching out? Something was up. "Put her through," Milgram told McIntosh.

Like the *New York Times*, Fischer wanted to know what Milgram thought of an insertion into the Transportation Bill, a multi-hundred-billion-dollar legislation that would keep funding for the nation's infrastructure. *"What does this have to do with me?"* Milgram thought. The congressional aide explained that Milgram and Marblegate had been found through a Google search as parties who might care about this arcane securities rule that was about to be gutted.

Then it all made sense. Marblegate's investment in $14 million worth of Education Management Corporation bonds and the subsequent lawsuit against the company had turned into a fight over the interpretation of the Trust Indenture Act of 1939. Marblegate's lawsuit had been getting traction in court, to the surprise of many in the restructuring community. Now Fischer was explaining to Milgram that the TIA had become a two-front war, migrating from the judicial branch to the legislative branch. Proposed changes to the TIA that would have undercut Marblegate's legal case had been slipped into the Transportation Bill. If enacted, they would retroactively apply to existing restructurings like Education Management.

Milgram's heart raced. If the bill became law, his lawsuit would be moot, and his investment wiped out. The TIA had nothing to do with transportation; this amendment was pure pork, a "rider" being inserted in the dead of night. Milgram's shock quickly turned into action, as he sent an SOS message to Bracewell LLP, the lobbying group that he used in Washington, DC. He explained the situation, and the Bracewell team went to work.

Bracewell learned that the amendment came from the office of Richard Shelby, the powerful Republican senator from Alabama who chaired the Rules and Administration Committee and who sat on the Senate Banking Committee. The TIA amendment language, which was just two pages—a mere 166 words—dropped into a 491-page bill, had been passed along from Shelby's office with eight other items deemed as "non-controversial." It was a fluke that it got back to someone like Milgram who cared enough to sound the alarm.

Milgram's partner at Marblegate, the legendary investment banker-turned-investor Henry Miller, alerted his friend Paul Singer at Elliott Management, while Milgram informed his other contacts in Washington, DC. Soon the word was out. Still, there was little time to get in front of the transportation bill, officially titled the Fixing America's Surface Transportation Act, or FAST Act—an apt name for the frenzy over re-writing the TIA.

When *Politico* contacted Milgram, he had a statement ready: "We were very concerned to learn that Senators working on the federal transportation bill have added a completely unrelated financial amendment that would retroactively overturn seventy-six years of legal precedent established under the Trust Indenture Act (TIA), directly impact several high-profile court cases pending adjudication and remove vital protections for minority investors for which the law was created. This amendment directly undermines legal due process and Constitutional procedure."

It turned out that Bracewell partner Scott Segal knew Bharat

Ramamurti, a top aide for Elizabeth Warren, the first-term senator from Massachusetts. Warren had a strong interest in consumer protection and had been investigating for-profit colleges. Warren also happened to be a former bankruptcy law professor at the Harvard Law School.

Warren did not like what she saw and objected to the amendment. Shelby did not feel strongly about the TIA legislation—the addition to the FAST Act was simply the result of usual horse-trading—so he dropped it at the first sign of controversy. On December 4, 2015, President Obama signed the five-year, $305 billion bill into law with just hours to spare before the scheduled expiration of transportation spending—without the TIA language.

Milgram breathed a sigh of relief. But the next day, Bracewell came back to him with bad news. The senator behind the TIA amendment was not Shelby, but one of the most powerful Democrats in Washington: Senate Minority Leader Harry Reid. Reid had the sway to bring back the TIA legislation.

Milgram's head was still spinning that week as he drove to a reception at Greenwich Country Day, a private school in one of the wealthiest enclaves in America. Milgram's long-time friend and fellow Greenwich resident Carney Hawks was at the same reception. Their kids both attended the school. Milgram relayed what he had discovered regarding this gambit to change the law in order to prevail in bankruptcy negotiations.

Hawks's firm Brigade Capital, a much larger hedge fund than Marblegate, had hundreds of millions of dollars at stake in the legislation. Brigade's bonds in question were in the Caesars OpCo, whose bondholders had their guarantee litigation lawsuits making their way through the courts as well. Any retroactive changes to the TIA would erase those suits.

But Hawks had a solution: Hawks's fraternity brother at the University of Virginia, Republican congressman Andy Barr of Kentucky, needed to hear about this, he told Milgram. If they could fight it in the House, they could halt any TIA reform that made it past the Senate.

KAJ VAZALES PRACTICALLY RAN DOWN the hallway in the Los Angeles offices of Oaktree Capital Management to reach the office of John Frank. A lawyer by training, Frank had been with Oaktree for more than fourteen years. As a vice chairman, he was one of the top four executives running the company along with Howard Marks, Bruce Karsh, and Jay Wintrob. A savvy political operator, he led any effort on behalf of Oaktree that would require pressing the flesh in Washington. He once had been an aide to Congressman Robert Drinan, who also happened to be a Jesuit priest.

"John, we've got a problem," said Vazales. "They're trying to change the law."

Vazales quickly explained that, while it was not clear exactly how or who, someone was trying to amend the Trust Indenture Act, the securities law at the foundation of Oaktree's own legal arguments in the Caesars Entertainment parent guarantee litigation. Frank figured Apollo was involved, and if that was how Marc Rowan wanted to play, Oaktree could, too. Oaktree had its own lobbyist in Washington, Jim Gould of Ogilvy Government Relations, and he would coordinate with the lobbyist working with Marblegate.

Frank and Gould learned that the lobbyist pushing the TIA amendment was none other than Brownstein Hyatt—which had been working with Caesars for years. The firm's co-founder Norm Brownstein was close with the Apollo founders, and the private equity firm had relied on Brownstein for work across many investments. Frank Schreck, the Nevada lawyer who had eased Apollo and TPG's path through the gaming licensing process, had even merged his practice into Brownstein Hyatt's. Apollo's fingerprints were all over this TIA legislation. Marc Rowan would eventually go himself to see California Representatives Maxine Waters and Kevin McCarthy.

Caesars had also needed a technical expert to craft the language and stump for them in the press. They hired Ken Klee, a legend of the bankruptcy bar. Klee helped write the Bankruptcy Reform Act of 1978, and had worked for years at Stutman Treister, the Los Angeles bankruptcy boutique where Bruce Bennett had cut his teeth, and was on the faculty at UCLA Law School. Klee had also become known in the bankruptcy world for his hobby of alternative medicine, specifically as a crystal healer. He told the *New York Times* that there was nothing untoward about the process to revise the TIA, saying the amendment was "just a correction to a recent misinterpretation of the statute—not a wholesale revision of the Trust Indenture Act."

By the time Oaktree's effort was in full swing, Milgram and Bracewell had already helped get the amendment removed from the Transportation Bill. Now, Oaktree was hearing chatter that Brownstein was trying to get it shoved into the Omnibus Appropriations Act, the required annual spending bill that was set to approve more than a trillion dollars in spending for the next year. The bill was up for vote in a matter of days. Harry Reid was pushing for it openly, and

Elizabeth Warren, who had helped keep it out of the transportation bill, had backed off in deference to her party leader.

When Frank met Gould in Washington and first started discussing it with lawmakers, they were told, "Look, if Harry Reid wants this, it's going to happen. It's a hopeless quest." Even worse for Oaktree's cause, the Brownstein lobbyists framed the amendment as something that they needed to save casino jobs in his state—a misleading claim, as the fight was really about private equity firms and hedge funds clashing over whose securities were more valuable. But Caesars had the home-field advantage and, like in the gaming commission hearings in 2014 where the second-lien bondholders tried to halt the Four Properties transaction, it was not easy to play the victim card.

Still, Frank was confident that if lawmakers simply read the amendment—it was just two pages after all—they'd drop it. Frank made the rounds to the offices of as many members of Congress as he could. Frank, with a deep authoritative voice, a firm grasp of the political process, and serious financial pedigree, would paint it as something that might embarrass a lawmaker later. "This is absurd. It's no way to draft legislation, literally in the middle of the night, literally with no notice," was his pitch. Howard Marks, the Oaktree founder, also made similar calls to the US senators he was acquainted with.

The counternarrative that Oaktree was driving was not only legislative, but also in the court of public opinion. Adam Levitin, a Georgetown University law professor and former student of Elizabeth Warren's at Harvard, wrote a letter to Congressional leaders, expressing concern that the TIA should not so rashly be amended. Co-signing the letter dated December 8 were sixteen other academic luminaries from across the US. They wrote, "...Several of us believe that the Trust Indenture Act should be amended, but not in the way proposed...There have been no hearings on the matter, no opportunity to hear from a diverse group of experts or the public, and no attempt to establish a legislative record...[W]e urge you to postpone any amendment of the Trust Indenture Act until after legislative hearings that enable more deliberate and careful considerations."

By this time, Carney Hawks had made good on his promise and connected Milgram's team with Rep. Andy Barr from Kentucky. Barr had helped convince enough Republicans that this was not the way they wanted law to be made now that they had the majority in the House and Senate, after the 2014 elections. Barr, along with twenty-two other Republican members of the House on December 10, sent a letter to Speaker Paul Ryan and Majority Leader Kevin McCarthy. "[S]everal Members of Congress are supporting inserting a policy rider that would retroactively narrow the rights of bondholders under the Trust Indenture Act under the guise of providing flexibility for corporate restructures," the letter stated. "While updating this Depression-era law might be warranted, to do so through an unvetted appropriations rider would be inappropriate."

Appaloosa's Jim Bolin wrote a letter to the heads of the House and the Senate, introducing himself as the "chairman" of the official second-lien noteholder committee in the Caesars bankruptcy. Bolin called out Apollo and TPG: "The primary beneficiaries of the amendment will be private equity sponsors of OpCo's parent company, Caesars Entertainment Corporation (CEC), which has been seeking to avoid liability for an 'irrevocable' and 'unconditional' guarantee by CEC that was offered to incentivize the purchase by investors of more than $10 billion in OpCo's debt."

Finally, John Frank of Oaktree corralled some of the largest bond investors in the country, including BlackRock, Pimco, and T. Rowe Price, to join the cause. Frank penned a letter to Mitch McConnell, Harry Reid, Paul Ryan, and Nancy Pelosi.

By the time the Omnibus Appropriations Act was signed into law on December 15, 2015, the TIA amendment had been rendered controversial enough that it was not included in the bill. The fight had been as fierce as anything experienced in the Chicago bankruptcy court. And it showed that both sides in Caesars were unafraid to take their conflict to any theater to gain a decisive advantage.

Though the TIA language did not make it into the final bill, the broader influence of the private equity firms in the legislative process continued to come to light. Caesars was not just lobbying Congress over changes in the TIA. And ironically, there was a piece of legislation that both the private equity firms and hedge fund creditors were in complete agreement on. The reorganization plan called for the creation of a new PropCo which would be structured as a "real estate investment trust." REITs avoided corporate-level tax, and that advantage made them attractive to all sorts of companies far afield from property. REITs were also viewed as a tax giveaway, and there was a push to close what was viewed as a loophole to unintended beneficiaries—a list which included Caesars.

On December 7, a provision was included in the Omnibus spending bill to restrict tax-free REIT spinoffs like the one Caesars was contemplating. Lobbyists including Norm Brownstein sprang into action, and even drafted the "fix" to save the tax-free Caesars REIT spin—along with one that was just approved at Energy Future Holdings, the Texas utility previously known as TXU, which was owned by

TPG and other private equity firms. According to a *New York Times* article, a familiar name had led the charge: "[Harry] Reid played a central role in getting the change made, participants in the process said…It was nicknamed by some involved as the 'Caesars/TXU carve out.'"

A "grandfather clause" that allowed REIT spinoffs already in the works made it into the final appropriations bill that was passed days later, and all sides of the Caesars fight breathed a sigh of relief.

AS BAD AS DC HAD been for Apollo, courtrooms in Chicago and New York had not been particularly friendly either. Judge Goldgar, even after Jim Millstein's "greatest messes of our time" warning in June 2015, had allowed the parent guarantee litigation to move forward. Caesars had appealed the decision to a federal district court, which in October 2015 affirmed Goldgar's decision to not implement an injunction. That district court decision was then appealed to the Seventh Circuit Court of Appeals. The appeals court ruled, in a decision written by the famed jurist Richard Posner, that Goldgar had erred in his reasoning. Posner wrote that "since successful resolution of disputes arising in bankruptcy proceedings is one of the [Bankruptcy] Code's central objectives," an injunction would be appropriate.

In February 2016, Goldgar relented and agreed to implement a temporary injunction to last for 60 days after the examiner's report was published. The injunction was paramount because both the Marblegate case and the Caesars MeehanCombs case had traction in the federal court system, and were on their way to forcing the Caesars parent to make good on its guarantee of $12 billion of OpCo bonds.

PART IV

ROLL OF THE DICE

The Examiner is a great job: Everyone is nice to you…until the report comes out. Richard Davis had grown sheepish as 2015 progressed and he started his work. His pending report on the string of deals Apollo and TPG executed at Caesars before the bankruptcy filing, whatever its conclusion, was primed to be the inflection point of the case. His findings very well could tip the scales on whether the hedge fund creditors or private equity firm owners were going to win or lose billions of dollars. For much of 2015, Davis's investigation was a shadow war running parallel to the bankruptcy proceedings in Chicago.

After being selected in March, Davis hired a team of lawyers and financial experts to assist his investigation. His legal team would come from the New York office of the Chicago-based firm Winston & Strawn. His finance consultants came from Alvarez & Marsal, a consulting firm that specialized in restructuring and valuation work. Each would contribute dozens of professionals working around the clock. Davis wanted to work fast and file a report within months. The various Caesars parties were waiting on his verdict on the pre-bankruptcy assets sales to inform their negotiations. But Davis slowly realized the sheer scale of the project—examining more than ten complex financial deals—was not going to happen that quickly, even with 50 people working for him.

The project was not just about crunching financial data and parsing bankruptcy and corporate law. Davis wanted to get a feel for the casino business. He visited Las Vegas and Atlantic City over the summer of 2015. John Payne, the longtime Caesars executive and then CEO of the OpCo, was Davis's tour guide. Davis noticed that Payne seemed to know all the employees' names at the properties, from the executive suite to the valets.

The documents Davis and his team needed to review and analyze totaled nearly nine million pages. But just getting key documents was its own ordeal. Paul, Weiss had for years simultaneously represented both the Caesars parent—owned by TPG and Apollo—as well as the Caesars OpCo. The law firm believed that joint representation entitled it to claim attorney-client privilege on a vast array of paperwork relevant to the investigation. The documents in question were expected to be among the most interesting and revealing in understanding all the controversial dealings before the bankruptcy. Davis was preparing to sue Paul, Weiss to force them to produce the material. The sides eventually came to a compromise: the disputed documents would be handed over on an "examiner's eyes only" basis, though Davis would be free to quote the material in his final report.

Beyond reading reams of documents, Davis could interview all the key players regarding their versions of events. The former Watergate prosecutor had some decisions to make on procedures. This was not a court of law. He needed witnesses to be candid while he asked difficult questions whose answers would be recorded in some manner. After Davis had been selected, he called previous bankruptcy examiners in other cases to get their advice.

One common recommendation: ensure that interviews were transcribed. Davis had elected not to put witnesses under oath because it added unnecessary tension. Transcripts, however, ensured that there would be no questions about the testimony, and it allowed Davis to share the results of the interviews with the creditors' committees, some of whom were interested in conducting their own parallel investigations. Davis would interview nearly 100 individuals from across Caesars, Apollo, TPG, Paul, Weiss, and the various investment banks and hedge fund creditors that had been involved in Caesars before the bankruptcy.

By fall, Davis, who had taken an office at Winston & Strawn's office in the MetLife building above Grand Central Terminal, had begun the formal interviews. He insisted that he do most of the key interviews himself. From his early days as a prosecutor, he had believed it was important to roll up his sleeves. Over the summer of 2015, Davis started out with some informal interviews as documents started to trickle in. These early interviews were not transcribed and were just for Davis and his team to start to understand the company and its situation.

Besides the interviews and document review, Davis wanted an

interactive process where all the players would make their respective case directly to him. Bruce Bennett viewed the examiner process as a form of litigation, a chance for him to zealously advocate for the second-lien bondholders. Jones Day and Houlihan Lokey made detailed presentations to the examiner team, arguing that damages from the Growth, CERP, and Four Properties transactions, along with several others, totaled more than $10 billion. These figures were clearly dramatized, but even a third of that figure would be a big victory. Kirkland's existing settlement contemplated only a $1.4 billion contribution from the Caesars parent—and nothing from Apollo and TPG specifically.

In early December, Davis had decided to share his preliminary findings with all sides in separate meetings. The final report was a few months away, and there were still follow-up interviews and new documents streaming in. But Davis wanted to at least give an indication of the direction he was headed. He prepared an identical thirty-two-page script to share with each side in the case. Davis even used the same jokes in each of the meetings, prompting David Neier—the lead partner from Winston—to tell him he should at least mix up his humor among the groups.

Davis would lead off saying, "All views [are] preliminary and assume that word 'preliminary' is present whenever I describe a conclusion. In a sense what I am presenting here can be viewed as my current working hypotheses as I work to complete the Investigation…I very much want input on what I identify as open issues as well as on whatever you disagree with—would like that by no later than 12/18. [The] purpose of today, however, is not to engage in those debates—today I will be devoting extensive time to outlining where I am."

Davis allowed the groups to provide any last feedback in January 2016 before he published his final report. After a tense, ugly year of fighting, there was also hope that the parties might decide to settle their differences before the Examiner's report saw the light of day.

"WE ARE JUST NOT GETTING there, Jim," Marc Rowan, calm as always, explained. Jim Millstein had hoped that cooler heads could prevail. Millstein and Brendan Hayes of Millstein & Co., in their latest shuttle diplomacy mission, were trying to find the appetite to settle the dispute between Caesars and the second-lien bondholders. Would forty-two cents on the dollar do it? Those junior bonds had traded down to around ten cents on the dollar before the bankruptcy at the time of the January 2015 filing. A year later, those bonds had rallied to above thirty cents. With Richard Davis's report due in weeks, it was worth a shot to try to preempt the findings.

But Apollo was not game, at least at a price above forty cents. That figure was far too rich for Rowan. The examiner's report may not be so unfavorable anyway, which would send those junior bond prices crashing and shift all the momentum back to Apollo.

Bruce Bennett's clients—Appaloosa and Oaktree—were as stubborn as Apollo. Tuck Hardie of Houlihan Lokey, the investment banking firm representing the group, was in touch with Steve Zelin, the Blackstone banker representing the Caesars parent. Would forty-seven cents do it, wondered Hardie? Forty-two cents was a non-starter so no, forty-seven cents was not going to work.

Low-grade settlement talks had gone on for some time, but there always seemed to be a ten-cent gap worth roughly $500 million. If Apollo offered twenty-eight cents, the bondholders were at thirty-eight cents. Apollo goes to thirty-seven cents, but now the ask had jumped to forty-seven cents. Neither side really wanted to compromise. Even with so many creditors in the Caesars capital structure, the central fight would continue to be a bitter grudge match with Apollo on one side and Appaloosa and Oaktree on the other.

For senior creditors or those, like Canyon Capital, who were holding multiple pieces of Caesars debt and equity, this duel was the nightmare scenario. Whatever the views on Mark Frissora as CEO, the Caesars business was undoubtedly recovering under his watch. Caesars' system-wide EBITDA had surged in 2015, up by a third. Average daily hotel rates in Vegas for the year jumped by 12 percent as the room refurbishment and implementation of resort fees took effect. 401(k) contributions and merit bonuses for employees were able to be restored. The best bet for these creditors to keep the momentum going was to get OpCo out of bankruptcy as quickly as possible without sweating the terms too much.

Appaloosa thought the group, based on their analysis of the value of the fraud claims, had a reasonable ask above seventy cents. Still, the second-lien committee had multiple members, and there was some diversity of viewpoints. Centerbridge was most willing to cut a deal. The bulk of its position was acquired in late 2014 when the second-lien bonds were trading below fifteen cents. At forty cents, Centerbridge would nearly triple its investment.

Even Kaj Vazales, Ken Liang's colleague at Oaktree, was on the fence. "Look how bad we are going to appear if we settle before the report. It was our idea for the examiner. It was our idea for the involuntary. We joined the second-lien committee. We've made our bet," Liang told Vazales in a pep talk.

The only thing left to do was wait for the report to land.

29

THE IDES OF MARCH

Howard Marks, the Oaktree co-founder, was busy on March 15, 2016. Oaktree was holding its biennial investor conference at the Beverly Hilton—the same place where Marks had attended Drexel's yearly Predator's Ball conference in the 1980s. The investor conference was a big deal to Marks. It was the chance to schmooze longtime clients and share his thoughts on the investment climate.

But March 15 would also be Caesars' judgment day, as the long-awaited examiner's report was expected to be released. (It was mere coincidence that the report's release would coincide with the anniversary of Julius Caesar's death. The report was originally expected in February.)

"Howard, do you want the PDF or should I just print it out for you?" Marks's Oaktree colleague Ken Liang asked.

During the festivities, Marks found the time to ping Liang about the status of the report every few hours.

Caesars had become personal. Marks's longtime friend Leon Black was on the other side, and the bad blood that had developed between the firms was very real. Even Marks's wife, Nancy, was periodically asking about the case since she was close with Black's wife Debra. "Tell Nancy that they sold our casinos for $1 to themselves and we are asking for it back. That's all," Liang would say.

Leon Black had, even in person, accused Marks of putting Oaktree's Caesars investment ahead of their personal relationship by not settling for the forty-cent offer on the table. Marks was taken aback: he wasn't then involved in the Caesars project. Moreover, Oaktree had been a longtime Caesars investor, not the opportunist Black accused the firm of being. Regardless, Oaktree had a fiduciary duty to its investors just as Apollo had a duty to its.

Marks wasn't surprised by Black's fury. When it came to business, he believed Apollo was ruthless and Black would put profits above all else. After the encounter with Black, Marks had his colleagues explain the details of the Caesars investment, a rare instance at this point in his career that he chose to get into the weeds. Marks then became convinced that the fight really pitted "blackhats"—Apollo—against "whitehats" —Oaktree and Appaloosa.

"Just email it to me," Marks instructed Liang, nearing midnight in Los Angeles. The report was posted to the bankruptcy docket earlier in the evening. Davis's effort would keep a lot of people up all night on March 15—perhaps for several nights.

The report clocked in at more than 1,800 pages, including all the exhibits and appendices. Given the millions of pages and thousands of hours of witness interviews, the sheer volume of work was not surprising. Yet in Davis's experience, even the most complex cases often hinged on just a handful of documents. In this case, Davis had his Eureka moment in late 2015, on the Amtrak returning from Baltimore where his daughter attended college.

In October 2012, Apollo had created a presentation that had described the creation of Caesars Growth Partners. In the presentation, Apollo discussed how Caesars Growth Partners would be a "'war chest' upon a potential restructuring event" and "a transaction like this is the only way we see it to 'have our cake and eat it too.'" That deck was never shared with TPG, and the slide with these most inflammatory comments were excised as a part of a presentation shared with Loveman. This was the smoking gun.

The presentation crystalized Davis's conclusions: Apollo's complex deals at Caesars—the Growth transaction, CERP, the Four Properties deal, the B-7 term loan, the Unsecured Notes deal—while nominally designed to help Caesars generate cash and extend runway, were really about positioning Apollo against creditors in an inevitable restructuring fight.

Davis opened his report dated March 15, 2016, stating, "The principal question being investigated is whether in structuring and implementing these transactions assets were removed from OpCo to the detriment of OpCo and its creditors. The simple answer to this question is 'yes'…The potential damages from those claims considered 'reasonable' or 'strong' range from $3.6 billion to $5.1 billion."

It was simply a devastating finding for Apollo. Davis estimated the maximum liability from the Growth transaction at $593 million, the CERP transaction at $427 million, and a staggering $1.7 billion for the Four Properties and B-7 deals combined. Davis said several of these big transactions gave rise to claims for the grave "actual fraudulent transfer" where there was intent to "hinder," "delay," or "defraud" creditors.

The report was not legally binding and was not admissible into court. Still, it was an attempt at independent fact-finding where all sides had the chance to make their case to Davis. And Davis, who had spent the previous year hearing Apollo's version of events, ended up buying very little of it.

The findings in the report were not just about Apollo and TPG selling casinos cheaply to themselves. Rather, Davis developed an intricate narrative about a massive corporate governance failure driven by Apollo. The Caesars OpCo, according to Davis's analysis, had been insolvent since the end of 2008, the year the buyout closed. Once in this so-called "zone of insolvency," the OpCo legally deserved a board of directors distinct and independent from the Caesars parent board—dominated by Apollo and TPG—to safeguard the interests of creditors.

The multi-billion-dollar liability estimate not only reflected fraud charges, but also included charges of breaches of fiduciary duty against the directors of the Caesars parent and the OpCo as well as "aiding and abetting" those fiduciary duty breaches by Apollo and TPG. These allegations about fiduciary duty were grave. The transactions were then to be held to "entire fairness," a higher standard of legal review in Delaware corporate courts. Under the entire fairness standard, Caesars would have to demonstrate that the transactions both met the test for a "fair price" and a "fair process," an exceedingly high bar. Moreover, the breaches of fiduciary duty that Davis identified—the duty of loyalty—exposed Rowan, Sambur, Bonderman, Loveman, and other Caesars directors to personal liability.

While the eye-popping numbers garnered the most initial attention, the report was most damning in its description—painstakingly detailed—of how Rowan and Sambur had executed each transaction. Even when there was no finding of liability, each was to Apollo's benefit. Davis wrote, "in assessing the actions of the Caesars parent and the Sponsors it is important to remember that the Sponsors are among the most financially savvy investors in the country and both TPG and Apollo have extensive experience in dealing with financially troubled companies. This expertise was applied in connection with their investment in Caesars and, indeed, during the relevant period Apollo was the *de facto* chief financial officer of the Caesars OpCo."

Davis continuted, "In the transactions at issue, the chief executive officer of the Caesars parent [Loveman] and the Caesars OpCo and other senior management also deferred to the Sponsors on key issues...Indeed, it appears that the Sponsors' past success in successfully negotiating resolutions involving troubled companies was a factor in their assuming they could do so here without the need to pay adequate attention to the requirements associated with being fiduciaries of an insolvent entity."

Davis's work confirmed the domination of Caesars by Rowan and Sambur in particular. In his liability estimates, Davis stated the claims against Apollo for aiding and abetting breaches of fiduciary duty could be worth between $2.6 billion and $3.8 billion, while the same claims against TPG were worth just $1.6 billion to $2.6 billion.

Davis harshly criticized Apollo, TPG, and Caesars' management and board over their understanding of solvency, the fundamental issue that should have determined how the private equity firms should have acted as the business deteriorated. According to one of Davis's analyses, the Caesars OpCo, between 2008 and 2014, was insolvent by a magnitude ranging from nearly $3 billion to $12 billion. Three formal arithmetic tests existed for insolvency—the balance sheet test, the cash flow test, and the adequate capital test.

"...[I]n many cases the Caesars parent and the sponsors either indicated ignorance of the relevant legal tests or simply seemed to ignore them based on their view that they believed the OpCo's long term debt could be addressed over time although...there was no realistic possibility that the debt could ever be repaid at anything close to face value."

Marc Rowan, for example, said in a November 2015 interview with the examiner, "...to me I look at normalized EBITDA and normalized growth rates, does the company have an opportunity to have assets equal or exceed liabilities as [the economic cycle] turns..."

Whatever the technical definitions of solvency, Davis's review of documents, emails, and presentations showed to him that Apollo, TPG, and Paul, Weiss had been aware for years that the Caesars OpCo was almost certainly doomed. Yet the company and its owners did little to protect creditors, choosing instead to favor their own equity investment.

One key subtext of the report was just how much Apollo had taken over Caesars. TPG had largely ceded the financial functions to Rowan and Sambur. Davis did not care much for David Bonderman, the TPG co-founder, after interviewing him. Davis found him to be like an eccentric uncle who was not sharp on the details surrounding Caesars.

Davis did take special notice of one comment Bonderman had made in his session. "What, as I understand it, we were trying to accomplish was to maximize the ability to pay debt, and to fund the capital needs of the Company. And the way to do that we were contemplating at that time was to take those assets which had excess cash flow, you might call it, or weren't in need of influx of cash flow, and put those in a place where they may be used to pay debt," Bonderman said, explaining the formation of Caesars Growth.

To Davis, this was tantamount to a confession. Apollo and TPG indeed were attempting to pluck the best assets out of the Caesars OpCo for themselves. Bonderman's view that those hand-picked casinos could pay off OpCo debt made little sense, since $18 billion of debt remained in the entity those casinos had just left.

On the other hand, Davis was highly impressed with Marc Rowan. Of the nearly 100 witnesses who were interviewed, the Apollo co-founder was the person Davis enjoyed the most. Rowan was razor sharp, charming, glib, warm, friendly, unpretentious, and displayed zero defensiveness about Apollo's conduct. Davis knew if this case ever went to a trial, the billionaire would be an extremely persuasive figure.

But even Marc Rowan, for all his gifts, could not save Apollo from Davis's wrath. All the contemporaneous evidence, in the form of emails, memos, and presentations, was overwhelming. But perhaps Apollo's biggest problem would be Rowan's young henchman, David Sambur. If Rowan was the person Davis enjoyed speaking with the most, then Sambur proved to be his least. In his interview, Sambur came off as slick and arrogant with a too-cute answer for everything.

The veracity of Sambur's testimony proved troubling enough that Davis had the Apollo executive sit for interviews on multiple separate occasions between October 2015 and January 2016, more than any other witness. His early interviews had been problematic. Davis and Winston & Strawn considered putting Sambur under oath, though they decided against it. Sambur's explanation of the circumstances of the 2014 $1.75 billion B-7 term loan financing proved to be most controversial. As a part of the transaction, the Caesars OpCo had released the parent guarantee on more than $10 billion of bonds. Davis was curious to learn whose idea it was first to release the guarantee—Apollo or the key lenders, GSO and BlackRock.

Sambur had insisted the release was the loan investors' idea, and that Apollo was forced to comply in order to get the much-needed infusion of cash. It was clear that releasing the guarantee was a bad outcome for bond investors and a huge boon for shareholders in the Caesars parent, like Apollo, who were suddenly relieved of a multi-billion-dollar obligation that would have wiped them out. The loanholders themselves also were beneficiaries since they kept their own guarantee and no longer had to share it with bondholders.

Sambur's problem was that Davis had accumulated a pile of other documents and presentations that indicated Apollo had contemplated releasing the guarantee as early as the fall of 2013.

Ryan Mollett of GSO and a BlackRock executive had insisted it was Apollo's idea to release the guarantee, and were furious that Sambur tried to pin it on them. The bond guarantee release, even if a benefit to lenders, was not a high priority to those firms because, as the most senior creditor, there was enough collateral in the form of casinos to cover their investment. When he re-called Sambur to ask him again about the B-7, Davis hoped that Sambur would correct himself. Instead, Sambur doubled down. At that moment Davis knew much of Sambur's testimony was not credible. Many believed the overall harshness of the examiner's report toward Apollo stemmed from Davis's personal distaste for the young executive half his age.

Davis also took aim at the machinery around Apollo and TPG, particularly the investment bankers and corporate lawyers who had blessed all the wheeling-and-dealing. Davis was shocked to see white shoe firms attach their brands to analysis he found lazy and shoddy.

The report noted how in the Growth transaction, Evercore's final fairness opinion used financial projections that were nearly a year old. Evercore had then failed to account for the Britney Spears/Planet Hollywood residency cash flows in an attempt to quickly close the deal. In the CERP transaction, Perella Weinberg had twisted itself into a pretzel to sign off on the transfer out of OpCo of the Linq and Octavius Tower for peanuts. And in the Four Properties sale, Centerview had used the downwardly revised projections in its analysis to complete the deal at a cheap valuation.

Davis also was sufficiently outraged enough by the investment banks to spend a section of the report explaining the structural problems that undermined the credibility of their financial analysis: The bankers relied on the projections that management provided, often doing little independent due diligence surrounding the reasonableness of the numbers. The fairness opinions were full of disclaimers where bankers avoided being accountable for their work. Moreover, the deal fees often ratcheted upwards when a deal was closed, creating implicit pressure to agree on valuations that were just good enough to get the parties to sign on the dotted line.

Still, Davis's harshest views toward the professional advisors were not toward a Wall Street investment bank, but rather a law firm.

THIS IS UNUSUAL; LEWIS CLAYTON *is going to help defend depositions and then going to have to testify himself?* This strange situation developed in 2015 as Richard Davis realized Paul, Weiss's legal advice to Caesars over the years was going to be the key storyline in his investigation. Paul, Weiss and its superstar, curmudgeon litigator, Lewis Clayton, were, simultaneously, representing Caesars in the examiner process. Davis had met Clayton for the first time on a flight to Chicago in March 2015, and he noted that Clayton had a first-class seat while he was flying in economy at the back of the plane.

Paul, Weiss and its core team who had been representing Apollo for years had been advising both the Caesars parent and the Caesars OpCo. There was not necessarily anything improper about concurrently working with a parent and subsidiary under ordinary circumstances. But as the financial problems at Caesars cascaded, the interests of Apollo and the two Caesars entities diverged into three distinct directions.

It had also become a tricky situation in the examiner investigation, as Paul, Weiss became one of Davis's targets while actively defending its client, the Caesars parent. The law firm had initially objected to sharing all the documents that Davis requested and only a lengthy negotiation prevented Davis from going to court to get the papers he wanted (document production delays had been a general issue as 350,000 pages from Apollo/TPG arrived in late January).

By the time his report had been published, Davis had devoted a subsection in his executive summary to Paul, Weiss's role in the string of transactions he had investigated. The section proved to be as explosive as any allegations made toward Apollo. In the December preview meetings prior to publication, Davis had not telegraphed any specific emphasis on Paul, Weiss. But just before the report was published, Davis, as a courtesy, called Brad Karp, the Paul, Weiss chairman whom he knew well, to tell him where the report would come out. It was a message of bad news and good news. Davis said he had concluded that the law firm was conflicted in representing both the Caesars Parent and the OpCo. Still, any legal claims against Paul, Weiss—which by now had retained an outside law firm, WilmerHale, to represent it—would be weak.

"During this entire period Apollo also was a very significant client of Paul, Weiss on matters unrelated to Caesars. This fact was not known to the independent directors of the Caesars parent. The Caesars General Counsel was aware of this and believed that Paul, Weiss was more responsive to the Apollo (and TPG) directors than they were to him. Neither O'Melveny & Meyers [where several Paul, Weiss lawyers had represented Apollo] nor Paul, Weiss has identified any retention letter relating to its representation of the Caesars OpCo, and it appears that none exists…the Examiner has concluded that probably by the Fall of 2012 and more clearly by the Fall of 2013 Paul, Weiss did have a conflict of interest in representing the Caesars parent and the Caesars OpCo in at least some of the relevant transactions…once such a divergence of interests occurs, a lawyer can only undertake or continue representing multiple clients if it is clear that the lawyer can competently represent both clients and if both clients provide informed consent based on a full disclosure by the lawyer of the issues involved in the simultaneous representation. Here it does not seem that either requirement was satisfied."

Importantly, Davis also detailed why any legal claims against Paul, Weiss would be "weak": any judgment against the firm would require the firm to have had knowledge at the time it was acting improperly. Still, the damage was done. Davis detailed multiple instances starting in 2012 when Paul, Weiss was in possession of financial information or presentations that showed that the Caesars OpCo was on notice about a possible insolvency, or was even advising the Caesars management and board on legal risks associated with bankruptcy and insolvency.

Davis even broaching the idea of malpractice, not to mention the aiding and abetting of breaches of fiduciary duty, was extraordinary. The report appeared to describe a lengthy conspiracy between Apollo and its trusted law firm to siphon value from creditors. And Paul, Weiss had either participated in the conspiracy or its advice was not good enough to prevent its key client from facing billions of dollars of potential liability.

The most concerning Paul, Weiss revelation from the report came from its ostensible client, the Caesars company. Tim Donovan, the Caesars general counsel, shared his view with Davis that Paul, Weiss was working more for Apollo than for the company. Apollo had become Paul, Weiss's largest single client by 2016, accounting for nearly a tenth of its revenue. The broader ties between the two firms were only growing. The firm had effectively become in-house counsel to Apollo with Paul, Weiss lawyers working Apollo deals, fund formation activities, and litigation matters.

Lawyers from Paul, Weiss were being "seconded" to Apollo and working out of the private equity firm's offices at 9 West 57th Street. Paul, Weiss had even created an "Apollo practice group," where several lawyers within the firm worked on routine legal matters for Apollo. There was an enormous amount of work generated for Paul, Weiss—by 2015, Apollo was managing more than $100 billion, had multiple funds and strategies, and owned dozens of portfolio companies. Deal lawyers even described what had become the de facto path to partnership at Paul, Weiss: Achieve excellence in two of three areas—public company M&A, private equity transactions, or Apollo work.

Apollo was a demanding client. The work had to be done quickly and perfectly. But it was often interesting, highly lucrative work, particularly for a firm that was relatively less prominent in blockbuster deal flow. The downside to this arrangement was now evident. Apollo was an aggressive firm that liked to push the envelope. And with Paul, Weiss's fortune now so tied to the firm there was the risk that the tail was wagging the dog. Even fans of Karp and Paul, Weiss in the legal community had been shocked at how it appeared Paul, Weiss had sold its soul.

Even as Apollo and Paul, Weiss were close, the law firm's official client was Caesars, which had minority public shareholders who were relying on Paul, Weiss to keep it out of trouble. Now Gary Loveman, who had been a Caesars OpCo director, was suddenly facing personal liability for the transactions that Apollo and Paul, Weiss had designed.

The culpability of Loveman, and the other Caesars executives, was an interesting question. Davis believed Loveman, in his testimony, had tried to walk a fine line between brilliant casino CEO and financial neophyte who had deferred to the wizards at Apollo. Loveman had also signed off on every deal under scrutiny, as a director and CEO.

Loveman had been a director at other big public companies like Coach and FedEx, and was a boardroom veteran. In addition, he had a PhD from MIT and faculty appointment at Harvard Business School, making any naiveté a tough sell. Loveman had been concerned enough about the transactions at the time to confront Lewis Clayton, the Paul, Weiss litigator, and confirm everything was above board. Loveman's ultimate view was that the Caesars transaction structures were so novel that there was no way to benchmark them to his knowledge and experience. Creditors, however, had not forgotten how they believed Loveman was intentionally evasive on conference calls and in investor meetings. Davis was largely unimpressed with the command of all the non-private equity Caesars directors on the complex deals they were approving, and such criticism started with Loveman.

If Davis had decided to assign liability to every one of the transactions he investigated, then Caesars and Apollo could have argued that he had been prejudiced against them. However, in the more than a dozen transactions investigated, Davis chose to absolve their conduct in nearly half the instances. This apparent evenhandedness made it impossible for the company and the private equity firms to simply dismiss the report out of hand.

Ironically, Apollo's transaction that Davis disliked the most was one he assigned no liability to whatsoever: the bare majority unsecured notes repurchase from August 2014 that resulted in the MeehanCombs lawsuit. Davis called the deal "ugly," given that it happened in secret and damaged nearly half of the noteholders. But Davis could not conclude any wrongdoing.

The terms of the Unsecured Notes deal, unlike Growth, CERP, and Four Properties, had been approved by the newly appointed independent OpCo directors Ronen Stauber and Steve Winograd. Kirkland & Ellis had spent hours explaining to the two their fiduciary duties as directors. Because the governance process was clearly done by the book, the so-called Delaware "business judgment" rule was in effect. Davis could not second-guess the board's decision making, and had to defer to their judgment—no matter how poorly he thought of the deal terms.

The Unsecured Notes deal became the perfect control experiment. Once Apollo had decided the OpCo required independent directors, nearly anything the OpCo board decided to do afterward would be beyond reproach. The problem was that every other controversial deal had occurred prior to the Unsecured Notes deal, and therefore faced a much harsher glare. If Apollo and Paul, Weiss had been wiser, Caesars' current predicament could have been avoided. Since Stauber and Winograd were willing to wave through the egregious Unsecured Notes deal, they probably would have been willing to go along with anything Rowan and Sambur had cooked up. Not bringing the pair on board just a year earlier was looking like as much as a $5 billion blunder.

IN THE LATE EVENING OF March 15, the Caesars team hastily arranged a conference call to discuss their response to the examiner's report. Rowan was exasperated enough to go to bed, and told the group that he was fine with whatever response everybody else came up with. Apollo simply did not buy that there had been any corporate governance failures at Caesars. Rowan liked to point out that Norwegian Cruise Lines, another Apollo company, had 600 subsidiaries. "Did each one of those entities require independent directors?" he would ask rhetorically.

The next day, Caesars put out a press release that in part said, "These transactions provided immense and indisputable benefit to OpCo and its creditors, who received billions of dollars in principal and interest payments. This is ultimately a dispute about valuation, process and whether OpCo was solvent at the time of each of the transactions. We disagree with the Examiner's subjective conclusions and opinions on these financial issues. Indeed, the Examiner's conclusions are completely inconsistent with the careful analysis and considered opinions of the independent and highly regarded investment banks and law firms who advised on these processes."

It was odd for Caesars immediately to use the efforts of law firms and investment banks as a shield, as Davis had meticulously dismantled their work product. But for now, Apollo did not have much more of a defense to offer.

"BEST EXAMINER'S REPORT IN THE history of mankind!" exalted Bruce Bennett.

Davis's findings were not just a boon for Bennett's clients' negotiating posture, but they served as a personal vindication for Bennett himself. He had been crusading for an examiner since the Delaware involuntary filing. When the case made its way to Chicago, the Caesars parent had argued in its papers that an examiner would confirm the propriety of Apollo and TPG's actions in the years before bankruptcy. In fact, the opposite had just happened.

Examiner reports historically tended to be nuanced and equivocal. Davis had written a towering narrative that was clear and decisive. Paul, Weiss had called Bennett when he was in a car on the way to LAX in the days before the report's publication suggesting the report would be unremarkable and that it might be worth settling in advance. Bennett was relieved he had not entertained that offer.

Bennett also took pleasure in how foolish Kirkland appeared now. The independent counsel to the Caesars OpCo had argued for a narrow examiner in front of Judge Goldgar in February 2015. Kirkland claimed that its Special Governance Committee had already negotiated a fine deal where the Caesars parent had agreed to contribute just $1.4 billion to a settlement. Kirkland had then tried to disband

Bennett's second-lien committee. And while Bennett had failed to disqualify Kirkland, with Davis now ascribing as much as $5 billion in wrongdoing, Bennett's views about Kirkland's alleged bias toward Apollo and TPG suddenly looked more interesting.

By coincidence, there was a March 16 hearing in Judge Goldgar's Chicago courtroom to discuss multiple matters, giving Bennett an early chance to make hay over the examiner's reports which had dropped less than 24 hours earlier.

David Zott of Kirkland opened his remarks by noting that Kirkland was still reviewing the 1,803-page document. "Speaking for myself, I haven't got through it yet."

"No, me neither," admitted Goldgar, who later in the hearing referred to the report as "Tolstoyesque."

Zott tried to get in front of the massive differences in conclusions between the investigation of the OpCo independent directors, which had been led by Kirkland, and what the examiner had concluded. "The [restructuring] plan will be predicated on enhanced contributions from the Caesars parent. Among other things, that's supported by recently produced documents we think are material to the overall analysis of the potential claims. It's also confirmed by the examiner's report insofar as we've gotten through it, and we're just beginning the process."

Kirkland was insisting that Apollo and TPG's late document dump from January was going to prompt it to increase its demands on Apollo and TPG, and that it had agreed to settle in 2015, for what was obviously now an inadequate figure, due to that tardiness.

Kirkland's restructuring plan was also at the center of another topic at the hearing: the retention of the financial advisor to the Caesars OpCo Special Governance Committee. What should have been a straightforward motion had turned into a huge mess in recent months. The committee had hired Mesirow Financial as its finance expert. The team was led by Melissa Kibler Knoll, a well-respected bankruptcy consultant. Knoll was, however, having an extramarital affair with Vincent Lazar, a bankruptcy partner at the law firm Jenner & Block. Their personal lives would normally have remained a private matter; however, Jenner & Block had been retained by the Caesars parent as local counsel in Chicago. Mesirow was investigating the actions, on behalf of the OpCo independent directors, of the Caesars parent. Knoll and Lazar were on opposite sides, with a clear conflict of interest.

The affair had only come to light from sheer dumb luck. Knoll had not mentioned the relationship in retention applications

Mesirow had made earlier in the case. But in a chance encounter, Denise DeLaurent, a lawyer in the US Trustee's Office in Chicago who happened to be assigned to the Caesars case, witnessed the pair in a private moment at a June 2015 industry conference in Traverse City, Michigan.

Knoll left the client team when the affair came to light, and Mesirow did all it could to address the conflict. The team at Mesirow that had done the work for the Caesars governance committee had already left the firm, forming a new firm called Baker Tilly, which was now seeking to be retained. Only a fraction of the 29 Baker Tilly professionals on the Caesars case were even on the project at Mesirow.

Goldgar, however, opposed the retention of Baker Tilly. "While it may be that the personnel from Mesirow were not tainted, I think the SGC's investigation has been or at the very least we can't know… So I think there is a problem with the SGC investigation, and I think there is a good question whether additional work on that investigation is even warranted."

Goldgar then asked Bennett to offer his thoughts, noting that the second-lien committee had not previously taken a position on the retention of Baker Tilly. Bennett wanted to undermine the Special Governance Committee investigation in any way possible, and Goldgar had given him the opening. "…I don't know how much reading you did last night, and I don't know how much access you had to Mesirow's prior work. And I feel comfortable telling Your Honor that it was partially the basis for the debtor's settlement that they are now retreating from with the Caesars parent. And the numbers that Mesirow produced are dramatically at variance with those contained in the examiner's report. So there is ample reason for concern about these materials…there will be an asterisk next to this report."

Zott of Kirkland then pointed out that the original Mesirow investigation was completed before Jenner & Block had been hired. As such, Bennett's theory about the affair impacting the original Mesirow report did not make sense, and the SGC's analysis was being updated anyway.

Regardless, Goldgar continued his screed against Mesirow and Knoll. "I don't get to worry about everybody's morality…I mean let's remember what happened here. She was having an affair that she did not disclose with counsel for the very company that her employer was investigating. She was sleeping with the enemy."

Knoll had erred in not initially disclosing her relationship with Lazar on Mesirow's application. But most in the case believed the firm had followed the correct procedures in remedying the conflict and were comfortable with Mesirow's role in the case. Goldgar's harsh comments struck most as gratuitous. In 2008, Goldgar had made comments about the attire of women in his courtroom that had made national news. He was again obsessing over a woman's behavior. Baker Tilly would go on to withdraw its application for retention.

Bruce Bennett had acted since the beginning of the bankruptcy like he owned the case, and now perhaps he finally did. He and his clients had been on their heels for fifteen months, but suddenly the momentum had shifted. Bennett did not get everything he wanted in the report. For example, Caesars had transferred the World Series of Poker intellectual property in 2009 and 2010 for peanuts, and it eventually became the billion-dollar CIE business. Bennett had wanted a huge fraud finding but Davis, given the years that had passed, did not do so. Still, $5 billion of potential liability was an almost unprecedented finding.

Bennett thought his job was not just to devise a legal strategy and to go fight in court, but also to serve as a coach and psychologist. He had to keep his clients patient and disciplined. In long, tough cases there was incredible pressure coming from all directions to settle quickly, cut losses, and save face. It had been exactly a year since Goldgar had approved the examiner's motion. There had been ebbs and flows since. But their wager in waiting for the report had paid big dividends. The case remained far from over; Apollo would continue its campaign to buy off as many creditors as possible in an attempt to leave the second-lien holders isolated. But the examiner's $5 billion headline value was now a powerful cudgel the group would be happy to swing.

"WHERE DO YOU THINK THIS case settles?" asked Appaloosa's David Tepper.

The second-lien bondholders had organized a call in the wake of the publication of the examiner's report, to gauge the group's reaction. Tepper left the day-to-day to his trusted deputy, Jim Bolin. But given the significance of the report, he decided to join this discussion. Appaloosa had been the swing player in the saga. Its hardline stance alongside Oaktree and its imperviousness to Apollo's high-pressure tactics were the key reasons this case remained a brawl.

Tepper liked to joke that the second-lien bondholders were going to take Leon Black's house in the Hamptons and that he was already deciding what curtains he was going to hang when he moved in. There was another running gag about putting Rowan and Sambur in "orange jumpsuits"—that the pair's Caesars hijinks would land them in prison (fortunately for Apollo, Richard Davis had specifically written in his report that there was no hint of criminality in his findings).

"Personally, I think we are par," replied Oaktree's Ken Liang, the junior bondholders' other key zealot. Liang had told David Sambur that only one or two out of a dozen Caesars transactions needed to be flagged by Richard Davis for second-lien bondholders to take control of the case. Davis had now given them much more than that.

"Maybe there is a settlement below that. I don't want to undercut Jim [Bolin] but I want to fight for par."

A year ago, their bonds were trading at ten cents. Now they were above fifty cents.

"I could go for par," Tepper laughed, as he contemplated getting 100 cents, an astronomical number that would mean more than a half billion dollars in profit for Appaloosa's position.

30

OLD FRIENDS

"**S**omebody tell me where Ken Liang's breakfast is so I can dip my balls in it," yelled David Sambur.

Sambur did not seem too bothered for a young man facing potentially more than $1 billion in personal liability. In the wake of Richard Davis's March examiner's report, the remainder of the Caesars case had been clarified. Bruce Bennett and his second-lien bondholders were going to use the examiner's findings to press their scorched-earth strategy in court. Meanwhile, Apollo was going to keep trying to pick off the assorted remaining holdout creditors groups to create momentum for a cramdown where the second-lien group would have unfavorable recoveries forced on them. And Kirkland and Millstein were going to plot their middle ground in the off chance that cooler heads could prevail.

One such attempt at promoting reconciliation was a formal mediation process, which had brought combatants Liang and Sambur into the same room this morning in the summer of 2016. Mediators in bankruptcies often did lead to breakthroughs, but the timing and conditions had to be ripe. The warring parties had to be interested in peace, fearful of failure, and have differences close enough to be bridged. It was not clear that would ever be the case with Caesars, but it was worth a shot.

The concept of a mediator was first broached with Judge Goldgar in February, a month before the examiner's report was published. Goldgar again took an unorthodox approach: He highly encouraged mediation but would not formally approve a motion, saying that if the parties wanted it then he couldn't stop them.

244 • MAX FRUMES AND SUJEET INDAP

"...This is a private matter. You don't need my permission to do this [mediation]. You can just do it...You're wearing the ruby slippers, Mr. Seligman. Just click your heels together three times and say there's no place like mediation," Goldgar quipped to David Seligman of Kirkland during a February 2016 hearing.

Goldgar's handling of the case over the first year had been unpredictable, to say the least. The worst concerns about him had not quite been borne out. But he ran Caesars more like a Socratic method law school seminar than a complex bankruptcy case seeking a resolution. Rather than ruling quickly on either easy or unimportant topics—like fees, or the Kirkland retention—he liked to have mini trials that were time-consuming and unproductive. Goldgar had been hard on Kirkland—as the debtor counsel they were most in his line of fire. But he had kept Bruce Bennett and everyone else off-balance, too.

The practical consequence was that court had become a vacuum. The only space for progress to be made was outside the courtroom walls. The main combatants, Apollo and Appaloosa/Oaktree, had little respect for Millstein's and Kirkland's authority, and were not particularly motivated to back down from their hardlines. Maybe a mediator could break the logjam. However, judging by Sambur's intentions for Liang's granola, Apollo was not quite ready to hug it out.

Joseph James Farnan Jr., the former chief judge of the District of Delaware, was the mediator chosen to oversee the ongoing tussle. Judge Farnan was now running his own firm in Wilmington, Delaware, and was well-known in bankruptcy circles. He had served as mediator in the complex Los Angeles Dodgers bankruptcy where Bruce Bennett had been representing the team.

The actual mediation was a mix of shuttle diplomacy and speed dating. There were some bilateral sessions conducted between specific groups, but there were also large gatherings at Kirkland & Ellis's office, for the private equity firms and the creditors. Kirkland's office space was a maze of both sweeping and abbreviated conference rooms. Each group was to camp out in its own dedicated room, and Farnan would jet between them ferrying offers and counteroffers. Sessions would last eight to nine hours, and even the likes of Marc Rowan would show up to show Farnan their sincerity.

Farnan, like Millstein, tried to get the second-lien group to back off their ask: a recovery greater than sixty cents.

"If you pursue that number, that will be litigated for years," Farnan said in one session. "If you want to settle, you need to move off your number."

Jim Bolin, Appaloosa's lead negotiator, represented the

second-lien group, along with Ken Liang, and he saw through what was happening. Apollo was just using mediation as a tactic to stall while they tried to strike deals with every other creditor group. Bolin believed Apollo was marshalling a cramdown by buying off Elliott and GSO and then hiding behind the mediation fig-leaf to hold the prospect of compromise in front of Goldgar. Oaktree and Appaloosa's plan was to hold firm even in the face of immense peer pressure. "Our legal claims are good. Stay patient and do not succumb to the pressure," had become their mantra.

Sessions with other creditors were not all that productive either. A group of the senior bondholders, which included lawyers from Kramer Levin along with Adam Sklar from Monarch Alternative Capital, met with Farnan hoping to juice their already-signed deal for something that exceeded 100 cents on the dollar. Caesars was in far better shape than it had been when they signed their deal in December of 2014, and they were entitled to more, they argued.

Farnan had formed a different view. "What makes you think they'll be able to sustain this level of EBITDA?" Farnan asked. The advisors explained some of the adjustments, including the freebies given to customers that actually delivered value back, but Farnan took it in a completely anecdotal direction. "Well I can tell you, I used to go to the Baltimore Horseshoe and play slots and I would get a free buffet and free crab legs. Then they stopped with the complimentary buffet and I'd have to pay $26, and then they took away the crab legs! Now I don't go there anymore. How can you be sure this cutting of the crab legs is not going to take away business?"

The first-lien notes group walked away confused. Later, they regrouped and were determined to make progress. The next time the group met at the offices of Miller Buckfire, the first-lien notes representatives had crab legs brought in especially for Farnan for the dinner served that evening. By the time the meal was over, Farnan had not touched the seafood.

The constant bloodshed was wearing out Jim Millstein and Brendan Hayes. In February, just prior to the publication of the Examiner's report, Millstein met Bruce Bennett, who he had known since the 1980s, for a drink in Chicago before a hearing with Goldgar. As they sat down, Bennett snarled, "You're here to get me to settle for forty cents, aren't you?"

Millstein replied, "No, I'm here to get you to settle. I don't care what the number is."

The examiner's report would only embolden Bennett, and it seemed the gap had widened.

But Millstein and Hayes had an idea to start making some headway in the wake of the examiner's report. Aside from the percentage recovery Appaloosa and Oaktree had been offered by Apollo, the pair were not happy about its form. The second-lien bondholders were set to get a quarter ownership of PropCo, the new vehicle that would own casinos and then lease them back to the Caesars operating company. In their view, PropCo would have way too much debt. Moreover, they were going to be on the other side of Apollo, who would own a piece of the OpCo—which was exactly how they ended up in this unenviable position in bankruptcy.

What if the entirety of PropCo equity just went to Elliott and the senior bondholders, wondered Millstein? PropCo originally had been an Elliott idea, and the senior bondholders were going to own a majority anyway. The second-lien group would get their recovery strictly in cash and securities in OpCo. The dollar amounts could be sorted out later, but this simplification could open up a dialogue.

Rowan and Sambur were lukewarm on the idea. Millstein did get enough buy-in to start freelancing with Elliott and Oaktree and Appaloosa, though they came around over time. Apollo and Oaktree/Appaloosa remained at war. But the PropCo solution was a building block, and could be pivotal down the road.

The plan of reorganization filed by Kirkland on June 7, 2016, showed progress. Because of the damaging revelations in the examiner's report, Apollo and the Caesars parent juiced their contribution to the pot nearly threefold to $4 billion. The recovery to the second-lien group represented just thirty-nine cents and Bennett disputed much of the math behind the offer. But the deal terms did include all of PropCo going to the Elliott group, while the second-lien group's equity would only be in the new Caesars OpCo. It was not nearly enough to satisfy their demands, but thanks to Millstein and Hayes, there appeared to be a path forward.

"I think we saw the light!" Marty Bienenstock beamed in a June 2016 hearing in Goldgar's courtroom. Bienenstock was the lawyer from Proskauer Rose representing the official committee of unsecured creditors—a motley crew of Caesars' vendors, unsecured bondholders, pension claims, and more at the bottom of the Caesars totem pole. Bienenstock had been a zealot at the beginning of the case in early 2015, even challenging the independence of Kirkland and conducting his own investigation of Apollo alongside the examiner.

But on this day in June 2016, he was here to declare peace. The UCC had decided to settle with Caesars for forty-two cents. Fifteen months earlier that number was nine cents, so they had improved substantially. But Bruce Bennett was furious that the UCC and his once law partner Bienenstock had cut a deal so cheaply and so early. Bienenstock represented an official creditors committee, and its acceptance of the current restructuring plan was a big deal. If the most junior group, albeit a smaller one in terms of dollar claims, was willing to stand down, it made the second-lien group look like greedy obstructionists. By virtue of representing an official commit-tee, Bienenstock's fees were even getting paid by the Caesars estate. Bennett wondered why the UCC lost its nerve.

Bienenstock's announcement about finding religion was at the hearing over a so-called "disclosure statement." Kirkland was racing to get Goldgar to schedule a confirmation hearing for its restruc-turing plan. A hearing would put pressure on the parties to settle or at least start a process for ending the case. As a part of the confir-mation hearing scheduling, Kirkland needed to draft a disclosure statement, which detailed the restructuring plan—including every-thing from contemplated creditor recoveries to a chronicle of key events in the bankruptcy process. With exhibits and appendices, disclosure statement drafts in this case easily exceeded 1,000 pages. Dissidents challenging the plan also had the chance to include their views opposing the agreement. The document would then be mailed to creditors for review before they voted to accept or reject the restructuring.

Kirkland suggested January and Goldgar set the date for January 17, 2017. "And there's something poetic about that," Goldgar com-mented, "because it will be almost two years to the day since the case was filed. So in the interest of poetry, as well as my own preparation, that's what we're going to do."

Ideally for Bennett, the UCC and second-lien bondholders needed to form a united front. Now that Bienenstock had "seen the light"—and other minor creditors like the $500 million Subsidiary Guarantee Notes had also settled—Apollo had successfully isolated Bennett's group. $14 billion of the $18 billion Caesars debt stack had shook hands with Rowan and Sambur. Whatever the quality of Ben-nett's legal claims, virtually everyone in the case was ready to move on. And bankruptcy judges confronted with that level of consensus were not inclined to stand in the way.

BRUCE BENNETT WAS GETTING TENSE. With essentially every creditor now on Apollo's side, he needed to find some way to keep his legal fight relevant. His clients—Oaktree, Appaloosa, Centerbridge, and

Tennenbaum—were facing daily peer pressure to settle like everyone else had. The examiner report and its $5 billion in liability claims would remain his cudgel. His best shot remained getting the injunction against the parent guarantee litigation lifted so the Caesars parent would be staring down $11 billion of liability. On June 8, Judge Goldgar was once again taking up the issue.

Kirkland and Millstein would yet again side with Apollo in advocating for the injunction to remain, leaving Bennett with only a few, tiny unsecured bondholders supporting him. The examiner's report had clarified his litigation strategy. With the likes of Apollo, TPG, and their executives looking at personal liability, he was going to make it clear that Caesars had, unfairly in his eyes, asked those parties to put nothing into the settlement pot while they each received "get out of jail free cards." Jim Millstein had to persuade Judge Goldgar that progress was being made and that the right thing to do was keep the injunction in place in order to finish off the negotiations—so Bennett had to shred Millstein's credibility.

"Good afternoon, Mr. Millstein. I'm going to try, but we have a lot to cover. First of all, you mentioned the examiner's report in your earlier testimony. Did you review the examiner's report?" Bennett asked casually.

"I read the executive summary," replied Millstein. Bennett's eyes widened. He looked at Millstein astonished at the banker's casual indifference to the most important moment thus far in the bankruptcy.

"So you didn't read—So you only read the first hundred pages?" Bennett shrieked. "You didn't read the valuation?"

"I read the valuation," Millstein replied, trying to temper Bennett's scolding.

"So you read the appendices?" Bennett probed.

"I read *some* of the appendices," Millstein told him.

Millstein's father, Ira, was close with Richard Davis, as both had been legends at Weil, Gotshal together. Jim Millstein had known Davis for almost forty years so it was ironic he had not put much time into his report.

Bennett was just getting warmed up.

"That's okay. All right. Good. By the way, you are a lawyer by training, I gather, correct?"

"You know my experience."

"That's true. But that's not admissible."

"Yes, by training."

"Okay. You don't have any business training in school, correct?"

"No."

Bennett and Millstein had known each other for nearly thirty years, and it was surreal to see them jousting. Like most people in the restructuring world, Millstein found Bennett to be obnoxious at times, and Millstein was one of the handful of people to have the stature to mock Bennett. Even though they were friendly, Bennett thought Millstein was just another Apollo lackey. Millstein's testimony would do him no favors.

"Based upon your examination, at least of the executive summary of the examiner's report," Bennett could not help but point out Millstein's abbreviated reading, "will you agree with me that the examiner determined that other persons and entities are potentially liable with the Caesars parent on account of the many claims that the examiner identified as claims against the Caesars parent?"

"I think that was the examiner's conclusion."

Bennett was trying to show that Millstein could target multiple deep pockets for settlement money.

"If the Caesars parent does not spend as much...to settle with OpCo, for whatever reason, it will have greater resources to pay its other creditors, whoever they may be; is that a correct or incorrect statement?" Bennett asked.

"I think it's just logic."

"Okay. Yes or no will get you out of here."

"I'm trying to help you."

"One more time."

At this point, Goldgar started to show his own frustration with Millstein. "Don't help. Just answer the questions," Goldgar interjected.

"Yes," Millstein said.

Bennett, sensing his advantage, proceeded to reference fine details of the examiner's report he knew that Millstein would not have handy.

"Okay. Isn't it true that the examiner determined that Growth Partners is potentially liable to one or more of the debtors for between $1.519 billion and $2.1 billion?...So how much did you determine Growth Partners could contribute toward payment of the claims?" asked Bennett.

"I don't have the analysis in front of me, Bruce," Millstein replied, now irritated enough to address Bennett by his first name.

"And I'm asking you how much money did you determine that Growth Partners could contribute toward payment of those claims?" Bennett pressed again.

"I didn't make that determination."

"So you didn't come up with a number?" Bennett said more incredulously.

"No."

"Did you come up with a range?"

"We—"

"That's a yes or no," Bennett interrupted.

"Once again, I'm trying to answer your question. The, we have not—I didn't make a determination as to what any individual defendant could contribute," Millstein now clearly pushed back onto his heels.

"One more time, Mr. Millstein. You're going to be here for a long time if we're going to do it this way. How much did you determine Growth Partners could contribute toward the payment of these claims? Are you saying you did determine or are you saying you didn't determine it?"

Bennett was relentless.

"The reason I am struggling is we have done a valuation evaluation of the Caesars parent and its component parts. And, therefore, we have done a valuation of Growth Partners. And so I could answer the question if I had the valuation in front of me."

"Isn't it true that the examiner determined Apollo entities are potentially liable to one or more of the debtors for between $3.2 billion and $4.7 billion?"

"I don't recall. I don't recall the numbers specifically."

"Do you remember that the examiner's report determined that the Apollo entities were liable to one or more of the debtors for billions of dollars?"

"I don't think he ever said liable, he said potentially liable, among the defendants that could be sued," Millstein tried to slow the Bennett barrage.

"Okay. Do you remember if the examiner determined that the Apollo entities are potentially liable to one or more of the debtors for billions of dollars?"

"Yes."

"How much did you determine the Apollo entities can contribute toward payment of those claims?"

"I did not investigate them. I investigated with regard to the—their ability to pay us funds."

"Have you obtained comprehensive financial information from all of the relevant Apollo entities?

"No."

"Why not?"

"Why not? We were—we were given a target for contributions that would…And I believe that that—that that—I believe a value, I think, at the time between $1.9 and $6.3 billion, with a mid-point of $4 billion, to satisfy a contribution claim that—"

"How much did you determine that the TPG entities can contribute toward payment of these claims?" Bennett would not let up.

"I don't believe I've assessed that," Millstein replied.

"Isn't it true that the examiner determined that David Sambur is potentially liable to one or more the debtors for between $2.8 billion and $4 billion?"

"I don't recall."

"How much did you determine that Mr. Rowan can contribute toward payment of these claims?"

"I made no independent investigation of his financial wherewithal," Millstein admitted.

"How much did you determine that Mr. Loveman can contribute toward payment of these claims?"

"No independent assessment."

"Does the name Mr. Hession mean something to you?"

Hession was the chief financial officer of Caesars, mentioned more than 300 times in the examiner's report. Hession was a member of the Caesars board and had approved some of the controversial transactions. Like Rowan and Bonderman, Hession was facing liability himself.

"No," Millstein said.

Goldgar then jumped in with his own question. "What was the Caesars parent reaction to the issuance of the examiner's report? Was there a great big mea culpa, or did they say, we think we did everything just fine?"

"I can testify hearsay, I suppose, as to what I saw. I think that they—what I heard—you want me to testify to what I heard?" Millstein stumbled.

"They issued a public statement, didn't they?" Goldgar provided.

"No. I mean, they were—they issued public statements. They—I think that they…yes, they did, and they're intending to vigorously defend."

Millstein's testimony had been disappointing for Caesars. Even if most of the creditors were happy with the settlement terms, the second-lien bondholders were entitled to pursue litigation over fraudulent transfers. Bennett's clients, for the right price, were willing to settle. But Bennett was determined to show that Millstein, the man in charge of the negotiations, was not trying so hard.

Truthfully, Millstein was never morally indignant over Apollo's actions. To him, hedge funds and private firms were equally greedy and opportunistic. His job was not to mete out justice but to cut a deal. It was strictly a technical exercise. Bennett had intimated that Millstein had sympathy toward Apollo, which was also untrue. Rowan and Sambur had hardly been helpful in getting to a deal, and Sambur had been deeply unpleasant to both Millstein and his team.

Millstein always had a plan. He was going to methodically agree to terms with as many creditor groups as possible, starting at the top and working his way down. Where the settlement money came from was not critical to him, and there were easier places to get it than Marc Rowan's pocket. Money was money to Millstein. Eventually, Rowan and Bennett were going to have to decide whether their brinksmanship was worth blowing up a fair deal. Millstein was betting, assuming Goldgar gave him the time to do his job, that neither would dare be so foolish.

Goldgar was pleased enough that almost all the creditor groups had now joined the settlement. But he also was beginning to believe that the biggest names in the case—Apollo, TPG, Rowan, Bonderman, Sambur—were getting a free ride. Goldgar wanted the sides to settle but was not going to wait forever. He implemented a 74-day injunction with a warning: "There better be some talking and it better happen fast. By the same token, I do not wish to hear that the Caesars parent has refused to sit down with the second-lien noteholders because they set conditions. I'm not interested in those conditions unless they involve suffering some form of bodily harm. You know, if they want you to sit on red hot coals, don't show up. But other than that, there better be some conversations. I am not telling anybody they need to reach a settlement in this case, but the premise of the injunction was to gain time to talk settlement and reach one. You have got that time. Use it."

IN ONE OF HIS BETTER moments during Bruce Bennett's onslaught during the June 8 injunction hearing, Jim Millstein said, "I think it was you who said that the *New York Times* today said that people are grossly underestimating the number of Trump voters, that they're underreported in the polls. I think the number of second-lien holders who will vote for this plan is grossly underreported."

Millstein had a point. Bennett had a math problem. The four committee members—Appaloosa, Oaktree, Centerbridge, and Tennenbaum—together owned just under $2 billion of the $5.5

billion of outstanding second-lien bonds. The clear hardliners on the committee were the two largest holders, Appaloosa and Oaktree. Still, the group was cohesive and aligned on strategy and tactics. But what they were not was a majority, and so the group needed to be sure that there were enough other holders of second-lien bonds who were on their side. Apollo knew the math, too, and were experts at picking off a hedge fund here and there to sign on to their settlement.

There were also so-called crossholders funds who were desperate for a settlement; since they owned multiple Caesars securities, they were hedged and simply needed the company to come out of bankruptcy as soon as possible to profit.

Chaney Sheffield of Canyon Capital was furiously backchanneling with Kaj Vazales and Dave Miller to see if a compromise was there. Canyon owned first-lien bonds, second-lien bonds, and equity in the Caesars parent, and simply needed the ordeal to be over.

Oaktree and Appaloosa were consistently getting the hard sell, too. Rowan and Josh Harris of Apollo even made the trek from Manhattan to New Jersey to plead with David Tepper and Jim Bolin, only to get stonewalled.

The second-lien committee had no intention of settling on the terms that were on the table, so it needed to shore up support to prevent Caesars from getting to a majority of second-lien bondholders. Bennett and Houlihan Lokey started calling up second-lien bondholders. The plan was to form a so-called "cooperation agreement," where a group of holders would commit to refuse to sign an RSA. Such agreements were not easy to corral. Few funds wanted to make quasi-binding commitments and sacrifice control over their holdings to others.

In late June 2016, a group of more than 10 holders of second-lien bonds gathered at Houlihan Lokey's offices on Park Avenue just north of Grand Central Terminal. Among the firms in attendance were: Paulson & Co, a major crossholder; Warlander Asset Management, run by a David Tepper protégé; Avenue Capital; Contrarian Capital Management; and CQS, a large, London-based manager. Paulson did not sign the cooperation agreement, but enough did to exceed 50 percent. Apollo, at least arithmetically, had successfully been stymied for now by Bennett. The joke was that the document was really a "non-cooperation" agreement, given they'd promised to keep saying "no."

In a July hearing, Goldgar learned of the cooperation agreement. He advised the sides to take control of finishing the case, otherwise he would do it himself. "In my experience, when parties are at an impasse like the one they are at in this case, it usually means at least one side is making a major miscalculation," Gold-gar said.

31

THE HOLE AND THE GAP

"**W**hy am I not going to hear from Mr. Millstein at the hearing? He has been your star witness all along. You know, as time goes on, your case peters out. I was quite surprised to see that I was not going to have a chance to question him," Judge Goldgar said to Kirkland's Jeffrey Zeiger at an August 17, 2016, hearing in Chicago.

Jim Millstein, the OpCo's investment banker, had always testified in the injunction hearings, consistently arguing that Judge Goldgar should prevent the parent guarantee lawsuits from proceeding in the New York federal court and Delaware state court. In June—now nineteen months into the bankruptcy—Goldgar, who had never warmed to Millstein, had reluctantly extended the injunction for seventy-four days through August 29, in the hope the extra time would lead to a final deal.

Goldgar had grown impatient and he telegraphed exactly whom he felt was responsible for the paralysis. "The estates here have claims—large ones the examiner found—against some of these entities, entities that include Apollo and TPG, as well as a host of other companies and individuals. The plan the Caesars OpCo want to confirm would release those claims…In fact, Mr. Millstein, the debtors restructuring advisor, from whom apparently, we will not hear, testified as recently as this past June that he had not even considered whether these entities could contribute anything."

In June 2015, Millstein had made his famed "greatest messes of our time" speech, referring to a possible Caesars parent bankruptcy if the guarantee litigation went forward. Millstein's admonition by now had even become a running punchline in Goldgar's courtroom. Then in the June 2016 hearing, Millstein was forced by Bruce Bennett to admit he had not even carefully read the examiner's report.

Judge Jed Rakoff had taken over the parent guarantee cases in New York federal court for Judge Shira Scheindlin, who had retired in March. Judge Rakoff was anxious to rule in the cases and had scheduled his proceeding for four p.m. on August 30, signaling to some that he was going to immediately trigger $11 billion in summary judgment for bondholders. The OpCo advisors, Kirkland and Millstein, needed to convince the skeptical Goldgar to extend the injunction. And since Millstein had been sidelined by a medical procedure, it was going to fall to Brendan Hayes to do it.

Hayes would be the sole witness put on by Kirkland. Given Millstein's difficult ordeals on the witness stand in previous injunction hearings, there were snickers that the legend was ducking out to avoid further embarrassment. Hayes did not have Millstein's experience. The mild-mannered Hayes, who resembled the actor Luke Perry, was just thirty-nine years old and had been a Managing Director for less than four years. Much of Hayes's career had been spent as a junk bond banker at Lehman Brothers and Barclays before he made his jump to restructuring. Hayes, however, had been doing the heavy lifting on Caesars and would be sharper on the details than Millstein—which mattered to Goldgar.

Testifying in bankruptcy court was a big deal. Expert witnesses were supposed to simplify complex issues for a judge and make a persuasive case for their side. Bankers put the reputation of themselves and their firms on the line. The Caesars case was both complex and extremely contentious. And it would happen to be the first time Brendan Hayes had testified in any case.

At nine a.m. on August 23, Goldgar opened the proceedings. "This is the hearing on the debtors' motion to extend the Section 105 injunction. Once more unto the breach, I guess. Are we ready to proceed?"

Hayes, who had flown to Chicago in the midst of a family vacation in New Hampshire, was called to the witness stand to be first examined by Jeff Zieger of Kirkland & Ellis. Hayes had to convince Judge Goldgar that there had been major progress toward a deal since June, and that the court should not blow up the case by lifting the injunction. Hayes opened by explaining the creditors representing $14 billion out of $18 billion of OpCo debt had signed on to the deal. And because the senior loan and bondholders had negotiated for accrued interest payments and were receiving well over 100 cents on the dollar, the agreed-upon creditor recovery currently totaled $17 billion.

There were holdouts—notably a slight majority of the $5.5 billion of second-lien junior bonds outstanding—represented by the second-lien committee. Still, Hayes believed he had progress to report. Caesars had settled with Frederick Barton Danner, an individual holder of unsecured notes. Unfortunately, Danner owned less than $20,000 of bonds. And bizarrely, he took a deal for 52 cents which was less than the trading price of the bonds. Even stranger, his lawyer, Gordon Novod, received a fee totaling seven million dollars. Also, a splinter group of second-lien bondholders had signed an RSA with Caesars weeks earlier. It called for fifty-five-cent recovery, up from the previous thirty-nine cents on the table. There were, however, major shortcomings in that deal as well.

The splinter second-lien group included familiar names who held debt and equity all across Caesars: Canyon Capital, Mason Capital, Paulson & Co., Soros Fund Management, and even Silver Point Capital, the once-militant member of the loan group that had—like Canyon—come to believe the entire Caesars system was cheap relative to true value. They cumulatively held about $2 billion of the second liens, but this added up to just 37 percent of second-lien debt, which was not close to a majority. Moreover, the additional payment required to fund the settlement totaled a whopping $950 million, and it was not clear who would fork over that money. Then there were those funds who had signed up for the Jones Day "cooperation agreement," who had agreed not to sign any second-lien deal with Caesars not approved by the Appaloosa/Oaktree committee. Still, the chasm was closing, and Hayes believed his non-stop shuttle diplomacy would soon lead to a final breakthrough.

Hayes explained to Judge Goldgar that the summer's other big development was the sale of Caesars Interactive Entertainment for $4.4 billion in cash to a Chinese buyer. CIE was the social gaming business whose popularity had exploded under the leadership of Mitch Garber. The World Series of Poker intellectual property had formed the origins of CIE and had been one of the first asset transfers out of the Caesars OpCo. CIE then became the prize asset of Caesars Growth Partners, the new entity created in 2013.

As a part of the latest restructuring plan, Humpty Dumpty was being put back together again with all the Caesars appendages reuniting into a single company—including CIE. But the $4.4 billion in cash proceeds had blown everyone away. That figure was double previous predictions. The cash haul meant that creditors could take less new debt and equity in their recoveries. CIE was a game-changer, all sides agreed. Hayes pleaded with Goldgar for time to figure it all out.

"So if you are suggesting that something is close, then presumably you know a number that you know would satisfy the second-lien noteholders who are currently not signatories to the RSA," asked Goldgar.

"I do," said Hayes.

Now it was Bruce Bennett's turn to throw cold water.

"WE'RE GOING TO RUN INTO numbers a lot of times, so during the break, I left you a calculator, a pad of paper, and a pen if we ever need to redo them, but you should be able to eyeball these," Bruce Bennett explained to Brendan Hayes. Bennett had eviscerated Hayes's boss Jim Millstein on cross-examination at the June hearing, and would try to do the same with Hayes today.

Millstein was asking that the Caesars parent shareholders give up half the company's new equity to creditors. Apollo and TPG's interest, because of the issuance of new shares, would fall to 30 percent. Millstein had valued the equity of the new Caesars at roughly $6 billion. Based on this theoretical value, the two private equity firms were making a $2 billion settlement contribution by diluting their stake by 50 percent. The overall settlement, made of tangible and intangible components, was worth $4 billion.

Bennett was having none of it. Apollo and TPG were not writing their own check and putting in real cash currency. Rather, all shareholders of the Caesars parent were simply taking a smaller stake in the new company. Bennett believed this would not settle serious claims of fraud.

In fact, he thought it was a windfall to Apollo and TPG. The trading value of Caesars implied the stake of the two firms that day was worth $1.7 billion—the market seemed to believe that the two firms were going to throw in $2.3 billion, not the $2 billion proposed—somehow, they would make $300 million profit on the current settlement terms.

Hayes explained the discrepancy to Bennett: "Noted in our demonstrative, our expectation is that there will be further contributions."

The math was confusing, and even Goldgar had difficulty following the numbers. But Bennett's core argument was about to become crystal clear.

"So, it was a Millstein decision to not seek settlement consideration from anyone other than the Caesars parent until two weeks ago?" asked Bennett, growing more incredulous by the minute.

"We are dealing with a negotiation where the Caesars parent is the best contributing party because of all the valuable assets, cash and equity, and ability to incur debt that it has. So until recently, you're right, we have not requested contributions from other parties."

The Caesars OpCo, via its lawyers at Kirkland, just two weeks earlier had filed an extraordinary 196-page complaint against the Caesars parent. It included more than sixty affiliates and persons associated with the Caesars parent, including Marc Rowan, David Sambur, David Bonderman, Gary Loveman, Eric Hession, Lynn Swann, and several other Caesars directors. The charges were related to the fraudulent transfers that Richard Davis had investigated, and the lawsuit was to maintain the chance for the OpCo to seek damages over the fraud charges.

At the same time, Millstein, the financial advisor to the OpCo, was only asking a single party, the Caesars parent, to put money in the pot to settle charges against all the defendants.

"But the fact remains that only two weeks ago—I'll try to pin it down in a second—no one made demands to any of the 67 defendants and 6 tolling parties with respect to the estate claims litigation other than the Caesars parent."

Hayes explained that the Millstein team had a meeting two weeks prior with Steve Zelin and Josh Abramson, the bankers for the Caesars parent at PJT Partners, the boutique firm that had recently acquired Blackstone's advisory business. Hayes had broached the idea of a broader contribution from parties other than the Caesars parent. Blackstone only responded a few days before this August 23 hearing, said Hayes.

"And what did they say?" asked Bennett.

"I figured you'd ask the question. They said it's something that they are taking upon themselves at the Caesars parent and view as a Caesars parent issue from the standpoint of there are independent shareholders, there are sponsors, there are insurance companies that provide insurance to the directors and officers of the Caesars parent."

"So, in other words the sponsors are not interested in contributing anything?" asked Judge Goldgar.

"No," confirmed Hayes.

"You don't think that's the correct interpretation of that," Goldgar followed up.

"Well, I don't think they would love to contribute anything. But I do believe that this is a—this is an issue that the Caesars parent needs to resolve from the standpoint of taking value that otherwise the Caesars parent could contribute on behalf of all of their shareholders and allocating it on the basis of certain claims against some of those shareholders, sponsors, officers and directors, etc."

"Well it sounded to me as if the question was what the sponsors could contribute and in what form. And the answer that you got after waiting a couple of weeks was, that's not our problem; that's a Caesars parent problem. Is that what you testified?"

"Yeah," said Hayes.

"Okay," confirmed Goldgar.

Hayes wanted to elaborate: "Yeah, I don't particularly agree with that," meaning that Hayes thought Apollo and TPG could independently put money into the pot.

"But that's what they told you?" reiterated Goldgar.

"That's what we heard," conceded Hayes.

"All right," said Goldgar.

Bennett's questions had touched a nerve with Goldgar, and the judge was intent on figuring out why Millstein and Kirkland had not been more aggressive in shaking down the private equity firms. Bennett's theory from the beginning of the case was that Kirkland and Millstein—who were supposed to be representing the best interests of all Caesars stakeholders—would not have the courage to take on Apollo and TPG.

"We're 20 months into this case. How could this not have occurred to somebody until just in the past few weeks?" Goldgar indignantly demanded.

"Because we have—our focus has been on total contributions and we have not, we have not necessarily concerned ourselves with whether it comes out, you know, person A's pocket or person B's pocket provided that the overall settlement currency is sufficient," Hayes said, now on his heels.

Hayes tried again to explain Millstein's negotiating strategy, but it was tedious enough that Goldgar threw up his hands. "Okay. At a certain point you could pay 100 cents and we can all go home. Just a thought."

Unfortunately for Hayes, Bennett still had questions.

"What's Marc Rowan worth?" asked Bennett.

"I don't know," answered Hayes.

"Based on his position in Apollo and any other information to you—I think an article in the [*New York*] *Post*—do you believe Mr. Rowan is worth more or less than a billion dollars?"

"I try not to rely on the *Post* but okay, likely more."

"So on account of a $1.7 to $2.8 billion claim against a person worth more than a billion, why aren't you seeking more than a fraction of $300 million?"

"Because we are seeking amounts in aggregate that provide reasonable recoveries, maximize value and allow us to get a deal done."

In his report, Richard Davis had estimated that Apollo's liability could be between nearly $2 billion and $3 billion. The Caesars board of directors had an insurance policy and discussions about that payout had started. But the problem was that the insurance was capped at $300 million—for the entire board, which had several members like Rowan, Sambur, Bonderman, and Loveman facing liability. The insurance pocket would not be nearly enough.

But Kirkland and Millstein believed they had already secured a hefty $4 billion contribution. Were Apollo, TPG, and their senior partners reaching into their pockets and writing checks? No, but their $2 billion equity contribution was enough for what they believed was a fair deal. Oaktree and Appaloosa were simply being greedy, they thought. Unfortunately for them, Goldgar had been ice cold toward that argument for months now.

Once Bennett had Hayes off-balance, the lawyer slyly pointed out the banker's relative youth.

"And is it true that you also don't have any experience at all in a case where there's a lawsuit against a third party that would provide a contribution to the debtor?"

"I believe that's correct."

"And you've never been qualified as an expert in any case."

"That's correct," agreed Hayes.

By the time Bennett had finished his cross-examination of Hayes, it was 4:50 p.m. Hayes still had to face questioning from a lawyer representing the unsecured notes, and then have a redirect with Zieger from Kirkland, followed by Bennett's final questions.

"I'm sorry about people who have plane reservations and I'm sorry about people who have vacations, but we're going to stop at 6:15. I haven't had a vacation since before this case began and I'd like to go home because my attention is waning," Goldgar said, perhaps speaking for everyone in that courtroom.

DAVID HILTY'S JOB WAS TO disagree with essentially everything that Brendan Hayes had said the day before. Hilty, the co-head of restructuring at Houlihan Lokey, represented the second-lien bondholders, and he was hoping to get the injunction of the bond guarantee litigation overturned by Judge Goldgar. While Tuck Hardie, the affable Southerner, had been leading the case for Houlihan, they believed Hilty would be a better expert on the stand and, as it turned out, Hardie had been disposed on another case in Australia.

Hilty was in his late forties and had far more experience as a restructuring banker than Hayes. In his spare time, he was the co-owner of the Southampton Social Club, a late-night hot spot in eastern Long Island. This day in court, he was to convey the view that the injunction which Caesars sought had nothing to do with negotiating in good faith with the junior creditors. Sidney Levinson of Jones Day would first examine him.

"If there is an injunction put in place," Hilty explained, "that basically stays the guarantee litigation, so that cannot move forward in any way, and yet the plan is moving forward. And the current plan of the debtors is a plan that is a cramdown plan, since it's not consensual, and seeks releases for third parties that at least the examiner report alleges has potential liability. That really, in my mind, still creates a free option for the Caesars parent and those parties to move that forward, while they don't face any risk of the guarantee litigation moving forward in any way."

According to him, Apollo's game was simply to get to the January confirmation hearing and force a settlement on the dissident creditors.

Hayes had trumpeted the RSA that had been signed with the four hedge funds who owned the second-lien bonds comprising 37 percent of the total. Hilty explained to Levinson that their support for a deal was deceptive. Canyon Capital, the one-time ally of Oaktree, had become a major investor across the Caesars capital structure. Canyon had its own interests. It owned roughly $400 million of the first-lien bonds as well as some senior bank debt and Caesars equity, compared with just $200 million of second-lien bonds. Because Canyon was involved across the Caesars capital structure, it was effectively hedged against whatever the precise terms of the second-lien recovery would be. A dollar lost on the second-lien bonds was a dollar made in Caesars stock. What mattered most to Canyon was to get the company out of bankruptcy as soon as possible, on whatever terms.

"So when you own both, you're actually receiving consideration on your second-lien notes and you're also receiving consideration for your Caesars parent equity. So you just need to know their perspective of getting value in both pockets…That clearly drives some motivation you know if you own so much of them to for example just try to reach a settlement so you can try to move forward," explained Hilty.

The costs of staying in bankruptcy were very real. The company had estimated that between accrued interest being paid to senior creditors along with "administrative expenses"—professional fees—the total was over $1 billion. The Caesars business had rallied, however, and its EBITDA had climbed $800 million so the net annual "cost" of the Chapter 11 was $300 million. A lengthy, contested confirmation would only make things worse.

David Zott of Kirkland was now cross-examining Hilty.

"...Between now and confirmation as both parties gear up for World War III, the administrative expenses are going to go up, right?" asked Zott.

"There's been a lot of litigation, including this hearing, but I don't actually know. But I would assume as we get closer to confirmation, they would be getting higher, correct," said Hilty, with the understatement of the day.

Zott was trying to get Hilty to concede that it was in everyone's interest to cut a deal as quickly as possible, even the recalcitrant second-lien bondholders that Hilty represented.

Everyone could agree that apart from the bad blood, the sheer mathematical exercise of evaluating ParentCo, OpCo, REITs, convertible bonds, take-back debt, preferred stock backstops, CEC/CAC mergers, and the like was making it impossible for everyone to follow, including the most important person in the courtroom—Judge Goldgar.

"Okay. I'm hearing 'gap' and I'm hearing 'hole,'" Goldgar interjected in one exchange between Zott and Hilty. The two were discussing the differences that had to be bridged for a deal between Caesars and the second-lien bonds. The "hole" and the "gap" were distinct but important concepts.

Goldgar offered his understanding. "And I actually think they have different meanings here. The hole was the $950 million under the 2L RSA that has not been funded. The gap is the $250 million that would be necessary in excess of $950 million to make members of the 2L committee happy. Have I got that right?"

Hilty concurred. "I agree with your terminology that the hole is the $900 million or so which needs to be filled for the 2L RSA to be funded."

"Right," said Goldgar.

The fifty-five-cent deal with Canyon and the three others didn't actually specify where an additional $950 million would come from to acquire that level of recovery. The 2L's whole point was that the RSA was meaningless because of the "hole" and the unwillingness of Apollo and TPG to put any money into the pot.

Hilty went on. "The gap, I believe you are correct. I believe that is what Mr. Hayes testified to yesterday in his view of the gap." The

$250 million gap was simply the aggregate difference between the fifty-five-cent offer on the table and the sixty cents the 2L committee was asking for. In all, another $1.2 billion needed to be unearthed to finish this case.

The complexity of the case had become an excuse for the lack of progress. In the days before the hearing, there was hope that the Caesars and the second-lien committee would meet with the mediator to discuss settlement proposals that had been swapped on August 2, nearly three weeks before. But Judge Farnan said such a meeting was premature. He had asked the Millstein team to run some numbers to get everyone on the same page.

In an email in the days before the hearing, Judge Farnan wrote, "as you all know, our discussions yesterday focused on different financial models of various settlement numbers. Before we adjourned, I detailed my plan for continuing to move forward. This morning I discussed with Jim [Millstein] and Brendan [Hayes] the various models and math corrections I needed for future meetings I plan to schedule with others and you in the coming weeks."

Those corrections did not arrive until Sunday, August 21, just two days before the hearing when Judge Goldgar was demanding to see progress. In reality, neither Caesars and Apollo nor the 2L group really were serious about settling the case through mediation, instead taking their chances with Judge Goldgar.

Hilty was making every attempt to destroy the credibility of Brendan Hayes but, at times, overreached. When Hayes had come up with his $6 billion theoretical equity value for the new Caesars, he called it an "intrinsic value." Bruce Bennett and David Hilty both attacked that approach.

While Hilty was testifying, Judge Goldgar asked him directly what he thought of Hayes's methodology.

"So intrinsic value is not a technical term in corporate finance circles; it's a Brendan Hayes term from his testimony here?" Goldgar asked Hilty.

"I don't commonly use the word 'intrinsic value' when I'm…talking about shares or anything like that."

It was a bizarre exchange. "Intrinsic value" was, in fact, a common term and basic concept, both among practitioners and in textbooks. Like Millstein & Co., Hilty's firm, Houlihan Lokey, had prepared its own "intrinsic value" analysis, and reconciling the models was part of what the mediator Farnan had been seeking to do. It should have been embarrassing to Hilty, but he caught a lucky break. Goldgar admitted he had never heard of "intrinsic value" either.

On the third day of the trial, David Zott cross-examined Hilty. Among Zott's goals was to show to Goldgar that it was Hilty, not Hayes, who was ignorant.

"So let me ask you the question, though I know you don't use the term 'intrinsic value.' Is that a common and accepted generally used corporate finance term?"

"I don't believe it is, no."

"Okay. Now are there treatises that are written about corporate finance and corporate valuations, sir? Authoritative treatises that you would recognize as authoritative?"

"Yes, there are."

"Have you heard of Graham and Dodd...their treatise or a book on securities analysis?"

Benjamin Graham and David Dodd were Columbia University professors in the 1930s and were the pioneers of corporate finance and valuation theory. They had inspired Warren Buffett, who had been a student of Graham. Buffett had even written the foreword for updates to their classic textbook, *Security Analysis*.

They were as famous as finance thinkers could be, but apparently not famous enough for the co-head of restructuring at Houlihan Lokey.

"I actually have not," admitted Hilty.

"You have not heard of that?" asked a startled Zott.

Zott had a copy of *Security Analysis*, which explained the concept of intrinsic value that Hilty had already denied any knowledge of. A lengthy discussion of the book's relevance ensued between Zott, Sid Levinson of Jones Day, and Judge Goldgar. Zott argued that it went to the "knowledge and expertise" of Hilty.

Unsurprisingly, Goldgar admitted he also had never heard of *Security Analysis*. "The fact that this book, which I have never heard of either, but then I'm not a securities analyst, as probably everyone is aware, the fact that it says it's a great thing doesn't make it a great thing." Kirkland was once again the victim of Goldgar's quirks.

After several minutes, Judge Goldgar was at the end of his rope. "Well, I think the problem now is that whatever probative value any of this has is outweighed by a waste of time...I think we should just move on, Mr. Zott."

After the hearing, Kirkland & Ellis shipped a copy of *Security Analysis* to Hilty's office in New York.

ZOTT ALSO NEEDED TO REHABILITATE Brendan Hayes's analysis of who was contributing to a Caesars settlement.

"I'd like to turn to a subject that we're all going to regret, before I'm done. And that is—and probably me more than you. That is the—whether other parties besides the Caesars parent are making a contribution to the plan. Okay?"

Kirkland and Millstein were intent to show that even if the $4 billion contribution did not come with Apollo, TPG, Rowan, or Bonderman writing checks, it still was a legitimate way to settle the case. And remarkably, Zott got a major concession from David Hilty.

"Now just to be clear, if the noteholders were receiving what they considered to be fair, satisfactory, and ample recovery, you don't care where the money is coming from, right?" pressed Zott.

"Ultimately, I think that's correct, if it was providing a recovery that people felt was reasonable," conceded Hilty.

Unfortunately for Kirkland and Caesars, Goldgar seemed to have already made up his mind on what was reasonable, and the final witness would not boost the Caesars view.

Kirkland did not want Ronen Stauber to testify at this injunction hearing. Stauber was one of the two independent directors added to the Caesars OpCo board in the summer of 2014. His job was to represent all the stakeholders of the OpCo, including creditors owning $18 billion of debt. Stauber, like his fellow independent director Steve Winograd, had ties to the Apollo founders, and the creditors believed both were Marc Rowan's stooges.

Over the two years, the company and the OpCo advisors got to know both men well. And while Winograd was respected by Kirkland and Millstein for his seriousness, Stauber was regarded as a lightweight. Stauber once received a *Wall Street Journal* news alert involving the French company, Casino. He sent the alert along to the Millstein team, telling them it could be a comparable transaction they could use for their analysis. Except Casino was a supermarket chain, not a gaming company.

Another time, Stauber was visiting the Harry Potter theme park in Florida. He sent a photo to the OpCo email working group, joking that he was looking for consideration that could be paid to Caesars creditors. Stauber was even having junior Millstein bankers do financial analysis for his own personal projects and investments until he was told that was inappropriate.

Geoff Stewart of Jones Day explained to Goldgar that Stauber was valuable to understanding Apollo and TPG's seriousness in contributing to a settlement. "But according to Mr. Hayes and others, the Caesars parent actually isn't doing the negotiating. The negotiating is being done by Mr. Rowan and by Mr. Sambur...This has led to the almost comic situation, almost mindful of the Marx Brothers scenario, where Millstein and Mr. Hayes approach Mr. Rowan and Mr. Sambur saying, 'we would like Mr. Rowan and Mr. Sambur to make a contribution.' At which point Mr. Rowan and Mr. Sambur say, we'll check. They come back two weeks later saying, we checked, and the answer is 'no,'" said Stewart. Goldgar let the deposition proceed.

Stauber's job was to show that he and Winograd—each being paid $40,000 a month—were indeed negotiating hard on behalf of the OpCo creditors.

Stauber's testimony proved disastrous. He provided no confidence that a vigorous negotiation was happening with Apollo, or even that he understood what the case was about. Stewart repeatedly asked Stauber how the committee came to its settlement and how specific allegations were addressed. Stauber could only keep repeating words such as "totality" and "holistic" as if he had been trained.

"We looked at the claims and our approach to it in its totality."

"We've looked at the totality of the case and arrived at our conclusions as the best way forward, in our opinion."

"We've looked at the totality of the case and arrived at our conclusions that way."

Stauber finally threw up his hands. "I've answered the question to the best of my ability."

Stewart eventually asked Stauber if he was willing to target Apollo since they were on the hook for liability based on the examiner's report.

"…have you ever had any discussions with anyone from Apollo about the possibilities that debtors might file a complaint against them?" asked Stewart.

"I don't recall."

"Have you personally reached out to Apollo since the June 15 injunction order and requested an additional contribution?"

"No."

"Are you aware of whether anyone representing the debtors has done so?"

"I don't know."

"Are you aware of any request by the debtors or their representatives seeking an additional contribution from either Mr. Rowan or Mr. Sambur?"

"I don't know."

"If the debtors wanted to make a demand to a particular defendant, whose responsibility would [it] be to approve that?"

"I don't know. It's a pretty hypothetical situation, so I'm not sure."

There was nothing hypothetical about it. It was Stauber's job to pursue claims against such parties as Apollo, Rowan, and Sambur.

"Have any demands been made upon Paul, Weiss to make a settlement contribution?"

"I don't know."

By revealing how clueless he was, Stauber, more than any other witness, had incinerated the case for the injunction—and worse, the case for the settlement plan Kirkland and Millstein had assembled. As the second-lien group saw it, Stauber's fecklessness implied that Rowan had simply put together the restructuring plan himself, for Apollo's and his own benefit. The logical conclusion was that was what Rowan intended when he hand-picked Stauber to be an independent board member.

END GAME

"As far as I can tell, the examiner's report has had essentially no effect, at least on the plan sponsors…Poor Mr. Davis, at least he was paid. Because it sounds as if it was a total waste of his time," lamented Goldgar.

David Zott was in the midst of his closing argument and Judge Goldgar was apparently also wondering why this case was proceeding after Davis's damning findings. Zott was doing his best to save the injunction and, by this point, had been reduced to begging.

"I represent all the creditors, 70 to 80 percent, saying please stay…the fact is the majority of this capital structure is asking for a stay to protect the hard work that's occurred over a year and a half with values and contributions that they think are fair. And they shouldn't all be put at risk by allowing one disgruntled group to go forward with [lifting] an injunction."

This was Zott's best—and essentially only—remaining argument. Everyone except a slight majority of the second-lien bondholders had agreed upon a deal, and letting them crash the case was simply unfair to the supermajority.

Frank Velocci, a Drinker Biddle lawyer who, with Jim Millar, represented the Unsecured Notes holders, also had the chance to address Goldgar. "…the individuals behind the sponsors, Your Honor, they are the architects of this mess, yet they sit here in situations where you can't demand anything of them. They don't come to court and explain to Your Honor why they are entitled to the release or what they're contributing to the plan. And I haven't seen them here in the three hearings that I've been here, trying to explain to the court why any of this is fair."

Jim Johnston, Bruce Bennett's colleague of more than twenty years, then summarized the second-lien case by saying, "...the evidence shows that there is nothing about the Caesars parent's actions that indicates that the injunction is or was about trying to reach a deal...the denial of an injunction, we think, first and foremost, will result in a settlement that will get this case over."

Zott got the final word and ominously told Goldgar, "The risk of miscalculation here could be catastrophic, catastrophic for this plan, catastrophic for the creditors that support it."

Goldgar then asked Kirkland and Jones Day how quickly they wanted a ruling, in the off chance they were going to settle on the courthouse steps. "I mean, I've seen Mr. Bennett and Mr. Sprayregen in here for forty-eight hours now, basically just eyeing each other across the room, during which time they were not apparently talking settlement unless they are telepathic. So if people are going to talk, I won't rule until Monday. But if they're not going to talk, then I'll rule tomorrow."

Jones Day and Kirkland conferred in a recess and decided they wanted a ruling as soon as possible.

"All right, 3:00 tomorrow," proclaimed Goldgar.

"Thank you, Your Honor."

"You're welcome. It will be from notes. It will not be something beautifully written, but I'll do my best. You have thanked me for my time. You are welcome. You and the other taxpayers, however, pay for it. Let me say, though, that I appreciate, as I hope I said before, I think I have, the high quality of the advocacy that I've seen in the past couple of days, and that I've seen since this case began. I don't see it all the time. You make a lot of work for me, but what goes on in here is a pleasure."

Goldgar's sentimentality seemed to portend that this case, one way or another, would soon reach its crescendo.

"FOR THE REASONS I WILL now discuss, the debtors' motion to extend the existing injunction is denied," Judge Goldgar said, wasting no time in sharing his ruling on Friday. After nearly 20 months, the head-to-head clash that would define this case—the immovable object, Apollo, and the unstoppable force, Appaloosa/Oaktree—had been decided. Goldgar's decision did not shock anyone who had been paying attention, but it was a stunning moment nonetheless. The case had been a slow burn, but everything had changed in an instant.

"I'm no longer convinced, as I have been in the past, either an injunction is likely to enhance the success of reorganization or that its denial will endanger that success…Most of the deal-making that has happened here has occurred when no injunction was in effect. This is particularly true of events late in May and early June of this year. The progress on settlement that I found justified a second injunction this past June all took place when the Caesars parent had no protection from an injunction and deadlines in the guarantee case that were looming."

Judge Goldgar had just trashed Kirkland's core argument that a timeout was necessary to promote settlement talks. He had observed that the most progress occurred when there was no safe harbor from the parent guarantee lawsuits.

"As for what happened after June 15: not that much," Goldgar went on to criticize the RSA that had been struck with the minority of the second-lien holders, noting the $950 million gap. The judge then ripped Apollo for slow-walking the mediation session. "The pace of discussions does not show that the current injunction is helping or that its expiration gives the parties much cause for concern. Given this history, in fact, it appears that it isn't injunctive relief that promotes settlement but rather its absence."

Goldgar then pummeled Apollo and TPG over their contempt for the process. "Particularly disturbing is that none of the targets of the estates' claims arising from the disputed transactions—targets that include the ultimate owners of the Caesars enterprise, Apollo and TPG—are making any financial contribution to the reorganization although the proposed plan would release all claims against them. Incredibly, the testimony this week was that the targets of these claims were not even approached about making a contribution until two weeks ago…Asked at his deposition whether any of these parties had been approached, Ronen Stauber testified, 'I don't know.' This from a member not only of the Caesars OpCo board but the board's restructuring committee.

"Worse still, Brendan Hayes, another of the debtor's restructuring advisors, testified that when Apollo and TPG were at last approached about funding the $950 million hole in the second-lien RSA, they refused, essentially saying it was a 'Parent problem.'"

Goldgar's hottest fury seemed to be reserved for the Caesars OpCo guardians. Caesars had always been a corporate governance case where creditors never had their interests safeguarded. But more than two years after OpCo added independent directors to their own lawyers and bankers, those groups still had failed to protect creditors. Bruce Bennett had tried and failed to show Kirkland's blind spots. But now Bennett's theory had been at least partially vindicated.

In his closing argument the day before, Zott had pleaded with Goldgar not to blow up a deal that most of the Caesars creditors had agreed to. Goldgar explicitly rejected that reasoning as well. "…the point of an injunction has always been to not only to protect the Caesars parent contribution but to gain time to reach a settlement. And to be clear, a settlement means a consensual plan. It does not mean a cramdown plan confirmed after a contested confirmation."

Goldgar took sharp exception to Caesars' congressional lobbying effort, pointing out that while it wanted a timeout on the injunction litigation, it was also trying to change the law. "But it's unseemly and so inequitable for the Caesar parent to employ an injunction in its favor to gain an advantage in litigation over parties whose hands the injunction had tied."

Goldgar closed the loop on the concept that had defined the four injunction hearings that began in June 2015. Creditors "face the possibility that a Caesars parent bankruptcy will indeed produce one of the 'great messes of our time.' But how great are these risks? Not so great."

Bennett, Appaloosa, and Oaktree had, more than anything, resented the arrogance of Apollo, Rowan, and Sambur, who believed that the case would be settled on their terms at a time and place of their choosing. This afternoon, Appaloosa and Oaktree had flipped the script. They were fully in control now.

Goldgar closed by reiterating his hope that the decision would prompt the resolution of the case. "The injunctions here have provided the Caesars parent, Apollo, and TPG a comfortable, free ride on the debtors' coattails. They have shown no keen sense of urgency to resolve the outstanding disputes that gave rise to the bankruptcy case—and frankly, neither have the debtors, at least where the disputed transactions are concerned. The Caesars parent, Apollo, and TPG have evidently felt no particular pressure to expedite the reorganization process. Now perhaps they will."

Goldgar's ruling was not flawless. He referred to Brendan Hayes's $4 billion intrinsic value of the reorganized Caesars equity as a "fiction." Hayes's valuation and the corporate finance principles embedded within were sensible. However, explaining the difference between the market price of Caesars and the Millstein "intrinsic value" was a nuance that Goldgar did not grasp. Bruce Bennett in his cross-examination, and then David Hilty, had successfully exploited Goldgar's confusion on the complex topic. When Hayes admitted that Millstein had not seriously asked Apollo and TPG for money, Goldgar effectively dismissed Hayes's views on all matters.

As momentous as it was to face the guarantee litigation in Judge Rakoff's court on August 30, Apollo and TPG had a bigger problem than the injunction expiration. Goldgar had specifically stated that he was not inclined to give the private equity firms and their executives coveted liability releases in a cramdown scenario. The private equity firms were going to have to cut a deal with the second-lien bondholders, who suddenly were holding all the cards—and were not inclined to be gracious.

In bankruptcy, holdout junior creditors like the junior bondholders usually got steamrolled. But Goldgar had been so offended by the arrogance of Caesars' negotiating tactics that he had completely upended that dynamic. Though it seemed that things could not get any worse, Sambur and Rowan had no idea about the kind of pressure they were about to face.

33

"PONY UP THE PAPER"

"**M**aybe it makes sense to talk," Paul Aronzon told Bruce Bennett. Aronzon was the senior bankruptcy partner at Milbank, the law firm brought on to replace Paul, Weiss in representing the Caesars parent after the disastrous March 2016 Examiner's report. Judge Goldgar's ruling earlier in the afternoon of Friday, August 26, 2016, had allowed the parent guarantee litigation to proceed. Within minutes, Apollo and TPG were thinking about throwing in the towel. Judge Goldgar had taken apart their approach to the case, and it would be smart to cut their losses. Aronzon had been empowered to find an off-ramp.

By coincidence, Aronzon lived no more than a mile from Bennett. They had known and respected each other for years. Aronzon drove over in the late afternoon, bringing a bottle of pinot noir which they opened as they sat on Bennett's patio.

Bennett may have been frustrated that his Los Angeles base kept him from achieving the celebrity he could have found in New York all these years. But his second-city blues faded whenever he was at home. His mansion was perched on a hill overlooking the Riviera Country Club. Riviera's golf course was one of the ten best in America, and the club's membership consisted of Hollywood stars and power players. (Bennett himself was not a member, though he had joined Brentwood Country Club down the street. His client, Kaj Vazales of Oaktree and the former golf mini-tour player, belonged to Riviera.) Bennett's house had massive windows that maximized the view of the golf course. The backyard had multiple levels, which included a lawn, a covered patio, and

an infinity swimming pool. One of his neighbors was the come-
dian, Larry David.

Aronzon opened by bemoaning the performance of Kirkland and
Millstein before the two got to the matter at hand.

"We are not going up, but we are not going down either," Bennett
informed Aronzon. The second-lien committee's ask was going to
be sixty-six cents. Aronzon asked if the final negotiations could start
the next day, Saturday. Bennett told him there were threshold issues
the advisors needed to flesh out before their respective clients could
get involved. First, the two sides needed to agree on a common valuation model for the company. Second, the terms on a new $1 billion
convertible bond going to the second-lien bondholders had to be
finalized in writing.

As the late summer sun began to set , Aronzon and Bennett agreed
the advisors—Milbank, PJT, Jones Day, and Houlihan Lokey—would
speak on Saturday. If that proved productive, Rowan and Sambur
could connect with Appaloosa and Oaktree on Sunday.

In a jubilant call among the second-lien committee, Oaktree and
Appaloosa swapped stories of Apollo frantically calling to settle.
David Tepper said Apollo was begging him to speak with Leon Black.
He said he told the private equity firm that it would get a far better deal talking with Appaloosa colleague Jim Bolin. Tepper then,
half-jokingly, said on the call that whatever the group's most recent
settlement proposal was, to "knock it higher by ten cents."

"THERE CAN BE NO SERIOUS dispute that Paul, Weiss, acting for the
Caesars parent, and/or the sponsors, not only facilitated the Fraudulent Transfers but was intimately involved in their formulation and
implementation," Bruce Bennett claimed. Kirkland & Ellis was not
the only legal powerhouse Bennett was targeting with full fury.

The parent guarantee litigation was the preeminent legal fight
in the bankruptcy. But there were several other ongoing skirmishes
where both the second-lien bondholders and Caesars were posturing
to win additional negotiating leverage. Few of these battles would lead
to a tipping point in the broader case, but they were part of the game
lawyers played to knock the other side off balance and perhaps get
a surprise victory. Caesars had, for example, challenged the second-
lien committee's decision over the involuntary bankruptcy. This led
to a multi-day trial held by Judge Goldgar in late 2015. In 2016, Goldgar said he had even drafted the first thirty-five pages of a ruling
which he ultimately never shared.

And Bennett was deploying his own litigation tactics. In May 2016, less than two months after the publication of the examiner's report, Jones Day filed a lawsuit in the bankruptcy court asking for "standing" to sue the Caesars parent on behalf of the Caesars OpCo over the fraudulent transfer allegations. That lawsuit named not only the Caesars parent but Apollo, TPG, their executives, Loveman, other Caesars directors, and Paul, Weiss, among many others.

More significantly, because of the confirmation hearing scheduled for January over the Caesars restructuring plan that he opposed, Bennett was entitled to broad discovery on all aspects of that plan. In particular, he was interested in the legal releases being granted to Caesars and all in its orbit. Bennett was seeking to force Paul, Weiss to hand over the most sensitive documents that Richard Davis had received on an "Examiner's Eyes only" basis to form his opinions on the fraudulent transfers. Normally, such documents would be protected under attorney-client privilege. But Bennett saw an opening. In the filing, Jones Day wrote that Apollo, TPG, and Paul, Weiss were "now trying to conceal from the Court their roles in these frauds—by hiding behind the attorney-client privilege. But the law is clear: a party who engages in fraud cannot rely on the attorney-client privilege."

Bennett wasn't just accusing Paul, Weiss of being complicit in the alleged fraudulent transfers—he was also accusing the firm of creating a scheme to cover it up. The latter assertion was based on handwritten notes that a Kirkland lawyer had taken during a conference call with Paul, Weiss in 2014. Paul, Weiss was outraged at the accusation. In its written response rejecting the motion, the firm noted that Richard Davis had written in the examiner's report that "the evidence does not support a conclusion that Paul, Weiss lawyers knowingly acted at any time to injure or prejudice the OpCo or its creditors."

The firm was also unhappy about being accused of orchestrating a cover-up. "That accusation rests on the Committee's tendentious speculation about a few words in a set of incomprehensible handwritten notes, an interpretation inconsistent with common sense, contrary to the Examiner's conclusion quoted above and refuted by the accompanying sworn declaration of the Paul, Weiss partner [Lewis Clayton] who is the target of the accusation."

Even as damning as Richard Davis's report was toward Paul, Weiss, plenty of others in the case thought he had let them off easy for their role in the $5 billion of potential fraud at Caesars. Davis had said that sustaining any charges against Paul, Weiss would be difficult. But that was not going to stop Bennett from making his case and applying maximum pressure against his adversaries to get leverage. And his case against Paul, Weiss was far better than anything he ever had on Kirkland.

"ALL RIGHT. LET ME ADDRESS the motion. And I have a couple of questions. And I'm going to give you some impressions and then I'm going to give you some work to do and that work will be done here today," dictated Judge Goldgar. It was September 14, 2016, and Goldgar was presiding over a hearing over one of Bruce Bennett's more extreme pressure tactics. In the summer, the second-lien committee had served subpoenas on six Caesars individuals: Apollo's Marc Rowan and David Sambur, TPG's David Bonderman and Kelvin Davis, and Caesars' Gary Loveman and Eric Hession.

The group had been Caesars directors and would receive liability releases as part of any settlement. Bennett simply wanted to determine their wealth, should it be needed to satisfy any potential judgment against them.

The subpoenas that Jones Day had served in late June asked for 17 types of documents, including tax returns, bank and brokerage accounts statements, property records—essentially anything that could demonstrate net worth. When negotiations over the subpoena terms broke down, Bennett filed a motion to compel the production of those documents.

Rowan and Sambur noted in their response papers that multiple layers of indemnification and insurance existed for them, from both Caesars and Apollo itself. There would be no need for their personal fortunes ever to be tapped, they explained. Apollo wrote that "the Committee's goal is not to obtain information but to harass the people on the other side of a settlement negotiation…to illustrate the egregious overreaching involved here, the subpoenas by their terms would require the Apollo Individuals to produce all receipts and instruction manuals for their children's toys."

Any bankruptcy judge experienced in large cases would have laughed Bennett's motion to compel out of court. Five of the six individuals were famously wealthy. Moreover, the settlement contribution could come from multiple sources—Caesars stock, insurance, or the firms they worked at. But Goldgar has demonstrated that he was an earnest judge not deferential to powerful law firms or private equity firms simply out of convention.

But Bennett's timing was fortuitous. Just three weeks earlier, Goldgar had lifted the injunction on the guarantee litigation though Caesars had won a delay on enforcement while it appealed. Bennett was laser focused on how little the private equity firms were directly contributing to the settlement. And Goldgar was ready to rule quickly on Bennett's motion, having just read all sides' previously submitted papers.

Goldgar asked Kirkland's David Seligman what the OpCo's position on "collectability" of a liability judgment was.

"Your Honor, the settlement contemplated in the plan, from our perspective, is a merits-based settlement. We did not discount for collectability [of] these individuals. We are not going to be arguing that these defendants don't have the ability to pay."

The core argument against allowing the discovery centered on the idea of "collectability." If liability, say, was estimated at $100 but defendants only had $60 in their pocket, then the settlement demand could be discounted to $60. If a defendant did not have the money to pay the ultimate damages, a collectability discount could be appropriate. Bennett wanted to know if the settlement that Kirkland and Millstein struck had been discounted, and if the defendants had the resources to satisfy potential judgments.

Seligman pushed back hard, arguing that since collectability was not an issue OpCo was raising, there was no need to allow Bennett's discovery motion. The $4 billion settlement that Kirkland and Millstein struck was based on their view regarding the fair value of the potential damages from the asset transfers, and nothing else.

Goldgar then asked if Seligman could "stipulate" that the defendants could satisfy any judgments against them. "Because if you could stipulate to that, then I could deny the motion and send you all home."

With no way of knowing what a judgment would be in court, there was no way Seligman could concede that point.

"But I'm not going to do that now. So that's what I needed to know," said Goldgar.

The dam had burst. One of the ugliest brawls in the history of corporate America would come to its shocking conclusion.

"I don't think that we can rule out discovery on this issue because the debtors didn't consider it. The debtors don't get to essentially legislate out of existence a particular legal issue. The legal issues are what they are."

Marc Rowan, David Bonderman, and Gary Loveman—three historically important men in their fields—were ordered by a federal judge to turn over their most sensitive personal financial information to creditors pursuing them on multi-billion-dollar charges of fraudulent conveyance and breaches of fiduciary duty.

The only thing Judge Goldgar wanted to do was tweak Bennett's document request. Goldgar wanted all sides to figure out together how to tailor the order most sensibly after he gave his own feedback.

"But I'm going to tell you some things that I think have to be changed here, and that will aid you in your conversations. And then there's a conference room right across the hall, and it's unlocked. And I'll be here all day long. And you'll be here until we get this fixed, because there's no ability to continue this motion. We're on too tight a timeline," Goldgar said, referring to the January confirmation hearing in just four months.

The courtroom was stunned as Goldgar simply went down the request list and offered his initial feedback. "Document request number two, the committee is requesting documents sufficient to show all income from any source whatsoever. You know that could be I sold my lawnmower to my next-door neighbor for $25. I mean there has to be some kind of floor on what's relevant here…and then in ten, ten not only concerns transfers, it also concerns purchases, sales, or uses. I just don't think Dr. Loveman, if he got his lawnmower repaired, has to produce a document relating to the lawnmower repair…"

Goldgar finished with his feedback and told the lawyers to get to work finalizing the document request.

Rowan and Sambur's attorney could not stand idle. "This is Marc Wolinsky for Apollo, and Mr. Rowan and Sambur."

Wolinsky was an acclaimed litigator from Wachtell Lipton who had represented Apollo in the Hexion/Huntsman case nearly a decade earlier, and was again back to protect the privacy and personal fortunes of the firm's founders.

"Are you interested in hearing argument on the merits?" he asked, hoping to get Goldgar to reconsider.

"Not particularly, because I've read the papers and I've read the TMT case and I think these are the relevant considerations."

David Bonderman's lawyer, David Rosner from Kasowitz Torres, jumped in to reiterate David Seligman's argument that collectability was not an issue.

Goldgar again disagreed with the argument. "The [second-lien] committee's position is that entering into settlement in which a host of claims in which only the Caesars parent is making a contribution is not fair and equitable. And part of that argument is going to be that these judgments could have been collected. There were judgments that could have been obtained and there were people out there that could have satisfied them and showing that Mr. Bonderman, for example—and you're shaking your head. But I mean, I've read the briefs and I'm sorry but I buy this argument that the idea that Mr. Bonderman potentially has, you know, six old masters displayed in his garage that could be grabbed and sold. I mean, I think that's relevant…"

"That's not the issue," Rosner snapped back.

"It is the issue!" Goldgar retorted.

"But here the debtors are not saying they made the settlement on the basis of their being judgment proof of $4 in a bank account or $40 million in a bank account," Rosner pleaded.

"Then perhaps I should deny confirmation right now," Goldgar shot back.

Rosner asked Goldgar to consider balancing the reasonableness of the request with how intrusive the discovery would be. That also went nowhere.

"I've balanced it. The balance weighs in favor of the committee. If these gentlemen don't want to be released under the plan, I'll quash the subpoenas today…But these folks are going to have to pony up the paper, okay?"

Goldgar then took a recess. Marc Kasowitz, the legendary litigator and founder of Kasowitz Benson, was irate with Goldgar's decision, along with everyone else on the Caesars side in court. Word quickly filtered back to the shocked Apollo offices in New York. In Los Angeles, Ken Liang at Oaktree headquarters was listening to the hearing on the phone and pumped his fist, as he had been leading the charge to get these bank account records.

After the break, the hearing resumed with Sidney Levinson of Jones Day telling Goldgar that the sides chose not to confer—as the judge had requested—because the defendants were going to appeal.

As Goldgar was set to end the hearing, Loveman's own lawyer, Richard Strassberg, a former federal prosecutor now at law firm Goodwin Procter, jumped in and asked Goldgar to consider the unique plights of Loveman and Eric Hession, who were not private equity tycoons. Strassberg argued that the two Caesars executives' financial resources could be gleaned from Caesars public filings where their compensation was disclosed, rendering the intrusive subpoena unnecessary.

"And for the last five years that income is publicly disclosed. So this is not an instance where, respectfully, there's any reasonable allegation that there are master paintings in the garage, right?" said Strassberg.

Loveman's indignities continued. His dreams of a windfall from the LBO had been dashed, and he would lose much of the millions he had invested in the deal. He spent several years after the buyout trying to fix both the balance sheet and the business, only to get replaced by a man he could not stand. Now Mark Frissora, a man he viscerally loathed, was getting credit for the Caesars turnaround and would keep the CEO job when Caesars emerged from bankruptcy.

"Oh, I don't know. My employer doesn't know about my art collection," dryly noted Goldgar.

Goldgar ordered the production of documents to begin on September 21. He marked up the subpoena request by hand with his edits scribbled in the margins, which were then filed to the court docket.

Everyone in the case was numb. The bewilderment was not just over what had transpired in court that day but rather the six-month sweep by the second-lien group who had, against all odds, prevailed on virtually every crucial matter in the case. Bruce Bennett had simply been a wrecking ball.

In March, the examiner's report laid in devastating detail pre-bankruptcy wrongdoing with damages estimated in the billions of dollars. Bennett slowly but surely worked to get Judge Goldgar to lift the injunction on the guarantee litigation, which he finally accomplished in late August. And in the longest of longshots, Judge Goldgar now had ruled the unthinkable, ordering two of the richest men in the world to hand over their most intimate financial information.

In an early September court filing challenging one of Bennett's legal maneuvers, the Caesars parent wrote that the second-lien group "wants to use these cases to play a reckless game of 'chicken' with the rest of the capital structure." Jim Bolin and Ken Liang kept dismissing settlement offers and Bennett remarkably kept winning in court, so there was never reason to back down—2016 had been a game of chicken, and Apollo was about to blink first.

Shortly after the September 14 ruling, David Sambur called his longtime nemeses, Kaj Vazales and Ken Liang at Oaktree. After being tortured for years by Sambur, this surrender overture filled the pair with sweet vindication—but less graciousness.

"We're going to rent a blimp and have it hover over Times Square with all your bank account information," Liang ribbed Sambur. For once, Sambur was in no position to retort.

MARC ROWAN WOULD INSIST THAT the real inflection point in the Caesars case was not Goldgar's decision to allow creditors access to his private financial information. Goldgar's approval of the discovery motion—had Apollo not yet settled—would have allowed Bennett's second-lien group to dig into the intricate details of Rowan's personal fortune to determine just how much money he had, where he had it, in order to satisfy any judgment against him brought by creditors.

Rowan brushed off such a notion by pointing out how the Caesars board members had gone through invasive scrutiny in the gaming licensing process, and anything they had to turn over now was nothing they hadn't already submitted to enter the casino business. Still, the prospect of dozens of Jones Day partners and associates flipping through their most sensitive information was unnerving.

Rowan was more upset about the parent guarantee litigation. Apollo viewed the examiner report findings about the solvency of OpCo and the asset transfers as an argument over valuation, which Rowan believed Apollo could ultimately win in court. The guarantee litigation, however, was what he thought of as "binary." Either the releases of the guarantees were legally permissible under the bond indentures or they were not. Apollo believed its interpretations were correct. But the Marblegate decision—bad law, in Caesars' view—indicated that Caesars was sure to lose the New York and Delaware cases, probably on summary judgment. Once Goldgar lifted the injunction Apollo had little choice but to capitulate, even as a Marblegate appeals court ruling was expected at any moment.

The negotiations with the junior bondholders were ongoing since August 26, and it looked like Apollo and TPG were going to keep a small but meaningful stake in the New Caesars. Even if peace would break out, the restructuring required a series of complex steps, including billions of dollars of new debt. The sooner that got done, the better for everyone. It did not happen often, but Rowan and Apollo had been defeated on the field.

Rowan had always been philosophical about deal making. LBOs were risky deals; some worked out, others did it. And sometimes you lost because there were things out of your control—like a random federal judge in New York blowing up decades of case law on bond restructurings. Apollo had fought the good fight at Caesars on behalf of its investors well longer than any other firm would have dared. It was time to tip their caps to the other side and move forward.

On September 21, one week after the ruling over personal financials discovery, the parties returned to court. Judge Goldgar would deny Bruce Bennett's crime-fraud exception motion to compel privileged documents from Paul, Weiss ruling that Bennett's legal theory was incorrect. But the motion mattered less since a settlement was nearing after Bennett had won in court on all the other big issues in the case.

David Seligman reported that a deal was coming together. "I can report that there's been significant activity over the past couple of weeks. Most recently, Your Honor, this past weekend, the Caesars parent, the sponsors, and potentially liable directors and officers provided the debtors and the major creditor groups with a best and final proposal for a global resolution of the case," Seligman explained to Judge Goldgar.

"Best and final" was a perhaps fitting term. For years, creditors had been hearing that phrase from David Sambur. Dave Miller from Elliott remembered how unnerved he was the first time Sambur uttered the threat in 2014. But he quickly realized that it meant little, and it became a running gag among all the creditors. With Kirkland saying it, however, "best and final" was finally accurate.

The total contribution to the settlement pot now would rocket from $4 billion to $5.6 billion, ahead of the high end of Richard Davis's estimated liability range. The $950 million "hole" that Brendan Hayes described at the August injunction hearing would be completely filled by Apollo and TPG, who would give up their $2 billion in Caesars parent equity, handing it back to creditors. This move was to address Goldgar's hot button issue that the private equity firms feel real pain in exchange for getting their prized releases. As Kris Hansen and Ryan Mollett had implored Rowan more than a year earlier, Apollo should have worried less about keeping a penny in Caesars and instead focused on getting their release.

The other public shareholders of the Caesars parent would contribute only an incremental $92 million of equity, the idea being that Apollo and TPG would do the heavy lifting in order to get the benefit of the liability release.

The negotiations around these equity contributions proved extremely complex. First, the Caesars parent and Caesars Growth had to re-merge, bringing all the transferred casinos back. Caesars Growth, which had benefited from the controversial transfers of casinos and the interactive business, theoretically could have been on the hook for damages.

All in all, Caesars creditors—in addition to the cash and takeback debt in the PropCo they were getting—would own roughly two-thirds of the New Caesars equity. The $950 million incremental contribution would wipe out the entirety of the original TPG and Apollo investment in Caesars. The pair would collectively keep around 14 percent of the New Caesars, reflecting their 2013 investment in Caesars Growth. They would lose their collective $2.65 billion original investment. The rest of the New Caesars would be divided up among the current public shareholders of the Caesars parent and the Caesars Growth.

Board of directors' insurance would kick in $100 million of cash into the settlement pot. The senior loan and bondholders would kick back a couple of pennies of their well-above-100-cent recoveries, which amounted to a couple hundred million dollars.

The second-lien creditors would be getting a recovery of roughly sixty-six cents—not bad for a group that had a nine-cent offer at the outset of the bankruptcy. Rowan had told Jim Millstein at the beginning of 2016 that a forty-two-cent offer was excessive and gave Oaktree and Appaloosa far too rich a recovery for their claims. The deal now had a gross value more than $1 billion greater than that forty-two-cent number, with most of that profit being a straight transfer from Apollo and TPG to the junior creditors.

The second-lien committee members were not the only winners. Marty Bienenstock had famously said in June that he had "seen the light" when he accepted a forty-six-cent settlement for his Unsecured Creditors Committee. That deal had angered Bruce Bennett. But because of a "most favored nation" clause Bienenstock negotiated, the unsecureds were now, ironically, entitled to the sixty-six cents Bennett's group had received.

This "best and final" deal had been assembled, without mediator Judge Farnan. In the latest bizarre twist in the case, Farnan had given his letter of resignation on September 9. When Goldgar lifted the injunction last August, he had criticized Farnan and the mediation process. Farnan, feeling unfairly attacked, wrote in his resignation, "Apparently the court did not find my progress report helpful because I didn't breach the confidentiality of the mediation and testify in open court or describe the discussions and proposals exchanged and detail the status of the differences among the parties. I believe the court either misspoke or doesn't understand how such disclosures would be viewed by participants and the markets."

It was the perfect ending for the mediation process. While Farnan may have been earnest through the sessions, Apollo and the second-lien committee had not. Bennett twisted the knife: "The fact that the mediator resigned has had no impact at all."

The hearing that day represented a first in the nearly two-year-old journey: all sides essentially coming together to put this case to bed. David Seligman of Kirkland explained to Goldgar that the deal he had outlined was going to be completed by midnight, Friday, September 23. Thomas Kreller, Paul Aronzon's colleague at Milbank, warned that Apollo and the Caesars parent, after coughing up another billion dollars, were done contributing any more money, though there was about $130 million needed to finish the deal.

Bruce Bennett pointed out that, according to his math, the stake that Apollo and TPG held remained sizeable enough that the private equity firms had the wherewithal to close the gap if they wanted to.

Ken Eckstein, the lawyer for the senior bondholders, echoed the sentiments for shared pain. "There should be a meeting tomorrow. That's what people should be doing, sitting down in a room. The debtor should call a meeting tomorrow morning. Everybody could be in the same office and ask the question, is there an ability for everybody to absorb the pain?"

After all the brutality over a $30 billion LBO, every creditor group stood to make a fortune on their speculation, due to their victories in the courtroom and negotiations, the steady turnaround in the Caesars business, and the Chinese buying CIE for $4 billion. All they had to do was put down their weapons and kick in literal pennies.

A meeting would be set for two days later on Friday morning, September 23, 2016, at the Manhattan office of Kirkland & Ellis.

Eckstein lamented to Judge Goldgar, "Nobody is going to be happy."

34
KNOW WHEN TO FOLD 'EM

"They want more money. We told them, 'no fucking way.'"

Kaj Vazales and Ken Liang were standing outside of Casa Lever, talking on speaker with Vazales's phone. It was September 23, 2016, and they had just departed from the supposedly final settlement negotiation in the Kirkland & Ellis conference room. On the other end of the line were their bosses, Oaktree founders Howard Marks and Bruce Karsh.

Paul Singer had just called the Oaktree royalty. Elliott's employees, Dave Miller and Jon Pollock, had just been in the same room with Vazales and Liang. Every Caesars creditor group had agreed to give back a pittance of their massive recoveries to settle the deal—except Oaktree. With everyone still set to make a fortune, Oaktree's intransigence shocked the room. It was also potentially destructive, as the settlement expired at midnight if everybody was not on board. Miller and Pollock had quickly phoned Paul Singer, asking him to intervene. There was too much money at stake, and the brinkmanship had gone on too long.

"You guys have been vindicated," Karsh offered. The sixty-six-cent offer for the second-lien bonds was more than seven times where they traded at the start of the Chapter 11. Even the heavyweight firms like Elliott and GSO had steered clear of the second-lien bonds, too leery of the fight with Apollo that would have come with owning those bonds. But by pressing their legal case and withstanding the massive peer pressure to settle early, Oaktree and Appaloosa had stared down Apollo and clinched one of the great upset victories in the history of Wall Street.

"It's not a big dollar amount. Let's be constructive and pitch in," said Marks.

But Vazales was not interested in taking the high road. Every creditor group in that conference room had played rough for years until they squeezed Apollo for the terms that they wanted. On top of that, Apollo and TPG were keeping a stake in Caesars worth nearly a billion dollars. It was their treachery that had led to the ugly fight, and now they were getting full liability releases. Let everyone else plug the $130 million hole, Vazales insisted.

It was an intensely personal experience for Vazales. Dave Miller, his best friend for more than half his life, had been one of the multiple creditors who had been browbeating him. Earlier that week in advance of the Friday meeting, Miller had even called Vazales.

"Look, you guys are heroes," Miller tried to reason with or at least flatter his friend. "You have crushed Apollo. You are gods in the eyes of the Street. Do you really want to blow this up over a few cents?"

It was a tense enough conversation that Vazales pulled his car off of San Vicente Boulevard not far from the Pacific Ocean. Vazales was tired of the psychological warfare. When the case had intensified in 2014, Vazales was nervous about a fight with Apollo, and only comforted when Appaloosa joined the fray. By now, however, he had proved his mettle.

"Dave, you haven't done us any favors. You contractually agreed to side with Apollo to crush us and now you are asking us to put back a piece of our hard-earned recovery? You can go fuck yourself."

Liang and Vazales were disappointed that their bosses did not want to make one last point. The two even reminded Marks and Karsh that the others in the room that morning did not exactly have clean hands themselves. Dave Miller and Ryan Mollett had their credit default swaps side bet about when Caesars would file for bankruptcy. Miller had then concocted the notorious convertible preferred stock for Elliott and its allies in the senior bondholder group. All these other players, including Apollo, could—and should—plug the hole Liang and Vazales insisted.

Enough was enough, however. Marks and Karsh appreciated the context but decided the second-lien group would throw back its $30 million or half a penny. The paper gain from the initial nine-cent offer to 65.5 cents on $5.5 billion of second-lien bonds outstanding was still roughly $3 billion. It was time to take the money and declare victory.

Millstein and Kirkland got word that the second-lien bondholders were, begrudgingly, making their concession. The lawyers spent the weekend hashing out the details. On Monday, September 26, Caesars announced that, at long last, all major creditor groups had agreed to term sheets on the restructuring. For the next several days, the lawyers would work around the clock on revising RSAs and the plan of reorganization.

But there was still, remarkably, the matter of one last holdout.

"SO IN AUGUST, IN OTHER words, people beat the house more often than not?" asked Judge Goldgar.

"Correct," Brendan Hayes confirmed.

"I thought that never happened."

"From time to time that happens."

It was October 4, 2016, and a Caesars creditor was, for what felt like the millionth time, trying to lift the injunction on the parent guarantee litigation.

Hayes explained to Judge Goldgar that while the Caesars business had trended well all year long, August had been an anomaly where the house did not win. It felt like it was a metaphor that described the case. It was during the August injunction hearing when Goldgar had rebuked Apollo and TPG and paved the way for the second-lien creditors' victory over the house.

Brendan Hayes would avoid another Bruce Bennett inquisition as the second-lien group had agreed to their 65.5-cent deal. The only party left fighting now was Trilogy Capital Management and its $9.4 million of the unsecured notes trying to hold up a deal among $18 billion of debt. Its executive, Barry Kupferberg, told Judge Goldgar he simply wanted either the same sweetheart deal that Goldman Sachs cut in the summer of 2014, or his day in federal court.

Trilogy, a small fund out of Westchester County, had taken over the fabled MeehanCombs parent guarantee lawsuit after Meehan-Combs had folded as a fund. In multiple negotiations with David Sambur and Marc Rowan, Kupferberg had been told he was not that important. Still, Kupferberg was upset enough about his Caesars ordeal that he wondered why no one was going to jail and he was not giving up without a fight.

It was perhaps fitting that Trilogy was holding out, as its lawsuit brought by Jim Millar had upended the case—even if the hedge funds behind it were minnows.

Minor holdouts like Trilogy were usually squashed like a bug at this stage of a bankruptcy. Undaunted, Kupferberg insisted on going to court. Hayes now had to convince Judge Goldgar that the injunction needed to remain in place so the hard-fought settlement could be approved.

Hayes would have to convince Goldgar of two things: first, the settlement was a great deal for creditors. (From Apollo's point of view, this was more than true. David Sambur by now was blaming Kirkland and Millstein & Co. for their defeat. "You're fucking this up," Sambur would tell the Millstein team. Hayes would sarcastically reply, "Oh yeah, it's definitely our fault.") And second, the deal was fragile; the judge needed to keep Kupferberg out of court so his $9 million claim would not topple $18 billion.

This time, Goldgar concurred with Hayes, pleased that the original $18 billion of debt at the Caesars OpCo would be slashed to less than $8 billion. Goldgar implemented an injunction through the confirmation hearing in January, calling the reorganizational plan "eminently confirmable." The same day, Caesars put out a press release that RSAs had been signed by all creditor groups.

Three weeks later, Trilogy got on board for their own settlement: 65.5 cents plus a few million in fees for Millar. It was a bittersweet moment for the hedge fund and Drinker Biddle. The Meehan-Combs/Trilogy lawsuit, even if it was brought by minor investors holding de minimis amount of debt with a minor law firm, had proved to be the most consequential lawsuit in the case—even if it was never adjudicated.

Millar liked to point out that he spotted the Trust Indenture Act issue well before Bennett and his phalanx of lawyers at Jones Day. "Am I doing a good enough job for you?" Bennett would taunt Millar outside the Chicago courtroom. Millar was frustrated that bankruptcy outcomes were usually determined by the richest firms in the case, a reality he was now tasting in Caesars. Still, there was some satisfaction knowing that his insight had helped slay the giants.

35

VENI, VIDI, VICI

The heavy lifting was over. It was January 17, 2017, the official cessation of hostilities in the Caesars bankruptcy. Two years and two days after the Chicago Chapter 11 filing, Judge Goldgar would preside over what should have been an uneventful confirmation hearing now that all sides had agreed to a deal.

Presenting the confirmation order in court for Kirkland & Ellis would be Joe Graham—a Midwesterner with both undergrad and law degrees from Notre Dame. As a senior associate soon to be partner, he was involved in every part of the Caesars transaction and had billed thousands of hours on the case, more than any other Kirkland lawyer. The last three months had been a blur of hundred-hour weeks getting all the paperwork done so Caesars could get on the path to formally emerge from bankruptcy later in 2017. Graham had cobbled together a confirmation order that Judge Goldgar could sign today.

At nine thirty a.m., Graham checked his phone.

"Motherfucker!" Graham let out. *Why today of all days?*

He had a message that the Second Circuit Court of Appeals had overturned the New York district court ruling in the Marblegate case. According to a two to one decision, the 2014 restructuring that Education Management Corporation had executed was not a violation of the Trust Indenture Act.

The Marblegate case loomed over Caesars like a specter. The original lower court decision in *Marblegate* basically guaranteed that the Caesars creditors would win a judgment, forcing the Caesars parent to make good on the parent guarantee.

Marblegate was largely considered bad law, and it was only a matter of time until the Second Circuit overturned the ruling. The Second Circuit had heard arguments in May 2016. A ruling could have come at any moment and would have altered the course of the Caesars case. Apollo and Caesars were so concerned about the issue they spent millions lobbying Congress to change the TIA. And now, just before the clock struck midnight, they got their wish. Marblegate had determined the outcome in Caesars, and had this ruling come any time before this day, the fate of Apollo and TPG would have been far different.

Graham's phone immediately started ringing.

"Have you heard anything?" It was Chris Shore from White & Case, who represented the SGN bondholder group. They had a nice deal for eighty-three cents on the dollar that they did not want disrupted at this late date.

Graham told him he had not heard anything.

As soon as Graham hung up, his phone lit up again.

"Hey, it's Sid. Have you heard anything?"

This time it was Sidney Levinson of Jones Day. The second-lien bondholders had been the biggest beneficiaries of the original lower-court Marblegate decision, and they did not want anything to upset the applecart.

Graham got several more calls from other creditor groups, all of whom had the same advice: Get in that courtroom and get Goldgar to sign off on the confirmation before Apollo tried anything crazy.

SINCE THE SETTLEMENT WAS STRUCK in October 2016, America had elected a failed casino operator as its forty-fifth president. It seemed perfect that Donald Trump, the self-proclaimed "king of debt," would take office three days after this hearing.

The Caesars combatants were now gathering in the Chicago courthouse where the lively first-day hearing had taken place two years before. Rows of wooden benches were about to be packed with hundreds of people who either had billions in debt or millions in professional fees riding on the case's conclusion.

As Judge Goldgar's "Oyez Oyez" intro sounded—for the last time for most of the capacity crowd—the judge walked in and sat down in the middle seat of the long judge's bench. The imposing Great Seal hung on the wall behind Goldgar, with an American eagle grasping arrows in one talon and an olive branch in the other. The latter had been extended only very late in this case.

After a few housekeeping matters, Graham presented the order to the judge. He expected Caesars lawyers to rise and tell the court that the deal was off at any moment.

"I think that brings us to the main event, plan confirmation," Graham set up.

The Caesars and Apollo representatives remained silent. Goldgar commenced with his usual fastidiousness, marking up the already skinny confirmation order Kirkland had prepared.

"Okay. I'll ignore all the throat clearing on the first two pages. I'll let you get away with that," Goldgar began. "And paragraph one says this plan is confirmed seems to be appropriate, but you don't need paragraph two."

"Okay," Graham said, mentally calculating which party wanted these lines.

"And you don't need paragraph three, and you don't need paragraph four...Paragraph five is fine. Paragraph six is not necessary and should come out. Paragraph seven needs to be revised, and the prefatory material needs to be changed, and it needs to be changed because I would like the releases and the exculpation clause and the release of liens to come out."

It became clear that all these changes required some discussion and a reprinting of the order.

The Kirkland team walked into the room nearby, set up with a printer for just this occasion, and everyone had something to say. It was a tense reunion for the key legal teams in the case. Thomas Kreller was there from Milbank. Kris Hansen from Stroock was there for the first-lien banks. Sid Levinson was there from Jones Day for the second-liens. Chris Shore and Tom Lauria chimed in for the SGNs. Ken Eckstein and Danny Eggerman from Kramer Levin spoke for the first-lien noteholders. Marty Bienenstock's partner Vincent Indelicato from Proskauer gave it a once over for the unsecured committee. Even Paul, Weiss, who had taken a back seat after the examiner's report, had several attorneys in the courtroom. Each firm had someone to review and approve the language.

Finally, they had an order all sides were comfortable with. Graham took it to the printer—which then promptly stalled. David Seligman impatiently asked, "Why is this taking so long?"

"The printer is slow! I can't help it," Graham responded. There was still no word from Apollo.

After what had been effectively three years of trench warfare, the peace treaty could not get signed quickly enough.

Everyone re-entered the courtroom. Goldgar read over the order, fixed one more thing by hand, and then looked expectantly at Graham, who almost forgot to ask Goldgar to sign the order.

"Don't you want me to sign your order?"

"Oh, yes, yes, Your Honor. Sorry. Sorry. I thought it was basically done." Graham rushed over to hand him the order.

Goldgar signed it right there, and it was finally over.

"All right. The plan is confirmed." The words floated in the air. A collective weight lifted throughout the room and across the country as news spread from Oaktree's offices in California to Elliott's in New York.

There indeed had been a discussion between Apollo and its advisors that morning about what to do with the Marblegate ruling. Marc Rowan was annoyed but had decided it was time to move forward. Apollo and TPG were keeping a small stake in the company and they had persevered longer than any other private equity firm would have. There was honor in that.

Goldgar offered some closing remarks.

"I have no particular profundities to offer today. I didn't prepare any orations," Goldgar said to a murmuring crowd. "But I did want to compliment you all and congratulate you. This plan, as everybody knows, is a great big settlement…Given the number of players and the number of different interests involved in this case, that you could reach something like this I think is extraordinary. I think it is really a monumental achievement. And it is a testament to your skill and sophistication and energy as lawyers, and also your flexibility and the flexibility of your clients, too, because the lawyers don't simply get to settle out from under clients…And so I wanted to make clear that although I did not see a lot of what was going on, I saw the product of what all of your energies produced, and it really is to your credit. It's a magnificent job. And certainly for creditors it's a great recovery… So congratulations to you all."

Not one to dwell on sentimentality, Goldgar softened the mood with a joke.

"All right. Final fee petitions, do let us know so that we can save our printer from destruction when you're about to file those." Everyone quickly gathered themselves.

"We will do that, Your Honor," said Graham.

Those fees paid for by the Caesars estate totaled $273 million, with $79 million for Kirkland alone. Jones Day was set to make $28 million for getting their clients $3 billion more in recovery than had been secured at the start of the case.

Bruce Bennett considered his ironic good fortune. For all his courtroom triumphs in Chicago, he had wanted the case in Delaware. In Wilmington, he now believed, his clients would have been pushed into perhaps a thirty cent settlement. Goldgar was maybe the one judge in America who gave Bennett the room to make his case. Jim Millstein's client, the Caesars OpCo, was often on the wrong side of Goldgar decisions. Still, Millstein conceded that in the end that the unorthodox judge had done his job and had guided the parties to fairly settle the dispute.

"All right. Very good. Thank you all," Goldgar concluded the hearing.

IT TOOK CAESARS AND ITS creditors two years in bankruptcy of all-out war to get a restructuring plan in place. Now the bloodied and exhausted combatants had to join forces to make it work. Caesars had to get sign-off from multiple state regulators. At the same time, there were billions in complex exit financings to be raised. For a decade since the financial crisis, Caesars' survival had relied on frothy debt and equity markets. It needed Wall Street to scoop up its paper one last time.

The 2014 machinations of Elliott's Dave Miller had helped push Caesars into bankruptcy; fittingly, a clean exit from bankruptcy was going to require his consent. The senior bondholders were set to own the PropCo that would house the Caesars real estate and rent it back to the operating company. The wrinkle was that Elliott had skillfully crafted the "backstop" financing for PropCo. The upshot of that was finally clear: Elliott's convertible preferred bond was effectively a flesh-eating bacterium. PropCo was to be a publicly traded company, but most of the spoils were going to Elliott and friends. There was no way its stock would function among ordinary investors. As the market discovered this late in 2016, the non-backstop bonds traded down and hedge funds like Solus and Och-Ziff swooped in with the thesis of cutting a deal.

The hedge funds in the backstop were going to buy $300 million worth of equity for just $250 million. The preferred stock, however, also came with the equivalent of a 15 percent "payment in kind" coupon. Rather than getting paid cash dividend, Elliott and friends got paid in more stock—so over time, their chunk of PropCo kept compounding at the expense of everyone else. PropCo could not function as a company like this. But Dave Miller could fix things, for a price.

Brendan Hayes of Millstein vowed that the backstop convertible preferred would never see the light of day. A tense negotiation session ensued, that included an awkward dinner meeting at Caesars Palace. Elliott and its allies in the backstop group, which included Pimco, JPMorgan, Monarch, and Canyon, would get their preferred stock taken out at 224 cents. The senior bondholders not in the backstop group, which now included Solus and Och-Ziff, also got a concession, swapping some PropCo debt for more equity. Everyone concluded that it was better to quickly solve this issue—even if they could have held out for more. Las Vegas was hot, gaming was hot, and this new company was going to be a rocket ship. Another extended fight would be foolish for everyone.

Elliott was allocated $80 million of the $300 million of the convertible preferred. It purchased that $80 million for just $66 million. It was then swapped for $179 million worth of PropCo stock. In addition, Elliott owned $686 million of bank debt and $1.25 billion of first-lien bonds, which had received recoveries well above 100 cents. There were also the hundreds of millions of dollars made in the credit default trade. All in all, it was estimated that the firm made roughly $1 billion in Caesars. Dave Miller had assiduously avoided the high risk/high reward second-lien bonds that his best friend Kaj Vazales owned, yet had made, so far, the biggest Caesars fortune of all.

"WILL ANYONE EVEN KNOW WHAT SPQR means?" Samantha Algaze of Elliott said out loud what everyone was thinking.

PropCo needed a formal name before it started trading. So the PropCo's new management hired consultants and then ran some of the options by the creditors who would now own the company, namely the first-lien noteholders. PropCo's hired consultants had winnowed the list to two final choices: SPQR—short for Senatus Populusque Romanus, the government of ancient Rome—and VICI, from Julius Caesar's Latin catch phrase, "I came, I saw, I conquered."

The PropCo board liked SPQR, but Elliott was less enthusiastic. It sounded weird and also resembled "SPDR," the ticker for exchange-traded funds affiliated with Standard & Poor's. Ultimately, VICI was chosen for its simplicity and symmetry with "Caesars".

David Sambur believed VICI had been specifically selected by Dave Miller. Sambur wondered if Miller, his long-time antagonist, was taunting him one last time. This was silly and apocryphal—Elliott would quickly sell out of VICI, locking in its profits—but Sambur's paranoia perfectly captured the intense emotions that had defined the case for years.

On October 6, 2017, Caesars formally emerged from bankruptcy as creditors received the consideration for their debt on the terms agreed to the year before. The US economy remained strong, as did the stock price, and the Caesars enterprise value only continued to jump. And because much of the creditor recoveries were in either stock of the new Caesars parent or VICI, hedge fund payouts were far higher than the nominal terms that had been negotiated.

The second-lien bonds exemplified the turnaround in the business. At the outset of the bankruptcy in early 2015, those bonds were trading at roughly ten cents. At the time of emergence, the value of the final negotiated recovery had jumped from 65.5 cents to essentially 100 cents because some of the recovery came in Caesars shares. The ninety-cent increase, from bottom to peak, was worth a staggering $5 billion in value. Houlihan Lokey had even designed a commemorative deal toy for the second-lien group that showed successively rising stacks of poker chips to depict how settlement offers kept steadily rising through the course of the Chapter 11. Marc Rowan and David Sambur had, in a perverse way, been vindicated: Caesars was destined to come back, and it did. The only problem was that all that value creation was seized by the creditors.

36

THE HANGOVER

"**M**ark, good to talk to you today." CNBC anchor Contessa Brewer welcomed Caesars Entertainment CEO Mark Frissora to *Power Lunch* just before three p.m. Eastern time on August 1, 2018.

"So, you're in the middle of this earnings call and all of a sudden we see your stock start to plummet at one point down 24 percent based on guidance around the third quarter. Did Wall Street get it wrong?"

"Well, I think so," Frissora deadpanned into the camera. "I think all of the analyst headlines would support the fact that we had a great quarter and we continue to have great prospects."

The stock had actually opened fifteen cents higher than the previous day's close. Though Frissora couldn't tell—he was being filmed live from Las Vegas—CNBC was overlaying a chart showing that Caesars' stock plunged around twelve thirty p.m. Eastern, smack in the middle of the disastrous conference call that started at noon Eastern that day. The CNBC interview was a chance to calm the market. Unfortunately, it only made matters worse. Frissora was, once again, not sharp—and investors were stampeding out of Caesars stock.

Earlier that morning, Caesars had released its second quarter results, which were solid. However, there were worries about its revenue guidance for the rest of the year. Frissora's confused, sometimes contradictory, comments had shocked investors. The company had admitted that RevPAR—revenue per available room—would only be flat or just above in the third quarter, far less than the expectation. The worry was that Las Vegas was unexpectedly softening—though Frissora tried to claim the weakness was due to a dearth of big-ticket events like the previous year's Floyd Mayweather prize fight. He went on to blame the volatility on the hedge funds in the stock who had come in after the bankruptcy.

Caesars needed someone who was ready for primetime. In mid-2018, Caesars' two largest shareholders were Canyon Capital and Senator Investment Group, who together owned nearly 20 percent of the stock. Other hedge funds with big stakes included Soros Fund Management, Silver Point, and Appaloosa.

The new boardroom had also become its own powder keg. As creditors took control of the company as a part of the restructuring, they suddenly had the right to name directors. Each of the first-lien loan holders, first-lien bondholders, and second-lien bondholders got to name a director. Apollo had argued that in 2013 and 2014 the chaos of handing the company to creditors would have been value destructive a point that years later was proving to be true.

David Sambur and Rick Schifter represented Apollo and TPG on the board, and together the firms owned roughly 15 percent of the company—yet still were trying to call the shots.

By late summer, Caesars's hedge fund shareholders had lined up behind a sale of the mighty Caesars empire to Eldorado Resorts, a small operator of regional casinos. Caesars was suddenly vulnerable after the recent stock price drop and its backers were losing patience. The feeding frenzy was beginning. There was one final indignity coming for Apollo at Caesars, and an old friend was going to deliver it.

CARL ICAHN LOVED CASINOS. IT was the one legal business that the mafia got into, he would joke. He had largely steered clear of the Caesars mess during the years after the LBO.

Icahn had, however, taken advantage of other buying opportunities in Las Vegas. Before the financial crisis, he had scooped up the Stratosphere out of bankruptcy, then flipped it to Goldman Sachs for a $1 billion profit. After the crisis, he bought Fontainebleau and flipped it, still unfinished, netting nearly $500 million.

In February 2019, Icahn announced he had taken a 20 percent stake in Caesars, between stock and derivatives. He was now the biggest shareholder of the company and his vision was about to win out.

In April, the company announced that Tony Rodio would become Caesars CEO—a choice engineered by Icahn. Rodio had been boss at Tropicana Entertainment, the Atlantic City-based gaming chain. Icahn had first become involved at Tropicana in 2010, later selling it for $1.8 billion to none other than Eldorado Resorts in 2018.

In June 2019, Caesars announced its planned sale to Eldorado Resorts. The acquisition was not inevitable, as the board held out for a blowout price. The $12.75 per share value was more than double where shares had bottomed out six months earlier. Caesars shareholders would get $8.40 per share in cash and the rest in Eldorado shares. Nearly twelve years after a $28 billion buyout, the enterprise value of Caesars and VICI was in that neighborhood.

The Eldorado transaction would be the final affront to Gary Loveman. Eldorado was a bare bones operation with little of the sophistication he had pioneered in the 1990s. He was personally offended that a rinky-dink operator like Eldorado was taking the keys to the storied Harrah's franchise that he'd turned into the biggest gaming company in the world.

Apollo and TPG even mismanaged their exit (though TPG had sold half its shares in 2018 at above $12/share). By early spring, the firms had decided to sell out. Icahn was taking greater control of the board and the company's direction, and the firms had better things to do. It was a testament to their belief in the company that they had held on all these years, well after any chance to make a decent return on their investment. The two sold their remaining Caesars shares—most of which were purchased by Icahn himself—in March of 2019. The sale price was just above eight dollars per share, a third less than the deal price struck three months later.

Some Caesars executives and directors thought Sambur would remain useful on the board and after more than a decade of being at the center of Caesars. Sambur was open to the idea of staying on. Icahn was dubious, however, as Apollo had sold its shares. Sambur would resign from the board in early April.

Icahn had teased Leon Black during walks in Central Park about overpaying for Caesars. Black would later quip to Icahn, "At least one of us made money on Caesars."

After SEC filings showed that Apollo had sold all its Caesars shares, Kaj Vazales of Oaktree wrote a formal, courteous email to Sambur, expressing that the years of bitter combat had never been personal to him. "Despite being on opposite sides of the table throughout a very difficult and contentious negotiation, I hope our paths cross again and just wanted to say there is no lingering ill will on my part," Vazales wrote.

Sambur replied with a single word: "thanks."

EPILOGUE
LEAVING LAS VEGAS

At the close of the Caesars case, Apollo had not only been defeated but also humiliated. In virtually no other bankruptcy had a company's private equity owners been on the brink of billions of dollars of personal liability. And no bankruptcy judge had ever ordered private equity titans to turn over their personal bank account details to show their ability to pay up.

Yet Caesars turned out to be less a cautionary tale than a roadmap for the private equity community. Apollo had built a reputation as the private equity firm that pushed the envelope further than any other. Post-Caesars, the rest of the industry noticed Apollo scarcely suffered any serious repercussions and if not for Appaloosa showing up, would have likely prevailed. Leon Black did admit in a 2017 investor conference call that the firm had "stumbled" in paying too much for Caesars, and vowed to stick to cheaply priced buyouts where Apollo had made its name. (Black also lamented in the same breath that the firm in 2007 had overspent in acquiring another company, Realogy. But that investment, unlike Caesars, Apollo eventually salvaged through canny distressed debt maneuvers.)

In 2017, Apollo went on to raise a $25 billion private equity fund that year, the largest ever. And while the headlines around Caesars were not pretty, institutional investors noted how tenaciously David Sambur and Marc Rowan had fought to save Apollo's position, and were happy to commit new capital. The rest of the industry would ultimately adopt an ethos of "What would Apollo do?" This phrase was explicitly offered by a top restructuring banker at a 2017 industry conference when asked to summarize the state of the distressed debt environment.

With as many headaches as it experienced as Apollo's lead co-investor in Caesars, TPG was among the first to replicate Apollo's financial engineering, even before the resolution of the Caesars case. TPG, along with another private equity firm, Leonard Green & Partners, had bought J.Crew in 2011 and loaded it up with debt. As the preppy retailer struggled to stay in vogue and cash flows began to dip, in 2016, the company executed a brazen play to shift its brand and other intellectual property to new subsidiaries away from creditors. The transaction was just the beginning of a long line of aggressive actions where companies found room in the credit documents to simply move assets away from the grasp of certain creditors, who could have sworn their investment was secured by those assets. When the private equity owners of PetSmart and Neiman Marcus replicated this maneuver, the industry publication *Covenant Review* would popularize a new term: that these copycats were "pulling a J.Crew."

"Pulling a J.Crew" exploited weak or non-existent covenants that were commonplace in debt documents. Credit funds, desperate for high-yielding paper, had little ability to push back on borrower-friendly terms. Trillions of dollars worth of high-yield bonds and leveraged loans, the riskiest types of corporate credit, are now outstanding. Most credit documents now allow for the removal of collateral or create vulnerability to get pushed down by other debt. US leveraged loan issuance, whose annual volume topped $1 trillion in recent years, was increasingly driven by complex "securitizations," where dozens of bundled loans were bought up by insurance companies and banks. These buyers liked the attractive interest rates but were ill-equipped to fight with private equity firms and hedge funds in distressed situations. The debt markets had come to feel like the Wild West, rife with disorder and lawlessness where regulators and courts were struggling to keep up with constant shootouts.

Even as TPG suffered from a string of disastrous pre-financial crisis LBOs, it would make a name for itself in 2010 in a new type of deal called "growth capital." It had put money to work in the likes of Airbnb and Uber, tech "unicorns" who were expanding quickly but burning cash. These deals had new pitfalls. David Bonderman would get caught up in the ugly corporate drama at Uber, the ride-sharing company. The company was already under siege over what was widely considered a broken corporate culture instituted by founder Travis Kalanick. Bonderman resigned from the Uber board after he was caught making an irreverent, sexist comment to fellow director Arianna Huffington.

If private equity firms had become more brazen in their tactics, hedge funds were not far behind. The credit default swap faceoff in Caesars, between Dave Miller of Elliott and GSO's Ryan Mollett, would augur even grander side wagers in distressed situations. In 2017, Mollett had designed a "manufactured default" at homebuilder Hovnanian. GSO would lend to the company cheaply if it simply defaulted on a particular piece of existing debt that would also allow GSO to profit on its CDS.

The seller of the CDS was none other than Solus Alternative Asset Management. While Solus was one of GSO's fellow first-lien bank loan holders in Caesars, there was still bad blood over the side-pocket investment that came to light late in negotiations, creating a rift between Mollett's first-lien group and Solus's lead negotiator in Caesars, Patrick Hambrook. Now it was Hambrook sitting on the other side of the GSO's Hovnanian CDS bet, and the litigation got ugly before they settled.

The uproar over manufactured defaults designed to benefit hedge funds led to a call for greater oversight and regulation in the CDS market. Blackstone was concerned enough about the reputational damage that it reined in GSO's tactics. Ryan Mollett would leave GSO in the aftermath of Hovnanian. Solus netted a nearly $425 million profit in Caesars alone. Hambrook joined a new credit investing firm, Hein Park, formed by veterans of George Soros's hedge fund including Soros's lead negotiator in the Caesars bankruptcy, Courtney Carson (Soros was quietly another big winner in Caesars).

If the manufactured default was not enough, "net short debt activism" became the next distressed investing innovation. In 2018, Aurelius Capital Management had taken a large position in the bonds of a telecom company, Windstream. Aurelius had been founded by Elliott alum Mark Brodsky. Brodsky believed that Windstream had violated a covenant when it spun off a subsidiary, and thus was in default on its debt. Elliott—also a large bondholder of the company—believed the precise opposite.

In a remarkable 2019 ruling, a federal judge in New York agreed with Aurelius' position. Windstream was ultimately forced to default and file for bankruptcy. Though Aurelius never confirmed, it was widely believed its biggest position was in Windstream CDS. Its strategy was simply to go to court and force a default of an otherwise healthy company to collect on its CDS. It profited spectacularly, even if its bonds were rendered near worthless. Elliott had done deep legal analysis, as it had in Caesars, and was confident in its position; but the loss in the case stung the firm.

The steady economy and low interest rates had limited distressed opportunities to fading retailers and volatile energy companies, and the flood of billions into the distressed debt funds left the industry as cutthroat as ever. David Tepper, whose firm, Appaloosa, made a profit approaching $1 billion on its Caesars position had little to prove on Wall Street. Tepper would buy the Carolina Panthers football team in 2018 for a record-setting $2.3 billion. Appaloosa converted itself into a family office, which essentially managed Tepper's wealth alone. Andrew Milgram's Marblegate Asset Management, had even moved into speculating in New York City taxi medallions.

Bruce Bennett's string of novel assignments continued. The Northern California utility, PG&E, filed for bankruptcy in early 2019, hoping to use the court process to sort out $30 billion of liability for wildfires that had killed dozens and destroyed thousands of structures. PG&E was hardly worthless—its value was estimated to be more than $50 billion—and Bennett's hedge fund clients who were PG&E shareholders believed they could pay off fire victims cheaply and be left holding a highly profitable utility. The sheer size of the company meant many of the same players from Caesars were involved. Ken Liang was named to the board of PG&E. Elliott and Apollo had taken a position in PG&E bonds, trying to take over the company themselves, though ultimately Bennett's clients prevailed in the fight.

Jim Millstein was advising California Governor Gavin Newsom on PG&E. Millstein, who had been traumatized by the Caesars case, had sold his firm to Guggenheim Partners, the financial service conglomerate, in 2018. It gave his team a safe landing spot. Millstein would become a co-chairman of Guggenheim. He was then able to spend more time pursuing his civic and public policy interests, leaving the next generation of bankers to mediate the latest brawls.

While the Caesars nightmare unfolded, Apollo mastermind Marc Rowan was planting the seeds for his greatest professional triumph. In 2009, Rowan noticed that life insurance companies were in big trouble due to poor underwriting and falling interest rates in the wake of the financial crisis. Apollo began buying up distressed insurance assets and eventually created its own life insurance company, Athene. Rowan's insight was that Athene could buy up distressed insurance asset cheaply and then have them invest in credit securities that Apollo itself created.

Athene went public in 2016 at a multi-billion-dollar valuation with Apollo as its largest shareholder. Apollo would eventually draw nearly $500 million in annual fees from Athene by managing its more than

$100 billion in assets. Apollo would create an entire banking business around originating vanilla corporate loans that earned a modest 5 to 7 percent a year, far less than the 25 to 30 percent expected in leveraged buyouts.

But the fees from Athene were steady and predictable, and by 2020 Apollo's own market capitalization exceeded $20 billion—largely based on this revolutionary credit and insurance unit that Rowan had built from scratch. Perhaps unsurprisingly, Athene was also plagued by questions over corporate governance, and some of the same directors that Apollo had relied upon at Caesars showed up in Apollo's insurance activities.

Rowan's outside interests proliferated too as he announced in the summer of 2020 he would step back from day-to-day work at Apollo. He donated $50 million to his alma mater, Wharton, and had become the chair of its board of overseers. He also had become a real estate and hospitality tycoon in the Hamptons. However, even that was not free of controversy. Rowan was caught in a frenzy of litigation with the town of Montauk over permits for his lobster shack, Duryea's.

Despite Apollo's continuing financial success, the headlines had been less kind for Leon Black. Black in 2018 and 2019 had admitted to having ties with the disgraced financier Jeffrey Epstein, who had been convicted of sex crimes in 2008 and who was later arrested in 2019 on federal charges of sexually abusing girls. Epstein who committed suicide later in 2019 while in custody, had once been a trustee of Black's family foundation. Epstein had also facilitated Black's donations to Harvard and MIT. In 2019, the *New York Times* reported that Black had paid Epstein at least $50 million after Epstein's 2008 conviction.

Black insisted that the payments were for personal financial advice. Apollo itself said it never had never done business with Epstein. (Apollo had settled in 2016 for $52 million charges from the SEC that it had misled its fund investors about fees and that it had failed to supervise a senior partner who had billed nearly $300,000 in personal expenses to Apollo funds.) Still, several institutional investors expressed their concerns about the revelations of Black's relationship with Epstein. Apollo announced in October 2020 that its independent directors would investigate Black's characterization of his relationship with Epstein.

Apollo's ties to President Trump also became an issue during his administration. Apollo had been a lender to the family real estate company of Jared Kushner, Trump's son-in-law. *The New York Times* reported that Josh Harris had even discussed a job in the White

House. During 2016, Rowan had kept a red *Make America Great Again* hat on his desk at 9 West 57th Street. In 2020, Leon Black's name figured prominently in a final installment of the report from the Senate Intelligence Committee on President Trump's ties to Russia. Black and Trump had visited Moscow together during the 1990s to consider business opportunities. And according to Black's testimony, Trump and Black "might have been in a strip club together." The Senate report even included a photo of the two from the trip.

It was ironic that the Donald Trump presidency began just as the Caesars case was ending. Trump, the self-styled "king of debt," had bounced back from multiple bankruptcies of his Atlantic City casinos. And his administration was filled with successful distressed investors, including Wilbur Ross and Steve Mnuchin. The influential *Financial Times* journalist Gillian Tett noted in a 2017 column how the cold, transactional politics that defined Trump resembled that of Wall Street vulture investors. It was hardly a surprise when President Trump pardoned Michael Milken in 2020.

Howard Marks would no longer be a friend Black could lean on. The decades-long relationship would be a victim of the Caesars saga after Black, during the case, had accused Marks and Oaktree of playing rough. When one of Black's children was to be married, an invitation arrived for Nancy Marks, but not for Howard. (The Markses, however, would invite both Leon and Debra Black to a subsequent wedding of one of their children.)

Oaktree had gone public like Apollo. But Oaktree never enjoyed the same success as its rival, and was acquired for nearly $5 billion in 2019 by the Canadian asset management giant, Brookfield. Oaktree continued as a standalone unit, and Marks continued to write his periodic public letters on financial markets. Ken Liang retired from Oaktree in 2018 and moved to Seattle to become a tech investor. In 2020, Kaj Vazales was promoted to co-head of the Oaktree North American distressed debt group.

As the impact of the coronavirus tore through the global economy in early 2020, Apollo would pounce, always priding itself as a canny buyer in times of tumult. It quickly struck rescue financing deals for the likes of Expedia and United Airlines. David Sambur, who in 2019 had been promoted to co-head of Apollo's private equity group, was the key player in many of these deals.

As 2020 wore on, troubled companies were forced to confront opportunistic creditors. Apollo's historic playbook had become the de facto law of the jungle: Exploit the letter of the credit documents to the furthest extent possible at the detriment of your adversary.

And like in Caesars, Apollo would be, at least once, hoisted by its own petard. Apollo teamed with Angelo Gordon and another fund to buy a chunk of mattress-maker Serta Simmons' existing debt, then to offer a rescue financing package that was essentially "pulling a J.Crew."

None other than Ryan Mollett was leading the investment for Angelo Gordon, where he had ended up after leaving GSO. Serta Simmons instead took a rival package that subordinated all of Apollo and Angelo Gordon's senior debt, halving its value instantly—a loss that reached into the hundreds of millions of dollars. It was eerily similar to the Caesars Unsecured Notes deal where MeehanCombs and Trilogy had been cut out of a sweetheart repayment engineered by Sambur.

Apollo and Angelo Gordon sued in New York court, arguing that Serta Simmons had violated their rights and that such a deal would wreak havoc in the capital markets. The irony was rich that Apollo was complaining about aggressive private equity behavior, a circumstance that was noted in Serta Simmons' court filings. The schadenfreude only grew when Apollo and Angelo Gordon's effort to block the transaction went on to lose in court (Oaktree, which described itself as an honorable player in Caesars, would itself later in 2020 rely on the edgy transaction structure that Apollo and Angelo Gordon had fought in court).

In another instance, Apollo even went so far as to demand an examiner in the bankruptcy of Houston-based energy company Sable Permian, where it had a stake. Apollo, displaying no hint of irony, argued: "Conflicts of interest are a defining feature of the Debtors' organizational structure...The Debtors corporate governance at all levels is dominated by the Sponsors, who may be incentivized to use the restructuring process to their advantage..."

Kirkland & Ellis reached even greater domination, seemingly snagging every key debtor assignment leading up to and during the pandemic. Its capabilities were so in demand that large corporations appear to have largely ignored a growing string of controversial outcomes. The firm developed a reputation for keeping a stable of "independent" board of director candidates who could parachute in to bless controversial deal making intended to avoid the corporate governance pitfalls that had doomed Caesars. Kirkland learned to avoid Chicago as a venue for its biggest Chapter 11 cases (Judge Goldgar in 2020 was elevated to chief judge of the U.S. bankruptcy court based of the Northern District of Illinois). Lawyers learned that New York, Delaware, Texas, and even Virginia had judges who were considered more user-friendly and did not often object to high fees.

In the 2020 bankruptcy of Neiman Marcus, there had been credible allegations of "asset stripping" prior to bankruptcy in transactions Kirkland had designed. The creditor, Dan Kamensky, who had accused the private equity owners of Neiman Marcus of fraudulent transfers had been a part of the Paulson & Co. team that invested in Caesars. Kamensky after helping secure a $172 million settlement for Neiman creditors was arrested by federal authorities accused of an act of corruption in the bankruptcy process. His downfall was a rare moment where criminal allegation entered into the Chapter 11 process and brought widespread, negative attention to the corporate bankruptcy world which was already reeling from many intense litigation fights.

Kirkland's overall business had prospered beyond its historical strengths in litigation, private equity, and bankruptcy as it poached top talent to become a corporate M&A powerhouse. Paul, Weiss continued to benefit from its close relationship with Apollo, though it has also had a big business representing creditors who at times had been victimized by private equity. Paul, Weiss also made a big splash in diversifying its client base when in 2016 it lured Scott Barshay—perhaps the top corporate M&A lawyer in America—away from Cravath, Swaine & Moore. Both Kirkland and Paul, Weiss now ranked among the most profitable law firms in the world.

Nothing went smoothly for the Caesars Entertainment business while suffering the indignity of being bought by regional rival Eldorado Resorts. It felt like déjà vu when financial markets seized up in March 2020, hearkening back to the early days of the Apollo/TPG buyout during the 2007 financial crisis. There was a question, once again, about whether the big banks would fulfill their lending commitments to ensure the deal could be funded. Several state regulators also were taking a hard line on the competition effects of the merger.

Still, even as casinos across America were largely shuttered by the coronavirus lockdowns, the nearly $10 billion in deal financing, as well as state regulatory approvals, finally came through, and the deal closed in July 2020. Canyon Capital, the LA-based hedge fund that had bet big on both gaming and the bankruptcy of Caesars, would net over $1 billion in profits by remaining patient in its Caesars trade. Many key players in the Caesars bankruptcy fight, such as Elliott, quickly sold their holdings to lock in profits as the company emerged from bankruptcy. However, Canyon kept all the Caesars paper, including VICI stock, that rocketed up in recent years.

Summer news reports also indicated an upcoming big deal in the works for another former part of the Caesars empire: Playtika. The mobile gaming business, whose $4 billion sale in 2016 had cinched the bankruptcy settlement, reportedly was looking to go public in 2021 at a whopping $10 billion valuation—a figure that demonstrated how much of the future of gaming and gambling was going to be online. Caesars announced in the autumn of 2020 that it would purchase the U.K. betting company William Hill for nearly $4 billion to take on the burgeoning sports betting market in the U.S. Caesars beat out a rival bid from, of all firms, Apollo. (Apollo, ironically, had remained prominent within Caesars Palace given it was, coincidentally, also a prominent mythological name. One of the property's pools was named the "Apollo Pool." And in one Caesars Palace corridor hung a replica painting of Boticelli's *Birth of Venus* created in the style of a Lichtenstein comic. The word bubble from the goddess said, "Where's Apollo when you need him?")

Mark Frissora's fortunes were not so bright. In August 2020, Gary Loveman's replacement settled charges with the SEC over the inflated profits at Hertz during his tenure, agreeing to pay back $2 million to the car rental company. These charges had helped lead to Frissora's departure from the car-rental company, and it had always seemed odd that Apollo had scooped him so quickly to lead Caesars.

Since leaving Caesars, Gary Loveman never returned to visit Las Vegas. He maintained Boston as his home base, but had a beach home in North Carolina he visited via his own turboprop plane (which had a green stripe on its tail in the same shade as the Boston Celtics logo, the NBA team of which he and David Bonderman were part owners).

After spending decades using his knowledge of data science to get Americans to gamble more, Loveman perhaps found a more noble use of his talent. In 2015, he worked for a time at health insurer Aetna, trying to see how data could be used to promote better health outcomes—a topic that had interested him since managing tens of thousands of casino workers in his CEO days. In 2019, after leaving Aetna the previous year, Loveman would co-found a healthcare startup also looking to use analytics to better health care outcomes.

In 2017, Harvard Business School would publish one of its fabled case studies on the Caesars bankruptcy. Kristin Mugford, a former distressed debt investor and former student of Loveman at HBS, co-wrote the case and used it in her course "Creating Value Through Corporate Restructuring." Mugford noticed that her students always were highly critical of Apollo's scorched-earth tactics at Caesars. Loveman himself would return, part-time, to HBS. But rather than teaching marketing, as he had during his original stint nearly thirty years before, in 2018 he took on a first-year finance course.

Messy bankruptcy fights between and across private equity firms and hedge funds had now become a core part of the American business scene. Still, with the billions of dollars that were at stake, the byzantine maneuvering, and the bad blood among the combatants, the Caesars brawl remains unrivaled. As one of the key bankers involved in the case reflected afterward, "All these current situations are 'little league.' Caesars was the seventh game of the World Series."

ACKNOWLEDGMENTS

It took four years to sell, report, and write a book on the Caesars story. Only in a project of this length could we have the space to capture both the chess match and the cage fight that modern corporate restructuring and bankruptcy have become. And as first-time authors, it was something we could not have done without the support of too many to count.

We were blessed that what, at times, was a complex and tedious topic could be brought to life by incredible drama and this group of colorful and singular characters. The pleasure of this project was speaking with, often for hours at a time, the hundreds of characters now spread out across America who are a part of this Caesars story. Their recollections and opinions of precisely the same set of events often widely diverged; our job, then, was to create this resulting mosaic. The bulk of the reporting and writing of this book took place in 2019, two years after the Caesars bankruptcy wrapped up. Given the deep-seated passions and rancor that defined the case, this distance ultimately proved beneficial in our interviews.

From the group of restructuring industry veterans who initially encouraged Max to write a book on distressed debt, the loudest voice belonged to Andrew Milgram. When the book was just a concept, Andy Kifer and Daniel Kurtz-Phelan offered their advice on putting together an actual proposal to get an agent. Hilary Claggett of the Rudy Agency was the only book agent willing to take Max on as a first-time author pushing narrative nonfiction on an esoteric business niche.

Social media is part of our story, as the two of us met on Twitter discussing the Caesars case, and we ultimately decided to join forces on this book project. After more than a year and multiple proposal drafts later, Hilary found the single interested buyer of the project, Diversion Books. We are grateful to Scott Waxman, Diversion's founder, along with his colleagues Mark Weinstein and Lia Ottaviano for believing in this project when literally no other publisher did. Diversion's Keith Wallman's expert editing fashioned an unwieldy draft into the polished product it is today. Emily Hillebrand of

Diversion has been instrumental in the marketing and outreach phase in recent months.

We are especially grateful for the time and patience of all of our sources. Many generously met with us in person—whether at a private jet hangar, a suburban Las Vegas Denny's, a Caesars Palace hotel room, or a Park Avenue office, among other locations—and kindly responded to our constant barrage of emails and texts and got on the phone with us, day and night. Without their explanations, insights, and recollections, this book would not have been possible.

Individually, Max expresses gratitude to his colleagues from Fitch, who have shown remarkable flexibility and patience in allowing him to line up both parental leave and book leave in 2019. A special thanks to Steve Miller for his leadership at Fitch Solutions, as well as for being a genuinely good guy in a hard knocks business, providing guidance and support through successes and failures both in business and in life. Thank you to Deirdre Brill, who hashed out some of the more difficult co-author dynamics on long runs through Brooklyn, and gratitude to Tim Gray for always being there—from four years on the frontlines at a high-pressure start-up, to offering to chip in for a legal defense fund if any hedge funds or law firms became agitated. Max recognizes Larry and Sylvia Frumes, who have endured years of reading ridiculous levels of jargon as the parents of a trade publication reporter, and to Anna Frumes and Tasha Barbre, who've talked him through a number of low points to be able to complete what he started. And especially to Abigail, who continued to support the book even when it meant there were no free weekends for the first six months of Beatrice's life, and without whose proofreading Max's first drafts would have been unreadable.

Sujeet appreciates the support of his *Financial Times* colleagues who first let him cover the Caesars imbroglio, even before there was a bankruptcy filing, and have endured his constant allusions to this forthcoming book on the subject. In particular, Mark Vandevelde has been a trusted partner on a series of complex and tense stories featuring private equity, and often, Apollo Global Management. Sujeet's parents, Ramakant and Hema Indap, likely wish he had years ago accepted his admission to law school. Hopefully writing this book is close enough approximation of a legal career, but also a confirmation that the road not traveled has worked out just fine. Sujeet's brother, Amit, sister-in-law Abha, and their sweet girls, Aanya and Amara—far away in California—wisely have little interest in Wall Street, New York City, or the media. Their love, laughter, and ability to provide Sujeet a connection to the real world, however, have meant everything.

And finally, to Jocelyn Lee: Eight years ago, Sujeet told her he was going to try out being a journalist, a job defined by lower pay, erratic hours, and a healthy amount of self-absorption. For the last three years, Jocelyn has tolerated Sujeet's extended moodiness as he and Max first struggled to sell the Caesars book and then his frequent absences as the two toiled to complete it. Her encouragement and tolerance have been heroic. Jocelyn desperately wanted to watch the HBO show *Succession* together. Sujeet refused; he simply could not bring himself to enjoy someone else's corporate thriller until his own was completed. Jocelyn, we can watch now.

NOTES AND SOURCES

Writing the story of a lengthy and messy litigation strewn across multiple jurisdictions is like putting an intricate jigsaw puzzle together. Both of us enjoy writing about knock-down, drag-out legal battles like Caesars. They are not only inherently dramatic, there is also a rich paper trail to comb through to understand the narrative independent of relying on individuals' memories, recollections, and speculation.

For *The Caesars Palace Coup*, we reviewed thousands of pages of legal filings, transcripts of court sessions, transcripts of regulatory hearings, investment memos, emails, and many other documents. For the chapters that focus on the controversial pre-bankruptcy transactions at Caesars that became the defining issue in the Chapter 11 fight, we rely heavily on the exhaustive investigation of the examiner, Richard Davis, which culminated in a report approaching 2,000 pages.

Still, no good story can be complete without speaking with the participants, big and small, to understand their actions and motivations. The documents we mention above often turn into leverage with characters as they allowed us to quickly get up to speed and critically assess what we learned in interviews.

We attempted to speak with as many individuals involved in the Caesars story as possible. Ultimately, we spoke with close to 200 different individuals. Given the ugly legal fight at Caesars that lasted for years and resulted in immense ill will among the parties, virtually all the participants asked to speak "on background" and not to ever be formally identified.

The dialogue we capture from regulatory hearings and court-room sessions comes from publicly available transcripts. Separately, we have also attempted, where possible, to accurately capture the dialogue that occurred in meetings, phone calls, negotiating sessions, and other interactions. We have tried to carefully reconstruct these scenes using the recollections of as many participants as we could. We, however, acknowledge that memories of long-past events may be imperfect.

We have described this story to others as a car crash where the eyewitness testimony of the identical event or events differs simply by where one was standing. We have in good faith written a narrative which we believe is accurate and fair. But given the many strong, diverging views we encountered, we also have tried to acknowledge those other views—even when they may differ from our own conclusions.

Despite our repeated efforts to engage, the two most controversial parties in this story, Apollo and Paul, Weiss, both offered extremely limited direct participation. Through pursuing other avenues—including finding others in their orbit familiar with their actions and thinking—we did all we could to understand their views on all aspects of the Caesars case.

Surprisingly, this kind of standard, basic news gathering and reporting proved controversial. Paul, Weiss, after repeatedly ignoring our inquiries in 2019, eventually agreed to only respond to written questions. The set of limited responses it sent back to us in December 2019 was almost immediately followed by a remarkable letter that demanded that we turn over our manuscript as well as a list of Paul, Weiss sources that they believed we had approached outside of official channels. The letter went on to accuse us of acting in bad faith and culminated with a threat to sue us for defamation (all well before a first draft of this book existed).

As we describe in the book, Paul, Weiss is a law firm that actively takes pride in its ostensible liberal values and commitment to public service, civil rights, and pro bono legal work. Yet in subsequent letters and phone calls to us and Diversion Books, Paul, Weiss further attempted to pressure us to turn over a non-existent manuscript and provide them with details of our reporting that no serious journalist would—or even could—hand over. We share these events to underscore the strong feelings that underlie the Caesars story and to demonstrate how the news media continues to face undue harassment from powerful forces, like Paul, Weiss, for simply attempting to do its job.

The list below describes the publicly available sources we consulted in writing this story.

Chapter 1: A Numbers Game

- Lal, Rajiv, and Patricia Carrolo. "Harrah's Entertainment Inc." Harvard Business School Case 502–011, October 2001. (Revised June 2004.)
- Tanner, Adam. *What Stays in Vegas*. 2014, pg. 27.
- Loveman, Gary. "Diamonds in the Data Mine." Harvard Business Review, May 2003.
- Norton, David, "The High Roller Experience." 2018, pg. 48–49.
- Stanford Business School case study prepared by Victoria Chang and Jeffrey Pfeffer. "Harrah's Entertainment & Gary Loveman," 2003.
- Binkley, Christina. *Winner Takes All*. Hachette Books, 2008.
- Schwartz, David. *Grandissimo: The First Emperor of Las Vegas*. Winchester Books, 2008.
- "Every Light Was On: Bill Harrah and his Clubs Remembered." University of Nevada Oral History Program, 1999.

Chapter 2: Kings of Leon

- Marc Rowan remarks to Birthright Israel, posted to YouTube, May 19, 2009, https://www.youtube.com/watch?v=zH6b4xEl1Bk&t=9s.
- Bruck, Connie. *The Predator's Ball: The Inside Story of Drexel Burnham and the Rise of the Junk Bond Raiders*. Penguin Books, 1988.
- Stewart, James. *Den of Thieves*. Simon & Schuster, 1991.
- Eichenwald, Kurt. "The Collapse of Drexel Burnham Lambert." *New York Times*, February 14, 1990.
- Eichenwald, Kurt. "Milken Defends Junk Bonds As He Enters His Guilty Plea." *New York Times*, April 25, 1990.
- Board of Governors of the Federal Reserve. Enforcement Actions against Crédit Lyonnais. December 18, 2003.
- Simpson, Glenn. "Executive Life Indictments Brought." *Wall Street Journal*, December 18, 2003.
- Federal Bureau of Investigation. "Crédit Lyonnais and Others to Plead Guilty and pay $771 million in Executive Life Affair." December 18, 2003.
- Crowney, Paul. "Inside the Crédit Lyonnais Scandal." *Institutional Investor*, November 11, 2003.
- "The French Connection." Forbes, August 19, 2001.
- "State of California v. Altus Finance." Decided August 15, 2005.
- Girion, Lisa. "Crédit Lyonnais Fraud Suit Dismissed." *Los Angeles Times*, May 10, 2002.
- Carreyou, John. "Crédit Lyonnais's Defense in Lawsuit Takes Blow After U.S. Financier Agrees to Testify, *Wall Street Journal*, December 3, 2001
- Levin, Myron. "California Amends Crédit Lyonnais Suit." *Los Angeles Times*, February 1, 2002.
- Winninghoff, Ellie. "Dissecting the Deal." Mother Jones, January 17, 2002.
- State of California vs. Altus Finance, Apollo Advisors, et. al., complaint dated January 29, 2002.
- Maharaj, Davan and John-Thor Dalhburg. "Tycoon Has Law Hot on his Heels." *Los Angeles Times*, July 6, 2000.
- Malkin, Lawrence. "French Bank Seeks U.S. Industry Role." *International Herald Tribune*, October 11, 1991.
- Maharaj, Davan and John-Thor Dalhburg. "Fraud Alleged in Purchase of Executive Life." *Los Angeles Times*, June 20, 2001.
- Kristof, Kathy. "Eight Deadline Offers Made for Executive Life." *Los Angeles Times*, October 12, 1991.

- "California Executive Life Insurance Settlement Ends 16 Years of Litigation." *Insurance Journal*, July 10, 2015.
- "Executive Life Case Finally Closed." *San Fernando Valley Business Journal*, July 10, 2015.
- "Court Favors Pinault's Artémis in Insurance Suit." *The New York Times*, August 26, 2008.
- Rehfeld, Barry. "Leon Black, Dealmaker in the 1980s, Empire Builder in the 1990s." *New York Times*, February 21, 1992.
- *Dirks vs. the SEC.* Supreme Court of the United States, March 21, 1983 oral argument, transcript.
- Bass Brothers: A fourth brother, Edward Bass, did not going into business with the other three. Applebom, Peter. "A Younger Brother Steps Out on His Own." *The New York Times*, June 5, 1988.
- Sterngold, James. "The Men Behind the Biggest Stories on Wall Street and Washington: Henry R. KRAVIS, Kohlberg, Kravis, Roberts; RJR Nabisco Deal A Triumphant Work For Master of Buyouts." *The New York Times*, January 3, 1989.
- Holmstrom, Bengt and Steven N. Kaplan. "Corporate Governance and Merger Activity in the United States: Making Sense of the 1980s and 1990s." Journal of Economic Perspectives vol. 15, number 2. Spring 2001.
- Helyar, John. "Why Is This Man Smiling?" *Fortune* Magazine, October 8, 2004.
- Singh, Tej. "Jonathan Coslet and the TPG Story." *Medium*, October 23, 2018.
- Varchaver, Nicholas. "One False Move." *Fortune* Magazine, April 4, 2005.
- Oman, Anne H. "New Law Protects District Landmarks." *The Washington Post*. March 8, 1979.
- Bonderman, David. "Consequences for Agencies and Groups Responsible for Historic Preservation Programs." Pace Law Review, vol. 1 issue 3. April 1981.
- *Penn Central Transp. Co. v. New York City* (1978). US Supreme Court. 17 April 1978 to 26 June 1978. Landmark Preservation Law.
- Bryant, Adam. "Deal Maker Takes Aim at Skies." *The New York Times*, November 11, 1992.
- Hightower, Susan. "Will Airline Deal Fly? Investor David Bonderman Thinks So." *Los Angeles Times*, May 29, 1994.
- Jarzemsky, Matt. "Uber Gaffe Is Latest Drama in Storied Career of Billionaire Bonderman." *Wall Street Journal*, June 15, 2017.
- Morgenson, Gretchen and Riva D. Atlas. "Bass Family, in Need of Money, Forced to Sell 6.4% of Disney." *New York Times*, September 21, 2001.
- Vrana, Debora and James S. Granelli. "American Savings Sold to Seattle Thrift." *Los Angeles Times*, July 23, 1996.
- Norris, Floyd. "Q. Who Lost in Continental Airlines Deal?" *The New York Times*, January 28, 1998.
- Sender, Henry. "Texas Pacific Group is Looking for Bold Deals." *The Wall Street Journal*, December 28, 2004.
- Oregon State Treasury—Performance and Holdings—Quarterly.
- Lee, E. D. "Five Questions with Dick Boyce, Former Partner with TPG." The Operating Partner, September 25, 2017.
- Univision Board of Directors—David Bonderman—Founding Partner profile.
- University of Washington—About the Bonderman Fellowship.

Chapter 3: Waking up in Vegas

- Sterngold, James. "The Men Behind The Biggest Stories On Wall Street And In Washington." *New York Times*, January 3, 1989.
- Holmstrom, Bengt and Steven N. Kaplan. "Corporate Governance And Merger Activity In The United States: Making Sense of the 1980s and 1990s." Journal Of Economic Perspectives, vol. 15, number 2, spring 2001.
- Helyar, John. "Why Is This Man Smiling?" *Fortune* Magazine, October 18, 2004.
- Singh, Tej. "Jonathan Coslet and the TPG Story." *Medium*, October 23, 2018.

- Varchaver, Nicholas. "For years, investing legend David Bonderman could do no wrong. And then he tried to buy a utility from Enron." *Fortune* Magazine, April 4, 2005.
- Oman, Anne H. "New Law Protects District Landmarks." *The Washington Post*, March 8, 1979.
- Bonderman, David. "Consequences for Agencies and Groups Responsible for Historic Consequences for Agencies and Groups Responsible for Historic Preservation Programs." Pace Law Review, April 1981.
- *Penn Central Transp. Co. V. New York City.* Supreme Court Decision, June 26, 1978, Delivered by BRENNAN, William J.
- Bryant, Adam. "Deal Maker Takes Aim at Skies." *New York Times*, November 11, 1992.
- Hightower, Susan. "Will Airline Deal Fly? Investor David Bonderman Thinks So." Associated Press, May 29, 1994.
- Jarzemsky, Matt. "Uber Gaffe Is Latest Drama in Storied Career of Billionaire Bonderman." *Wall Street Journal*, June 15, 2017.
- Morgenson, Gretchen and Riva D. Atlas. "Bass Family, in Need of Money, Forced to Sell 6.4% of Disney." *New York Times*, September 21, 2001.
- Vrana, Debora and James S. Granelli. "American Savings Sold to Seattle." *Los Angeles Times*, July 23, 1996.
- Norris, Floyd. "Who Lost In Continental Airlines Deal?" *New York Times*, January 28, 1998.
- Sender, Henny. "Texas Pacific Group Is Looking for Bold Deals." *The Wall Street Journal*, December 28, 2004.
- Oregon State Treasury, Investment Performance and Holdings, Retrieved 9/5/20.
- Conti, Chris. "Five Questions with Dick Boyce, former Partner with TPG." The Operating Partner blog, September 25, 2017.
- Harrah's Entertainment press release on Apollo, TPG acquisition, December 19, 2006.

Chapter 4: Put Your Money Where Your Mouth Is

- Stutz, Howard. "Lawyer Had Hand in Shaping Nevada's Casino Licensing." *Las Vegas Review-Journal*, September 25, 2001.
- Crow, Kelly. "An Art Mystery Solved: Mogul Is 'Scream' Buyer." *The Wall Street Journal*, July 11, 2012.
- Markels, Alex. "Business; Vail Has Big Bets Riding Off the Beaten Slopes." *The New York Times*, December 29, 2002.
- Harrah's Entertainment Definitive Proxy Statement (Schedule 14A), dated March 8, 2007.
- Transcript of hearing of Nevada State Gaming Control Board, December 5, 2007.
- Transcript of hearing of Nevada Gaming Commission, December 20, 2007.
- Note: In 2012, Black spent $120 million to purchase one of the four versions of Edvard Munch's *The Scream*, according to the *Wall Street Journal*. He owned pieces from such masters as Picasso and Van Gogh and had been a collector for years.

Chapter 5: A Bridge Just Far Enough

- Gibbs and Bruns. - Huntsman Corporation v. Credit Suisse Securities (USA) LLC, Et. Al. - 23 June 2009. Case Summary.
- Texas Case Law - Credit Suisse Securities (USA) LLC and Deutsche Bank Securities, Inc., Appellants, v. Huntsman Corporation, Appellee. - 23 Oct 2008 - Case Summary.
- Court of Chancery of the State of Delaware. "Hexion, et al, v. Huntsman Corp." 18 June 2008 - Complaint, etc.

- Court of Chancery of the State of Delaware - Hexion, et al, v Huntsman Corp - 24 September 2008 - Defendant Huntsman Corp.'s Post-trial Brief.
- Court of Chancery of the State of Delaware - Hexion, et al, v Huntsman Corp - Pre-Trial Brief of Plaintiffs-Counterclaim Defendants.
- Court of Chancery of the State of Delaware - Hexion, et al, v Huntsman Corp - Post-Trial Brief of Plaintiffs-Counterclaim Defendants.
- Court of Chancery of the State of Delaware - Hexion, et al, v Huntsman Corp - Defendant Huntsman Corp's Post-Trial Brief.
- Huntsman Corp vs. Apollo Global Management complaint filed in District Court of Montgomery County in 2008
- Strasburg, Jenny, Patricia Kowsmann, and Max Colchester. "When Barclays's Jes Staley Went to Bat for an In-Law, a Powerful Client Cried Foul." *The Wall Street Journal*, May 2, 2017.
- "Merger Arbs: The Hexion-Huntsman Horror Show." *The Wall Street Journal*, June 19, 2008.
- Hexion Specialty Chemicals vs Huntsman Corp, Court of Chancery of the State of Delaware, decision dated September 19, 2008.
- Huntsman, Sr., Jon M. *Barefoot to Billionaire*. Overlook Duckworth, 2014.
- Davidoff, Steven M. *Gods at War: Shotgun Takeovers, Government by Deal, and the Private Equity Implosion*. John Wiley & Sons, 2009.

Chapter 6: Project Runway

- Lattman, Peter and Jesse Drucker. "Harrah's Plans to Cut Debt, Benefiting From Tax Break." March 2, 2009.
- Burton, Earl. "Former PartyGaming CEO Hired By Harrah's." *Poker News Daily*, April 14, 2009.
- Benoit, David. "Liberty Media's Charter Deal Cashes Out Apollo." *Wall Street Journal*, March 19, 2013.
- Lattman, Peter. "Treasure Hunters of the Financial Crisis." November 9, 2013.
- Bank of New York Mellon v. Realogy, Memorandum Opinion, Dec. 18, 2008.
- Apollo Global Management, LLC Form S-1, as filed with the Securities and Exchange Commission, April 8, 2008.
- Harrah's Entertainment, Inc. Form S-1, as filed with the Securities and Exchange Commission, November 5, 2010.
- Stutz, Howard. "Harrah's cancels stock offering." *Las Vegas Review-Journal*, November 19, 2010.
- Jinks, Beth. "Harrah's Gets Investment From Paulson, Apollo, TPG." *Bloomberg*, June 3, 2010.
- Segall, Eli. "10 years since Fontainebleau in Las Vegas went bankrupt." *Las Vegas Review-Journal*, June 7, 2019.
- Benston, Liz. "Culinary Union agrees to wage freeze." *Las Vegas Sun*, June 20, 2009.
- Chandan, Sam. "The Past, Present, And Future Of CMBS." Wharton Real Estate Review, Spring 2012.
- Commercial Mortgage Alert, CMBS Issuance Data, Retrieved Sept. 6, 2020.
- "UNLV and the Harrah's Foundation Announce Largest Corporate Gift in UNLV History." University of Nevada Announcement, September 10, 2007.
- Hamilton Lane Market Overview, LBO Study 2016/2017.
- Caesars Entertainment Corporation Form S-1 2012, as filed with the Securities and Exchange Commission, February 6, 2012.
- Bagli, Charles V. "Expanding Fight for Gamblers, a Revived Resort Adds Table Games." *New York Times*, August 2, 2010.
- Stevenson, Alexandra and Matthew Goldstein. "John Paulson's Fall From Hedge Fund Stardom." *New York Times Dealbook*, May 1, 2017.
- Stutz, Howard. "Harrah's cancels stock offering." *Las Vegas Review-Journal*, November 19, 2010.

- Glasser, AJ. "Playtika Acquired by Caesars Entertainment Casino Group for $80M to $90M." *Adweek*, May 19, 2011.
- Rinaldo, Sandie. "Mitch Garber rose from humble beginnings to head up a $2.5-billion empire." *CTV National News*, February 12, 2016.
- Randazzo, Sara. "Leading Questions: A Chat with Denver Attorney and Lobbyist Norman Brownstein." *Wall Street Journal*, June 15, 2015.
- Silva, Cristina. "Las Vegas still fumes over 2-year-old Obama remark." Associated Press, October 24, 2011.
- Atlantic City Gaming Revenue Study, University of Nevada, Las Vegas, Center for Gaming Research, January 2020.
- LVCVA Executive Summary of Southern Nevada Tourism Indicators, Visitor Statistics, Retrieved Sept 6, 2020.
- Davies, Megan. "Harrah's sued over Bahamas resort venture-filing." *Reuters*, November 24, 2008.
- Harrah's Entertainment, Inc, 2006 Form 10-K, as filed with the Securities and Exchange Commission on March 6, 2007.
- Harrah's Entertainment, Inc, 2010 Form 10-K, as filed with the Securities and Exchange Commission on March 4, 2011.
- Harrah's Entertainment, Inc, 2009 Form 10-K, as filed with the Securities and Exchange Commission on March 9, 2010.
- Harrah's Entertainment, Inc, 2008 Form 10-K, as filed with the Securities and Exchange Commission on March 16, 2009.
- Harrah's Entertainment, September 2008, Investor Presentation.
- Audi, Tamara, Peter Lattman, and Jeff McCracken. "Harrah's Changes Its Game." *Wall Street Journal*, October 27, 2008.
- Pierceall, Kimberly. "Nevada casino regulators scold Caesars for bankruptcy." Associated Press, March 27, 2015.
- "Penn National Gaming and PNG Acquisition Company Inc. Terminate Merger Agreement." Penn National Gaming company announcement, July 3, 2008.
- Crow, Kelly. "An Art Mystery Solved: Mogul Is 'Scream' Buyer." *The Wall Street Journal*, July 11, 2012.
- Segall, Eli. "Relationship with Dubai renewed with deal by MGM Resorts subsidiary." *Las Vegas Review-Journal*, March 24, 2017.
- Vardi, Nathan. "How Billionaires Lost And Made Fortunes In LyondellBasell." *Forbes*, March 11, 2011.
- Zuckerman, Greg. "The Greatest Trade Ever." Crown Business, 2009.
- Transcript, Nevada Gaming Commission Hearing to discuss Paulson transaction, February 18, 2010.
- Presentation slides to Nevada Gaming Commission from Harrah's, February 18, 2010.
- Lattman, Peter. "Birthdays are Still Big in Buyout Land." *The New York Times*, August 18, 2011.
- Cohan, William. "A Private Equity Gamble in Vegas Gone Wrong." *Fortune*, June 5, 2015.
- Report of the CalPERS Special Review, Steptoe & Johnson LLP, March 2011.
- Press Release regarding "2007 Party in the Garden." Museum of Modern Art, May 15, 2007.
- "Placement Agent Charged with Bribery in CalPERS Corruption Conspiracy." Department of Justice, August 7, 2014.
- "Former CalPERS CEO Sentenced to 54 Months' Imprisonment for Role in Corruption Conspiracy." Department of Justice, August 7, 2014.
- Apollo fee reduction agreement with CalPERS, April 16, 2010.
- "SEC Charges Former CalPERS CEO and friend with Falsifying Letters in $20m Placement Agent Fee Scheme." April 23, 2012.
- Lifsher, Marc. "Ex-CalPERS official Villalobos commits suicide." *Los Angeles Times*, January 15, 2015.
- Walters, Dan. "Two big deals and two big scandals." *Sacramento Bee*, July 15, 2014

Chapter 7: Not That Innocent

- Final Report of Examiner, Richard J. Davis, Substantially Unredacted, May 16, 2016 (initially filed March 15, 2016).
- Cimilluca, Dana. "Wachtell's Fairness Opinion." *Wall Street Journal*, Oct. 23, 2007.
- Smith v. Van Gorkom, Delaware Supreme Court, 1985.
- Clarke, Norm. "Britney Spears Confirms Two-year Residency At Planet Hollywood." *Las Vegas Review-Journal*, September 17, 2013.
- "Britney Spears father is named conservator." *The New York Times*, February 2, 2008.
- Phillips, Ray. "Brad Karp is the man behind the man in the hot seat." *Super Lawyers Magazine*, October 4, 2010.
- Adkins, Lenore. "Brad Karp: From Dreams of Congress to Chair of Paul Weiss." Bloomberg Law, January 13, 2017.
- Paul Weiss, Firm History, Paulweiss.com, retrieved Sept. 6, 2020.
- Kolz, Amy. "O'Melveny Loses Seven NY Partners to Paul Weiss, Two to Weil Gotshal." AmLaw Daily, May 10, 2011.
- Maiden Lane Letter regarding Hilton debt restructuring regarding Commercial Mortgage Backed Securities Trust 2008, as filed with the Securities and Exchange Commission.
- "Hilton Worldwide Completes Restructuring of Existing Debt." Blackstone company announcement, April 8, 2010.
- Heath, Thomas. "Christopher Nassetta: The man who turned around Hilton." *Washington Post*, July 6, 2014.

Chapter 8: CERP's Up

- Final Report of Examiner, Richard J. Davis, Substantially Unredacted, May 16, 2016 (initially filed March 15, 2016).
- Sorkin, Andrew Ross. "The Pressure of Great Expectations." *New York Times*, April 27, 2007.

Chapter 9: Four Properties of the Apocalypse

- Final Report of Examiner, Richard J. Davis, Substantially Unredacted, May 16, 2016 (initially filed March 15, 2016).

Chapter 10: Shot of B-7

- Final Report of Examiner, Richard J. Davis, Substantially Unredacted, May 16, 2016 (initially filed March 15, 2016).
- "Blackstone to Buy GSO Capital." *New York Times Dealbook*, January 10, 2008.
- Mikle, Jean. "State Takes $300 million pension gamble on Revel Casino Owner." *Courier Post*, March 16, 2016.
- Segal, Julie. "Blackstone Group's GSO Capital: Lenders of Last Resort." *Institutional Investor*, June 12, 2013.
- Carey, David and John Morris. "King of Capital." Crown Business, 2010.
- "Chatham Asset Management and Omega Charitable Partnership to Acquire American Media," company announcement, August 15, 2014.

Chapter 11: Pixie Dust

- Final Report of Examiner, Richard J. Davis, Substantially Unredacted, May 16, 2016 (initially filed March 15, 2016).
- Richard M. Goldman interview with Jamie Sprayregen on Debtwire's The Inside Track, March 26, 2019.
- Carey, David and John Morris. "King of Capital." Crown Business, 2010.

- Ronen Stauber profile on https://www.jenrocapital.com/about retrieved Sept. 6, 2020.

Chapter 12: Shell Game

- Final Report of Examiner, Richard J. Davis, Substantially Unredacted, May 16, 2016 (initially filed March 15, 2016).
- MeehanCombs Global Credit Opportunities Master Fund, LP v. Caesars Entertainment Corp. and Caesars Entertainment Operating Co., Inc., Case No. 14-cv-07091-SAS.
- Marblegate Asset Management v. Education Management - Nov 14, 2014 - Amended Opinion and Order.
- Federated Strategic Income Fund v. Mechala Group - Nov 2, 1999 - US District Court, SD New York.
- Segal, Steven. A Look at the Second Circuit Decision in Marblegate. February 28, 2017. Kramer Levin.
- Lobrano, John D. Second Circuit Reverses Marblegate Decision Regarding Trust Indenture Act. 28 Jan 2017. Harvard Law School Forum on Corporate Governance.
- U.S. District Court of the Southern District of New York - Marblegate Management, et. al., v Education Management Corp, et. al. Amended Opinion and Order. December 30, 2014.

Chapter 13: Chasing Waterfalls

- Stevenson, Alexandra. "How Argentina Settled a Billion-Dollar Debt Dispute With Hedge Funds." *New York Times*, April 25, 2016.
- Costa, Filipe R. "Fund Manager in Focus—Paul Singer." Master Investor, July 20, 2015.
- Leopold, Jason. "If You Keep Fucking With Mr. Trump, We Know Where You Live." BuzzFeed News, May 1, 2017.
- "Investor Howard Marks on Luck, Risks and the Job that Got Away." University of Pennsylvania, Wharton profile, March 17, 2014.
- Rose-Smith, Imogen. "Canyon Capital Thrives in a Transforming Financial Landscape." October 2, 2014.
- Final Report of Examiner, Richard J. Davis, Substantially Unredacted, May 16, 2016 (initially filed March 15, 2016).
- "First Lien Bondholder, Through its Counsel Kramer Levin, Discloses Information Provided by Caesars During Settlement Negotiations." Press release, December 11, 2014.
- "Informal Committee Of Certain First Lien Bank Lenders Of Caesars Entertainment Releases Information About Restructuring Discussions." Press release, December 11, 2014.
- Wilmington Savings Fund Society, FSB v. Caesars Entertainment Corporation, Case 15-01145, Delaware Court of Chancery, August 4, 2014.
- Caesars Entertainment Operating Company, Inc. and Caesars Entertainment Corporation v. Appaloosa Investment Limited Partnership I, et al, Case 652392-2014, August 5, 2014.
- Transcript, meeting of Louisiana Gaming Control Board of Directors Meeting, April 24, 2014.
- Transcript, meeting of Louisiana Gaming Control Board of Directors Meeting, May 19, 2014.

Chapter 14: Guitar Hero

- Sherlock, Ruth. "American Billionaire Builds Hamptons Mansion on land bought from boss who snubbed him." *The Telegraph*, September 23, 2015.

- Taub, Stephen. "Never afraid to be first, David Tepper's Appaloosa grossed $7.5 billion last year by betting on financials early on." *Institutional Investor*, February 1, 2010.
- Keller, Laura, "Caesars Lender Silver Point Said to Exit Reorganization Talks." *Bloomberg*, November 19, 2014
- Blinder, Rachel. "Billionaire completes Hamptons mansion after tearing down home of ex-boss Jon Corzine who wouldn't promote him." *Daily News*, September 23, 2015.
- Keller, Laura. "Caesars Restructuring Talks Stall as Highest-Ranked Lenders Exit." *Bloomberg*, December 12, 2014
- Zuckerman, Gregory. "Fund Boss Made $7 Billion in the Panic." *The Wall Street Journal*, December 23, 2009.
- Pressler, Jessica. "Ready to be Rich." *New York Magazine*, September 26, 2010.
- Caesars Entertainment Economic Deal Overview. November 22, 2014. Stroock Rothschild.
- "Informal Committee Of Certain First Lien Bank Lenders Of Caesars Entertainment Releases Information About Restructuring Discussions." December 11, 2014. PR Newswire.
- "First Lien Bondholder, Through its Counsel Kramer Levin, Discloses Information Provided by Caesars During Settlement Negotiations." Business Wire. December 11, 2014.
- Securities and Exchange Commission - Caesars Entertainment - Form 8-k, December 12, 2014 - New Support Agreement.

Chapter 15: First Derivative

- UMB Bank v. Caesars Entertainment Corporation, Delaware Court of Chancery, Case 15-01145, November 25, 2014.
- Tett, Gillian. *Fool's Gold.* Free Press, 2009.
- Keller, Laura, "Elliott Said to Bet on Caesars Default Amid Bankruptcy Talks." *Bloomberg*, December 4, 2014
- McDonald, Robert and Anna Paulson. "AIG in Hindsight." Federal Reserve Bank of Chicago, October 2014.

Chapter 16: Rubicon Crossed

- Caesars Entertainment - Press Release 4th Quarter and Full Year 2014 Results - March 2, 2015.
- Securities and Exchange Commission - Caesars Entertainment - Form 8-k/A (amendment 1), December 22, 2014 - Current Report.
- Caesars Entertainment Operating Co. - Caesars Entertainment Operating Co. Reaches Agreement with First Lien Noteholder Steering Committee on Debt Restructuring - No date.
- Securities and Exchange Commission - Caesars Entertainment - Form 8-k, December 15, 2014 - Current Report.
- Jarzemsky, Matt and Matt Wirz. "Apollo Plots Salvaging of Bad Caesars Bet." *The Wall Street Journal*, January 5, 2015.
- Sender, Henry. "Caesars owners seek way out of gambling debt." *The Financial Times*, January 7, 2015.

Chapter 17: Big Game Hunter

- Norris, Floyd. "Orange County Crisis Jolts Bond Market." *The New York Times*, December 8, 1994.

- Sullivan, Casey. "Top LA Bankruptcy Lawfirm to Close Doors." *Reuters*, April 22, 2014.
- Sterngold, James. "Orange County Creditors said to Accept Plan." *The New York Times*, May 3, 1996.
- Mydans, Seth. "Law Firm Takes Case With Two Million Clients." *The New York Times*, December 18, 1994.
- Wayne, Leslie. "Orange County's Artful Dodger; the Creative Bankruptcy Tactics of Bruce Bennett." *The New York Times*, August 4, 1995.
- Wilgoren, Jodi. "Orange County In Bankruptcy: Brain Trust: Lead Attorney In County Bankruptcy Earned A Whiz Kid Reputation By Resolving Big Cases." *Los Angeles Times*, December 11, 1994.
- Lait, Matt and Shelby Grad. "Its Overdue Debt Paid, O.C. Exits Bankruptcy." *Los Angeles Times*, June 13, 1996.

Chapter 18: Involuntary Reaction

- "$64-Million Claim Against O.C. Is Put Off." Associated Press, January 8, 1998.
- "Merrill Lynch Sued Over Release of Data on Notes." Bloomberg News, December 22, 1998.
- Stutz, Howard. "Bankruptcy judge approves Station Casinos reorganization plan." *Las Vegas Review-Journal*, August 27, 2010.
- Declaration of Joshua M Mester in Support of Brief Of Petitioning Creditors, US Bankruptcy court.
- Caesars Entertainment Operating Company, Delaware Bankruptcy Court, Involuntary Petition, January 12, 2015.
- Note: Technically, two different funds from the same firm could have been the different signatories to file the involuntary, yet this option did not imply sufficient buy-in for the group to pursue.

Chapter 19: Pride Goeth Before the Fall

- Puppel, Doug. *A Hero Named Gary*. The Public Education Foundation, 2013.
- CEOC Docket #915.
- "World Cup Gambling Hub Lands Ambassador in Vegas Court", *Bloomberg News*, August 5, 2014
- Kosman, Josh. "Leon Black will pay Caesars executives $81M in deferred pay." *New York Post*, May 12, 2015.
- Stutz, Howard. "Caesars retiree bitter after flow of pension checks stops." *Las Vegas Review-Journal*, March 24, 2015.
- Dezember, Ryan and Gillian Tan. "Apollo Goes on the Road to Appease Debt Investors." *Wall Street Journal*, April 30, 2015.
- Rohit, T. K. and Sagarika Jaisinghani. "Hertz CEO steps down after accounting errors." *Reuters*, September 8, 2014.
- Annual Report on Form 10-K of Hertz Global Holdings, Inc., as filed with the Securities and Exchange Commission on July 16, 2015.
- Stutz, Howard. "New Caesars CEO blamed for Hertz accounting failures." *Las Vegas Review-Journal*, July 18, 2015.
- Hertz Global Holdings, Inc. 8-K disclosure of Mark Frissora resignation, as filed with the Securities and Exchange Commission, September 19, 2014.
- Caesars Entertainment Corporation 8-K disclosure of Gary Loveman resignation, as filed with the Securities and Exchange Commission, February 5, 2015.

- CEOC Selected Financial Information, March 2015, Retrieved from Caesars website September 6, 2020.
- Caesars Entertainment Announces Management Transition, company announcement, February 4, 2015.
- Investigative Report For The Massachusetts Gaming Commission Applicant [Caesars], Sterling Suffolk Racecourse LLC, October 18, 2013.
- Transcript, Nevada Gaming Commission hearing, March 26, 2015.
- Letter from Nicole Houng to Judge Benjamin Goldgar, United States Bankruptcy Court, Northern District of Illinois, March 18, 2015, Document #915, CEOC bankruptcy docket.

Chapter 20: Split Screen

- Declaration of Randall S. Eisenberg, Chief Restructuring Officer of Caesars Entertainment Operating Company, in support of first-day pleadings, Document #6, CEOC docket.
- Clark-Flory, Tracy. "Judges Examine Lawyer Cleavage." *Salon*, May 23, 2009.
- Schwartz, John. "At a Symposium of Judges, a Debate on the Laws of Fashion." *The New York Times*, May 22, 2009.
- Marek, Lynne. "Federal Judges Grouse About Lawyers' Courtroom Attire." Law.com. May 21, 2009.
- Caesars Entertainment Operating Company, U.S. Bankruptcy Court for the Northern District of Illinois (Chicago), First Day Hearing Transcript, January 15, 2015.
- Caesars Entertainment Operating Company, U.S. Bankruptcy Court for the District of Delaware, First Day Hearing Transcript, January 15, 2015.

Chapter 21: Storm Juno is Gone

- Caesars Entertainment Operating Company, U.S. Bankruptcy Court for the District of Delaware, Transcript, Venue Determination, January 26, 2015.
- Caesars Entertainment Operating Company, U.S. Bankruptcy Court for the District of Delaware, Transcript, Venue Determination, January 27, 2015.
- Caesars Entertainment Operating Company, U.S. Bankruptcy Court for the District of Delaware, Transcript of Court Decision Re: Motion Of The Petitioning Creditors For Order Establishing Venue Before Judge Kevin Gross, January 28, 2015.
- "Exploring the Role of Creditors' Committees in Directing the Affairs of a Chapter 11 Debtor." Jones Day. July/August 2009.
- Tartaglione, Nancy. "21st Century Fox & Apollo In Joint Venture Talks For Shine, Endemol And CORE Media." *Deadline*, May 15, 2014.
- Koppel, Nathan. "Martin Bienenstock, A Weil Veteran, Shifts To Dewey & LeBoeuf." *The Wall Street Journal*, November 30, 2007.
- Spektor, Mike and Jennifer Smith. "Bankruptcy Specialist at Dewey Heads for Exit." *The Wall Street Journal*, May 11, 2012.
- Lattman, Peter. "Dewey's Bienenstock Discusses Law Firm's Demise." *New York Times Dealbook*, May 14, 2012.
- Rosen, Ellen. "A Lawyer Finds He Can Go Home Again." *The New York Times*, March 9, 2007.
- "Dewey Have Data on How Much Partners Got Paid? Yes —Thanks to the Partner Contribution Plan." Above the Law. August 16, 2012.
- Stewart, James B. "The Collapse." *The New Yorker*, October 14, 2013.

Chapter 22: A Thorough Examination

- Tarm, Michael and Kimberly Pierce. "Judge appoints examiner in bankruptcy of Caesars division." *Daily News*, March 25, 2015.

- Celarier, Michelle. "Case builds against former NY hedgie 'Buddy' Fletcher." *New York Post*, February 18, 2015.
- Wirz, Matt. "Icahn's Thwarted Plan for Dynegy." *The Wall Street Journal*, September 30, 2012.
- Caesars Entertainment Operating Company Docket, U.S. Bankruptcy Court for the Northern District of Illinois (Chicago):
  - o Notice of Debtors motion for order a) appointing an examiner and b) granting relief related, February 13, 2015, Document #363
  - o Notice of motion of official committee of second priority noteholders for appointment of examiner with access to and authority to disclose privileged materials, February 17, 2015, Document #367
  - o Debtor's preliminary joint objection to examiner, February 25, 2015, Document #442
  - o Omnibus objection of statutory of unsecured creditors to examiner, February 25, 2015, Document #445
  - o Response of Caesars Entertainment Corporation to motions for appointment of examiner, February 25, 2015, Document #461
  - o Objection of the official committee of second lien noteholders to debtors' motion for an examiner, February 25, 2015, Document #446
  - o Response of ad hoc committee of first-lien noteholders to motion to appoint examiner, February 25, 2015, document #470
  - o Statement and reservation of rights of the ad hoc committee of first-lien bank lenders with respect to the motions of each of the debtors and the official committee of second priority noteholders for the appointment of an examiner, February 25, 2015, document #472
  - o Order granting in part and denying in part motions to appoint examiner, March 12, 2015
- Transcript, Caesars Entertainment Operating Company Hearing on March 25, 2015, U.S. Bankruptcy Court, Northern District of Illinois.
- Transcript, Caesars Entertainment Operating Company Hearing on April 23, 2015, U.S. Bankruptcy Court, Northern District of Illinois.

Chapter 23: Next Man Up

- David, Javier E. "AIG Makes Final Repayment to Government for Bailout." CNBC. March 1, 2013.
- Ritholtz, Barry. "Transcript: Jim Millstein & Restructuring of AIG." October 28, 2018.
- Indap, Sujeet and James Fontanella-Khan. "Wall Street's battle of the bankers." *Financial Times*, January 24, 2016.
- Caesars Entertainment Operating Company Docket, U.S. Bankruptcy Court for the Northern District of Illinois (Chicago):
- Notice of debtors' application for entry of an order authorizing the employment and retention of Millstein & Co., LP as financial advisor and investment banker for the debtors, document, #665
- "Jim Millstein on lessons from the financial crisis," Financial Times Podcast, Alphachat, May 4, 2018.

Chapter 24: Give Peace a Chance

- Opinion and Order - MeehanCombs et. al. v. Caesars Entertainment. January 15, 2015. (TIA - Caesars 1)
- BOKF N.A. v. Caesars Entertainment Corporation Opinion-and Order. August 27, 2015. US District Court of New York SD. 2015. (TIA - Caesars 2)
- Marblegate Asset Management v. Education Management Corp Opinion and Order. US District Court of New York SD. June 23, 2015. (TIA - Marblegate 2)

- Caesars Entertainment Operating Company Docket, U.S. Bankruptcy Court for the Northern District of Illinois (Chicago):
  - Adversary Case No. 15-00149 Adversary to Stay Prepetition Litigation Transcript - June 3, 2015
  - Adversary Case No. 15-00149 Adversary to Stay Prepetition Litigation Transcript - June 4, 2015
  - Adversary Case No. 15-00149 Adversary to Stay Prepetition Litigation - Memorandum July 22, 2015

Chapter 25: The Meter is Running

- Transcript, Caesars Entertainment Operating Company Hearing on November 18, 2015, U.S. Bankruptcy Court, Northern District of Illinois.
- Caesars Entertainment Operating Company Docket, U.S. Bankruptcy Court for the Northern District of Illinois (Chicago):
  - Notice of motion regarding motion of the official committee of second priority noteholders to reconsider order granting debtors' application for retention of Kirkland & Ellis, document #2470
  - Notice of filing of the supplement to second interim fee application of Kirkland & Ellis, attorneys for the debtors for the period from June 1, 2015, through and including September 30, 2015, document #2930
  - Notice of first interim fee application of Kirkland & Ellis LLP for the period from January 15, 2015, through and including May 31, 2015, document #1903
  - Reply in support of motion to reconsider order granting debtors' application for retention of Kirkland & Ellis LLP, document #2575
  - Judge Goldgar order requiring Kirkland & Ellis to file supplement to second interim fee application, document #2830
  - Notice of motion of the official committee of second priority noteholders to reconsider order granting debtors' application for retention of Kirkland & Ellis LLP, document #2514
  - Judge Goldgar order construing the motion of second-lien noteholders committee to reconsider the retention of Kirkland & Ellis, document #2636
  - Declaration of Joshua Mester in support of motion of the official committee of second priority noteholders to reconsider order granting debtors' application for retention of Kirkland & Ellis, document #2471
  - Final fee application of Kirkland & Ellis for the period from January 15, 2015, through and including January 17, 2017, document #7620

Chapter 26: Don't Stop "Till" You Get Enough

- January 30, 2015 - Caesars 8k - failed negotiations with banks.
- July 21, 2015 - Caesars 8K - ad hoc 2L RSA.
- Keller, Laura, "Paulson Said Close to Deal for Caesars Unit's Restructuring." *Bloomberg,* July 9, 2015.
- August 21, 2015 - First Lien Bank RSA.
- Second Lien Evaluation of July 30, RSA.
- August 10, 2015 lawsuit for vote-buying.
- New York Real Estate Lookup.
- Till v. SCS Credit Corp. (O2-1016) 541 U.S. 465 (2004). 17 May 2004. Cornell Law School.
- Chapter 11 "101." American Bankruptcy Institute Journal.
- A Deep Dive into Till v. SCS Credit Corp.—Part I: An Overview of the Topic and the Facts of the Case. The Necessary and Proper Blog. January 3, 2014.
- ABI Commission Report—Cramdown Interest Rates. American Bankruptcy Institute.

- Vital Records for Oct. 1. Kokomo Perspective.
- Pacelle, Mitchell and Richard B. Schmitt. "Chaim Fortgang Defended Creditors, But Offended Many of his Colleagues." *The Wall Street Journal*, February 27, 2002.
- Bankruptcy Titan Hangs Shingle at Silver Point. Global Capital. March 19, 2004.
- Craig, Susanne, Ben Protess, and Evelyn M. Rusli. "The Goldman Sachs Diaspora." *The New York Times*, May 16, 2011.
- New York City Department of Finance Office of the City Register

Chapter 27: Mr. Rowan Goes to Washington

- Saul, Stephanie. "For-Profit College Operator EDMC Will Forgive Student Loans." *The New York Times*, November 16, 2015.
- Frumes, Max. "The Mysterious Shelved Amendment To The Transportation Bill That Would Divide Billionaires." *Forbes Magazine*, December 4, 2015
- White, Ben. "Big moments for the economy ahead." *Politico*, December 1, 2015.
- Dovere, Edward-Isaac. "The Kingmaker." *The Atlantic*, December 6, 2019.
- Corkery, Michael. "The $1,000-an-Hour Lawyer Moonlights as Energy Healer." *The Wall Street Journal*, August 27, 2013.
- "Rev. Robert Drinan, Ex-Congressman, Dies at 86." *The New York Times*, January 29, 2007.
- Klee, Kenneth N. "How Judges are Skewing Bond Law." *The Wall Street Journal*, November 8, 2015.
- Moyer, Liz. "Law Professors Ask Congress to Delay Debt Law." *The New York Times*, December 8, 2015.
- Senate Committee on Finance Hearing. July 31, 2007.
- Hulse, Carl. "Harry Reid to Retire from Senate in 2016." *The New York Times*, March 27, 2015.
- Kane, Paul. "Harry Reid considering new chief of staff." *The Washington Post*, January 7, 2015.
- Cohen, Stephen. "ADL and Aspen Institute Launch Civil Society Fellowship to Help Create Next Generation of Community Leaders." The Aspen Institute, April 25, 2019.
- Transcript, Caesars Entertainment Operating Company Hearing on November 18, 2015, U.S. Bankruptcy Court, Northern District of Illinois. August 24, 2016. Barry Kupferberg testimony.
- Grim, Ryan and Paul Blumenthal. "Harry Reid Directly Solicited Contribution From Private Equity Giant Before Controversial Rider." *Huffington Post*, December 17, 2015.
- Lipton, Eric and Liz Moyer. "Hospitality and gambling Interests delay closing of billion-dollar tax loophole." *The New York Times*, December 20, 2015.
- Josten, R. Bruce. EVP Government Affairs for the U.S. Chamber of Commerce letter to House Financial Services and Senate Banking Committees opposing the TIA rider, March 31, 2016.
- Brownstein Hyatt Farber Schreck, LLP Lobbying Reports, retrieved September 2019 from https://soprweb.senate.gov/index.cfm?event=selectFields&reset=1, Reports from 2014 to the end of 2017, regarding "Solvency and credit market issues."
- "Summary of Serious Flaws in Proposed TIA Amendment," Anonymous lobbying memo opposing the TIA rider.
- Letter to Congress opposing TIA rider, from Adam J. Levitin, law professor at Georgetown University Law Center, signed by 16 other academics, December 8, 2015.
- Asset manager letter to Congress opposing the TIA rider, signed by BlackRock, DoubleLine Group, Oaktree Capital Management, Pacific Investment Management Company (PIMCO), T. Rowe Price Associates, and Western Asset Management Company. December 14, 2015.

- Andy Barr, and twenty-two other Republican members of the House, letter to Speaker Paul Ryan and Majority Leader Kevin McCarthy opposing the TIA rider, December 10, 2015.
- Judah Gross, Lyuba Petrova, Michael Paladino, CFA, "Satisfaction Not Guaranteed," Fitch Ratings special report on corporate parent guarantees, August 28, 2018.

Chapter 28: Roll of the Dice

- Caesars Entertainment Operating Company Docket, U.S. Bankruptcy Court for the Northern District of Illinois (Chicago)
  - Final Report of Examiner, Richard J. Davis, Substantially Unredacted, May 16, 2016 (initially filed March 15, 2016), Document #3720

Chapter 29: The Ides of March

- Caesars Entertainment Operating Company, U.S. Bankruptcy Court for the Northern District of Illinois (Chicago), Transcript 3/16/16.
- Caesars Entertainment Operating Company Docket, U.S. Bankruptcy Court for the Northern District of Illinois (Chicago):
  - Final Report of Examiner, Richard J. Davis, Substantially Unredacted, May 16, 2016 (initially filed March 15, 2016), Document #3720
  - United States Trustee's comment on Mesirow Financial Consulting's final fee application
- Kosman, Josh. "Consultant who bedded the enemy ruins months-long corruption probe." *New York Post*, April 2, 2016.

Chapter 30: Old Friends

- "Cooperation agreement with second-lien holders not to sign the second amended plan." July 5, 2016.
- Caesars Entertainment Operating Company Docket, U.S. Bankruptcy Court for the Northern District of Illinois (Chicago):
  - Notice of filing of the disclosure statement for the debtors' second amended joint plan of reorganization, Document #4007
- Mintz, Douglas. "Seventh Circuit Holds Section 105(a) Permits Stay of Litigations Against Non-Debtor Affiliates."
- Rick Schifter case in front of Farnan. March 26, 1992.
- Kosman, Josh. "Caesars may sink because of alleged $3B typo." *New York Post*, December 14, 2015.
- Kosman, Josh. "Investor wants to freeze out fellow billionaire in Caesars fight." *New York Post*, June 26, 2016.
- Mediation of a Bankruptcy. American Bankruptcy Institute. May 2003.
- Caesars Entertainment Operating Company, U.S. Bankruptcy Court for the Northern District of Illinois (Chicago):
  - Transcript, hearing on Feb 17, 2016
  - Transcript, hearing on May 6, 2016
  - Transcript, hearing on June 6, 2016
  - Transcript, hearing on June 7, 2016
  - Transcript, hearing on June 8, 2016
  - Transcript, hearing on June 9, 2016

Chapter 31: The Hole and the Gap

- Caesars Entertainment Operating Company, U.S. Bankruptcy Court for the Northern District of Illinois (Chicago):
  - Transcript, hearing on August 17, 2016
  - Transcript, hearing on August 23, 2016

- o   Transcript, hearing on August 24, 2016
- o   Transcript, hearing on August 25, 2016
- o   Transcript, hearing on August 26, 2016

Chapter 33: "Pony Up the Paper"

- • Caesars Entertainment Operating Company, U.S. Bankruptcy Court for the Northern District of Illinois (Chicago):
  - o   Transcript, hearing on September 14, 2016
  - o   Transcript, hearing on September 21, 2016
- • Caesars Entertainment Operating Company Docket, U.S. Bankruptcy Court for the Northern District of Illinois (Chicago):
  - o   CEC objection to the motion of Official Committee of Second Priority Noteholders to Continue the Confirmation Hearing and Related Deadlines, Document # 4908, September 13, 2016
  - o   CEC Opposition to Motion of Official Committee of Second Priority Noteholders to compel Paul, Weiss, Rifkind, Wharton & Garrison, Apollo Global Management, TPG Capital, and CEC to produce documents pursuant to the crime-fraud exception, Document #4895, September 13, 2016
  - o   Paul, Weiss, Rifkind, Wharton & Garrison's opposition to the official committee of second priority noteholder's motion to compel production of privileged documents pursuant to the crime-fraud exception, Document #4900, September 13, 2016
  - o   Adversary complaint filed by CEOC against CEC and affiliates, Apollo, TPG, and their directors, Document #4619, August 9, 2016
  - o   Notice of motion of official committee of second priority noteholders' amended motion to compel respondents to produce documents and information in response to subpoenas, Document #4796, August 31, 2016
  - o   Order granting official committee of second priority noteholders' amended motion to compel respondents to produce documents and information in response to subpoenas, Document #4925, September 14, 2016
  - o   Notice of motion of official committee of second priority noteholders to compel Paul, Weiss, Rifkind, Wharton & Garrison, Apollo Global Management, TPG Capital, and Caesars Entertainment Corporation to produce documents pursuant to the crime-fraud protection, Document #4803, September 1, 2016
  - o   Notice of official committee of second priority noteholders' motion for an order compelling production of non-privileged communications between Apollo Global Management and the Debtors, September 16, 2016, Document #4991
  - o   Notice of Official Committee of Second Priority Noteholders' Emergency Motion for an Order compelling David B. Sambur and Marc J. Rowan to appear at their depositions and imposing sanctions on Apollo Global Management and Mr. Sambur for failure to appear at deposition, July 26, 2016, Document #4494
  - o   Notice of motion of noteholder committee for order granting standing to commence, prosecute, and settle claims on behalf of the debtors' estates. Document#3694, May 13, 2016
  - o   Opposition of Marc J. Rowan and David Sambur to motion to compel the production of personal financial information, Document #4846, September 7, 2016
- • "Caesars Entertainment and its sponsors to increase contribution to increase contributions to CEOC's restructuring." Caesars press release dated September 21, 2016.

- "Caesars Entertainment, Caesars Entertainment Operating Company, Announce Key Economic Terms of Proposed Consensual Restructuring Plan for CEOC." September 27, 2016.

Chapter 34: Know When to Fold 'em

- Caesars Entertainment Operating Company, Confirmation of CEOC's creditor groups' support for a term sheet that describes the key economic terms of a proposed consensual Chapter 11 plan, 8-K as filed with the Securities and Exchange Commission, September 27, 2016.
- Caesars Entertainment Operating Company announcement of RSA, 8-K, October 5, 2016.
- Caesars Entertainment Operating Company, U.S. Bankruptcy Court for the Northern District of Illinois (Chicago), Transcript, hearing 10/4/16.
- Confirmation Order, Caesars Entertainment Operating Company Docket, U.S. Bankruptcy Court for the Northern District of Illinois (Chicago).

Chapter 35: Veni, Vidi, VICI

- Caesars Entertainment Corporation, Schedule 14A disclosure of proposed merger with Eldorado Resorts, October 11, 2019.
- Caesars Entertainment Corporation, Schedule 13D disclosure of Apollo ownership, March 7, 2019,
- Caesars Entertainment Corporation, Schedule 14A proxy materials, May 15, 2019.
- Caesars Entertainment Corporation, Schedule 14A, proxy April 10, 2018.
- Prince, Todd. "TPG Capital, Apollo sell remaining stake in Caesars," *Las Vegas Review-Journal*, March 12, 2019.
- Caesars Entertainment Corporation, Robert Morse resignation, 8-K, Nov 26, 2018.
- Vardi, Nathan. "How Carl Icahn Made $1.4 Billion Playing The Booms And Busts Of Las Vegas." *Forbes*, August 30, 2017.
- Indap, Sujeet. "US casinos unlock the value in their real estate." *Financial Times*, July 18, 2019.
- Lombardo, Cara. "Carl Icahn All But Exits Casinos With Tropicana Entertainment Sale." *Wall Street Journal*, April 16, 2018.
- *CNBC Power Lunch*. "Caesars Entertainment CEO on plummeting stock price." Mark Frissora on CNBC, August 1, 2018.

Epilogue: Leaving Las Vegas

- Smith, Robert. "Investors cry foul at aggressive clause in euro high-yield sale." *Financial Times*, June 7, 2017.
- Indap, Sujeet. "Private equity firms' lawyers get creative." *Financial Times*, August 14, 2017.
- Indap, Sujeet. "Private equity gags on its own medicine in contentious debt battles." *Financial Times*.
- Isaac, Mike and Susan Chira. "David Bonderman Resigns From Uber Board After Sexist Remark." *New York Times*, June 13, 2017.
- Scurria, Andrew. "Home Builder Accused of Default Swap Scheme With Blackstone Unit." *Wall Street Journal*, December 2, 2017.
- Indap, Sujeet. "Windstream debt battle opens up 'Pandora's Box' for hedge funds." *Financial Times*, February 22, 2019.
- Parmar, Hema. "Tepper to Keep His Hedge Fund Alive for Handful of Key Investors." *Bloomberg*, October 5, 2019.
- Indap, Sujeet and Mark Vandevelde. "Private equity: Apollo's lucrative but controversial bet on insurance." *Financial Times*, October 31, 2018.

- McMorrow, T.E. "Marc Rowan's Million-Dollar View." *The Independent* (East Hampton), August 7, 2020.
- Chinese, Vera. "Town ups legal budget to handle lobster restaurant case." *Newsday* (Long Island), December 29, 2019.
- "Report Concerning Jeffrey E. Epstein's Connections to Harvard University," Harvard internal investigation, May 2020.
- Indap, Sujeet. "Apollo's Leon Black seeks to reassure investors over Epstein ties." *Financial Times*, August 1, 2019.
- Goldstein, Matthew and Jessica Silver-Greenberg. "Leon Black Plays Down Ties to Jeffrey Epstein but Is Silent on 2011 Deal." *New York Times*, August 1, 2019.
- Senate Intelligence Committee Report on Russian Interference with 2016 Elections, references to Leon Black.
- Tett, Gillian. "Distressed-debt players rule the roost in Trump's White House." *Financial Times*, April 27, 2017.
- Sen, Anirban and Joshua Franklin. "China-owned Playtika hires banks for $1 billion U.S. IPO." *Reuters*, June 2, 2020.
- "SEC Charges Hertz's Former CEO With Aiding and Abetting Company's Financial Reporting and Disclosure Violations." Securities and Exchange Commission announcement, August 13, 2020.
- "Wharton Receives $50 Million Gift from Marc J. Rowan and Carolyn Rowan for Teaching, Research, and Leadership." Wharton announcement, October 2, 2018.
- GLM DFW Inc. v. Windstream Holdings Inc. (In re Windstream Holdings Inc.), 19-4854 S.D.N.Y. March 3, 2020.
- Goldstein, Matthew, Steve Eder, and David Enrich. "Virgin Islands Will Subpoena Billionaire Investor in Epstein Case." *New York Times*, August 23, 2020.
- Mugford, Kristin and David Chan. "Bankruptcy at Caesars Entertainment," Harvard Business School case, February 20, 2017.
- Berger, Paul. "Investment Firm Forgives $70 Million in New York City Taxi-Cab Debt." *Wall Street Journal*, September 13, 2020.
- Indap, Sujeet and Mark Vandevelde. "Neiman Marcus: How a creditor's crusade against private equity power went wrong." *Financial Times*, October 4, 2020. Bakewell, Sally and Lisa Lee. "Oaktree Deal Crushed a Leveraged Loan and Exposed Market's Woes." *Bloomberg News*, October 7, 2020.
- "Goldstein, Matthew, Steve Eder and David Enrich. "The Billionaire Who Stood by Jeffrey Epstein." *New York Times*, October 12, 2020"
- "Vandevelde, Mark. "Leon Black on Epstein links: 'Any suggestion of blackmail is… untrue'" *Financial Times*, October 29, 2020.

INDEX

leveraged buyout, 2, 19, 26, 28, 34, 51, 77, 109, 307. *See also* LBOs
Levine, Dennis, 18
Levinson, Sidney, 114–15, 262, 265, 281, 292–93
Levitin, Adam, 217, 329
Lewinsky, Monica, 104
Liang, Ken, 2–3, 5–7, 117–22, 135, 137, 145, 153–55, 226–28, 241, 243–45, 281–82, 287–88, 306, 308
"lifetime value," 14
Liggett Group, 19
Liman, Arthur, 68
limited partnership financing, 65
Linq, 72, 79–84, 232
Lipton Tea, 149
Lipton, Marty, 189
liquidity, 48, 52, 66, 97, 140, 181
Little Caesars, 155
"locked-up" funds, 134
"lockstep" compensation model, 104
Lockyer, Bill, 23
Los Angeles Dodgers, 155, 165, 244
Louisiana Gaming Control Board, 115
Loveman, Gary, 11–16, 25–26, 28–30, 34–36, 38–41, 47, 50–51, 53–58, 63, 65–67, 72–73, 76–77, 82–83, 87, 129, 144, 157–60, 163, 228–30, 235–36, 251, 259, 261, 277–81, 301, 311
LyondellBasell, 57–58

M&A, 26, 30, 37, 42, 55, 68–70, 104, 149, 235, 310
Mae, Ginnie, 149
managing analyst, 17
managing director, 18
Mandalay Bay, 16
"manufactured default," 305
Marblegate Asset Management (Marblegate), 108–9, 175, 192–98, 213–16, 219, 283, 291–92, 294, 306
"Marks salad," 118
Marks, Howard, 3, 6–7, 118, 154, 215, 217, 287, 308
Marks, Nancy, 118, 308
Marland, Francois, 23
Marshall, Arthur, 40
Martin, Brad, 30
Marx Brothers, 267
Masters, Blythe, 139
McCarthy, Kevin, 216–17
McCartney, Paul, 58
McCoy, John M., 61
McIntosh, Sarah, 213
MeehanCombs Global Credit Opportunities v. Caesars Entertainment Corporation and Caesars Entertainment Operating Company, 108, 198, 211, 219, 236
MeehanCombs, 107, 175, 192, 198, 211, 219, 236, 289, 309
Melchiorre, Anthony, 98

Memphis (Tennessee), 11–14
Memphis Pizza Café, 14
Merrill Lynch, 31, 42, 150
Mestre, Eduardo, 70
MetLife, 224
MGM Grand, 16, 25, 56
Michael J. Fox Foundation, 35
Middle America, 13
Milgram, Andrew, 108–10, 213 -17, 306. *See also* Marblegate Asset Management
Milken Global Conference, 57
Milken, Michael, 3–4, 18–19, 24, 26–27, 29, 36, 53, 57, 68, 118, 308
  junk bond king, 16–17, 182
Millar, Jim, 107–8, 110, 175, 192, 198, 269, 289–90
millennials, 71, 79
Miller Buckfire, 126, 245
Miller, Bob, 30
Miller, Dave, 2, 5, 7, 11, 111–13, 121, 123–24, 127–28, 131, 133, 140, 143, 207–8, 253, 284, 287–88, 295–96, 305
Millstein & Co., 1, 190, 209, 225, 264, 290
Mirage, The. *See* Wynn, Steve
Mirman, Richard, 14
mobile phones, 56
Moelis, Ken, 26, 30, 32
Mollett, Ryan, 2, 5, 91–95, 116, 128, 131–32, 139–40, 145, 204, 206–7, 211, 232, 284, 288, 305, 309
MoMA, 58–60
Momentive Performance Materials, 204
Monarch Alternative Capital, 245
"most favored nation" clause, 285
movie theater chains, 119
Mugford, Kristin, 311
Museum of Modern Art. *See* MoMA
mutual non-aggression pact, 184

NAACP, 37
National Enquirer, 97
Neilander, Dennis, 39
Neiman Marcus, 304, 310
"net short debt activism." *See* "manufacture default"
Nevada Gaming Commission, 37, 39, 47, 162
Nevada Gaming Control Board, 37, 97
New Jersey Devils, 95
New York Stock Exchange, 64
New York Times, 58, 150, 213, 216, 219, 252, 307
Newsom, Gavin, 306
NFL, 68
"non-cooperation" agreement, 253
Non-Extending Creditors, 134
Nor'easter, 173
Norton, David, 14
Norwegian Cruise Lines, 237

ABOUT THE AUTHORS

SUJEET INDAP IS THE US EDITOR of the Lex Column of the *Financial Times* and contributes stories across the paper. He has written extensively on the intersection of corporate finance and corporate law. Indap was previously an investment banker before he joined the *FT* in 2013. He is a graduate of Pomona College and the Wharton School at the University of Pennsylvania. Indap lives in Manhattan with his wife.

MAX FRUMES LEADS A NEWS TEAM at Fitch Solutions covering corporate debt and restructuring. He previously was the founding editor of a leading publication covering corporate bankruptcy, and before that reported for S&P's Leveraged Commentary & Data and *The Deal*. Frumes received his undergraduate degree from the University of California, Berkeley, and an MSJ from Northwestern's Medill School of Journalism. He lives in Brooklyn with his wife and daughter.